NEW DIRECTIONS IN MUSIC

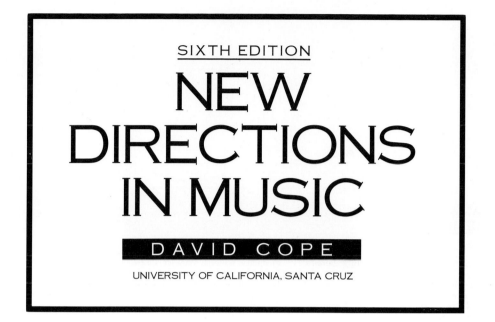

SIXTH EDITION

NEW DIRECTIONS IN MUSIC

DAVID COPE

UNIVERSITY OF CALIFORNIA, SANTA CRUZ

WCB Brown &
Benchmark
PUBLISHERS

Madison, Wisconsin • Dubuque, Iowa • Indianapolis, Indiana
Melbourne, Australia • Oxford, England

Book Team

Editor *Kathleen M. Nietzke*
Developmental Editor *Deborah Daniel Reinbold*
Production Editor *Kay Driscoll*

A Division of Wm. C. Brown Communications, Inc.

Vice President and General Manager *Thomas E. Doran*
Executive Managing Editor *Ed Bartell*
Executive Editor *Edgar J. Laube*
Director of Marketing *Kathy Law Laube*
National Sales Manager *Eric Ziegler*
Marketing Manager *Carla Aspelmeier*
Advertising Manager *Jodi Rymer*
Managing Editor, Production *Colleen A. Yonda*
Manager of Visuals and Design *Faye M. Schilling*

Production Editorial Manager *Vickie Putman Caughron*
Publishing Services Manager *Karen J. Slaght*
Permissions/Records Manager *Connie Allendorf*

Wm. C. Brown Communications, Inc.

Chairman Emeritus *Wm. C. Brown*
Chairman and Chief Executive Officer *Mark C. Falb*
President and Chief Operating Officer *G. Franklin Lewis*
Corporate Vice President, Operations *Beverly Kolz*
Corporate Vice President, President of WCB Manufacturing *Roger Meyer*

Cover image by Sailer & Cook Creative Services

Copyedited by Barbara Walsh

Consulting editor Frederick W. Westphal

Dedicated to my wife,
without whom this book
would not have been written;
and to my parents, whose
faith started it all.

CONTENTS

PREFACE

This sixth edition of *New Directions in Music* contains a number of significant changes. The book has been reorganized into what I feel represents a more logical succession of ideas and developments. "Analog Electronic Music" (chapter 8) now comes prior to "Digital Electronic Music" (chapter 9) for continuity ("Extended Media Resources" is now chapter 7). Chapter 11, "The New Conservatism," and chapter 12, "The Post-Avant-Garde," are reversed from the previous edition, reflecting what to me is a more logical closure for the text. New information will be found on compact discs (CD), MIDI interfaces, and sampling techniques, each with attendant charts of relevant equipment and software (as well as developer addresses listed in Appendix IV). Over one hundred new bibliographic citings for reference and further study have been increased and updated. In this latter area, I have included CDs and videos.

Chapter 10 ("Automated Music"; previously "Automated and Cybernetic Music") has been completely revised to reflect a more practical and less theoretical point of view. Sections on inference, artificial intelligence, and fractals have been removed and replaced with actual operational programs for pattern matching and composing. Also, a new section on neural networks, a fast-growing area of automated composition, has been included in this chapter.

The chapter bibliographies include not only materials discussed in the chapters but supplemental materials that will be of use to the reader seeking greater detail. Each chapter bibliography is divided into two main categories:

1. Further Readings: Books and articles relevant to the subject matter of the chapter. These are listed alphabetically by author following the subheadings of the chapter. Also included are reference materials for in-depth biographical study of the composers mentioned in the chapter.

2. Compact Discs, Recordings, and Publishers: These include record/CD/video numbers and publishers (when available) of works referred to in the chapter as well as other works I feel demonstrate chapter content (listed alphabetically by composer).

These bibliographies have been subdivided according to the subheadings of the associated chapter, and annotations have been removed since they are no longer particularly useful.

Though by no means all-inclusive, these bibliographies are sufficiently comprehensive to serve the reader. They are intended to be used as lists of information selected as examples of chapter material, and as *sources* in themselves for bibliographical information to support more intensive research. The bibliographies have been extensively updated and their scope broadened since the fifth edition. This, combined with the updating of the composer biographies (Appendix II), the expansions of terms and their definitions (Appendix I), and the source addresses of Appendix IV, should make the materials discussed more easily understood by and accessible to the reader. Composition or publication dates are included if available. They are mentioned with the first appearance of the name of the work and not thereafter (i.e., if the work is discussed and the date is listed in the body of the chapter, the date will not be included in the chapter bibliography under *Compact Discs, Recordings, and Publishers*).

One is often confronted by readers holding a variety of misconceptions, two of which this composer-author would like to dispel with brevity and singular decisiveness. First of all, just as writing about Greek mythology does not make one either a Greek or a believer in myths, so writing about various types of *avant-garde* music does not *necessarily* make one an admirer of this selfsame music. Second, due to the volatile nature of much of the subject matter under discussion, one must weigh carefully a most important statement in the *Preface* to the first edition:

> The lack of material herein related to more traditional (mainstream) techniques is not intended to reflect or suggest their unimportance (they are *most* important), but is rather due both to the fact that there is a wealth of material already available on these subjects, and to the necessarily limited scope of this text.

Whether one agrees or disagrees with the concepts, philosophies, and resultant sound activities and/or silences discussed herein is simply beside the point. This music *does* exist, and to avoid either their manifestations or significance is simply playing ostrich.

It is quite possible that more compositions have been brought into the world during the past 50 years than during the entire previous 120-year period. Many of these works are experimental, destined to become, like P. D. Q. Bach, "hopelessly lost," or to help found a broad and more creative base for artistic endeavor. In any event, they can no longer be considered external to the history of this era, or to its future existence.

Directions seem as numerous or as diverse as composers or works. And yet there exists behind these directions historical motives and constant aesthetic values, traceable and uniquely observable due to their singularly radical nature. Electronic instruments and techniques, aleatoric methods, adoption of scientific procedures and theatrical participation, once held as highly controversial and innovative, have entered a large number of current mainstream compositions, due in part to the recent sophistication of international communications media. It was not always so. Berlioz's innovations in orchestration waited half a century for recognition and acceptance. Charles Ives's experiments took many years to be discovered—many more to be considered even rational.

The purpose of this book, then, is to explore the history, philosophies, materials, composers, and works pertaining to those directions in music since the late 1940s that express a radical departure from tradition in concept and/or production, with special emphasis on the relationship of these to significant and realistic directions of style and thought.

New Directions in Music is intended as an introduction and general survey of *avant-garde* and post-*avant-garde* music in the twentieth century to the present, in the hope that it will stimulate the reader to further listening and research. Designed for music students at the college and graduate level, it may be suitably integrated into any course incorporating the study of various aspects of twentieth-century composition: forms, techniques, philosophy. It can be a valuable supplement to the well-rounded education of any serious musician. By the very fact that most of the years discussed have not yet become "history" in the academic sense, I have intentionally avoided the standard historical approach and rhetoric in order to develop the *concepts* of the *New Directions in Music*.

I would like to thank the following reviewers who reviewed this text: Edwin Childs, Biola University; Ken Keaton, Florida Atlantic University; Charles McKnight, Stetson University; Gary M. Potter, Indiana University; John Steffa, Murray State University; and Herbert C. Turrentine, Southern Methodist University.

David Cope

INTRODUCTION

As work neared completion on the fourth edition of *New Directions in Music,* I was struck with the notion of including an original Cage mesostic. I wrote to John in New York, half suspecting he wouldn't even receive my letter before the deadline passed. He responded in less than ten days (he is amazing in keeping up on correspondence) and promised something as soon as he could get to it. He had just returned from Europe and now had to fly to Oakland. Since I had thought to send a copy of the third edition with my request, I was overjoyed to think that he would now be able to contribute a mesostic to the book.

After a few days had passed, John phoned from Oakland. He was quite apologetic. It seems that he had placed *New Directions in Music* in a drawer in New York City. When he went to retrieve it for creating the mesostic, the drawer would not open; something was stuck between the upper shelf and the contents (probably *New Directions in Music*) and no subsequent pulling and tugging would pry it open. John called a carpenter. Time passed, however, and since he had to get to the airport to fly to Oakland, he left the book "locked" in the drawer.

I, of course, was aghast at this trick of fate but more than understanding of John's plight. In fact, I guess I was so delighted that he would *think* of doing a mesostic, I momentarily forgot that I was not going to receive it. I quickly mailed John a new copy of the third edition (actually not "new" since the only copy I had was the one in which I had made editorial changes for edition four). But time was getting short and my optimism was fast retreating. I did have hope, however, since it could have been worse: John could have read the will of fate into my book's active reluctance to allow his drawer to act normally.

Finally, John wrote a note and attached the following correspondence. While nothing could truly surpass a personal Cage mesostic, as far as I was concerned, this serial came close. The articulate and perceptive dialogue present speaks for itself. It does, I hope, give the reader a spirit of inquiry that accompanies the soul bent on these kinds of exploratory journeys. Mr. Berry's kind permission to use his letters is gratefully appreciated.

1 November 1982

Dear Mr. Cage,

What follows is the angry cry of a young composer demanding explanation and justification for what he perceives as folly in an older colleague. It is offered as a tossed gauntlet. I challenge you to defend yourself so I may understand you better. And be assured I sincerely prefer understanding over anger.

Mr. Cage: I accuse you for items #1 and #2, and hold you directly responsible for the situation described in item #3.

ITEM #1: You have systematically bastardized the art of music composition through the abuse of language. By redefinition of the word 'music', in a way which says, 'anything and everything is music' you have made the word 'music' meaningless. If everything is music, then *nothing* is music. And therefore, composers can no longer exist . . . there is simply nothing left for them to do.

ITEM #2: You have declared, 'My purpose is to eliminate purpose.' You would have all composers eliminate beauty, sincerity, joy, compassion, expression, and love from their music. You would have all composers ignore these basic qualities in music which humanity has enjoyed for several thousand years.

ITEM #3: As a result of your nihilistic philosophy of music, and your pointless musical-sociological experiments, most young composers have been completely alienated from other musicians and from concert audiences. Concert audiences (in the U.S.) are for the most part completely disinterested in New Music, having been convinced there is no purpose or sincerity in the work of most 20th century composers. You have caused a near-total collapse of musical culture in this country, and left nothing for us (the young composers) to work with. We have no patrons, and our motives for composing music are constantly suspect.

I believe the Great John Cage, 'grandfather of modern music', is a nihilistic comedian playing to an audience of indoctrinated sheep. His art is not art at all: it is blasphemy.

Sincerely,

Charles Berry

Charles Berry

JOHN CAGE
101 West 18 Street (5B) • New York,
New York 10011

MESSAGE	REPLY

TO Mr. Charles Berry
3571 Ruffin Rd. #238
San Diego, Calif. 92123

DATE Nov. 21, 1982

It seems that what angers you are my writings, my ideas. I suggest you drop interest in them and focus on your own. Turn your attention to what you believe in. That is what I did. Thus I found alternative compositional means that would permit the introduction of noises and sounds available through new technology into musical works. I rediscovered the traditional purposes for making music

a) to imitate nature in her manner of operation, and b) to sober and quiet the mind thus making it susceptible to divine influences. Thus I was freed from self expression. Music became a discipline, a way of life. I have always noticed that very few people are interested in New Music. I was 50 years old before there was any supportive acceptance of my work. I am now much older but my work remains controversial as your feelings testify.

Sincerely,

John Cage

Detach and File for Follow-up

8 Dec 1982

Dear Mr. Cage,

Thank you for your letter. It has given me a much better understanding of the intent and substance of your ideas and your music. For the present I will take your advice and concentrate on my own creative instincts. However, I do feel compelled to study your work further.

At some future date I may, quite possibly, approach your work from a different perspective and find it refreshing and enjoyable.

Sincerely,

Charles Berry

Charles Berry

THE CHALLENGE
TO TONALITY

1

Nineteenth-century humankind, reasonably cloaked in the gifts of the industrial revolution, entered the final one hundred years of the millennium with optimistic and exploratory vision. H. G. Wells' prophetic "War of the Worlds" (1898) introduced millions to the planet earth viewed finally as a sum of its parts, and to an electrical and even atomic future. It was an era of incredible change and challenge to established traditions. The very essence of its spirit rode tether with Orville and Wilbur Wright above a North Carolina beach in 1903.

The arts rarely detach themselves from social dynamics. The visual arts began (as early as the 1860s) to question the photographic realism of classicism with impressionistic and pointillistic explorations. Georges Seurat's 1886 oil painting *A Sunday Afternoon on the Grande Jatte,* for example, is composed of small dots of intense color systematically covering an enormous 6' 9" by 10' canvas (see Figure 1.1). The docile and immobile figures are relaxed in a timelessness almost antithetical to the passionate points that bring it forth. Poets Paul Verlaine (1844–1896) and Stéphane Mallarmé (1842–1898, whose poem *L'Après-midi d'un faune* was the source for Debussy's seminal Prélude of 1894) mirrored the sensuous and coloristic Impressionist painters.

The Expressionists contrasted this exotic lyricism with intensely personal and emotive concepts. Vincent Van Gogh's (1853–1890) visionary early work produced violent and often tormented canvases. Georges Rouault's *Head of Christ* (see Figure 1.2) gives an example of the Gothic brutality of Expressionism. T. S. Eliot (1888–1965) and James Joyce (1882–1941) exemplified these qualities in "stream of consciousness" novels and poetry.

Both Expressionism and Impressionism, while in their own right significant schools of art, served as precursors for the abstractionists of the twentieth century. Kandinsky's (1866–1944) *Sketch I for "Composition VII"* (see Figure 1.3) is a subtle Impressionist "shaping" *and* an Expressionist "personal insight" while avoiding any covert realism or objectivism. Ambiguity of representation thereby creates another level of viewing color and balance.

Concomitant to (possibly even subscribed within) abstractive art is Cubism with its principal exponent Pablo Picasso (1881–1973). If abstract art "removes" image, then Cubism "abstracts" the removal. While *Three Musicians* (see Figure 1.4) is

Figure 1.1. Georges Seurat (1859–1891): *A Sunday Afternoon on the Grande Jatte* (1886). Helen Birch Bartlett Memorial Collection. An example of Impressionism.

Figure 1.2. Georges Rouault (1871–1958): *Head of Christ* (1905). Walter Chrysler Museum, Provincetown. An example of Expressionism.

Figure 1.3. Wassily Kandinsky: *Sketch I for "Composition VII"* (1913). Collection Felix Klee, Bern. An example of abstract art.

Figure 1.4. Pablo Picasso: *Three Musicians* (1921). The Museum of Modern Art, New York; Mrs. Simon Guggenheim Fund. An example of Cubism.

Figure 1.5. Left to right: Jean Cocteau, French surrealist author and filmmaker; Pablo Picasso; Igor Stravinsky; Olga Picasso; 1925.

clearly that, the angular and often perspective-lacking juxtaposition of "cutout"-like figures distorts the view, creating an amorphous catalog of queries into the underlying rationale. Picasso, like so many of the century's artists and authors, pursued active relationships with composers, playwrights, and dancers.

By 1919 two endemically twentieth-century schools of art were born. The first, the Bauhaus, was a group of visual artists (both two- and three-dimensional) headed by Walter Gropius (a German-born architect) whose visionary work created a model for today's steel and glass skyscrapers. The second, the Dadaists, was formed by poets André Breton and Tristan Tzara and spawned the talents of (among others) Marcel Duchamp (1887–1968), Man Ray (1890–1976), and Salvador Dali (1904–1989). Dali also forged a third school called *surrealism*. His canvases (see Figure 1.6) often depict plastic figures melted into impossible shapes similar to Picasso's Cubism but lacking its formal line, and creating power through supernatural images.

Each development and contrary turn in the road, whether it be in the style or content of art or literature, reflects the tenacity of artists in times of great uncertainty. It is no accident that art parallels the tempo of world events. Contextualized by the "winds of change" in the visual and narrative arts, composers began similarly to divest themselves of the often unspoken presumptions of tradition and strike out for the edges of discovery.

An Overview of Tonality

The "common-practice" period of music history (roughly 1700–1900) witnessed a flowering of musical resources into an enormously rich and complex language. Its basic force, tonality, still pervades much of today's popular musics. While a just summary of tonal vocabulary and techniques could take hundreds of pages, there are three primal forces that are important to note. The inexorable challenges to these central concepts spawned "new directions in music."

Figure 1.6. Salvador Dali: *The Persistence of Memory* (1931). Collection, The Museum of Modern Art, New York. An example of *surrealism*.

First, concepts of "key" define the basic pitch vocabulary of tonality. Melodies reduced to source material become scales of ordered intervals. Figure 1.7 shows a melodic line and the projection of a scale. Tonality defines these pitches as *diatonic* and those foreign to the "key" as *chromatic*.

Second, concepts of consonance (relaxation) versus dissonance (tension) permeate the relationships of tonal materials. The overtone series (pitches present in acoustic sound) is often argued as the rationale for vertical consonance. This series (infinite; shown here through eight pitches) gives prominence in its lower (more audible) spectrum to three primary intervals: octaves, fifths, and thirds—see Figure 1.8. When projected as a simultaneity these create a triad (three-note chord built

Figure 1.7. Wolfgang Amadeus Mozart (1756–1791): *Theme and Variations: "Ah! Vous Dirai-je, Maman"* and a derived C major scale.

in thirds). Pitches outside these basic sonorities are called "non-harmonic" and typically resolve (move toward) a chord member. Most tonal music consists of these harmonic triads contextualized by key (e.g., *diatonic* or *chromatic*).

Figure 1.8. The overtone series on C with primary lower intervals marked and a derived C major triad.

Finally, subtle concepts of hierarchical relationships pervade most tonal music. Two primary pitches provide fulcrum and weight. The *dominant* note (or triad) is the fifth of the key. It begs resolution to the *tonic* note (or triad), which answers the dominant "question." The tonic is the first note of each key scale. Figure 1.9 shows the primary chords of tonic and dominant in tonal hierarchy with examples of other "secondary" chords. As well, the figure shows a fragment of a piece with the three tonal principles at work: key, consonance, and hierarchy.

The interplay of these and other tonal principles has provided a common language for thousands of composers. Their music, steeped in rich tonal traditions, parallels that of classic realism in the visual arts. So complex is the syntax of this language that relationships are often implied but not present.

As the century turned, tonal composers faced critical challenges with sophistication of syntax developing "slang" counterparts. The *chromatic* outweighed the *diatonic*, the non-harmonic overshadowed the harmonic, the hierarchy had become so implied as to become unreal. Figure 1.10 demonstrates the complex tonal ambivalences of late nineteenth century (Romantic period) music. Each of the three principal elements of tonality is barely perceivable. The very fabric of *diatonic* and *consonant* hierarchy is in crisis here. While many composers clung to tonal traditions (twentieth-century Romanticists such as Elgar, Rachmaninoff, etc.), many felt the need to strike out for new soil (though, as with all historical models, based on older techniques).

Expanded Scale Resources

Exploration of alternative scales was one of the initial ways composers sought for new order. Traditional and quasi-traditional modes, direct (sixteenth century) antecedents of tonality, returned in new guises. Impressionism in music (circa 1894–1915), as in the visual arts, chose methods of alluding to yet blurring classic realism (in this case tonality).

x = non-harmonic tones

Figure 1.9. (a) chords listed in tonal hierarchy; (b) Ludwig van Beethoven (1770–1827): *Sonata* Op. 2, No. 3.

Figure 1.10. Richard Wagner (1813–1883): *Tristan und Isolde* (Prelude)—1859.

Figure 1.11 shows six somewhat standard modes often used in impressionistic works, with their Renaissance (sixteenth century) nomenclature. Note that in each of the modes, the half-step patterns apply to different members of the series, giving a significantly different-sounding scale even though the pitch content of each is the same (piano white keys). Figure 1.12 shows Debussy's use of Aeolian mode on D as the basis for pitch materials.

Figure 1.11. The standard modes.

Figure 1.12. Claude Debussy (1862–1918): *Prélude, Des pas sur la neige* (Footsteps in the Snow) (1910). A. Durand, Paris. An example of modal composition.

Figure 1.13. Claude Debussy. Dover Publications, Inc. Permission granted.

The first four measures state the mode through repeated tonic (D in the lowest voice) and a scale-like melodic line. The B♭ creates a transposed mode with Aeolian half-steps between 2–3 and 5–6 (see Figure 1.11). The C♯, which was often common as a leading tone in the late Renaissance, is conspicuously missing here. Debussy is obviously concerned about establishing modal integrity so that the variances with D minor can be emphasized. The B♮ beginning in measure 5 might briefly suggest D melodic minor, but the constant use of C♮ clearly identifies a modulation to D-Dorian (half-steps between 2–3 and 6–7; see Figure 1.11). "Tonal" ears can often bend modal materials into tonal leanings. Debussy fights this tendency, avoiding leading tone implications wherever possible.

Another popular resource in early music of this century was the whole-tone scale. This scale divides the octave into six equal whole steps, creating an interesting and definitely non-tonal mode. Figure 1.14 shows a basic whole-tone scale beginning on C, and a second whole-tone scale beginning on D♭. In actuality these are the only two different possibilities, since beginning on any other pitch will duplicate the tones and intervals of one or the other of these scales.

Figure 1.14. Two whole-tone scales.

Composers discovered that this limitation, the lack of the real potential of modulating to different whole-tone "keys," is a severe drawback. As well, the characteristic sound of the scale soon wears thin. Figure 1.15 presents an example of the C whole-tone scale in use.

Composers of the early twentieth century adopted folk modes and materials as well as traditional modes and whole-tone scales. In Figure 1.17, Debussy employs a Spanish mode in *Habañera* style. The melodic line (here at the bottom) convincingly states a D-based mode different from any yet mentioned. The scale is clarified and established by repetition of the important intervals of difference between it and

Figure 1.15. Béla Bartók: (1881–1945): *Mikrokosmos* (1926–37) Volume 5, no. 136: "Whole-tone Scale." Boosey and Hawkes, New York City.

Figure 1.16. Béla Bartók. Dover Publications, Inc. Permission granted.

Figure 1.17. Claude Debussy: *Soirée dans Grenade,* from *Estampes* (1903). A. Durand, Paris. Use of folk modes in classical music.

Figure 1.18. Mode derived from Figure 1.17.

traditional tonality and modality. The augmented second suggests the harmonic minor on C♯, but the use of the D♮, which would be a half-step above the tonic, negates that possibility (See Figure 1.18).

Octatonic (eight-note) scales have been used often by composers like Igor Stravinsky and Béla Bartók. The octatonic scale is formed by alternating whole and half-steps. Thus C-D-E♭-F-F♯-G♯-A-B-C forms one octatonic scale. This and other forms of synthetic scales can form the template around which compositions or even styles can be created. The scale used can provide, as it does in tonal music, a consistency and predictability for the listener. Once established it is possible to modulate to other forms of the scale (as in C♯-D♯-E-F♯-G-A-B♭-C-C♯, the half-step-above version of the previously mentioned octatonic scale) as well as to create interesting chromatic chord functions and melodic shapes. Composers using synthetic modes, however, are more likely to emphasize the mode they are using by repetition than to vary it by including extensive chromatic notes from outside the mode itself. Scales such as the octatonic obviously also allow analysts the opportunity to postulate tonal parallels to contemporary styles. Function substitutes (as for the dominant, since G doesn't exist in the previously mentioned C octatonic scale) hold useful potential as do therefore substitute cadence types and implied harmony.

Pentatonic, or five-note, scales derive in part from simplified versions of *oriental* and *Indonesian* folk music. These latter folk traditions encompass complicated and exotic tunings as well as subtle cultural connotations. Western tradition, however, extracted the simplified scale elements of five notes as shown in Figure 1.19. The melody here is completely constructed of piano keyboard black notes as opposed to the white-key modal constructions of Figure 1.11. As with whole-tone scales, the lack of half-steps creates tonal ambiguity. As well, notice the reference to oriental temples in the title.

Synthetic scales involve the creation, usually by the composer, of unique scales for the purpose of composition. Figure 1.20 shows an example of a work, by an American impressionist, Charles Griffes, 1884–1920, based on a synthetic mode.

Figure 1.19. (a) Two pentatonic scales; (b) Claude Debussy: *Pagodes* from *Estampes* (1903). A. Durand, Paris.

Figure 1.20. Charles Tomlinson Griffes: *Sonata* (1918). G. Schirmer, New York. Use of synthetic modes in 20th century music.

Figure 1.21. Synthetic modes derived from Figure 1.20.

Here the scale used does not conform to traditional tonal-modal shapes. In Figure 1.21a, the scale based on F is clearly derived from these opening notes. In Figure 1.21b, the scale of the entire movement is shown. With synthetic scales, composers are able to freely determine their own functional relationships. This is accomplished through the same resources available to the common-practice composer: repetition and cadence. Unfortunately, real definition of expectancy and fulfillment, so characteristic of tonal music, can only be suggested here since often only one piece (or at best a few) exists in any particular synthetic scale. Moreover, the composer using such scales must constantly be aware of the tonally based experience of the listener. Synthetically derived materials can often be mistaken as tonal or modal in origin when this is not the case.

Any one of the scales mentioned herein, or an assemblage of two or more, might act as a tonal substitute were it not for the lack of a consistent body of work utilizing the materials and techniques. More often than not, these new scales were exploited and then abandoned, victims of yet newer devices in hopes that a stable system might surface to replace tonality. At the same time, the engaging qualities of works whose materials are unique cannot be overlooked. For further types of synthetic scales see Nicolas Slonimsky's *Thesaurus of Scales and Melodic Patterns* in the bibliography of this chapter.

Extensions of Tertian Harmony

As melodic materials developed into more complex and subtle variants, so too did their harmonic counterparts. In early Western tonal traditions, one finds triads used without a great deal of non-triadic dissonances. As the common practice developed, non-harmonic tones increased in number and, while still embellishing their harmonic function, began to pull gently at the triadic structure. As explorations continued, a hierarchy of dissonances surfaced. Some tones outside the triad itself seemed more consonant than others. Often these latter tones are extensions of building thirds upon thirds (the source of the triad itself). Figure 1.22 shows a series of triads with added thirds creating continuous seventh chords.

Figure 1.22. Eric Satie (1886–1925): *Trois Gymnopédies* (No. 1) (1888). G. Schirmer, New York. An example of seventh chords.

Note that non-harmonic tones "resolve" into the triadic structures while seventh-chord projections indicate no "resoluton." Figure 1.23 shows a series of expanded harmonic structures (seventh and ninth chords) with some tones resolving to chord tones and others not. This ambiguity is a trademark of turn-of-the-century impressionistic composers.

Figure 1.23. Maurice Ravel (1875–1937): *Sonatine* (1903). An example of seventh and ninth chords.

Further expansion of triads by thirds creates further complexity and depth of texture. Figure 1.24 shows a dominant thirteenth chord. Note how chord members do not resolve into a triad. Spacing is also a critical component. If the thirteenth chord of Figure 1.24 is collapsed within a single octave, a dissonant chord occurs where seconds rather than thirds seem to be the basic substructure as seen in Figure 1.25. These tend to resemble "clusters" of sound as discussed in chapter 3.

Figure 1.24. Claude Debussy: *Prélude à "L'Après-midi d'un Faune"* (1894). An example of a dominant thirteenth chord.

Figure 1.25. Collapsed thirteenth chord and resultant dissonance.

Because ninth, eleventh, and thirteenth chords are often vertically oriented (since non-harmonic movement is reduced with so many tones already present in the chord), constant contrary motion with chords of so many members can create contrapuntal chaos, with few of the voices distinguishable and often colliding with one another. Thus they are often used in parallel voice motion. This is called *planing* ("planes" or "levels" of register).

Planing basically involves "freezing" a chord structure and then moving it as if it were a single melodic line. Harmonies become a by-product of melodic movement and are heard as moving groups of notes rather than separate entities. Figure 1.26 is an example of diatonic planing.

Figure 1.26. Claude Debussy: *Feuilles mortes* "Dead Leaves," from the Préludes, Book II (1913). A. Durand, Paris. An example of diatonic planing.

While the intervals change (e.g., major to minor) and the functions could be said to change on each chord, it is the horizontal movement that carries the vertical structure along. To evaluate "tonics," "dominants," and other functions within this is to simply ignore the real meaning of the music.

Figure 1.27 shows a more substantial use of planing from the same composer. Here the *freezing* of the basic pattern remains so fixed that the passage obtains a great variety of chromaticism. Again, it would be possible to carefully go through

Figure 1.27. Claude Debussy: *La Soirée dans Grenade* from *Estampes* (1903). A. Durand, Paris. Another example of planing.

each and every harmonic structure and delineate function. The vertical sonorities are, however, simply a by-product of the melodic line and the resulting chords and chromaticism formed by this planing. The triads of Figure 1.28 create a full chromatic complement (all twelve tones) to the resolute "pedal point" G in the bass.

Composers also sought to create complex vertical structures (while hoping to retain some tonal identity) by combining two or more keys simultaneously. This "polytonality" produces a rich fabric of chromatic textures, especially when the keys

Figure 1.28. Maurice Ravel: *Le Tombeau de Couperin,* "Minuet" (1917). A. Durand, Paris. An example of triadic planing.

Figure 1.29. Maurice Ravel. Dover Publications, Inc. Permission granted.

Figure 1.30. (a) Igor Stravinsky (1882–1971): *Petrushka* (1911). (b) Scales of C and F♯ major.

Figure 1.31. Igor Stravinsky. Dover Publications, Inc. Permission granted. Stravinsky (seen here fourth from left) appears with the Hindemith Quartet (composer Paul Hindemith is standing).

have few common tones. Figure 1.30 (reduced from orchestral score) shows an example of polytonality using the keys of C major and F♯ major simultaneously. Note how the scales shown have only two notes in common: B and F [E♯].

The dissonance of the passage is greatly reduced by the simple use of triads in each key. The listener, though certainly pummeled with dissonance, can grasp the basic duality of the elements in this context. To create this counterpoint of keys, composers often establish strong key centers rather than allowing the variants to intermingle and reduce the bitonal recognizability. In Figure 1.32, Bartók uses different key signatures, different staves, and particularly different material for each key (B major melodic figuration versus C major harmonic planing).

Figure 1.32. Béla Bartók: *Out of Doors Suite* (1926). Universal Edition.

Some composers add the element of "collage" to polytonal techniques. This effect combines polytonality with quotation (usually popular or folk in origin). The result often creates polyrhythms, polymeters, polytextures, and polyconcepts from the overlapping of widely diverse musical types. Figure 1.33 shows this process in use. Here one idea is in B♭ major (flutes, clarinets, trumpets, bass, and lower violas), another in D minor (piano, violins, and horns), with a third suggesting F major (trombones). One line wavers slowly (top 'celli) around chromatic pitches B♭, A, and C♭. The result might be chaos, but because each idea is uniquely orchestrated and identifiable as quotation, the polytonality works effectively. Collage techniques are therefore viable procedures to clarify and establish polytonality.

Figure 1.33. Charles Ives (1874–1954): "Putnam's Camp," from *Three Places in New England* (1914).

Figure 1.34. Charles Ives. Dover Publications, Inc. Permission granted.

Figure 1.35. Charles Ives: *The Cage* (from *114 Songs:* 1884–1921). Published by the composer and later by New Music Edition. An example of chords built with fourths.

Composers also sought ways of constructing chords from intervals other than thirds. In Figure 1.35, the basic harmonic fabric is clearly fourth chords (four 4ths creating five notes). Only the first chord of the second measure (with the word "wonder") defies this analysis. Note how the melodic line contrasts with the harmonic structure by moving almost exclusively in seconds. The "stacked" nature of the chords makes planing almost unavoidable. There is no doubt of the non-tertian nature of these chords since no tones resolve or even hint of triads.

Figure 1.36 is a more complex interplay of non-tertian harmonies and develops a more contrapuntal basis of voice motion. The first chord is a "stacked" fourth

Figure 1.36. Paul Hindemith (1895–1963): *Le Cygne* (from *Six Chansons*) (1939). *B. Schott's Soehne, Mainz.* Contrapuntal techniques in non-tertian harmony.

chord (B—E—A) with a doubled B in the top voice. The third, fourth, and sixth chords are similarly stacked in fourths. Chords five and seven are inversions of fourth chords and need only an octave displacement of one pitch (B below E for chord five, and F♯ between C♯ and B for chord seven) to be seen as similar projections of fourths. Chords two, eight, and nine are ambiguous with either a note missing (e.g., chord two could be seen as stacked fourths if the B were in the bass and an E added just above it) or a triad with an added pitch. The final chord is a triad that by its simplicity seems almost dissonant (i.e., in its "contrary to context" meaning). Chromatic pitches here are not derived from tonal inflections but are the result of projections of "perfect" fourths.

Expanding triads into dense sonorities (ninth, eleventh, and thirteenth chords), using more than one key simultaneously (polytonality), and exploring new interval foundations for harmonies all expand the composer's menu of available materials for vertical simultaneities. Each of these avenues, while initially focused on as elaborations of tonality, helps to defuse its very center—the triad—and in so doing provides exit routes into less clearly interpretable vocabularies.

Musical Hierarchies

As harmonic cohesiveness seeps from tonality, hierarchical structure slips away. Subtle chromatic embellishing chords with complex but expected resolutions grow so distant from basic key concepts that recognition of tonic and dominant becomes obscured. Simply rhyming phrases of tonality appears too obvious, and phrases blur into a continuity that lacks clear hierarchical structure (i.e., primary structure: I, V; secondary: ii, iii, etc.; tertiary: chromatic chords, etc.). Busoni possibly says it more eloquently: "Let me take thought, how music may be restored to its primitive, natural essence; let us free it from architectonic, acoustic and esthetic dogmas; let it be pure invention and sentiment, in harmonies, in forms, in tone-colors (for invention and sentiment are not the prerogative of melody alone); let it follow the line of the rainbow and vie with the clouds in breaking sunbeams."[1]

With tonal superstructure gone, composers evolved uniquely "personal" languages that often did not last for more than a few works. As well, tonal emphasis on phrase structure and cadence imploded into a preoccupation with single events. Scriabin's *mystic chord,* for example, is a kind of fourth chord inclusive of both augmented and diminished forms (see Figure 1.37). This became the organic source for melodic and harmonic development. Figure 1.38 shows a brief sample of how this structure permeates the fabric of Scriabin's work.

Figure 1.37. Alexander Scriabin's *mystic chord.*

1. Ferruccio Busoni, *Sketch of a New Esthetic of Music* (New York City: G. Schirmer, Inc., 1911). Translated from German by T. Baker.

Figure 1.38. Alexander Scriabin (1872–1915): *Poème* Op. 69, no. 1 (1913).

The "event" concept, taken to the extreme, implies a momentary collapse of the lyric in music. The emphasis turns to the vertical subtleties of the event—its texture, timbre, and duration—with a focus separate from cadence-directed motion. Figure 1.39 shows how groups of events can be organized into linear direction. The texture here is fluid, yet shaped by a set of events or points of sound. Compare this to Figure 1.1 and note the differences between pointillism in art and music. In the former, the "points" group to form images; in the latter, the focus is on points of timbre.

Figure 1.39. Anton Webern (1883–1945): *Six Bagatelles* for string quartet (1913). An example of musical pointillism.

With music freed, as it were, from "architectonic" expectation, areas other than pitch also became available for experimentation. The rigor of the bar line relaxed into what some have called "time-suspension." Figure 1.40 shows two of the many ways composers used to free music from the "tyranny" of the beat. First, on-beats are avoided (especially downbeats) to diminish their import. Second, irregular small subdivisions of the beat are created to blur suggested beat accent.

The *atonal* (derogatory word often used to describe works of this century) qualities of the pitch material are similar to that of Scriabin's *Poème* (Figure 1.38) and

Figure 1.40. Arnold Schoenberg (1874 1951): *Scchs Kleine Klavierstucke* Op. 19 (1911). Universal Edition.

triadic references are rare. Public acceptance of these *atonal* works was quite mixed as the following review in the *Paris-Midi* of May 29, 1913 indicates:

> . . . musical cubism has made its appearance in the fair city of Paris. By singular irony of fate, it was in the venerable hall of the Conservatoire, the temple of all tradition, that this revelation took place . . . offering to its habitués the first performance of three piano pieces by Arnold Schoenberg. This composer hails from Vienna, preceded by an intriguing reputation. Every performance of one of his works in Austria and Germany has provoked disorders, police intervention, transportation of the wounded to the hospital and of dead bodies to the morgue. At the sound of the last chord the listeners would come to blows, and music lovers strewn on the floor would be picked up in bunches. So we waited with impatience the first contact of this explosive art with French sensibilities. . . . But all expectations were deceived. True, there were some uncomfortable smiles, some anguished sighs, some stifled groans, but no scandal crupted. Arnold Schoenberg would not believe it.[2]

Timbral explorations were likewise important, and composers continued to expand the repertoire of acceptable musical sounds. Percussion sections of orchestras often "wagged the dog," as in works by Edgard Varèse. *Amériques* (1922) for orchestra, for example, requires ten percussionists utilizing twenty-one different instruments. This work also expands the resources of the traditional orchestra with normal complements of winds often doubled in size (e.g., six trumpets, five trombones, etc.). He also employs the Hecklephone, contrabass tuba, and contrabass trombone. *Amériques* is a culmination of the post-Romantic tradition of gargantuan orchestras exemplified by Schoenberg's *Gurre-lieder* (1911, for five soloists, choir, and large orchestra).

While some composers clung to tonal inheritance, content to articulate their musical thoughts through revisions of Western music tradition, others saw this as a turning point for their musical styles. The common language was gone for them and each was free to pursue an experimental direction. For some this meant the construction of new vocabularies and/or a complete reexamination of the very nature of sound and the complicated way in which the human animal acts and interacts in its presence.

2. Nicolas Slonimsky, *Lexicon of Musical Invective: Critical Assaults on Composers since Beethoven's Time* (2d ed.) Seattle: University of Washington Press, 1969, pp. 310–11.

Vectoral Analysis:
Edgard Varèse:
Density 21.5

Vectoral[3] *analysis* will be used for all larger in-depth analysis throughout the text. Its seven-pronged view of each piece provides the perspective and thorough analysis necessary to understand contemporary music more fully, especially that of recent experimental vintage.

The following is a basic synopsis of the analytical process to be used.

1. Historical Background: This includes information of relevance to the piece under discussion relating to period of composition, school of composition (if any), inclusive dates of composition, country of origin, historical influences, and the composer's important teachers.

2. Overview, Structure, and Texture: This includes general formal analysis and a careful look at composite structures (e.g., homophonic, monophonic, contrapuntal), general notational principles used, rhythmic ideas generated, compositional techniques influencing structure (e.g., mobile forms, graphic notation), and texts employed.

3. Orchestration Techniques: Basic timbre analysis, general instrumentation, unusual techniques (e.g., multiphonics, preparations), extreme ranges, unusual balance and/or inverted structures, relevant relation of timbre to form, and structure.

3. From *vector,* a quantity with both force and direction, here defined as a three-dimensional analytical technique rather than two-dimensional form analysis or one-dimensional harmonic analysis.

Figure 1.41. Edgard Varèse. BMI Archives. Used by permission.

4. Basic Techniques: Includes pitch organization (e.g., tonal), motivic structures, and rhythmic detail.

5. Vertical Models: Presentation of significant samplings of vertical structures from the piece, including chord roots, centers, and voice leading between chord structures.

6. Horizontal Models: Presentation of significant samplings of horizontal melodic structures including cadence, balance, and motion.

7. Style: A summary of the stylistic parameters employed by the composer; any relevant material not discussed above; general summation of harmonic, melodic, rhythmic, and formal techniques used; and their correlation.

Limitations of space do not allow for extensive dissertations for each of these categories (which indeed becomes a possibility when one begins to delve deeply into most contemporary works), but rather a synoptical summary of the techniques and applications found under each reference.

1. Historical Background: Edgard Varèse (1883–1965) was born in Paris of Italian-French parents and studied principally mathematics and science at school until he was 18. He then entered the Schola Cantorum where he studied composition with Vincent d'Indy, Albert Roussel, and Charles Widor, becoming as well a very close friend and confidant of Ferruccio Busoni. He came to the United States in 1915, organizing both orchestras and concert societies for new music in New York City. Many of his early works were destroyed by fire. The greater part of the music we are now aware of was written during the twenties and thirties; for example, *Octandre* (1924), *Intégrales* (1925), and *Ionisation* (1931). From that time until the early fifties Varèse did not compose. The fifties brought *Déserts* (1954) and *Poème électronique* (1958) into existence, both works involving electronic forces. Varèse was clearly influenced by the iconoclastic Busoni and Carlos Salzedo, with whom he founded the Internatonal Composers' Guild in 1921. As well, his work shows marked influence of Stravinsky's early "primitive" period.

2. Overview: *Density 21.5* was completed in 1936 and written for Georges Barrere for the inauguration of his platinum flute (21.5 is the density of platinum). The work was revised in April of 1946 for a *New Music Quarterly* release in July of that year, and subsequent performances follow this latter form. The work is in three main continuous sections, with the first and last having similar lyric qualities. The middle section is event-oriented.

   It is interesting that the first note of each of these sections when taken out of context but grouped together become the first three notes of the piece (F—E—F♯) as shown in Figure 1.4. This kind of "organic" writing (all materials flowing naturally from a single seed) replaces some of the tonal expectations of key, triad, and hierarchy and provides a kind of consistency that gives a natural sense of flow to the work.

3. Orchestration Techniques: Most timbral features available on the flute are explored in this piece: range differences, dynamics within the various

registers, articulations, and so on. Figure 1.42 shows an excerpt employing "slapped" keys, a percussive effect produced by playing softly and hitting the key simultaneously (+).

4. Basic Techniques: The motive of the piece is clearly stated and separated from the body of the first phrase: F—E—F♯ (see Figure 1.43). Note that this motive also implies a concept of statement (F), new statement (E), and return to the first statement with variation (F♯), which characterizes the work's form. Within the first section, one finds constant references to the opening motive. Measure 2 continues the first phrase with basic expansion of intervals and extension (four notes instead of three). The second phrase begins exactly as the first, but continues with variations based on inversion (F♯—G—F♯) and repetition. The third phrase retrogrades the extension of the first phrase and intervallically expands the motive to G—B♭—G. Every note of the first section can realistically be evolved from the opening three-note motive. Some are extensive variations, while others are simple inversions. However, all reflect in some way the concept of statement—new statement—return, with variation implicit in the motive of the piece. One can also note the synthetic scale used at the beginning and throughout the work based on the eight-pitch base of the opening eight bars. Also

Figure 1.42. Opening materials of each section for *Density 21.5.* © 1946 by Colfranc Music Publishing Corp.

Figure 1.43. The opening 8 bars of *Density 21.5* © 1946 by Colfranc Music Publishing Corp.

noteworthy is the way in which Varèse "saves" important notes—notably D, which does not occur until bar 11; and B, which does not occur until bar 18.

The second section establishes a contrasting pointillistic theme (see Figure 1.42). However, note the "real" material here: E—C♯—E is clearly a variant of the opening motive. Even the highly contrasting and repetitive climax of the work is an extended inversion of the opening motive. The third section returns to the opening lyric style, with pitch content based on opening materials.

Varèse may have even attempted numerical relationships with the title of the piece. Interestingly, 70 out of the first 83 intervals of the piece are seconds (2) primes (1) or fifths (5). Whether Varèse intended such relationships is really beside the point; such extreme consistency of intervallic structure contributes to the overall tightly integrated structure of the piece.

5. Vertical Model: One does not expect to find vertical possibilities in a work for solo flute. However, it is interesting to note how figure repetition, after a period of time, blends and begins to suggest vertical simultaneities. In Figure 1.44 two of the prominent intervals (seconds and fourths) are underscored by notable repetition. The passage emphasizes tonal ambiguities (non-resolution of tritones) and contrasts these with highly directed dynamics. Note as well how the D♯ is "saved" and finally reached in an explosive *fortississimo*.

Figure 1.44. Repetition in *Density 21.5*. © 1946 by Colfranc Publishing Corp.

6. Horizontal Models: The expansion of the original motive is prevalent. Figure 1.45 shows how the interval of a second expands to the augmented fourth (as mentioned in vertical models). Note how the passage is a kind of "suspension" of musical time. Only the opening note is a downbeat, with the remainder of the phrase freely sculpted from available duration rather than splintered from beats and sub-beats.

7. Style: Varèse's *Density 21.5* is a three-part work consistently hewn from an initial three-note motive of major and minor seconds. The instrument's range and available effects are explored as are the concepts of augmentation and diminution of intervals, saving pitches for intense climaxes. A "free" phrase

Figure 1.45. Expansion techniques in *Density 21.5*. © 1946 by Colfranc Publishing Corp.

structure dominates but without marked tonal references or resolutions. Lines are freely spun through time in a musical and balanced manner. The musical language used, however separate from a tonal sphere, is articulate and consistent. Varèse belongs to that group of composers intent on creating a new syntax from rich vocabularies of sound.

Readers should compare this vectoral analysis with those of the next two chapters (for the extraordinary differences) and then the last two chapters of the book (for the similarities). The chromaticism of the Webern example in the next chapter compares favorably except in its serial approach. The line of the Varèse contrasts significantly with the pointillism of the Webern. The Glass example in chapter 11, however, is comparable in the latter case and not in the former.

Bibliography— Chapter 1*

Further Readings

Prelude

Austin, William. *Music in the Twentieth Century.* New York: W. W. Norton, 1966.

Gagne, Cole, and Tracy Caras. *Soundpieces: Interviews with American Composers.* Metuchen, N.J.: The Scarecrow Press, Inc., 1982.

Griffiths, Paul. *A Concise History of Avant-Garde Music.* New York: Oxford University Press, 1978.

Harder, Paul. *Bridge to Twentieth Century Music.* Boston: Allyn and Bacon, 1973.

Hartog, H. *European Music in the Twentieth Century.* New York: Praeger, 1957.

Machlis, Joseph. *Introduction to Contemporary Music,* 2d ed. New York: W. W. Norton and Co., 1979.

Martin, W. R. and Drossin, J. *Music of the Twentieth Century.* Englewood Cliffs, N.J.: Prentice-Hall, 1980.

Mellers, Wilfred. *Romanticism and the Twentieth Century.* New York: Schocken, 1969.

Myers, Rollo W. *Modern French Music from Fauré to Boulez.* New York: Praeger Books, 1971.

Rochberg, George. *The Aesthetics of Survival. A Composer's View of Twentieth-Century Music.* Ann Arbor: The University of Michigan Press, 1984.

Salzman, Eric. *Twentieth-Century Music: An Introduction,* 3d ed. Englewood Cliffs, N.J.: Prentice-Hall, 1988.

Satie, Erik. *Écrits (réunis, établis et annotés par Ornella Volta).* Paris: Editions Champ Libre, 1977.

Schillinger, Joseph. *The Mathematical Basis of the Arts.* New York: The Philosophical Library, 1948.

———. *The Schillinger System of Musical Composition.* New York: Da Capo Press, 1978.

Simms, Bryan R. *Music of the Twentieth Century, Style and Structure.* New York: Schirmer Books, 1986.

Slonimsky, Nicolas. *Music Since 1900,* 4th ed. New York: Charles Scribner's Sons, 1971.

Sternfeld, F. W., ed. *Music in the Modern Age. Praeger History of Music.* Vol. V. New York: Praeger Books, 1973.

*Addresses for record companies, periodicals, and music publishers mentioned in this Bibliography can be found in Appendix IV.

Stuckenschmidt, H. H. *Twentieth-Century Music.* New York: McGraw-Hill, 1969.

Thompson, Oscar. *A Dictionary of Twentieth-Century Composers (1911–1971).* London: Faber and Faber, 1973.

Yates, Peter. *Twentieth-Century Music.* New York: Pantheon, 1967.

An Overview of Tonality

Aldwell, Edward, and Carl Schachter. *Harmony and Voice Leading.* New York: Harcourt Brace Jovanovich, 1978.

Backus, John. *The Acoustical Foundations of Music.* New York: W. W. Norton, 1969.

Benade, Arthur. *Fundamentals of Music Acoustics.* New York: Oxford University Press, 1976.

Benward, Bruce. *Music in Theory and Practice,* 2d ed. Dubuque, Iowa: Wm. C. Brown Publishers, 1982.

Forte, Allen. *Tonal Harmony in Concept and Practice,* 3d ed. New York: Holt, Rinehart and Winston, 1979.

Hall, Donald. *Musical Acoustics.* Belmont, Calif.: Wadsworth Publishing Co., 1980.

Hartog, H. *European Music in the Twentieth Century.* New York: Praeger, 1957.

Roederer, Juan. *Introduction to the Physics and Psychophysics of Music.* London: The English University Press, Ltd., 1974.

Stuckenschmidt, H. H. *Twentieth-Century Music.* New York: McGraw-IIill, 1969.

Expanded Scale Resources

Fink, Robert, and Robert Ricci. *The Language of Twentieth Century Music.* New York: Schirmer Books, 1975.

Forte, Allen. *Contemporary Tone Structures.* New York: Columbia University Press, 1955.

Kostka, Stefan. *Materials and Techniques of Twentieth-Century Music.* Englewood Cliffs, N.J.: Prentice-Hall, 1990.

Slonimsky, Nicolas. *Thesaurus of Scales and Melodic Patterns.* New York: Coleman-Ross, 1947.

Tenney, James. *Meta (+) Hodos: A Phenomenology of Twentieth-Century Musical Materials and an Approach to the Study of Form.* Oakland, Calif.: Frog Peak Music, 1986.

Extensions of Tertian Harmony

Dallin, Leon. *Techniques of Twentieth Century Composition,* 3d ed. Dubuque, Iowa: Wm. C. Brown Publishers, 1974.

Howat, Roy. *Debussy in Proportion.* Cambridge: Cambridge University Press, 1983.

Kupbovic, L. "The Role of Tonality in Contemporary and 'Up-to-date' Composition." *Tempo* 135 (1980): pp. 16–19.

Lester, Joel. *Analytic Approaches to Twentieth-Century Music.* New York: W. W. Norton, 1989.

Persichetti, Vincent. *Twentieth Century Harmony.* New York: W. W. Norton, 1961.

Musical Hierarchies

Hindemith, Paul. *The Craft of Musical Composition.* New York: Associated Music Publishers, 1937.

Lerdahl, Fred, and Ray Jackendoff. *A Generative Theory of Tonal Music.* Cambridge, Mass.: MIT Press, 1983.

Narmour, Eugene. "Some Major Theoretical Problems Concerning the Concept of Hierarchy in the Analysis of Tonal Music." *Music Perception* 1, no. 2 (1983): pp. 129–99.

Schenker, Heinrich. *Five Analyses in Sketchform.* New York: David Mannes School of Music, 1933.

Schillinger, Joseph. *The Mathematical Basis of the Arts.* New York: The Philosophical Library, 1948.

————. *The Schillinger System of Musical Composition.* New York: Da Capo Press, 1978.

Schoenberg, Arnold. *Structural Functions of Harmony.* New York: W. W. Norton, 1969.

Edgard Varèse

Schuller, Gunther. "Conversation with Varèse." *Perspectives of New Music* 3, no. 2 (1965): pp. 32–37.

Varèse, Louise Norton. *A Looking Glass Diary.* New York: W. W. Norton, 1972.

Wen-Chung, Chou. "The Liberation of Sound." In *Contemporary Composers on Contemporary Music,* ed. Barney Childs and Elliott Schwartz, pp. 308–15. New York: Holt, Rinehart and Winston, 1967.

————. "Varèse: A Sketch of the Man and His Music." *Musical Quarterly* 52 (1966): pp. 151–70.

Compact Discs, Recordings, and Publishers

Bartók, Béla. *Mikrokosmos.* Volume V (1935). Boosey and Hawkes. Hungaroton HCD 31156–56.

————. *Out of Doors Suite.* Universal Edition. DG 423 958–2.

Beethoven, Ludwig van. *Sonata* Op. 2, No. 3, C. F. Peters. Philips 420 153–2PH.

Busoni, Ferruccio. *Fantasia contrappuntistica* (1915). Continuum CCD 1006.

Debussy, Claude. *La Soirée dans Grenade.* International Music Corporation. Denon CO-1411.

————. *Pelleas and Melisande* (1907). A. Durand. Pierre Verany PV 788094/4.

————. *Preludes* Books I and II (1910–1913). A. Durand. Nonesuch 73031.

————. *Prélude à "L'Après-midi d'un faune."* A. Durand. EMI Eminence CD-EMX 9502.

Griffes, Charles Tomlinson. *Sonata.* G. Schirmer. Gasparo GSCD 231.

Hindemith, Paul. *Chansons* (6). B. Schott's Soehne, Mainz.

Ives, Charles. *Concord Sonata* (1915). Associated Music Publishers. New World 378–2.

————. *114 Songs* (1884–1921). New Music Edition. Nonesuch 9 71325–2.

————. *Three Places in New England.* Mercury Music Corporation. DG 423 243–2GC.

Mozart, Wolfgang Amadeus. *Theme and Variations: Ah! Vous Dirai-je, Maman* (K. 265). Kalmus Edition. Accent ACC 58018.

Ravel, Maurice. *Daphnis et Chloe Suite #2* (1913). A. Durand. London 400055–2 LH.

————. *Le Tombeau de Couperin.* A. Durand. Decca 400 051–2DH.

————. *Sonatine* (for piano). International Music Publishers. Denon CD-7805.

Satie, Erik. *Trois Gymnopédies.* Kalmus Edition. Decca 410 220–2DH.

Schoenberg, Arnold. *Pierrot Lunaire* (1912). Universal Edition. London Enterprise 425 626–2LM.

————. *Sechs Kleine Klavierstücke* Op. 19. International Editions. DG 423 249–2.

Scriabin, Alexander. *Poème* Op. 69, No. 1. C. F. Peters.

Stravinsky, Igor. *Petrushka.* Edition Russe de Musique. EMKI CDC 7 49053 2.

Varèse, Edgard. *Density 21.5.* Colfranc Corporation. Nonesuch 73028.

————. *Octandre.* Colfranc Corporation. Reference Recordings RR 29 CD.

Wagner, Richard. *Tristan und Isolde.* Eulenberg Scores. DG 423 613–2.

Webern, Anton. *Six Bagatelles* (for string quartet). Universal Edition. Nonesuch 9 79181–2.

2 SERIALISM

12-Tone Techniques

As artists stretched ever outward to explore new visions, musical traditions continued to collapse. Audiences groped for tangible indications of commonality of style. Stravinsky remarks: "Is it any wonder, then, that the critics of today should be dumbfounded by a language in which all of the characteristics of their aesthetic seem to be violated?"[1] Natural too is the composer's desire for new order to be able to spend more time "composing" and less "experimenting" with new materials and techniques.

During the first two decades of the twentieth century, a number of mainstreams derived from Romantic traditions of the nineteenth century developed. The Germanic style (often presented as a Beethoven-Wagner-Mahler-Schoenberg lineage) was steeped in motivic microdevelopment and metatonal (chromatic) concepts. The Franco-Russian composers (particularly Debussy, Ravel, and Stravinsky), the Primitivists (especially Béla Bartók), and the Iconoclastic composers (particularly Charles Ives in America) developed more fluid, less systematic techniques, often effecting fewer works in freer application.

One of the more important developments during this time was twelve-tone composition (often called *serialism* or *dodecaphony*). It was derived from a base of Germanic tradition, and presented composers with the prospect of a common language and context. The twelve-tone approach was developed primarily by Arnold Schoenberg during the years 1917 to 1923, during which time he wrote little music, devoting his energies to performance and development of the new techniques and applications he had discovered. Serialism seemed to him to be the natural conclusion of the extended complex chromaticism that had been developing in Western European music during the previous 140 years (since mid-Mozart).

One of the basic properties of twelve-tone writing is the creation of a row. The only basic requirement of this line of twelve notes is that they all be different (i.e., the row must contain all twelve notes of the chromatic scale). Figure 2.1 shows how three different serial composers applied this principle. Note how Schoenberg's row (a) tends to void suggestions of tonal centers (i.e., successive notes tending not to exist in the implied key signature of the previous note). On the other hand, Berg's row (b) holds strong tonal ties with continuous triadic reference (the first seven

---

1. Igor Stravinsky, *An Autobiography* (New York: W. W. Norton, 1936), p. 176.

Figure 2.1. (a) Schoenberg: *Variations for Orchestra*, Op. 31; (b) Berg: *Violin Concerto*; (c) Webern: *Symphonie*, Op. 21.

Figure 2.2. Arnold Schoenberg. Dover Publications, Inc. Permission granted.

Figure 2.3. Alban Berg. Dover Publications, Inc. Permission granted.

notes, moreover, existing in the G melodic minor scale). Webern (c) tends to develop certain integrated cross-referencing within the row itself (i.e., the second half of the row is a reverse of the first half).

Once a composer has created a row, called "prime," certain variants are created: *retrograde* (the row played backward), *inversion* (the row played upside down), and *inversion-retrograde* (the row played both upside down and backward). Each of these is shown in Figure 2.4 based on the Schoenberg row of Figure 2.1. It is important to note from the outset that interval integrity must be maintained throughout (i.e., each interval is reproduced exactly with each version). However, it is not necessary for the new pitch to remain in the octave shown. Once determined, the pitch belongs to a "class" of pitches with the same name. Therefore, all C's belong to the same "pitch class."

The numbers above each note of the prime version (Figure 2.4) indicate the position of the notes in the row. The number to the right of the version letters are

Figure 2.4. Prime, retrograde, inversion, and inversion-retrograde of row for Schoenberg's *Variations for Orchestra*, Op. 31.

Figure 2.4. Prime, retrograde, inversion, and inversion-retrograde of row for Schoenberg's *Variations for Orchestra*, Op. 31.

Figure 2.5. Transpositions (beginning on successively lower notes) of row for Schoenberg's *Variations for Orchestra*, Op. 31.

intervals in chromatic scale order; the initial pitch is labeled "0" and the last "11," accounting for the eleven half-steps between the twelve different notes present. Each of these variants can now exist in twelve transpositions (each beginning on twelve different notes, again keeping their respective interval integrity intact). Figure 2.5 shows the original row beginning on B♭, then A, then A♭, and so on, clearly demonstrating the different levels. Notice that the variations Schoenberg chose to develop his row properties are extensions of motivic development that German composers (particularly since Beethoven) used with extreme vitality. Again, the arabic numeral next to the "P" indicates a new beginning pitch referenced to the interval above "P_0."

One way composers chose to show all the versions of a row at once is called a *matrix*. This "box" of 144 squares is created by cross-thatching twelve vertical lines with twelve horizontal lines (actually thirteen in each case to provide the outer layers of the box itself). If the original row is placed across the top of the box from left to right and the inversion placed down the left of the matrix from top to bottom a frame can be created to define the interior rows. To complete the matrix, one fills in left to right the transpositions of the original, allowing the notes of the inversion to dictate the beginning notes. Figure 2.6 shows a completed matrix based on the Schoenberg row of Figure 2.1. Note that one can now quickly read any version of the row

	I_0	I_6	I_8	I_5	I_7	I_{11}	I_4	I_3	I_9	I_{10}	I_1	I_2	
P_0	Bb	E	Gb	Eb	F	A	D	Db	G	Ab	B	C	R_0
P_6	E	Bb	C	A	B	Eb	Ab	G	Db	D	F	F#	R_6
P_4	D	Ab	Bb	G	A	Db	Gb	F	B	C	Eb	E	R_4
P_7	F	B	Db	Bb	C	E	A	Ab	D	Eb	Gb	G	R_7
P_5	Eb	A	B	Ab	Bb	D	G	Gb	C	Db	E	F	R_5
P_1	B	F	G	E	Gb	Bb	Eb	D	Ab	A	C	Db	R_1
P_8	F#	C	D	B	Db	F	Bb	A	Eb	E	G	Ab	R_8
P_9	G	Db	Eb	C	D	Gb	B	Bb	E	F	Ab	A	R_9
P_3	C#	G	A	F#	Ab	C	F	E	Bb	B	D	D#	R_3
P_2	C	F#	G#	F	G	B	E	Eb	A	Bb	C#	D	R_2
P_{11}	A	D#	F	D	E	G#	C#	C	F#	G	Bb	B	R_{11}
P_{10}	G#	D	E	C#	D#	G	C	B	F	F#	A	Bb	R_{10}
	RI_0	RI_6	RI_8	RI_5	RI_7	RI_{11}	RI_4	RI_3	RI_9	RI_{10}	RI_1	RI_2	

Figure 2.6. Matrix of row from Schoenberg's *Variations for Orchestra*, Op. 31.

from the completed matrix (originals, left to right; inversions, top to bottom; retrogrades, right to left; retrograde-inversions, bottom to top). The matrix can become an extremely important tool for use in analysis or composition of twelve-tone music.

A row seen in a matrix is void of absolute register. The Bb (upper left corner) could appear in any octave. Each pitch becomes part of a distinct and related (by octave) "set" of pitches (all Bb's in this instance). As mentioned earlier, they belong to the same "pitch class." Composers are able to choose freely from any member of a certain pitch class and not be restricted to a given octave. Notes that are enharmonically equivalent (i.e., Bb, A#) belong to the same pitch class.

Composers typically utilize rows in two ways in serial composition. The first (here called category A) derives all successive notes from one version of the row at a time. Figure 2.7A shows a category A type of composition using the Schoenberg row. Notice that all notes of both melody and harmony are extracts from the single version of the original form of the row. In order to show this, numbers here refer to row ordering and not interval relationship to the initial pitch. The work could continue from this point with a repeat of this version or any other version used in a similar manner.

A second type of twelve-tone composition employs more than one version of the row at a time and is called category B. Figure 2.7B shows three versions of the

Figure 2.7. Category A (a) and category B (b) types of twelve-tone composition using Schoenberg row from *Variations for Orchestra*, Op. 31.

Schoenberg row used simultaneously. Unlike the category A composition, it is difficult here to maintain a twelve-tone integrity (e.g., notes are frequently repeated immediately or simultaneously, often creating non-row-centered sonorities).

Early in the development of twelve-tone theory, Schoenberg and others adopted a variety of techniques that aid the composer in expanding the potential of the approach. These create interesting anomalies that can eventually lead to unique styles and works. The most simple of these variations is *repetition*. Since most music includes repetition of individual notes as inherent to an important motive or line, this same attribute can be utilized in twelve-tone composition. Therefore, repeated notes and chords are acceptable and not considered deviations from the basic structure of twelve-tone concepts. Patterns of notes (e.g., two-, three-, and four-note groupings) may also be repeated immediately after they have sounded, making it possible for the composer to initiate individual stylistic motives.

Overlapping one version of the row with another is also fairly common in twelve-tone compositions. Typically in this variant, the last note of one version becomes the first note of the next. Composers also use *anticipations* of coming material, creating interesting implosions of row contents. Figure 2.8 has the first eight notes of the row in the voice part. The ninth through twelfth notes of the row are stated in the piano part even before the voice part begins. These then are repeated with variation as accompaniment until they fall in their right place numerically.

Combinatoriality

Category B twelve-tone composition poses problems of harmonic continuity and homogeneity. While these problems do not exist in category A composition, composers seem more interested in the complexities available in the contrapuntal use of

Figure 2.8. Arnold Schoenberg: *Sommermud.* Example of note repetition and anticipation in twelve-tone composition.

many variants of the row used simultaneously. Combinatoriality mechanics tend to absorb the discontinuities resulting from category B usage.

One of the first steps in understanding combinatoriality involves applying principles of subsetting. A *subset* is a group of notes, smaller than twelve, that is an evenly divisible integer of the whole (e.g., 2, 3, 4, and 6 are each evenly divisible into 12). Terminology includes *hexachord,* a group of six notes (two in a twelve-tone row); *tetrachord,* a group of four notes (three in a twelve-tone row); *trichord,* a group of three notes (four in a twelve-tone row); and *dichord,* a group of two notes (six in a twelve-tone row).

Combinatoriality, the combining of versions of mutually exclusive note contents, is best understood when carefully observing the matrix. Looking back at Figure 2.6, one notices that the second hexachord of the original row (i.e., D, D♭, G, A♭, B, C of P_0 in that order) equals the pitch content of the first hexachord of the inversion of the row beginning on G (I_9 top to bottom beginning in the ninth square from left to right). Important, however, is that the order of the notes involved has changed (i.e., they now read G, D♭, B, D, C, and A♭; 9, 3, 1, 4, 2, 10 instead of 4, 3, 9, 10, 1, 2). As would be expected, the second hexachord of this inversion has the same note content as the first hexachord of the original nontransposed version. This feature becomes important when one realizes that combining these two versions in a category B type composition provides a continuous twelve-tone (category A type) continuity and homogeneity, while at the same time providing the explorations possible in the contrapuntal environment of category B frameworks.

In Figure 2.9 the top voice uses the twelve notes of the original form of the row, with the twelve notes of the inversion from G used in the bass voice. Note, however, that unlike Figure 2.7B where the vertical chromaticism often produces irregularities such as octaves and repeated notes, this example does not. Clearly the first bar contains twelve different notes as does the second bar. This kind of hexachordal subsetting in the right combinations provides the basis for combinatorial composition.

Figure 2.9. Combinatoriality using the original (top voice) and the inversion (bottom voice) of the row from Schoenberg's *Variations for Orchestra*, Op. 31.

Pitch class sets									
		5-7	0,1,2,6,7	6-18	0,1,2,5,7,8	7-Z17	0,1,2,4,5,6,9	8-28	0,1,3,4,6,7,9,10
		5-8(12)	0,2,3,4,6	6-Z19	0,1,3,4,7,8	7-Z18	0,1,2,3,5,8,9	8-Z29	0,1,2,3,5,6,7,9
3-1(12)	0,1,2	5-9	0,1,2,4,6	6-20(4)	0,1,4,5,8,9	7-19	0,1,2,3,6,7,9	9-1	0,1,2,3,4,5,6,7,8
3-2	0,1,3	5-10	0,1,3,4,6	6-21	0,2,3,4,6,8	7-20	0,1,2,4,7,8,9	9-2	0,1,2,3,4,5,6,7,9
3-3	0,1,4	5-11	0,2,3,4,7	6-22	0,1,2,4,6,8	7-21	0,1,2,4,5,8,9	9-3	0,1,2,3,4,5,6,8,9
3-4	0,1,5	5-Z12(12)	0,1,3,5,6	6-Z23(12)	0,2,3,5,6,8	7-22	0,1,2,5,6,8,9	9-4	0,1,2,3,4,5,7,8,9
3-5	0,1,6	5-13	0,1,2,4,8	6-Z24	0,1,3,4,6,8	7-23	0,2,3,4,5,7,9	9-5	0,1,2,3,4,6,7,8,9
3-6(12)	0,2,4	5-14	0,1,2,5,7	6-Z25	0,1,3,5,6,8	7-24	0,1,2,3,5,7,9	9-6	0,1,2,3,4,5,6,8,10
3-7	0,2,5	5-15(12)	0,1,2,6,8	6-Z26(12)	0,1,3,5,7,8	7-25	0,2,3,4,6,7,9	9-7	0,1,2,3,4,5,7,8,10
3-8	0,2,6	5-16	0,1,3,4,7	6-27	0,1,3,4,6,9	7-26	0,1,3,4,5,7,9	9-8	0,1,2,3,4,6,7,8,10
3-9(12)	0,2,7	5-17(12)	0,1,3,4,8	6-Z28(12)	0,1,3,5,6,9	7-27	0,1,2,4,5,7,9	9-9	0,1,2,3,5,6,7,8,10
3-10(12)	0,3,6	5-Z18	0,1,4,5,7	6-Z29(12)	0,1,3,6,8,9	7-28	0,1,3,5,6,7,9	9-10	0,1,2,3,4,6,7,9,10
3-11	0,3,7	5-19	0,1,3,6,7	6-30(12)	0,1,3,6,7,9	7-29	0,1,2,4,6,7,9	9-11	0,1,2,3,5,6,7,9,10
3-12(4)	0,4,8	5-20	0,1,3,7,8	6-31	0,1,3,5,8,9	7-30	0,1,2,4,6,8,9	9-12	0,1,2,4,5,6,8,9,10
4-1(12)	0,1,2,3	5-21	0,1,4,5,8	6-32(12)	0,2,4,5,7,9	7-31	0,1,3,4,6,7,9		
4-2	0,1,2,4	5-22(12)	0,1,4,7,8	6-33	0,2,3,5,7,9	7-32	0,1,3,4,6,8,9		
4-3(12)	0,1,3,4	5-23	0,2,3,5,7	6-34	0,1,3,5,7,9	7-33	0,1,2,4,6,8,10		
4-4	0,1,2,5	5-24	0,1,3,5,7	6-35(2)	0,2,4,6,8,10	7-34	0,1,3,4,6,8,10		
4-5	0,1,2,6	5-25	0,2,3,5,8	6-Z36	0,1,2,3,4,7	7-35	0,1,3,5,6,8,10		
4-6(12)	0,1,2,7	5-26	0,2,4,5,8	6-Z37(12)	0,1,2,3,4,8	7-Z36	0,1,2,3,5,6,8		
4-7(12)	0,1,4,5	5-27	0,1,3,5,8	6-Z38(12)	0,1,2,3,7,8	7-Z37	0,1,3,4,5,7,8		
4-8(12)	0,1,5,6	5-28	0,2,3,6,8	6-Z39	0,2,3,4,5,8	7-Z38	0,1,2,4,5,7,8		
4-9(6)	0,1,6,7	5-29	0,1,3,6,8	6-Z40	0,1,2,3,5,8	8-1	0,1,2,3,4,5,6,7		
4-10(12)	0,2,3,5	5-30	0,1,4,6,8	6-Z41	0,1,2,3,6,8	8-2	0,1,2,3,4,5,6,8		
4-11	0,1,3,5	5-31	0,1,3,6,9	6-Z42(12)	0,1,2,3,6,9	8-3	0,1,2,3,4,5,6,9		
4-12	0,2,3,6	5-32	0,1,4,6,9	6-Z43	0,1,2,5,6,8	8-4	0,1,2,3,4,5,7,8		
4-13	0,1,3,6	5-33(12)	0,2,4,6,8	6-Z44	0,1,2,5,6,9	8-5	0,1,2,3,4,6,7,8		
4-14	0,2,3,7	5-34(12)	0,2,4,6,9	6-Z45(12)	0,2,3,4,6,9	8-6	0,1,2,3,5,6,7,8		
4-Z15	0,1,4,6	5-35(12)	0,2,4,7,9	6-Z46	0,1,2,4,6,9	8-7	0,1,2,3,4,5,8,9		
4-16	0,1,5,7	5-Z36	0,1,2,4,7	6-Z47	0,1,2,4,7,9	8-8	0,1,2,3,4,7,8,9		
4-17(12)	0,3,4,7	5-Z37(12)	0,3,4,5,8	6-Z48(12)	0,1,2,5,7,9	8-9	0,1,2,3,6,7,8,9		
4-18	0,1,4,7	5-Z38	0,1,2,5,8	6-Z49(12)	0,1,3,4,7,9	8-10	0,2,3,4,5,6,7,9		
4-19	0,1,4,8	6-1(12)	0,1,2,3,4,5	6-Z50(12)	0,1,4,6,7,9	8-11	0,1,2,3,4,5,7,9		
4-20(12)	0,1,5,8	6-2	0,1,2,3,4,6	7-1	0,1,2,3,4,5,6	8-12	0,1,3,4,5,6,7,9		
4-21(12)	0,2,4,6	6Z3	0,1,2,3,5,6	7-2	0,1,2,3,4,5,7	8-13	0,1,2,3,4,6,7,9		
4-22	0,2,4,7	6-Z4(12)	0,1,2,4,5,6	7-3	0,1,2,3,4,5,8	8-14	0,1,2,4,5,6,7,9		
4-23(12)	0,2,5,7	6-5	0,1,2,3,6,7	7-4	0,1,2,3,4,6,7	8-Z15	0,1,2,3,4,6,8,9		
4-24(12)	0,2,4,8	6-Z6(12)	0,1,2,5,6,7	7-5	0,1,2,3,5,6,7	8-16	0,1,2,3,5,7,8,9		
4-25(6)	0,2,6,8	6-7(6)	0,1,2,6,7,8	7-6	0,1,2,3,4,7,8	8-17	0,1,3,4,5,6,8,9		
4-26(12)	0,3,5,8	6-8(12)	0,2,3,4,5,7	7-7	0,1,2,3,6,7,8	8-18	0,1,2,3,5,6,8,9		
4-27	0,2,5,8	6-9	0,1,2,3,5,7	7-8	0,2,3,4,5,6,8	8-19	0,1,2,4,5,6,8,9		
4-28(3)	0,3,6,9	6-Z10	0,1,3,4,5,7	7-9	0,1,2,3,4,6,8	8-20	0,1,2,4,5,7,8,9		
4-Z29	0,1,3,7	6-Z11	0,1,2,4,5,7	7-10	0,1,2,3,4,6,9	8-21	0,1,2,3,4,6,8,10		
5-1(12)	0,1,2,3,4	6-Z12	0,1,2,4,6,7	7-11	0,1,3,4,5,6,8	8-22	0,1,2,3,5,6,8,10		
5-2	0,1,2,3,5	6-Z13(12)	0,1,3,4,6,7	7-Z12	0,1,2,3,4,7,9	8-23	0,1,2,3,5,7,8,10		
5-3	0,1,2,4,5	6-14	0,1,3,4,5,8	7-13	0,1,2,4,5,6,8	8-24	0,1,2,4,5,6,8,10		
5-4	0,1,2,3,6	6-15	0,1,2,4,5,8	7-14	0,1,2,3,5,7,8	8-25	0,1,2,4,6,7,8,10		
5-5	0,1,2,3,7	6-16	0,1,4,5,6,8	7-15	0,1,2,4,6,7,8	8-26	0,1,2,4,5,7,9,10		
5-6	0,1,2,5,6	6-Z17	0,1,2,4,7,8	7-16	0,1,2,3,5,6,9	8-27	0,1,2,4,5,7,8,10		

Figure 2.10. A chart of unordered pitch class sets.

Set Theory

A number of composers have employed theories of unordered pitch sets in their compositions. This theory suggests that contiguous pitch groupings (whether melodic or harmonic) can be recognized regardless of their order or transposition. Only 220 unique pitch class (pc) sets exist mathematically (shown here in Figure 2.10).

The name of each set derives from the number of pitches in the set and its number in the series. The numbers that follow equate to 0 = C, 1 = Db, 2 = D, and so on in ascending numerical order, with intervals reduced within the octave (12 = pitch class equivalency). Two pitch-class sets are equivalent if they are reducible to the same prime form by transposition or by inversion followed by transposition. Figure 2.11 shows how such reductions demonstrate similarities between otherwise (apparently) dissimilar harmonies. Figure 2.11a shows two harmonies that seem to be different. Using set theory, however, they reduce to the same pc set. The process follows:

1. Eliminate all octave doublings and place the results within a single octave range as shown in Figure 2.11b. One does the same thing, either implicitly or explicitly, when analyzing tonal music.

2. Represent each note by its equivalent number as previously described (e.g., C = 0, D♭ = 1, etc.) as shown in Figure 2.11c. This helps clarify intervals.

3. Rearrange the order of numbers by first placing them in ascending order and then transposing them (as necessary) so that the first number is zero (i.e., subtracting the first number from each number in the series, or transposing to C) as shown in Figure 2.11d. This effectively transposes all chords so that they are in ascending order above the note C.

It is immediately clear that both chords reduce to the same set. Usually at this juncture the set is identified in the list of sets given in Figure 2.10. Unfortunately, however, this set is not to be found in that list. For this to occur the set must be placed in its best normal order or "prime form." This is accomplished by the following steps:

1. Permutate the row by rotating the first number to the last and add 12 to it as shown in Figure 2.11e. This is similar to finding the root of a triad by successively placing the bass note an octave up.

2. Find the difference between the first and last numbers of the set and select the set with the least difference as shown in the right-hand portion of Figure 2.11e. This finds the chords with the smallest overall range and is similar to finding a triad from its inversions.

3. If more than one set has the same least difference, as is the case here, determine the prime form by finding the difference between the first and second numbers of the equal remaining sets and select the one with the smallest difference as shown in Figure 2.11f. If more than one set has the same smallest difference, then find the difference between the first and third numbers, and so on. This is not necessary in this case, as 3, 5, 6, 9, 12 proves smallest. This is similar to removing the 6/4 and 6/3 versions from more than one version of triads.

Figure 2.11a. Chords from (respectively) works by Berg and Stravinsky.

a)

Figure 2.11b-l. Process for reducing a pitch class set to its prime form.

b) 1) F, F♯, A, C, E♭
    2) D, F, G, A♭, B

c) 1) 5, 6, 9, 0, 3
    2) 2, 5, 7, 8, 11

d) 1) 0, 3, 5, 6, 9
    2) 2, 5, 7, 8, 11 = 0, 3, 5, 6, 9

e) 0, 3, 5, 6, 9   = 9
       3, 5, 6, 9, 12   = 9
          5, 6, 9, 12, 15   = 10
             6, 9, 12, 15, 17   = 11
                9, 12, 15, 17, 18 = 9

f) 0, 3, 5, 6, 9   = 3
       3, 5, 6, 9, 12   = 2
                9, 12, 15, 17, 18 = 3

g) 3, 5, 6, 9, 12   =   0, 2, 3, 6, 9

h) 0, 2, 3, 6, 9   =   0, 10, 9, 6, 3

i) 0, 3, 6, 9, 10

j) 0, 3, 6, 9, 10   = 10
       3, 6, 9, 10, 12   = 9
          6, 9, 10, 12, 15   = 9
             9, 10, 12, 15, 18   = 9
                10, 12, 15, 18, 21 = 11

k)   3, 6, 9, 10, 12   = 3
          6, 9, 10, 12, 15   = 3
             9, 10, 12, 15, 18   = 1

l) 9, 10, 12, 15, 18 = 0, 1, 3, 6, 9   = set number 5-31

If the set is still not on the pc set list, it is necessary to do the following:

4. Transpose the set (as necessary) so that the first number is zero (i.e., subtract the first number from each number in the series) as shown in Figure 2.11g.

5. If the set is still not present, as is the case here, subtract each number of the set from 12 as shown in Figure 2.11h.

6. Place the set in ascending order as shown in Figure 2.11i.

7. Again, find its best prime form as in steps 1 to 3 above and as shown in Figure 2.11j and 2.11k.

8. Transpose the set as in step 4 (above) so that the first number is zero as shown in Figure 2.11l.

This set correlates to the prime form 5-31 in Figure 2.10.

Often, only the first four steps above are actually necessary since many chords will fall naturally into the chart. A description of why each of these steps is necessary would be extensive and cumbersome. Suffice it to say that this process roughly parallels that of reducing and transposing inversions of triads to demonstrate their similarity (i.e., root position, 6, and 6/4 inversions).

Figure 2.12 shows another more contextual example. The pc-set analysis below the example demonstrates the interrelationships between unordered sets of pitches (repeated pitches count only once). Note the number of comparable pitch set names. The 6–5 set located in the top voices of both phrases is not readily apparent without using the pc-set manipulations. The music hints at it, however, in the E♭–D♭ dichord (two-note set) at the end of each phrase. The harmonic repeat of 7 Z18 (the Z stands for pitch-class sets that have the same total interval content, but are unrelated by transposition or inversion) and the very consistent 4–16 harmonic vocabulary related to the first tetrachord (four-note set) of the melody suggest serious motivic interweavings.

Pitch-set theory is not without its critics. Many argue against composer intention while others claim that these relationships, for the most part, are unheard and hence useless. In Berg's *Wozzeck,* for example, pc-set analysis of the themes of each character is serious evidence of composer-intended relationships (understood only by a thorough set analysis). Pioneering work on Stravinsky's *Rite of Spring* by Allen Forte suggests serious intent by the composer to draw links between various pitch sets (principally harmonic) in the work. Regardless of past intention or future use, set theory has caused a number of mathematically inclined composers to define their work by the use of unordered pitch sets. The more works under set theory scrutiny, the more that seem to be thus composed.

Serialism

Pantonality (this, not *atonality,* was the term used by Schoenberg), or "inclusive of all tonalities," is important not because of chromaticism, but in its extreme control over compositional elements, a control that is predominantly inaudible and recognizable in general stylistic terms only. Serialization of the other parameters of

Figure 2.12. Opening of Schoenberg's Op. 11, No. 2 with analysis using set theory.

motive a

6-5: (8,9,0,1,2,3)

4-16: (8,9,1,3)

Top Voice: Db A Eb Ab D C Eb Db

F

D

Bottom Voice:

7-Z18: (0,1,2,3,5,8,9)

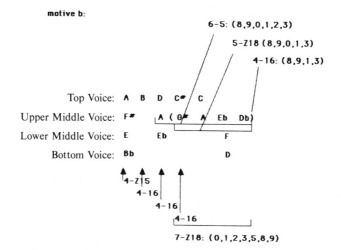

motive b:

6-5: (8,9,0,1,2,3)

5-Z18 (8,9,0,1,3)

4-16: (8,9,1,3)

Top Voice: A   B   D   C# C

Upper Middle Voice: F#   A (G# A Eb Db)

Lower Middle Voice: E   Eb   F

Bottom Voice: Bb   D

4-Z15

4-16

4-16

4-16

7-Z18: (0,1,2,3,5,8,9)

musical composition begins as it does in pitch organization, with the creation of a row and extended by the basic variant sets.

Anton Webern's *Variations for Piano,* Op. 27 (second movement) employs a dynamic row of nine values as shown in Figure 2.13. Webern follows this prime

ƒ p ƒ   p ƒ p   ƒ p ƒƒ

Figure 2.13. Anton Webern: *Variations for Piano,* Op. 27, second movement. Dynamic row.

order with a variation of the retrograde (the third trichord—now the first—left in original order shown in Figure 2.14). Articulations are directly related to individual

ƒ p ƒƒ   p ƒ p   ƒ p ƒ

Figure 2.14. Retrograde (variation) of the dynamic row of Figure 2.14.

1. ⌒   7. >
2. •   8. >
3. - / • / ⌒   9. ⌒ ‿ / •
4. ⌒ / •   10. ⌒ ‿
5. • / - / •   11.
6. >   12. ⌒ ‿

Figure 2.15. Articulation row of Webern's *Variations for Piano,* Op. 27.

pitches of the row. Figure 2.15 shows how this is accomplished. For example, the second note of every version of the row used in the second variation is staccato, and so forth. Careful analysis of rhythm and form (a cyclic mirror canon) shows that these are also related serially to the basic structure of this piece. Whether any of these elements are audible is beside the point. Most tonal composers worked with intricate motivic and chromatic techniques that become evident to the ear only after repeated listening and score study. Some critics of these techniques claim that their basic use is inherently "non-musical." Here again, the point relates to the particular composer using them; if used musically, they aid in the creation of good music. If used as a crutch to simply produce notations of mathematical import and interest without real aural meaning, then certainly they are "non-musical."

The piano composition by Milton Babbitt shown in Figure 2.16 demonstrates serialized control of dynamics, rhythm, and pitch. The pitch content of this piece is based on combinatorial principles. The basic row is shown in Figure 2.17. Note that this form of the row appears in the lower voice of the first two bars. Babbitt carefully observed that the first hexachord of the original form of the row beginning on E contained notes that were mutually exclusive of those in the first hexachord of the original beginning on B♭. Therefore, by combining this version (as the upper voice) with the original nontransposed version, he was able to create combinatoriality. Note

Figure 2.16. Milton Babbitt: *Three Compositions for Piano,* 1947 (measures 1–8, Piece No. 1). Published by Boelke-Bonart, Inc., Hillsdale, N.Y.

Figure 2.17. Row for Milton Babbitt's *Three Compositions for Piano.*

that the first bar contains twelve different notes as does the second bar, thus avoiding inconsistent repetitions or octave-unison doublings.

The rhythm of the piece also involves serial principles. If one looks carefully at the hexachordal subgroupings within each bar of the composition, it becomes clear that a held note contrasts the other notes. In the bass voice, for example, the held tone (fifth in the six-note sequence) suggests a five grouping followed by a single note. The same is true of the first hexachord of the row in the upper voice (i.e., 5/1). In the second bar, the grouping is distinctly different. Here the held note (fourth of the sequence) divides the hexachord into groups of four and two notes each. The rhythm clearly follows a pattern based on the principle of 5/1/4/2; each voice holds that row intact. In the upper voice in bar 3 one encounters the order 2/4, with the next bar developing 1/5 (again, in the upper voice). This ordering (2/4/1/5) is the retrograde of the original rhythmic row.

To create an inversion of such rows becomes obviously different from similar groupings in tone rows. Babbitt creates such "inversions" here (see Figure 2.18) by inverting dichordal subsets (i.e., reversing the order of the outer groups of two numbers each). Therefore, the inversion of 5/1/4/2 becomes 1/5/2/4 and the inversion retrograde, 4/2/5/1. Examining Figure 2.16, bars 3 and 4 (bass voice), one can immediately recognize that the rhythm here is an inversion retrograde of the original row. Serialization of rhythmic principles continues in this manner for the remainder of the piece.

Dynamic serialization, while simpler in this piece, is still important to its basic structure. Here, each version of the row links with a dynamic (i.e., original, *mp;* retrograde, *mf;* inversion, *f;* and inversion retrograde, *p*).

In his now-famous article "Who Cares If You Listen," Milton Babbitt speaks of this "high degree of determinacy":

> In the simplest terms, each such "atomic" event is located in a five-dimensional musical space determined by pitch-class, register, dynamic, duration, and timbre. These five components not only together define the single event, but, in the course of a work, the successive values of each component create an individually coherent structure, frequently in parallel with the corresponding structures created by each of the other components. Inability to perceive and remember precisely the values of any of these components results in a dislocation of the event in the work's musical space, an alteration of its relation to all other events in the work, and—thus—a falsification of the composition's total structure. For example, an incorrectly performed or perceived dynamic value results in destruction of the work's dynamic pattern, but also in false identification of other components of the event (of which this dynamic value is a part) with corresponding components of other events, so creating incorrect pitch, registral, timbral and durational associations.[2]

Babbitt speaks of the confusion surrounding his article in an interview:

> I gave a lecture at Tanglewood in 1957 about the state of the contemporary composer. The then-editor of *High Fidelity* heard it and asked me to write it down. I had been improvising it and didn't want to write it down, but they had a copy of the tape and asked me if I would take it and put it in some kind of publishable shape. The title of the article as submitted to *High Fidelity* was "The Composer as Specialist." There was no imputation whatsoever of "who cares if you listen," which as far as I am concerned conveys very little of the letter of the article, and nothing of the spirit. Obviously the point was that I cared a great deal who listened, but above all how they listened. I was concerned about the fact that people were not listening. But theirs of course, was a much more provocative title, and journalists are concerned to provoke, and do. It wasn't "who cares if you listen." It was this: If you're not going to take our activities in as serious and dignified a manner as we take them, then of course we don't want you to listen.[3]

2. Milton Babbitt, "Who Cares If You Listen," *High Fidelity* 8, no. 2 (February 1958) pp. 38–40, 126–27.

3. Cole Cagne and Tracy Caras, *Soundpieces: Interviews with American Composers* (London: The Scarecrow Press, Inc., 1982), p. 37.

Figure 2.18. Rhythm rows for Babbitt's *Three Compositions for Piano.*

P: 5 - 1 - 4 - 2
I: 1 - 5 - 2 - 4
R: 2 - 4 - 1 - 5
IR: 4 - 2 - 5 - 1

Olivier Messiaen (b. 1909 in France) was one of the first to use rhythmic augmentation, diminution (by one-half, one-third, one-fourth, etc.) of the original material. His *Quatre études de rhythme* (especially number 2, *Mode de valeur et d'intensités),* published in 1949, was one of the first works to include integral organization of the "whole." Though based more on modal than twelve-tone principles, all of the basic musical components are serialized (36 sounds; 24 durations; 7 dynamics; 12 articulations).

Messiaen's influence over the younger composers of France, combined with twelve-tone theory, enabled Pierre Boulez to arrange twelve different durations, twelve articulations, and twelve dynamics in row forms, thus creating serialization possibilities over more compositional elements. This is particularly effective and noticeable in Boulez's *Structures* (1952) and *Second Piano Sonata* (1948). Figure 2.19 shows each of the series he used.

Figure 2.19. Boulez: *Structures* Serialization of parameters.

Bernd Alois Zimmermann's *Perspectives* for two pianos (1956) is row controlled from an aggregate of procedures pertaining to pitch, density, rhythm, dynamics, attacks, and pedaling, representing somewhat of a landmark in its degree of systematic composer control (see the article on the work in *die Reihe* #4 for complete analysis). Ruth Crawford's (1901–53) innovative String Quartet (1931) employs procedures of serialism. The third movement of this work includes an obvious systematic procedure of control in which the compositional elements (pitch, duration, dynamics, and rhythm) are related and serialized. The foundation of the movement is a double canon in dynamics only (first canon in the viola and 'cello and the second in the two violins). The resulting dovetailing of dynamics (one voice in crescendo and the other in simultaneous diminuendo) foreshadows yet another technique of experimentation: timbre modulation. The opening intervals are major and minor seconds with the undulating dynamics creating timbre movements from one instrument to another.

These mathematical approaches are new only in their applications, for since Pythagoras and his followers, music theory has evolved through a process of scientific formulas applied during, though more often after, the compositional process. The increased requirements on both performer and audience must certainly have

Figure 2.20. Pierre Boulez.

been in part responsible for the replacement of the performer by tape music, and the diminishing size of the audience—leaving even fellow professionals interested, but often confused bystanders. Even without serialism, performance conflicts appeared to Charles Ives who, in the Postface to his *114 Songs* (1922), explained: "Some of the songs in this book, particularly among the later ones, cannot be sung, and if they could, perhaps might prefer, if they had to say, to remain as they are; that is, 'in the leaf'—and that they will remain in this peaceful state is more than presumable."[4]

In America, colleges and universities have replaced the courts, the church, and patrons of earlier times, offering the composer the only realistic terms for survival. The need in this academic environment to present composition as an ordered and intellectual pursuit, and the close physical proximity of so-called "disciplines" of scientific teachings, have contributed no small part to the large volume of systems and aesthetics of the past forty years. Pierre Boulez, in an interview with the author, referred to this environment:

Yes, academic, and in the strong sense of the word. It does not matter whether the academic is after Schumann, after Bach, after Wagner, or after a new serial type; the academic is something which I cannot accept at any time. The main problem, to my mind, is to find a purely musical way of thinking and not something which is parascientific.[5]

4. Charles Ives, "Postface to 114 Songs," in *Essays before a Sonata, and Other Writings*, ed. Howard Boatwright (New York: W. W. Norton & Co., 1961), p. 131.

5. Galen Wilson and David Cope, "An Interview with Pierre Boulez," *Composer* 1, no. 2 (September 1969), pp. 79–80.

Clearly, then, composers began to define their actions and reactions in terms of highly intellectual processes. By the late forties, the lines between "more" control and "less" control had been clearly drawn and defined. The roots of this disagreement seem to lie, both nationalistically (Europe vs. America) and compositionally, in the concept that extremely highly organized music sounds very often like extremely unorganized music, with the row and total serialization representing the parting of the ways (see Figure 2.21).

Figure 2.21. An *avant-garde* mobile.

This mobile shows the turn-of-the-century experimental tradition to the left of the *mainstream* composers, or those continuing tonal or quasi-tonal models of the nineteenth century. In the mid-thirties the experimental tradition branched and accelerated into a flurry of activity at the forefront of discovery and ever-reaching into the unknown: the *avant-garde*. (For information on vectoral analysis and procedures see chapter 1.)

**Vectoral Analysis:
Anton von Webern:
Symphonie, Op. 21**

1. Historical Background: Webern was born in Vienna in 1883 and died in Mittersill (near Salzburg), where he had moved to avoid the Allied bombings. He studied with Guido Adler at the University of Vienna and received a doctorate in musicology in 1906. He conducted in the provincial theaters and the Vienna Workers Symphony Concerts (organized by the then-socialist city). He stayed in Germany during the Second World War, even though performances of his music were banned by the Third Reich. He worked as a proofreader for a Viennese publisher. He died in 1945 of gunshot wounds delivered accidentally by an American occupation troop stationed in Mittersill.

2. Overview: This work is in two short movements. The first movement is a kind of two-part (each is repeated) "binary" form with the second a large canonic development of the first. The second movement is a theme and seven variations.

3. Orchestration Techniques: The *Symphonie* (1929) is scored for nine solo instruments: clarinet, bass clarinet, two horns, harp, two violins, viola, and 'cello. The major difference between this and Webern's previous work (Op. 20) is *klangfarbenmelodien* (defined as a kind of *pointillism*—see chapter 1's discussion of origins in the visual arts—that involves timbre). Note that in the opening of the work, Webern casts few notes without range, rest, or timbre separations (e.g., horn vs. harp vs. pizzicati 'cello, etc.; see Figure 2.23).

Figure 2.23. First 14 bars of Anton Webern's *Symphonie,* Op. 21, first movement. Beginning of double canon shown in first 7 bars.

4. Basic Techniques: The row of the piece is shown in Figure 2.24. This palindrome row (one that reads with the same intervals in both directions) makes the initial series identical with its retrograde (transposed) and the inversion identical with the inversion-retrograde (transposed). Therefore, only twenty-four forms of the row are actually possible (not the usual forty-eight).

The work begins with a double canon in inverted motion in four parts. Horn 2 begins the original on A with imitation beginning in measure 4 (the

Figure 2.24. Row for Webern's *Symphonie,* Op. 21 showing palindrome characteristic.

Figure 2.25. Frozen notes and rotation around "A" in opening section of Webern, *Symphonie,* Op. 21.

original a major third higher) in the harp. The harp begins in measure 2 the inversion on F, which is imitated by the first horn in inversion beginning on A, measure 3. Note as well how the opening section "rotates" around A (shown in Figure 2.25). These thirteen notes (E♭ is doubled) are all register frozen. This is category B composition. All twelve notes do not appear until the twenty-third pitch (E♭) is sounded in the harp.

5. Vertical Models: Harmonic identities do not play a major role in this work. When more than one note sounds at a time, a consistent vocabulary appears that is based on the minor second (and concomitant projections, e.g., the ninth and seventh), augmented fourth, and the major sixth. These are the intervals most commonly found and provide a perceptible model for the category B compositional techniques.

6. Horizontal Models: The horizontal or melodic techniques are framed in the row itself reflected in the complex canonic treatment and the variants based on *klangfarbenmelodien.* The constant leaping of lines often voids a real linear function as do the rests that abound. Certainly the opening four bars in the second horn provide the frame or model for the entire work in terms of horizontal vocabulary.

7. Style: Webern's *Symphonie* (Op. 21) is an enormously complex twelve-tone work whose pointillism, *klangfarbenmelodien,* and canonic interweaving of lines project a highly intellectual approach to the compositional process. The miniature ensemble, in contrast to the late Romantic orchestras of one hundred or more performers, as well as short duration create a crystalline edge to each note, contributing critical material to the larger structure. The lack of doubling, the serial feel to articulations and dynamics, and the imitations of rhythmic developments all contribute to its synthesis of clarity and complexity.

Compare this work with the analysis of the Penderecki of chapter 3. Note that while the chromaticism compares favorably (in the twelve-tone clusters), Penderecki expounds dramatic gestures and thick textures while Webern centers explicitly on single-note pointillism. The Webern resembles the Xenakis example at the end of chapter 10 in that both pay serious attention to rigorous forms of serialism; the first by virtue of the twelve-tone base and permutations of other elements, and the latter because it has automated features based on stochastic principles. This points out the fact that the two seemingly opposed concepts of *serialism* and *indeterminacy* are not mutually exclusive.

Bibliography— Chapter 2*

Further Readings

12-Tone Techniques

Anderson, E. Ruth. *Contemporary American Composers: A Biographical Dictionary.* Boston: G. K. Hall, 1976.

Babbitt, Milton. "Set Structure as a Compositional Determinant." *Journal of Music Theory* 5 (1961): pp. 72–94.

Basart, Ann Phillips. *Serial Music: A Classified Bibliography of Writings on Twelve Tone and Electronic Music.* Berkeley: University of California Press, 1961.

Beckwith, John, and Udo Kasemets. *The Modern Composer and His World.* Toronto: University of Toronto Press, 1961.

Berg, Alban. "Why Is Schoenberg's Music So Hard to Understand?" *The Music Review* (1952): pp. 187–96.

Boretz, Benjamin, and Edward T. Cone, eds. *Perspectives on American Composers.* New York: W. W. Norton and Co., 1971.

———. *Perspectives on Contemporary Music Theory.* New York: W. W. Norton and Co., 1972.

Boulez, Pierre. "Aléa." *Nouvette Revue Francaise* 59 (1957).

———. *Orientations.* London: Faber and Faber, 1986.

———. *Boulez on Music Today.* Cambridge, Mass.: Harvard University Press, 1971.

Brindle, Reginald Smith. *The New Music: The Avant-Garde since 1945.* New York: Oxford University Press, 1975.

Chase, Gilbert. *The American Composer Speaks.* Baton Rouge: Louisiana State University Press, 1966.

Dallin, Leon. *Techniques of Twentieth Century Composition.* 3d ed. Dubuque, Iowa: Wm. C. Brown Publishers, 1974.

Griffiths, Paul. *Modern Music.* New York: George Braziller, 1981.

Hansen, Peter. *An Introduction to Twentieth Century Music.* Boston: Allyn and Bacon, 1967.

Hitchcock, H. Wiley. *Music in the United States: An Historical Introduction.* Englewood Cliffs, N.J.: Prentice-Hall, 1969.

Lang, Paul Henry, ed. *Problems of Modern Music.* New York: W. W. Norton and Co., 1960.

Machlis, Joseph. *Introduction to Contemporary Music,* 2d ed. New York: W. W. Norton and Co., 1979.

Neighbour, Oliver, Paul Griffiths, and George Perle. *The New Grove Second Viennese School.* London: Macmillan, 1980.

The New Oxford History of Music: The Modern Age 1890–1960. London: Oxford University Press, 1974.

*Addresses for record companies, periodicals, and music publishers mentioned in this Bibliography can be found in Appendix IV.

Perle, George. *Serial Composition and Atonality.* Berkeley: University of California Press, 1962.

———. *Twelve-Tone Tonality.* Berkeley: University of California Press, 1977.

Rossi, Nick. *Music of Our Time.* Boston: Crescendo Publishing Co., 1969.

Salzman, Eric. *Twentieth-Century Music: An Introduction.* 3d ed. Englewood Cliffs, N.J.: Prentice-Hall, 1988.

Schaefer, John. *New Sounds, A Listener's Guide to New Music.* New York: Harper and Row, Publishers, 1987.

Schoffman, Nachum. *From Chords to Simultaneities.* New York: Greenwood Press, 1990.

Schwartz, Elliott, and Barney Childs, eds. *Contemporary Composers on Contemporary Music.* New York: Holt, Rinehart and Winston, 1967.

Spinner, Leopold. *A Short Introduction to the Technique of Twelve-Tone Composition.* London: Boosey and Hawkes, 1960.

Straus, Joseph N. *Introduction to Post Tonal Theory.* Englewood Cliffs, N.J.: Prentice-Hall, 1990.

———. *Remaking the Past: Musical Modernism and the Influence of the Tonal Tradition.* Cambridge, Mass.: Harvard University Press, 1990.

Tremblay, George. *The Definitive Cycle of the Twelve-Tone Row.* New York: Criterion Music Corp., 1974.

Yates, Peter. *Twentieth Century Music.* New York: Pantheon Books, 1967.

Combinatoriality

Brindle, Reginald Smith. *The New Music: The Avant-Garde since 1945.* New York: Oxford University Press, 1975.

Lester, Joel. *Analytic Approaches to Twentieth-Century Music.* New York: W. W. Norton, 1989.

Lewin, David. *Generalized Musical Intervals and Transformations.* New Haven: Yale University Press, 1987.

Vinton, John, ed. *Dictionary of Contemporary Music.* New York: E. P. Dutton and Co., 1974.

Set Theory

Brindle, Reginald Smith. *The New Music: The Avant-Garde since 1945.* New York: Oxford University Press, 1975.

Forte, Allen. *The Structure of Atonal Music.* New Haven: Yale University Press, 1973.

———. "Pitch-Class Set Analysis Today." *Music Analysis* 4, no. 1 (1985): pp. 29–58.

———. *The Harmonic Organization of The Rite of Spring.* New Haven: Yale University Press, 1978.

———. *Contemporary Tone-Structures.* New York: Columbia University Press, 1955.

Lewin, David. *Generalized Musical Intervals and Transformations.* New Haven: Yale University Press, 1987.

Sherman, Robert W. *Concept and Design in Music.* New York: Harcourt Brace Jovanovich, 1989.

Serialism

Babbitt, Milton. "Set Structure as a Compositional Determinant." *Journal of Music Theory* 5 (1961): pp. 72–94.

Vinton, John, ed. *Dictionary of Contemporary Music.* New York: E. P. Dutton and Co., 1974.

Anton von Webern

Anderson, E. Ruth. *Contemporary American Composers: A Biographical Dictionary.* Boston: G. K. Hall, 1976.

Griffiths, Paul. *Modern Music.* New York: George Braziller, 1981.

Hansen, Peter. *An Introduction to Twentieth Century Music.* Boston: Allyn and Bacon, 1967.

Kolneder, Walter. *Anton Webern: An Introduction to His Works.* Berkeley: University of California Press, 1968.

Neighbour, Oliver, Paul Griffiths, and George Perle. *The New Grove Second Viennese School.* London: Macmillan, 1980.

Rossi, Nick. *Music of Our Time.* Boston: Crescendo Publishing Co., 1969.

Salzman, Eric. *Twentieth-Century Music: An Introduction,* 3d ed. Englewood Cliffs, N.J.: Prentice-Hall, 1988.

Compact Discs, Recordings, and Publishers

Babbitt, Milton. *Quartet No. 2* (1954). Nonesuch 71280.

———. *Quartet No. 3* (1969–70). Turnabout 34515.

———. *Three Compositions for Piano.* Boelke-Bonart. Harmonia Mundi 90560.

Berg, Alban. *Concerto for Violin and Orchestra* (1935). Universal Edition. DG 413 725–2GH.

Boulez, Pierre, *Le Marteau Sans Maître* (1955). Universal Edition. ADES 14122–2.

———. *Second Piano Sonata.* Heugel Publishers. DG 419 202–2GH.

———. *Structures.* Universal Edition. CBS MK 42619.

———. *Structures: premier livre for two pianos* (1951–52). Universal Edition. Wergo 60011.

Crawford, Ruth. *Quartet.* New Music Edition. Gramavision R21S–79440.

Dallapiccola, Luigi. *Canti di prigionia* (for chorus and orchestra) (1941). Carisch Publishers. Nonesuch 79050–2.

Krenek, Ernst. *Twelve Short Piano Pieces Written in the Twelve-Tone Technique* (1939). G. Schirmer.

Messiaen, Olivier. *Chronochromie* (1960). Leduc Publishers. Erato ECD 71580.

Rudhyar, Dane. *Granites* (for piano, 1929). Published by Lengnick. CRI S–247. Released in the July 1935 New Music Quarterly.

Satie, Erik. *La belle eccentrique* (1920). Sirene. Vanguard VECD 7527.

Schäffer, Boguslaw. *Introduction to Composition* (1976). PWM.

Schoenberg, Arnold. *Variations for Orchestra.* Op. 31 (1928). Universal Edition. DG 415 326–2.

Webern, Anton. *Symphonie.* Op. 21. Universal Edition. DG 423 254–2.

———. Piano Variations, Op. 27 (1936). DG 419 202–2.

SOUND-MASS AND MICROTONES

3

Sound-mass, in contrast to serialism, minimizes the importance of individual notes and their order, while maximizing the importance of texture, rhythm, dynamics, and/or timbre of broad gestures. This refocusing is of great significance in the development of the *avant-garde* movement. Sound-mass confronts one of the most profound technicalities of the music world—the fine differentiation between sound and noise, a derogatory term applied to sounds antithetical to music.

Mainstream composers utilized sound-mass (often called clusters) in a variety of ways. Gustav Mahler, for example, used two large panchromatic chords (inclusive of all twelve tones) in the first movement of his *Tenth Symphony* (1910). Béla Bartók employed clusters in his 1926 *Piano Sonata*. It is possibly most challengingly utilized, however, in Igor Stravinsky's *Le Sacre du Printemps* (1913), where driving and repetitive string massses of sound ("Danse des Adolescentes") are "charged" with harsh accents. The rhythm of the accents becomes the thrust of the work at this point, reducing the importance of pitch. Figure 3.1 shows the "dance" and the resultant increased importance of rhythm (accents) and decreased importance of pitch as integral linear (melodic) or vertical (harmonic) contributors to the work. Clearly this chord is an F♭ (enharmonically E) ninth chord. However, the repetitious use of this vertical sonority offers little pitch importance.

Sound-Mass Evolution

Figure 3.1. Igor Stravinsky: *Le Sacre du Printemps:* "Danse des Adolescentes." Piano reduction of the string parts.

Figure 3.2. Henry Cowell: *The Hero Sun* (1922). Page 3. © Copyright Breitkopf and Härtel, Inc. Permission granted by the publisher. Associated Music Publishers, agents in U.S.

Henry Cowell's *The Tides of Manaunaun* (1911) and Charles Ives's *From the Steeples to the Mountains* (brass qt., 1901) and *Majority* (piano and voice, 1921) present some of the first uses of traditional "noise" as an acceptable musical element. Cowell's *The Hero Sun* (1922) includes a right forearm cluster on the black keys (see Figure 3.2; note that the ♯ above indicates black keys while a ♮ indicates white keys), a striking use of sound-mass as both a melodic and percussive device against the open consonances of the left-hand harmonies. Cowell's notations for clusters differ occasionally from piece to piece, but the basics are shown and explained in Figure 3.3 taken from *What's This* (also 1922). These works, along with

Figure 3.3. Explanation of symbols from *What's This* (1922), by Henry Cowell. © Copyright Breitkopf and Härtel, Inc. Permission granted by the publisher. Associated Music Publishers, agents in U.S.

Cowell's innovative pieces such as *The Banshee,* discussed in chapter 4, impressed a large number of composers (Béla Bartók in particular) and culminated in authorship of *New Musical Resources* (1930). Figure 3.4 reveals the depth to which Cowell studied both the musical properties and notation of sound-mass. About this example he has written: "Clusters that do in a certain sense move are, however, quite possible, and it is interesting to consider the various ways in which such movement can be introduced."[1] He notes both additive and subtractive clusters (subtractive in Figure 3.4), and thus predates a great deal of music, especially that of Penderecki, and articles like Kagel's "Tone-clusters, Attacks, Transitions" in *Die Reihe* #5.

1. Henry Cowell, *New Musical Resources* (New York: Alfred A. Knopf, 1930), p. 126.

Figure 3.6. John Becker: *Symphonia Brevis* (Symphony No. 3), page 3. Copyright © 1972 by C. F. Peters Corporation. By permission.

John Becker (1886–1961), regrettably a relatively unnoticed innovator of the twenties and thirties, included large clusters in most of his works. His *Symphonia Brevis* (Symphony No. 3, which first appeared in Cowell's *New Music* in 1930) derives large sound-mass structures from long sustained chords built of seconds with instruments of similar color. In other sections the clusters twist sections of the orchestra into single percussion instrumental sounds by means of articulation (short, very loud, heavy accents). Figure 3.6 shows the final five bars of the opening section from this work. As lines are overlaid in the rich contrapuntal fabric, Becker uses all twelve tones of the chromatic scale simultaneously with the F♯ rooted chord spread over five octaves.

Edgard Varèse uses brass, organ, and Ondes Martenot in his *Equatorial* (1934) to achieve sound-mass. In reference to the work of Varèse, Robert Erickson writes: "These highly individual sound-blocks are images, icons, in their own right. They

Timp.

Perc.

Xylo.

Pno.

Vns. I

Vns. II

Va.

Vc.

Cb.

Figure 3.6. (*Continued*)

exist as entities in the same way as a melody can be felt to be an entity."[2] Many consider Varèse's music the extension of Stravinsky's "primitive" period (e.g., *Le Sacre du Printemps;* period extending to the mid-twenties of this century when Stravinsky's so-called *neoclassic* period began). The massive dissonances of his *Hyperprism* (1923) and *Octandre* (1924) are strikingly percussive.

In *Octandre,* Varèse creates mirror-type sound-mass as shown in Figure 3.7A and B. In A, Varèse balances the "stacked" chromatic pitches with a central B♮ a minor third from each end of the cluster. In Figure 3.7B, he separates two small groupings of chromatic half-steps by equal intervals, this time the major third. Each of these structures (bars 15 and 20, respectively) includes octave transpositions and inverted orchestration, with the flute more than an octave below the clarinet, for example, to create harsh dynamic thrusts of sound. The work abounds with similar vertical sonorities.

Wallingford Riegger's *Music for Brass Choir* (1949) is one of the first large ensemble works to use large "closed" clusters. The work opens with ten trombones, each with a different chromatic note, encompassing the range of a diminished seventh. The panchromatic final chord of ten trumpets, eight horns, ten trombones, two tubas, and percussion expresses subtle dynamic shadings with the final four bars being *lento e pianissimo.*

2. Robert Erickson, "Varèse: 1924–1937: Sound-Ikon," *Composer* 1, no. 3 (December 1969), p. 144.

Figure 3.7. From Edgard Varèse, *Octandre*.

Figure 3.8. Galen Wilson: *Sonate Harmonique.*

Twelve-note or panchromatic chords are logically derived from twelve-tone music. While wide spacing avoids "cluster chord" terminology, the effect is the same. *Sonate Harmonique* by Galen Wilson contains a near-panchromatic (nine-note) cluster effect (see Figure 3.8).

Luigi Nono's three choral works *Il canto sospeso* (1956), *La terra e la campagna* (1957), and *Cori di de Doni* (1958) are based almost entirely on twelve-tone aggregate choral clusters, creating masses of sound within which the voices move as "fish through water."

Apart from the aforementioned Becker work, sound-mass occurs in orchestral works like *Metastasis* (1955) by Iannis Xenakis, and *Threnody for the Victims of Hiroshima* (1960) by Krzysztof Penderecki. Probably one of the best-known orchestral works of the past forty years, *Threnody* employs a wide variety of string techniques (fifty-two string parts), surprisingly few of which are actually new. More immediately recognizable are the solid bands of sound that widen and contract by means of *glissandi*. These clusters, involving quarter tones, create a "white sound" effect resolved by movement to a single pitch, and contain such heavy overtone influence that, even though only the area of a fifth may actually be covered, the aural impression is one of all audible sounds occurring simultaneously.

Figure 3.9 is the final fifty-four seconds of *Threnody*. Even though the notation is proportional (see Appendix III), the visual cluster bands are similar to those that were suggested by Cowell in his *New Musical Resources* thirty years earlier (refer to Figure 3.4).

Iannis Xenakis utilizes sound-mass as a result of his stochastic procedures (see chapter 10 for more detailed discussion). Most of his works employ large "sonic-clouds" that sound incredibly dense as a result of large numbers of individual voices usually of like timbre (*pizzicato* or *glissandi* clusters, for example). Indeed it is difficult to pick out a single one of his works that does not demonstrate an elegant use of sound-mass both in terms of rhythm and pitch. Xenakis has had considerable impact in Europe and many have attributed Penderecki's and the Polish School's use of sound-mass to his influence. In a 1955 article "The Crisis of Serial Music," Xenakis remarks:

> Linear polyphony destroys itself by its very complexity; what one hears is in reality nothing but a mass of notes in various registers. The enormous complexity prevents the audience from following the intertwining of the lines and has as its macrocosmic effect an irrational and fortuitous dispersion of sounds over the whole extent of the sonic spectrum. There is consequently a contradiction between the polyphonic linear system and the heard result, which is surface or mass.[3]

Henryk Górecki's (b. 1933 in Poland) *Scontri* for orchestra (1960) includes graphically notated blocks and bands of tones on large black boxes overlapping entire sections of the score.

In *Sonant* (1960), Mauricio Kagel calls for speaking and whispering from the ensemble at various pitch levels *ad libitum,* the result being a block or "cluster" sound-mass. The consequence of such experimentations is not only new notations, but direct applications of partially indeterminate procedures: though clusters are inevitable, exact duplication of numerous highly variable factors creates unpredictable results.

---

3. Iannis Xenakis, "The Crisis of Serial Music," *Gravesaner Blätter*, no. 1 (1955), pp. 23–66.

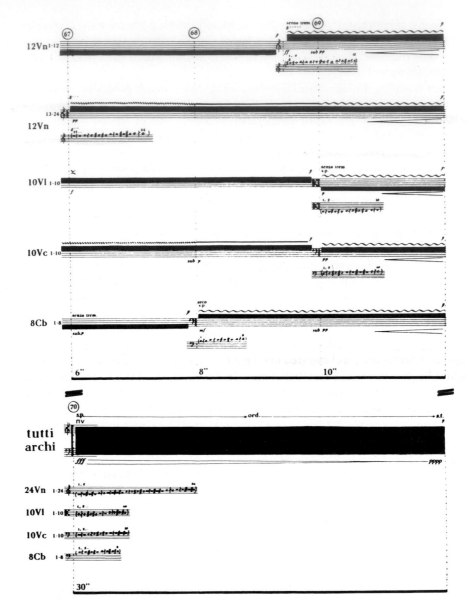

Figure 3.9. Krzysztof Penderecki: *Threnody for the Victims of Hiroshima* (final page of score). The notes for each cluster band are written out in traditional form beneath them in this proportional notation. Copyright © 1961 Deshon Music, Inc., & PWM Editions. Used with permission. All rights reserved. The two systems here are 24″ and 30″ in duration respectively.

In the last few years, it has become increasingly difficult to ascertain whether cluster effects have created improvisational (partially aleatoric) procedures or vice versa. *Improvisation ajoutée* (1962) by Mauricio Kagel, for four-manual organ and two or three adjunct performers, includes block clusters of sound, performed with hands, forearms, and feet, and rapid multichanges in registration with, as the composer states, "the improvisation arising through the statistical nature of timbre transformations."

The *Trois Poèmes d'Henri Michaux* for mixed chorus and orchestra (1963) by Witold Lutoslawski includes cluster chords derived of approximate pitch notation. The rhythmic clusters in the second part ("Le grand combat") are created by extremely complex composite rhythms.

Stockhausen's *Mixtur* (1964) demonstrates cluster effects spatially, as the five groups are placed around the audience with the notes only approximated by lack of staves or other exact pitch identification. Obvious motivic structures occur, yet each performer's independent decision regarding pitch and rhythmic variety results in extremely complex sound-mass structures.

Penderecki's *Passion According to St. Luke* (1965) compounds simple structures into dense bands of twelve-tone clusters. A continuous thread of contrapuntal material, even during these cluster effects, represents a unique approach to sound-mass construction. Half-sung, half-spoken backgrounds to crowd scenes create equally massive constructs of sound that owe their intensity to drama as well as to dissonance.

Pauline Oliveros's *Sound Patterns* (1961) demonstrates sound-mass effects with voices, employing whispers, tongue clicks, lip pops, and improvised pitches within areas of high, middle, and low registers. The results are often similar to the choral effects in Penderecki's *Passion,* yet exist more as timbre clusters than as pitch clusters.

György Ligeti's *Atmosphéres* (1961) involves the full complement of winds, strings, and percussion, orchestrated in such a manner as to create unique "clusters" of sound by overtones and resultant tones. In *Lux Aeterna* (1966) and *Requiem* (1965) for soprano, mezzo-soprano, two mixed choirs, and orchestra, Ligeti approaches effects in which instruments and individual voices are unrecognizable. Ligeti's *Lontano* (1967) for orchestra often employs over fifty separate instrumental voices (Ligeti's music, unlike Penderecki's, is traditionally notated), creating an ever-evolving and developing sonic texture. While seeming to lack recognizable melodic direction, this piece maintains an enormous musical impact in terms of the dynamics and timbre.

"The important tones, the ones that are most plainly heard, are those of the outer edges of a given cluster."[4] Thus both composer and performer realized that order and exact notation of clusters could be described verbally or graphically. Theodore Lucas, in *Aberrations No. VII* for piano (Figure 3.10), evolves a system of cluster notation (white and black keys) denoting duration by horizontal length. Graphic structures show only approximate pitch and relative motion. Note here that the two sets of clusters remain static. Various cluster effects are dramatically notated by Stanley Lunetta in his *Piano Music*. Notice especially with the indication "wiggle all fingers" in Figure 3.11 the interpretative possibilities for the performer. Karel Husa's *Apotheosis of This Earth* for concert band (see Figure 3.12) demonstrates another means of achieving sound-mass: rhythmic densities so thick as to produce vibrating columns of sound. This approach allows for continuous development of motivic and melodic fragments.

4. Henry Cowell, *New Musical Resources* (New York: Alfred A. Knopf, 1930), p. 122.

Figure 3.10. Theodore Lucas: *Aberrations No. VII* for piano. Copyright 1969 by the composer.

North/White by R. Murray Schafer was, in the words of the composer, "inspired by the rape of the Canadian North . . . carried out by the nation's government in conspiracy with business and industry." The title derives from "white light," which contains all visual frequencies: the piece then contains all audible frequencies producible by a symphony orchestra. The work begins and ends on single notes enclosing tapering clusters of sound. The form is a kind of "crab" structure with the first three main sections (slow cluster buildup; repeated notes; chromatic scales) presented in retrograde order in the second half of the piece. Schafer has created a dynamic and sometimes hostile work.

INSTRUCTIONS:

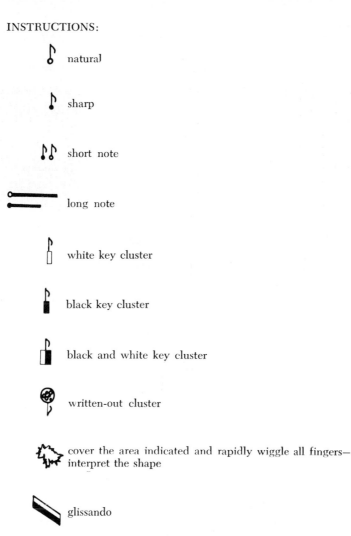

    natural

    sharp

    short note

    long note

    white key cluster

    black key cluster

    black and white key cluster

    written-out cluster

    cover the area indicated and rapidly wiggle all fingers—interpret the shape

    glissando

    spaced evenly

Great care has been taken to space all other notes to indicate the rhythmical relationships. After each page-turn play each system completely, following all instructions and playing all visible notes.

Figure 3.11. Stanley Lunetta: *Piano Music.* Performance instructions. Permission granted by *Source: Music of the Avant-Garde.* Composer/Performer Edition, Davis, California.

Microtones

While twelve-note scales and the search for a single *stable* tuning system have existed for many centuries,[5] it seems to many contemporary composers that this search is a fruitless one, which results in a hybrid intonation (equal temperament) lacking

5. Cf. Zarlino (1558), Salinas (1577), Mattheson (1725), Jackson (1726), Liston (1812), Delezenne (1827), Poole (1850), Drobesch (1855), Bosanquet (1875), and Keonig (1876), to name but a few. See Fred Fisher, "The Yellow Bell of China and the Endless Search," *Music Educators Journal* (April 1973): p. 30.

Figure 3.12. Karel Husa: *The Apotheosis of This Earth.* © Copyright 1971 by Associated Music Publishers, Inc. Used by permission.

the multifold potentials of flexible tunings. It is important to note here that while the piano may remain "fixed" in equal-tempered tuning, other instruments do not. Orchestral performers create a wide range and variety of tunings, usually a combination of *just* (based on the overtone series) and *equal* (each semitone equidistant from the next) temperaments applied at the discretion of their "musical ears." Similarly, tonal key regions with "leading tones," sevenths of dominant seventh chords, and the like call for *adjusted* intonations. Mozart, for example, worked and *taught* with a seventeen-note scale, clearly identifying microtones through spelling (e.g., C♯ and D♭ were quite differently tuned, the first being higher).

Julian Carrillo in "The Thirteenth Sound" divides the octave into ninety-five different pitches, numbering each pitch at the end of the stem where one would

Figure 3.12 *Continued*

ordinarily find the note head.[6] Harry Partch's forty-three-note approach (discussed as well in chapter 4) is much freer. Through his creation of an entirely new set of instruments he has created a virtually "infinite" variety of both timbres and tunings. Most of these approaches, however, seemed doomed to either extremely limited usage or complete neglect. The main problem is that most theorists and composers continue to search for new *systems* not realizing that the devising of any such system is little better than the *system* in present use. It is indeed the flexibility or "non-systematic" use of intonations that is most valuable. Composers such as Ben Johnston, Lou Harrison, James Tenney, Kenneth Gaburo, and many others have composed sections, movements, or works to multiple sets of intonations.

Ben Johnston's *Fourth String Quartet* uses a varying number of proportional octave divisions from five to twenty-two, thus creating a flexible set of intonations

---

6. Julian Carrillo, "The Thirteenth Sound," trans. Patricia Ann Smith, *Soundings* 5 (1972), p. 64. This volume also contains a number of works by Carrillo using his number notations.

Figure 3.13. Ben Johnston.

based on the composer's ear and musical intuitions. Johnston has written extensively on microtonal music, and in writing about his *Fourth String Quartet* he sums up a great complexity in a few concise words:

> Over the whole of the historical period of instrumental music, Western music has based itself upon an acoustical lie. In our time this lie—that the normal musical ear hears twelve equal intervals within the span of an octave—has led to the impoverishment of pitch usage in our music. In our frustration at the complex means it takes to wrest yet a few more permutations from a closed system, we have attempted the abandonment of all systems, forgetting that we need never have closed our system.[7]

Johnston further describes the situation quite accurately in "How to Cook an Albatross": "In our laziness, when we changed over to the twelve-tone system, we just took the pitches of the previous music as though we were moving into a furnished apartment and had no time to even take the pictures off the wall. What excuse?"[8]

The potential of microtones is bounded only by the ability of the composer to hear ideas, the notation to express these ideas (see Appendix III), and the performer to accurately perform the results. Microtonal tunings and other tuning systems are available on a number of synthesizers (see chapters 8 and 9 for examples).

7. From the April 28, 1974 program notes of a concert at the University of Wisconsin–Milwaukee by the Fine Arts Quartet.

8. Ben Johnston, "How to Cook an Albatross," *Source* 7 (1970), p. 65.

The first actual notations given in Appendix III present three examples of how composers utilizing microtonal resources notate what they wish. All of the microtonal notations in Appendix III represent quarter tones, with the first being the simplest and possibly the most clear.

Microtones do not correspond to pitches in equal temperament. Microtonal "systems" usually involve more than twelve tones per octave, thereby forcing one or more intervals to be less than an equal-tempered semitone apart. For example, quarter tones (twenty-four tones per octave) present a type of microtonal system with twelve pitches in equal temperament and twelve in the equidistant "cracks."

Many composers felt that the creation of equal temperament, and the resolution of the octave into twelve parts, created arbitrary musical systems. Scalular materials based on microtonal divisions date from the time of the Greeks (enharmonic genus), and interest in them revived in the Renaissance with N. Vicentino and his *archicembalo* and *archiorgano*. Gerhardus Mercator's (sixteenth century) fifty-three tones per octave scale is another particularly notable example. Alois Hába (1893–1972) constructed a quarter-tone piano in the early twenties[9] of this century and employed a sixth-tone system in the late thirties. Charles Ives (1874–1954) experimented with microtones in his *Three Quarter Tone Pieces* (1918?) for two pianos tuned a quarter tone apart. Harry Partch (1901–74),[10] in the process of working with an acoustical division of the octave into forty-three tones, developed new instruments necessary for the realization of his experiments. He worked more in isolation than Hába, but has received much attention in the past few years.[11] Composers such as Teo Macero, Calvin Hamilton, and Donald Lybbert have continued similar experimentation.

Though quarter tones were used sparsely by Bartók (especially in his *Violin Concerto,* 1938) and Milhaud in the late thirties and forties, their true import had not fully been discovered. The use of twenty-four or more divisions of the octave requires abandonment or total revision of techniques of traditional instruments, creation of new or revised systems of notation, and increasingly complex harmonic and melodic vocabularies. New instruments (e.g., the tape recorder), notations and scientific vocabularies developed in the early fifties, often as a direct result of experiments with tuning systems.

While microtones are used to embellish music and to provide variety in an otherwise strictly twelve-note vocabulary, tuning systems afford whole new territories for experimentation. The definition of a tuning system is that it rigorously applies its approach to *all* of the notes available. Such systems typically utilize fixed-tuned instruments (usually percussion). These systems divide into three basic types: "just" tuning systems, "equal" tuning systems, and "varied" tuning systems. In the first case, all of the information about the scale is derived specifically from the overtone series (see chapter 1). This series (infinite) possesses much information about tuning with the true resonance in its nature being the source of much of our music. Tonality,

9. See Alois Hába, *The Theory of Quartertones* (out of print).

10. See Harry Partch, *Genesis of a Music* (Madison: University of Wisconsin Press, 1949).

11. See also Elliott Friedman, "Tonality in the Music of Harry Partch," *Composer* 2, no. 1 (June 1970) pp. 16–24.

as shown in chapter 1, could be said to come from projection of the series; trombones and other wind instruments overblow into the series in order to complete a full range of notes, and so on. The second or "equal" tuning system simply divides the octave into equal intervals. These intervals consist of 100 "cents," a system developed by A. J. Ellis in the nineteenth century. An octave consists therefore of 1,200 cents. The cent system is logarithmic in nature: c (cent) = 1,200/log 2 × log 1 (interval in cents). Since the series is exponential in nature, the actual frequency divisions are small in the lower registers and large in the upper. Finally, combinations of these two approaches, or wholly new approaches not using either of these two, exist in the "varied" tuning systems characteristic of many used by world cultures. Western music, though couched in its secure twelve divisions of the octave, has (but to a much lesser extent) had its proposals, experiments, and protagonists for new intonations.

In Javanese music the gamelan uses many instruments involved with "varied" tuning systems. The *gambang* (xylophone), *gender, saron,* and *demoeng* (all bronze idiophones), and *bonang* (set of gongs) use either the *slendro* or the *pelog*. The *slendro* consists of wide intervals and the *pelog* of narrower steps. The *slendro* is constructed of a pentatonic scale consisting of five nearly equal intervals of 240 cents (somewhat close to whole-tone and quarter-tone scales) as shown in Figure 3.14. The *pelog,* in contrast, consists of two conjunct tetrachords, each of which is divided (approximately) into a half-step and a major third. The two-thirds are filled in by two additional tones, creating a septatonic scale shown in Figure 3.15. The + and − signs here indicate the lowering or raising necessary to achieve the correct pitch in the series.

Composers on the Pacific Rim have imitated such tuning systems and approaches to music. Lou Harrison, for example, has created what has been termed the American Gamelan, where his own versions of instruments in Southeastern Asian music are substituted in gamelans for which he composes. Such gamelans have produced a number of serious protagonists and composers including Jody Diamond, Vincent McDermott, Daniel Schmidt, Jarrad Powell, Jim Madara, Daniel Goode, David Demnitz, Jeff Morris, Shin Nakamura, and Laura Liben.

Figure 3.14. The *slendro* pentatonic scale consisting of five nearly equal intervals of 240 cents.

Figure 3.15. The *pelog* scale of two conjunct tetrachords, each of which is divided (approximately) into a half-step and a major third filled in by two additional tones, creating a septatonic scale.

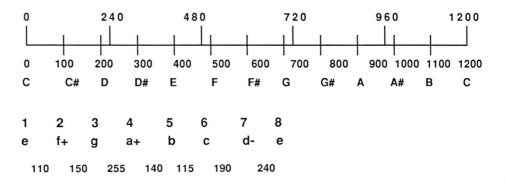

Figure 3.16. György Ligeti: *Lontano.* Typical rhythmic entrances.

Rhythmic Developments

Rhythm, viewed without the melodic or harmonic drive of most works prior to this century, is a rather simply used parameter of musical structure. It often seems strangled by the bar line or tied down to basic repetitions related to dance forms. Ligeti comments about freeing this in notes for *Lontano* (1967): "The bar lines serve only as a means of synchronization; bar lines and beats never mean an accentuation, the music must flow smoothly. . . ."[12] The score of Lontano is filled with double- and triple-dotted notes, entrances on inner positions of triplets, quintuplets, septuplets, and so on, as shown in Figure 3.16. Ligeti diffuses the bar line and beat and gives the rhythm a development and tangible diversity.

Boulez speaks to this point in *Boulez on Music Today:*

> The rational use of the opposition between multiplication and division of the [beat] unit will, moreover, give rise to striking contrasts due to the broader span of values brought into play . . . interaction of these various methods of organization can be extremely fertile, and will create an inexhaustible variety of objects—in the same way as in the field of pitch.[13]

Some composers turn to proportional notation to avoid the accent implications of bar lines and simplicity of beat structures. Thus a section is marked 30 seconds and the notations within performed as they reach the eye as if the visual action of reading would take 30 seconds. No accents, other than those specifically marked, are implied by such notation, creating a great deal of rhythmic variety. By the same token, this inexactness of notation disturbs some composers in that the results often differ markedly from one performance to another.

Olivier Messiaen, in both words (*The Technique of My Musical Language;* see Bibliography for this chapter) and music (notably *Livre d'orgue,* 1951), has developed complex rhythmic formulations such as non-retrogradable rhythms (rhythmic palindromes) and "added values" which are dots, rests, or notes added to complicate otherwise simple rhythmic patterns, especially with respect to the beat. His work has had considerable influence on his students (most notably Boulez) and on other composers throughout Europe.

Elliott Carter attempts the same goal, but from quite a different perspective. In *Flawed Words* and *Stubborn Sounds* Carter speaks of his directions: "The result in my own music was, first of all, the way of evolving rhythms and continuities now called 'metric modulation,' which I worked out in the composition of my *Cello Sonata*

12. György Ligeti, *Lontano* (New York: Schott Music Corp., 1969), from the performance notes in the score.

13. Pierre Boulez, *Boulez on Music Today* (Cambridge, Mass.: Harvard University Press, 1971), p. 58.

Figure 3.17. Metric modulations from Elliott Carter's *Double Concerto.*

bars 313-314: $\begin{smallmatrix}9\\8\end{smallmatrix}$ ($\textstyle\frac{}{}$. = 60) = $\begin{smallmatrix}14\\16\end{smallmatrix}$ (. = 60)

(= 105) = (. = 56)

bars 613-614:

Figure 3.18. Elliott Carter. BMI Archives. Used by permission.

of 1948." Later in the same book he speaks of new music in general: " . . . what is needed is never just a string of interesting passages, but works whose central interest is constituted by the way everything that happens in them happens *as* and *when* it does in relation to everything else."[14]

Metric modulation, though not an entirely new concept to Eastern music or music in the Western world prior to the advent of the so-called "common-practice period," is a highly complex procedure. In Carter's *Double Concerto* (1961) for harpsichord and piano with two chamber orchestras, there are many such modulations. As seen in Figure 3.17, the meter and the tempo often change at bar lines. This, combined with a rich variety of complex rhythmic development within the bar, achieves a highly structured yet "bar line"–free momentum of sounds; though many

14. Allen Edwards, *Flawed Words and Stubborn Sounds* (New York: W. W. Norton and Co., 1971), pp. 91–92.

of Carter's critics express grave doubt as to whether such "metric modulations" can actually be accurately performed. Carter's earlier *Cello Sonata* has surprisingly few metric modulations compared with the highly technical complexities of the renowned *Double Concerto*.

Most composers take a middle road between the proportional and "modulation" principles examined here, utilizing both within a single work as does Ligeti in his *Aventures* (see Figure 4.14 in the next chapter).

Electronic and computer music present an ever-growing potential source for complex rhythmic structures and rhythm freed from bar lines. The author discusses this in his own contribution to *Electronic Music: A Listener's Guide* by Elliott Schwartz:

> The major advantage to working with electronic equipment and sounds which seem undiminished by overdone "exploration" is rhythmic freedom. No other ensemble of instruments is equally capable of fractioning time into controllable particles as the components of a well-equipped electronic music studio. While some listeners feel that the opportunity to free rhythm from any immediately recognizable meters removes some inalienable musical basic, it must be pointed out that to a large degree meter was introduced only to keep performers together in ensembles; while necessary, it was certainly not particularly musical in itself. The disposition of time is much more controllable in the electronic studio.[15]

(For information on vectoral analysis and procedures, see chapter 1.)

Vectoral Analysis: Krzysztof Penderecki: *Capriccio for Violin and Orchestra*

1. Historical Background: Krzysztof Penderecki (*c* is pronounced as if it were an *s*) was born in Debica, Poland, in 1933. He studied at the Music Academy in Kracow, where he eventually taught. Influences on his style include Iannis Xenakis for sound-mass structures of thick multi-timbred densities and Luigi Nono:

> In 1957, Luigi Nono came to Poland, to visit. He brought some scores with him, and he gave me some. I remember the *Five Pieces* of Webern. I was already writing my own music at that time (1957 or 1958). He gave me some of his music also. I think it was *Il Canto di Spezzo, Varianti* for violin and orchestra, *Cori di de Doni,* the piece for chorus, then *Improvisation sur Mallarmé,* by Boulez. All this was very new for me, and I tried to incorporate these techniques in a very short time. This was in 1958, till the middle of 1959. And then I decided to go my way.[16]

15. Elliott Schwartz, *Electronic Music: A Listener's Guide* (New York: Praeger Publishers, 1972); from "Observations by Composers," p. 214.

16. David Felder and Mark Schneider, "An Interview with Krzysztof Penderecki," *Composer* 8, no. 1 (1977), p. 12.

Figure 3.19. Krzysztof
Penderecki.

Most of his early works require large forces for performance, and range from short experiments in sound (especially *Threnody,* 1960; *Polymorphia,* 1961; and *De Natura Sonoris,* 1967 for string orchestras) to large dramatic opera/oratorios (notably *The Passion According to St. Luke,* 1965, and *The Devils of Loudon,* 1969). The thread of intense drama linked with subtle mystical religious overtones weaves through his musical style until his more recent turn to neo-romanticism.

2. Overview: The *Capriccio for Violin and Orchestra* (completed in 1967) is a concise concerto-type work in an abbreviated rondo-variations form (i.e., a set of variations with alternate variants referring noticeably to the opening material). After the brief opening timpani roll, a sound-mass occurs softly in the winds. Out of this texture grow individual crescendi contrapuntally increasing in number. This serves as a conceptual model for the remainder of the work, with variations deriving momentum from a variety of parameters, such as timbre, dynamics, rhythm, and texture, rather than the more typical variants of pitch that one usually associates with this form.

3. Orchestration Techniques: The orchestra splits into sections (i.e., generally instruments of like timbre). Penderecki utilizes his large percussion battery (five players needed for performance) to create large slashes of sound (e.g., vibraphone, bells, triangles, chimes, harp, and piano used simultaneously on page 5 of the score for a bright attack of cluster material). Effects include playing on the other side of the bridge (strings) and bowing for noise (extra hard pressure on the string) with pizzicato used on the piano. Double- and triple-tongued repeated notes in the winds give rhythmic drive to stacked clusters.

4. Basic Techniques: *Capriccio* is a free twelve-tone work. This means free use of the serial concept (i.e., eleven-note rows), as well as continual development of new rows rather than clinging to a single series. Interval content evolves from the minor second (chromatic clusters from the outset) and resulting octave displacements (major seventh, minor ninth). The major second and various thirds become important as the work progresses. Throughout the piece there is the feeling of expansion, the result of intervals opening up, as well as general ideas becoming longer and more developed.

5. Vertical Models: Figure 3.20 demonstrates the kind of vertical clustering that is a mainstay of this work. Notation defines pitch content followed by duration in terms of thick black proportional lines.

> I had to write in shorthand—something for me to remember, because my style of composing at that time was just to draw a piece first and then look for pitch. . . . I just wanted to write music that would have an impact, a density, powerful expression, a different expression. . . . I think this notation was for me, in the beginning, like shorthand, really, coming from drawing the piece. I used to see the whole piece in front of me—*Threnody* is very easy to draw. First you have just the high note, then you have this repeating section, then you have this cluster going, coming—different directions from the one note, twelve, and back—using different shapes. Then there is a louder section; then there's another section, then there is the section which is strictly written in twelve-tone technique. Then it goes back to the same cluster technique again, and the end of the piece is a big cluster, which you can draw like a square and write behind it *fortissimo.* . . . I didn't want to write in bars, because this music doesn't work if you put it in bars.[17]

In Figure 3.20, the *arm* (*armonium* or "harmonium," a reed-type organ) and piano (using wire brushes on the inside) cover their approximate visual areas in the time allowed. The meter is 2/4, with the quarter note approximately equal to M.M. 76, though no tempo is given in the score; the author determined such by carefully dividing the number of bars into the duration (ten minutes), including combinations of *ritardandi,* and so on. The resultant vertical textures vary, but nonetheless continue the chromatic clusters. A third type of vertical structure is shown in the upper right-hand corner. A spread sound-mass moves by the use of microtonal (here, quarter tones) inflections in contrapuntal alternation.

Penderecki continually concentrates on the ever-widening possibilities of cluster techniques. In the opening sections, the work centers on minor second stacked clusters. Within the first minute he expands this to major second clusters (whole-tone). These eventually widen to octave-displaced minor second clusters.

6. Horizontal Models: As with the vertical concepts explored in this work, Penderecki concentrates on the use of seconds. Over 80 percent of the

17. Ibid., p. 13.

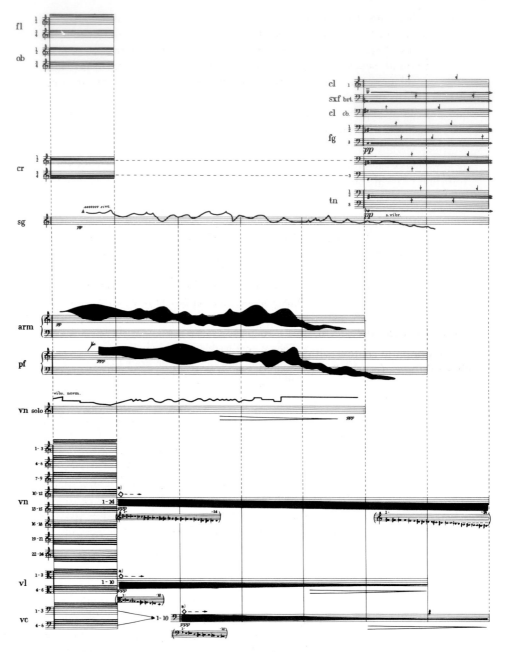

Figure 3.20. Krzysztof Penderecki: *Capriccio for Violin and Orchestra* (p. 29). Copyright © 1968 by Moeck Verlag. Used with permission. All rights reserved.

intervals in the opening solo violin line are half- or whole steps. Often even thirds are augmentations of seconds. These lines become more angular by octave displacement, creating sevenths and ninths. The improvisatory solo violin line of Figure 3.20 gives a strong impression of the "seconds" concept. Penderecki joins the vertical and horizontal developments so that one feels each proceeding at a similar rate of speed.

It is interesting to note Penderecki's own remarks concerning his linear writing for the violin in this piece.

Sometimes when writing a group of notes in a very fast tempo, like in *Capriccio* for example, I know it is impossible to play all of them. But I did it because then I had achieved a tension in the sound. If I would have written only four or five notes, he would just do it, you know, so you would lose all the tension I have in the piece. I know this exactly. Performers ask me all the time: "Please, this is impossible." I reply that it is absolutely possible—"You will do it." Maybe the player will miss two or three of them, but there is a tension here.[18]

7. Style: Penderecki's *Capriccio for Violin and Orchestra* is a tightly woven, freely chromatic work based on the exploration of the interval of a second (both melodically and harmonically). These explorations slowly expand through a variation form, over a rondo template.

The dramatic context within which the work proceeds depends on large orchestral forces (especially percussion), contrapuntal interweaving of nonpitch parameters (especially dynamics and rhythm), and various effects (including microtones). In contrast to the *Symphonie* of Webern (analyzed in chapter 2), Penderecki has produced a dramatic style packed with sound-mass, rhythmic development, and microtonal inflections. This example should also be compared to the Vectoral Analyses of chapters 4 and 12 for similarity in terms of reliance on dramatic elements and explorations in orchestration. Its lack of lyricism also contrasts with the outcome of the Cage (chapter 5). The clusters hold similarities to the performances of the Oliveros work in chapter 6 and the score and tape of Erb's *Souvenir* in chapter 7. Some of the textures, especially the thick sonorities where individual pitches lose distinction, resemble those used by Varèse in the Vectoral Analysis of chapter 8.

Sound-Mass Evolution

**Bibliography*—
Chapter 3**

Further Readings

Boatwright, Howard, ed. *Essays before a Sonata. The Majority, and Other Writings by Charles Ives.* New York: W. W. Norton and Co., 1962.
Burkholder, J. Peter. *Charles Ives: The Ideas Behind the Music.* New Haven: Yale University Press, 1985.
Cowell, Henry. *New Musical Resources.* New York: Alfred A. Knopf, 1930.

18. Ibid., p. 14.

*Addresses for record companies, periodicals, and music publishers mentioned in this Bibliography can be found in Appendix IV.

Dallin, Leon. *Techniques of Twentieth Century Composition,* 3d ed. Dubuque, Iowa: Wm. C. Brown Publishers, 1974.

Erickson, Robert. *Sound Structure in Music.* Berkeley: University of California Press, 1975.

Goldstein, Malcolm. "Texture." In *Dictionary of Contemporary Music,* ed. John Vinton, pp. 741–53. New York: E. P. Dutton and Co., 1974.

Higgins, Dick. "Henry Cowell: Some Personal Recollections." *Soundings* 14–15 (1986).

Marquis, G. Welton. *Twentieth Century Music Idioms.* New York: Prentice-Hall, 1964.

Persichetti, Vincent. *Twentieth Century Harmony.* New York: W. W. Norton and Co., 1961.

Riegger, Wallingford. "John J. Becker." *Bulletin of the ACA* 9, no. 1 (1959): pp. 2–7.

Rudhyar, Dane. "When Does Sound Become Music." *Soundings* 14–15 (1986): pp. 82–84.

Cluster Techniques

Burkholder, J. Peter. *Charles Ives: The Ideas Behind the Music.* New Haven: Yale University Press, 1985.

Christiansen, Louis. "Introduction to the Music of György Ligeti," *Numus West* 2 (1973).

Cowell, Henry, ed. *American Composers on American Music.* New York: Frederick Ungar Publishing Co., 1933.

Dallin, Leon. *Techniques of Twentieth Century Composition,* 3d ed. Dubuque, Iowa: Wm. C. Brown Publishers, 1974.

Garland, Peter. "Dane Rudhyar." *Soundings* 14–15 (1986): pp. 4–5.

Gilbert, Steven. "Carl Ruggles (1876–1971): An Appreciation." *Perspectives of New Music* 11, no. 1 (1972): pp. 224–32.

Kagel, Mauricio. "Tone Clusters, Attacks, Transitions." *Die Reihe* 5 (1959): pp. 40–55.

Kirkpatrick, John. "The Evolution of Carl Ruggles: A Chronicle Largely in His Own Words." *Perspectives of New Music* 6, no. 2 (1968): pp. 146–66.

Persichetti, Vincent. *Twentieth Century Harmony.* New York: W. W. Norton and Co., 1961.

Weisgall, Hugo. "The Music of Henry Cowell." *Musical Quarterly* 45 (1959): pp. 484–507.

Microtones

Balzano, Gerald J. "The Group-Theoretic Description of 12-Fold and Microtonal Pitch Systems." *Computer Music Journal* 4, no. 4 (1980): pp. 66–84.

———. "What are Musical Pitch and Timbre?" *Music Perception* 3, no. 3 (1986): pp. 297–314.

Boatwright, Howard. "Ives' Quarter-Tone Impressions." *Perspectives of New Music* 3, no. 2 (1965): pp. 146–66.

Partch, Harry. *Genesis of a Music,* 2d ed. New York: Da Capo Press, 1973.

Tuning Systems

Johnston, Ben. "Proportionality and Expanded Pitch Relations." *Perspectives of New Music* 5, no. 1 (1966): pp. 112–20.

Orga, Ates. "Alois Hába and Microtonality." *Musical Opinion* 91 (1968): p. 541.

Partch, Harry. *Genesis of a Music,* 2d ed. New York: Da Capo Press, 1973.

Rhythmic Developments

Babbitt, Milton. "Twelve-Tone Rhythmic Structure and the Electronic Medium."
Perspectives of New Music 1, no. 1 (1962): pp. 49–79.

Carter, Elliott. "The Rhythmic Basis of American Music." *Score* 12 (1955): pp. 94–102.

Creston, Paul. *Principles of Rhythm.* New York: Franco Columbo, 1964.

Edwards, Allen. *Flawed Words and Stubborn Sounds.* New York: W. W. Norton and Co., 1971.

Erickson, Robert. "Time Relations." *Journal of Music Theory* 7 (1963): pp. 174–92.

Hitchcock, H. Wiley. *Music in the United States: A Historical Introduction.* Englewood Cliffs, N.J.: Prentice-Hall, 1969.

Lewin, David. "On Formal Intervals between Time-Spans." *Music Perception* 1, no. 4 (1984): pp. 412–23.

Messiaen, Olivier. *The Technique of My Musical Language.* Paris: Alphonse Leduc and Cie., 1950.

Stockhausen, Karlheinz. ". . . How Time Passes. . . ." *Die Reihe* 3 (1957).

Stone, Else, and Kurt Stone, eds. *The Writings of Elliott Carter.* Bloomington: Indiana University Press, 1977.

Krzysztof Penderecki

Felder, David, and Mark Schneider. "An Interview with Krzysztof Penderecki," *Composer* 8, no. 1 (1977): pp. 8–20.

Robinson, Ray. *A Study of the Penderecki St. Luke Passion.* Germany: Moeck, 1983.

———. *Krzysztof Penderecki: A Guide to His Works.* Princeton, N.J.: Prestige Publications, 1988.

Vinton, John, ed. *Dictionary of Contemporary Music.* New York: E. P. Dutton and Co., 1974.

Sound-Mass Evolution

Compact Discs, Recordings, and Publishers

Bartók, Béla. *Sonata* (1921). Universal Edition. Hungaroton HCD–31051.

———. String Quartet No. 5 (1934). Boosey & Hawkes. Hungaroton HCD–12502/04.

Becker, John. *Symphony No. 3.* C. F. Peters. Albany Records TROY027–2.

Blackwood, Easley. *Symphony No. 1.* (1958). RCA LM–2352.

Blomdahl, Karl-Birger. *Aniara* (1959). Schott. Caprice CAP–2 2016/1–2.

———. *Le Marteau sans Maître* (1959). Universal Edition. Ades 14122–2.

Britten, Benjamin. *The Turn of the Screw* (1954). Boosey & Hawkes. London 425 672–2LH2.

Carter, Elliott. *Cello Sonata.* G. Schirmer. Nonesuch 71234.

———. *Double Concerto.* Associated Music Publishers. Elektra/Nonesuch H–71314.

———. *String Quartets* No. 1 (1951) and No. 2 (1959) AMP. Etcetera KTC 1065–6.

Constant, Marius. *24 Preludes for Orchestra* (1958). Ricordi. Heliodor HS–25058.

Crumb, George. *Black Angels* (1970). C. F. Peters. Elektra/Nonesuch 79242–2–P.

Curran, Alvin. *Home-Made.* CPE–Source.

Dempster, Stuart. *Standing Waves* (1976). 1750 Arch Records S–1775.

Erickson, Robert. *Ricercar á 5* (1966). Okra Music. DG–0654084.

Helm, Everett. *Concerto for Five Solo Instruments, Percussion and Strings* (1954). Schott.

Husa, Karel. *Apotheosis of this Earth* (1971). AMP. Golden Crest 4134.

———. *Music for Prague* (1968). AMP. CBS MK 44916.

Kagel, Mauricio. *Sonant.* C. F. Peters.

Liebermann, Rolf. *Concerto for Jazz Band and Symphony Orchestra* (1954). Universal Edition.

Ligeti, György. *Atmosphères.* Universal Edition. Wergo 60162–50.

———. *Lontano.* Schott. DG 429 260–2.

———. *Lux Aeterna.* C. F. Peters. Wergo WER 60162–RO.

———. *Nouvelles Aventures* (1965). Neues. Wergo 60 045–50.

———. *Requiem.* C. F. Peters. Wergo 60 045–50.

———. *Volumina* (1962). Wergo 60161–50.

Lutoslawski, Witold. *Concerto for Orchestra* (1954). PWM. London 425 694–2.

———. *Les Espaces du Sommeil* (1975). Published by Chester Music. Philips 416 387–2.

Messiaen, Olivier. *L'Ascension* (1934). Leduc. Erato ECD 71580.

———. *La Nativité du Seigneur* (1935). Leduc. Erato 2292 45470–2.

———. *Quatre études de rythme for piano* (1949). Durand. Nimbus NI 5090.

Moryl, Richard. *Chroma for Chamber Ensemble* (1972). Desto 7143.

Nono, Luigi. *Cori di Didone.* Schott.

———. *Il canto sospeso.* Schott.

———. *La terra e la campagna.* Schott.

Penderecki, Krzysztof. *Capriccio for Violin and Orchestra.* Moeck. RCA 60370–2–RC.

———. *Threnody for the Victims of Hiroshima.* Eulenberg. Conifer CDCF 168.

Persichetti, Vincent. *Symphony for Band* (1956). Elkan-Vogel. Coronet S–1247.

Riegger, Wallingford. *Music for Brass Choir.* Mercury Music. CRI S-229.

Ruggles, Carl. *Angels* (1921). Curwen. Turnabout 34398.

———. *Lilacs and Portals* (1926). AME. Columbia ML 4986.

———. *Sun Treader* (1932). DG 2530048.

Schafer, R. Murray. *East* (1972). RCI 434.

———. *Ra.* CMC 1283.

———. *Requiem for a Party Girl* (1966). BMI Canada. CRI S-245.

Schuman, William. *Credendum* (1955). Merion Music. CRIS-308.

———. *Symphony No. 8* (1962). Merion Music. DG 419 780–2.

Schwartz, Elliott. *Texture* (1966). A. Broude. Ars Nova AN-1002.

Stockhausen, Karlheinz. *Mixtur* (1967). Universal Edition. DG 137012.

Strandberg, Newton. *Xerxes.* Opus One Records 16.

Stravinsky, Igor. *Le Sacre du Printemps.* Boosey & Hawkes. Decca 400 084–2DM.

Trythall, Gilbert. *Entropy for Stereo Brass Improvisation Group and Stereo Tape* (1967). Golden Crest S-4085.

Varèse, Edgard. *Equatorial.* G. Schirmer. Nonesuch 71269.

———. *Hyperprism.* Columbia MG 31078.

———. *Octandre.* Ricordi. Reference Recordings RR 29.

Woodbury, Arthur. *Remembrances.* CPE-Source.

Cluster Techniques

Cope, David. *Iceberg Meadow* (1969). Carl Fischer. Capra 1201.

Cowell, Henry. *The Hero Sun.* Breitkopf & Härtel.

———. *The Tides of Manaunaun.* Breitkopf & Härtel. CRI 109.

—. *What's This.* Breitkopf & Härtel. CRI S-281.
Globokar, Vinko. *Ausstrahlungen* (1969). Peters. Harmonia Mundi HMU 933.
Ives, Charles. *Majority.* AMP.
—. *Sonata 2* (1915). AMP. New World 378–2.
—. *Songs.* New Music Edition. Etcetera KTC-1020.
Ligeti, György. *Aventures* (1962). C. F. Peters. DG 423 244–2.
Milhaud, Darius. *Piano Sonata* (1916). Salabert.
Rudhyar, Dane. *Stars* for piano. CRI–247.
—. *Tetragram 4* for piano. CRI–372.

Microtones

Carrillo, Julian. *Mass for Pope John XXIII in Quarter-Tones* (1962). CRI S–246.
Ives, Charles. *Chorale for Quarter-tone Piano.* Avant 1008.
—. *Three Pieces for Two Pianos Tuned a Quarter-tone Apart* (1924). C. F. Peters.
Johnston, Ben. *String Quartet No. 2* (1964). Nonesuch 71224.
Lybbert, Donald. *Lines for the Fallen* (1968). C. F. Peters. Odyssey 32–160162.
Macero, Teo. *One-Three Quarters.* Odyssey 32–160162.
Penderecki, Krzysztof. *Passion According to St. Luke.* Moeck. EMI Harmonia Mundi
    CDS 7. 49313–2.

4 INSTRUMENT
EXPLORATION

The Futurists

The desire for new and different sounds has not been the only driving force behind the experimental or *avant-garde* composers during the past sixty years. Yet it is new and different sounds that continue to provide the most serious division between audiences and composers. John Cage refers to this in his 1937 lecture "The Future of Music: Credo": "Whereas, in the past, the point of disagreement has been between dissonance and consonance, it will be, in the immediate future, between noise and so-called musical sounds."[1] Philosophically, it is not "new" sounds that have disturbed the music world, since no significant new sounds have been developed that had not coexisted with music since early times, but rather the fact that these sounds are considered musical. A group of Italian composers, called Futurists, wrote music for machine guns, steam whistles, sirens, and other "noisemakers" as early as 1912. Deriving their name from Marinetti's 1909 term *futurismo* (referring to extreme radicalism in all the arts), the Futurists were among the first composers to include noise as an inherent part of their music, not merely as a side effect. Francesco Pratella's theoretical "Musica Futurista" (reprinted in Nicolas Slonimsky's *Music Since 1900*) describes the "music" of steamboats, automobiles, battleships, railways, shipyards, and airplanes. Luigi Russolo (1885–1947), the most noted Futurist composer, constructed many of his own "noise instruments." Though his and most of the music of this movement was completely without popular success and approval, its significance lies in the fact that it proposed a concept and laid a foundation for other composers. Varèse, for example, employed sirens and anvils in *Ionisation*. Mossolov, in his more imitative *Symphony of Machines—Steel Foundry* (1928), included the constant rattling of a metal sheet throughout the work. Equally unsuccessful, the Futurist movement in France (*bruitisme*) enlarged the concept of noise as a viable musical source. George Antheil's *Ballet mécanique* (1924), probably the most "infamous" of noise pieces, was largely influenced by the French movement. Its first Carnegie Hall performance (April 10, 1927) brought about a violent audience reaction reminiscent of the first performance of Stravinsky's *Le Sacre du Printemps*.

1. John Cage, *Silence* (Cambridge, Mass.: The M.I.T. Press, paperback edition, 1961), p. 4.

Figure 4.1 George Antheil arriving in New York for the U.S. premiere performance of his *Ballet mécanique* (1927).

Antheil established the paradigm for the *avant-garde* to come, the "predictable" unpredictability of which is expressed in "An Introduction to George Antheil" by Charles Amirkhanian:

> Here is a man who once drew a pistol during a piano recital to silence a restive audience; a man who, in 1923, composed a piece of music calling for the sound of an airplane motor; a man who was mistakenly reported by the news media to have been eaten alive by lions in the Sahara Desert; and a man who collaborated with Hedy Lamarr in the invention and patenting of a World War II torpedo.[2]

Ezra Pound remarks that Antheil was possibly the first American-born musician to be taken seriously in Europe. This might explain John Cage's later successes there. The *Treatise on Harmony* by Antheil (a twenty-five-page book) repetitively dwells on the need for a reappraisal of rhythmic ideas equal to those of melody and harmony: "A sound of any pitch, or combination of such sounds, may be followed by a sound of any other pitch or any combination of such sounds, providing the time interval between them is properly gauged; and this is true for any series of sounds, chords or arpeggios."[3]

In few periods of music history has the performer played such an important role in the development of new sound resource and instrumental techniques. Many instrumentalists have, during the past forty years, created a significant impact in determining and exploring the sound capabilities of their respective instruments and have more than justified the claim that this immense potential can be applied as easily and as constructively as the use of computer-generated sound.

2. Charles Amirkhanian, "An Introduction to George Antheil," *Soundings* 7–8 (1973), p. 176. Originally printed in a KPFA Folio of November 1970.

3. Ezra Pound, *Antheil* (New York: Da Capo Press, 1968). p. 10.

Figure 4.2. Bertram Turetzky, bassist.

Bruno Bartolozzi, in his book *New Sounds for Woodwind,* states the concept of the contemporary performer's role in new music as well as the role of instruments:

> Their continued existence in the world of creative composition therefore depends to a very large extent on just what they have to offer the composer, just how much they can rouse his interest and provoke his fantasy. Some composers already show an obvious lack of interest in conventional instruments and have no hesitation in using the most unusual means in an effort to find new sonorities. . . .[4]

No traditional instrument has escaped the imagination of the composer's creative mind. Some performers, however, have steadfastly maintained that any other than traditional performance on their instruments violates inherent intention and should not be attempted. One must wonder why plucking (*pizzicato*) and muting (*con sordino*), two often-used traditional effects, do not violate inherent intention. Certainly, short of physical damage to the instrument itself, even the most critical of traditionalists must admit that the history of traditional performance techniques is riddled with experimentation. Donald Erb sums it up well:

> Music is made by a performer. It comes from him rather than from his instrument, the instrument being merely a vehicle. Therefore it seems logical that any sound a performer can make may be used in a musical composition.[5]

4. Bruno Bartolozzi, *New Sounds for Woodwind* (New York: Oxford University Press, 1967), p. 1.
5. Quoted in Bertram Turetzky, "Vocal and Speech Sounds—A Technique of Contemporary Writing for the Contrabass." *Composer* 1, no. 3 (December 1969), p. 169.

Chapter 4

Four major additions to string techniques have evolved:

1. percussive effects such as knocking, rapping, tapping, or slapping the strings or body of the instrument (especially in the works of Meyer Kupferman, Eugene Kurtz, and Sydney Hodkinson);

2. singing, speaking, or humming while playing (particularly apparent in the works of Russell Peck, Jacob Druckman, Charles Whittenberg, and Richard Felciano);

3. unusual bowings inclusive of circular bowing, bowing on or across the bridge, bowing between the bridge and tailpiece, bowing directly on the tailpiece, and *undertones* (subharmonics) created by bowing with great pressure on a harmonic node (actually creating notes well below the lowest open string of the instrument); these devices are used extensively in the works of Krzysztof Penderecki, Karlheinz Stockhausen, Mauricio Kagel, and George Crumb, among others; and

4. combinations and extensions of traditional techniques (e.g., harmonics, glissandi, fingering without bowing, pizzicati, etc.), especially notable in the works of Krzysztof Penderecki, György Ligeti, Donald Erb, and Mauricio Kagel.

Figure 4.3 shows Krzysztof Penderecki's use of playing between the bridge and tailpiece (⊤ and ⫴), highest-note pizzicato (↑), and irregular tremolo (⫫) among others in his *Threnody for the Victims of Hiroshima* (for explanation of the proportional notation, see Appendix III).[6]

Notable performers of innovative works for strings are Paul Zukofsky and Max Pollikov (violin), Walter Trampler (viola), Siegfried Palm ('cello), and Bertram Turetzky and Alvin Brehm (contrabass). String groups particularly dedicated to new music and techniques include the Fine Arts Quartet and the Kronos Quartet, among others.[7]

Though there is a difference between the ways in which innovative techniques are applied to sections (brass and woodwind) and to individual instruments, particularly

6. For a more detailed discussion of new string techniques, see Bertram Turetzky's articles "The Bass as a Drum," *Composer* 1, no. 2 (September 1969), pp. 92–107; and "Vocal and Speech Sounds: A Technique of Contemporary Writing for the Contrabass," *Composer* 1, no. 3 (December 1969), pp. 118–34; and his book *The Contemporary Contrabass* (Berkeley: University of California Press, 1974).

7. It should be noted that throughout the course of this chapter the mentioning of performers' names is necessarily incomplete due to space limitations. Apologies to those many highly dedicated and talented performers of contemporary music, whose names are not included here.

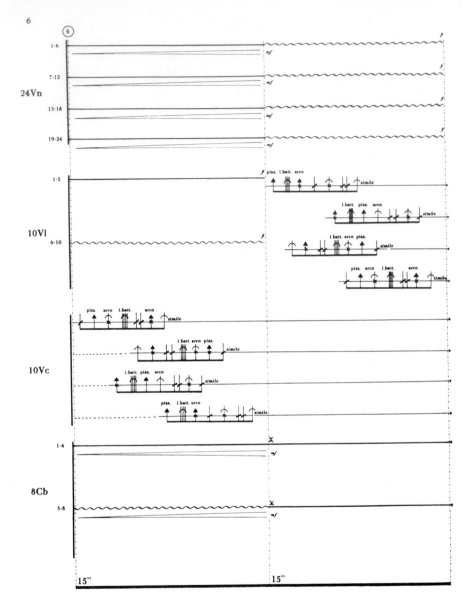

between the various single-reed, double-reed, and non-reed instruments of the wood-wind section, they are combined here due to their basic similarities. The author has grouped similar effects within six major categories:

1. multiphonics, or the creation of more than one pitch simultaneously on one instrument, are created by either of two basic methods: singing along with playing and/or forcing the strong overtone content of a given fundamental to become audible by altering embouchure, fingerings, overblowing, dynamics, and a combination of these. Figure 4.4 shows Toru Takamitsu's use and

notation (in terms of open and closed holes for fingering) in his *Voice* (1971) for solo flute (also found in works of Donald Erb, Roger Reynolds, Russell Peck, and Jacob Druckman, among others);

2. fingerings involving pitch and timbre fluctuations by changing the available fingerings on the instrument for the same note (particularly notable in the works of George Crumb);

3. jazz effects, which include a large variety of hitherto avoided sounds such as *rips, fall offs, bends,* and so on (see particularly the brass works of William Sydeman, Phil Winsor, Donald Erb, and David Cope);

4. percussion effects such as rapping, tapping, fingering without blowing, fingernails on the bell tremolo, and hand-pops (the palm of the hand slapping the open bore of the mouthpiece) as noted in the works of Aurelio de la Vega, Iannis Xenakis, and many others;

5. use of mouthpiece alone or instrument without mouthpiece, both performable with actual or approximate pitch (see works by Donald Erb, Krzysztof Penderecki, and György Ligeti, among others); and

6. extension of traditional techniques such as glissandi, harmonics, speed rates of vibrato, pedal tones, flutter tongue, circular breathing, and many others (see works by composers listed under 1–5 as well as works by Luciano Berio, Lukas Foss, and Gunther Schuller).

Donald Scavarda's *Matrix* for solo clarinet (1962), shown in Figure 4.5, contains a wide variety of new wind techniques including multiphonics (one of the very first such usages), smears, breath noise, overtone clusters, inverted mouthpiece, and undertones. Scavarda speaks to this point:

> It was in trying to find sounds that were most natural to the clarinet that I discovered what are now called *multiphonics* in April 1962. Gradually I began to realize the exciting potential of the simultaneity of sounds that could be produced by the instrument. It was necessary first, however, to discard old habits and attitudes about what the clarinet should sound like. It required an open mind and much hard work and patience to explore and 'mine' these rich, natural complex sounds and eventually to bring them to the surface.[8]

Notable performers of woodwind and brass works of the *avant-garde* include Aurèle Nicolet, Pierluigi Mencarelli, Savarino Gazzeloni, and Harvey Sollberger—flute; Joseph Celli, Lawrence Singer, and Heinz Holliger—oboe; Phillip Rehfeldt, Detalmo Corneti, and William O. Smith—clarinet; William Scribner and Sergio Penazzi—bassoon; Ken Dorn and James Houlik—saxophone; Gerard Schwarz, Robert Levy, and Marice Stith—trumpet; James Fulkerson, Stuart Dempster, and Vinko Globokar—trombone; and Barton Cummings and Roger Bobo—tuba.

8. From notes to the score by the composer. *Matrix* (1962) published by Lingua Press (1980).

Figure 4.5. Donald Scavarda. *Matrix* (1962) for clarinet.

It is in the percussion section that the maximum degree of enlargement and experimentation has taken place. Composers using more traditional instruments (timpani, snare drum, xylophone, etc.) developed a wide variety of unusual techniques, and especially experimented with various sizes and types of beaters (metal, wood, cloth, glass), to increase timbral resources. Exotic or foreign folk instruments were added mostly for particular effects and used sparingly. Surprisingly, in considering the "noises" percussion instruments such as the "whip" emit, many mainstream composers who use them nevertheless refuse to consider the musical potentiality of other less "noisy" instruments. For a number of years, the most unusual and philosophically significant of these additions to the percussion section was the brake drum. The fact that a part of a car (or truck) had found its way into the standard percussion section of the symphony orchestra seemed to go unnoticed. Its use clearly

Percussion

Figure 4.6. An example of traditional (left) *vis à vis* contemporary (right) percussion notation.

implied that any object could act as a usable sound source.[9] Early experimenters in percussion music include John Cage, Edgard Varèse, Carlos Chavez, and especially John Becker, whose *Abongo* (1933) marks one of the first serious efforts in true percussion music. Percussion sections, since the late nineteenth century, have also required new notation systems, necessitated by the fact that performers must read as many as six instrumental parts simultaneously, and five-line staves are often impractical (see Figure 4.6).

The increasing need for explicit performance directions indicating type of mallet to be used, the action of the mallet, and its exact placement on the instrument requires vastly new and different notations. Figure 4.7A shows the exact movement of the mallet across a timpani head. Figure 4.7B demonstrates the exact performance direction on the striking surface of crash cymbals. Figure 4.7C notates the sweep action of wire brushes on a bass drum. Since widely variable timbres can result from mallet direction and placement on each of these three percussion instruments, as well as from direction and amount of crash for cymbals, new notation becomes inevitable and increasingly more graphic.

An actual listing and numbering of percussion effects would create a book twice the size of this volume for just the unusual uses of the "standard" orchestral percussion instruments. The codification of the percussion section defines any instrument, no matter whether string (e.g., piano), air (e.g., slide whistle), or others similar in kind to the orchestra "staples," as within "percussion" classification. This is particularly true when non-Western instruments are used with an orchestra—no matter what the context, the nature of the instrument, or the method of producing sound.

Notable *avant-garde* composers for percussion include Larry Austin, Karlheinz Stockhausen, Frederic Rzewski, Harry Partch, Edward Miller, Mario Bertoncini, Peter Garland, William Kraft, and many, many others. Performers include Max

---

9. The brake drum is described and pictured in a number of contemporary orchestration books (e.g., Reed and Leach, *Scoring for Percussion* [New York: Prentice-Hall, Inc., 1969]).

A

Timpani: mallet motion

B

Cymbals: striking procedure

C

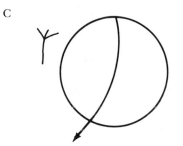

Bass drum: wire brush motion

Figure 4.7. *Avant-garde* percussion notations.

Figure 4.8. William Kraft. Photo by A. A. Friedman.

Figure 4.9. Blackearth Percussion Group.

Neuhaus, Christoph Caskel, Willy Winant, and William Kraft. Often, as here indicated (and more often than in any other section of the orchestra), percussionists tend to be composers as well. William Kraft is both a percussionist and a gifted and well-known composer for all instruments which includes his extensive percussion solo and ensemble literature. The well-known Blackearth Percussion Group (see Figure 4.9) performed *avant-garde* music until disbanding several years ago.

Vocal

The voice, in both solo and choral situations, has in recent years become a focal point of innovative development realized both in terms of dramatic emphasis of text and as an instrument separate from verbal associations. Its ability to be a "percussively stringed wind instrument" gives it nearly all of the timbre potentials of all the aforementioned instruments. Only the physical limitations of individual performers become obstacles to the composer's available resources (few can equal Roy Hart's eight-octave range and multiphonic abilities).

Most vocal experimentation has taken place in three basic areas:

1. effects, such as panting, whistling, sucking, kissing, hissing, clucking, laughing, talking, whispering, and so forth (especially in the works of Hans Werner Henze, Krzysztof Penderecki, György Ligeti, Karlheinz Stockhausen, Mauricio Kagel, Pauline Oliveros, Folke Rabe, Richard Felciano, Luciano Berio, and David Cope);

2. multiphonics (especially notable in the *Versuch über Schweine* by Hans Werner Henze); and

3. muting in the forms of humming, hands over mouth and slowly opening and closing the mouth (employed well in works by Donald Erb and Robert Morris).

Figure 4.10, the *Aventures* of György Ligeti, shows the breathing in and out (measures 1–5 shown by symbols ▶ = inhale and ◀ = exhale) as well as muting (closed mouth *m* in the second brace). This work is notable for its many other effects, its lack of text (replaced by a 112–letter alphabet for creating sounds), and the exchanging metric and proportional notations shown clearly here between braces one and two. Hans Werner Henze's *Versuch über Schweine* (1969) for voice and orchestra is equally impressive in its incredible use of dramatic vocal gymnastics.

Singers who are known for their performance of new music include Roy Hart, Randy Wong, Catherine Rowe, Bethany Beardslee, Elaine Bonazzi, Joan La Barbara, Neva Pilgrim, Paul Sperry, and the late Cathy Berberian and Jan DeGaetani. The New Music Choral Ensemble (NMCE), founded by its director (Kenneth Gaburo) in 1966, stood for a decade as one of the world's foremost choral ensembles dedicated to the performance of new music.

David Hykes, founder and developer of the Harmonic Choir (1975), practices the art of Harmonic Chant, or the singing of more than one note simultaneously. While Tibetan Buddhist monks and Mongolian "throat" (or *hoomi*) singers have produced music in this manner for centuries, Western singers have only begun using this approach in the past few decades. By performing and recording only in highly resonant spaces such as large churches and abbeys, including New York City's Cathedral of St. John, the Harmonic Choir is able to take advantage of certain singing techniques to pronounce high harmonics simultaneously with sung fundamentals. With his colleague Timothy Hill, Hykes has developed five types of Harmonic Chant. These move from drones based on subharmonic pitches through sung fundamentals, as drones over which singers produce melodies based on the overtone series, to contrapuntal harmonic movements of both fundamentals and derived melodies from various related harmonic series.

Keyboard Instruments

The early experiments and compositions for piano by Henry Cowell (e.g., 1925, *The Banshee,* which involved plucking and stroking the strings inside the instrument), John Cage (e.g., 1938, *Bacchanale,* and 1946–48, *Sonatas and Interludes* for prepared piano) and Christian Wolff (whose *For Prepared Piano* appeared in *New Music Quarterly* in April, 1951) aroused great interest. At least a few performers became aware of the fantastic array of new sound resources that were available, and that these resources, combined with variable performance techniques, were just as viable as more traditional ones.

The prepared piano (a technique first explored by John Cage in the mid-thirties) involves the placement of objects such as nuts, bolts, and nails on, around, and between the strings, thus converting the piano into an instrument with an almost limitless variety of new timbres. Figure 4.11 shows a number of typical preparations. Resulting timbres can be altered by (a) location of preparation in regard to string length (e.g., placing at harmonic nodes creates a very different sound from

Figure 4.11. From Richard Bunger: *The Well-Prepared Piano.* Examples of piano preparations. Used by permission of the author and illustrator, Richard Bunger. Second Edition. Litoral Arts Press, 35 Firefly Lane, Sebastopol, California 95472 (1981).

that resulting when one places the object between these nodes); (b) striking techniques (i.e., initiating the sound via the keyboard creates a sound distinctly different from that obtained if one strikes the preparation directly with a mallet or similar instrument); and (c) elasticity and density of material utilized. Such preparations should do no damage to the instrument whatsoever if proper precautions are used (see Figure 4.12, which shows the use of a screwdriver covered with masking tape to insert preparations, thus avoiding any harm to the strings).

Aside from preparation, the following new techniques are currently being used and explored:

1. muting (usually done by placing a finger on the string inside the piano between the pin and the dampers and playing the notes on the keyboard with the other hand) is notated with a + above the note (used particularly in the works of George Crumb and David Cope);

2. harmonics (produced by touching a node of the string inside the piano with one hand and striking the corresponding key with the other) are employed much like those of string instruments (used in works by George Crumb, Larry Barnes, and many others);

3. bowing the strings (produced by making bows of fishline, threading them around and between the strings, and then drawing back and forth as one would on a string instrument), found particularly in the works of Curtis Curtis-Smith;

4. stroking, rapping, tapping, striking, or plucking the strings or preparations between the strings directly for a variety of different timbres (used primarily in the works of Henry Cowell, George Crumb, David Cope, Donald Erb, and others); and

5. using other parts of the instrument by knocking, tapping, rapping, and so on, particularly on the wood of the lid and body, the metal of the internal crossbars and soundboard, and so on, with mallets, hands, and various other objects (notable in works like *Knocking Piece* by Ben Johnston, and works by John Cage, George Crumb, Donald Erb, and many others).

Stephen Scott has developed a "bowed piano" influenced by Curtis-Smith's invention. Scott has created sets of miniature "piano bows" similar in design to regular violin bows. Constructed of popsicle sticks with horsehair glued to both sides, these bows are able to produce rich and vibrant continuous sounds on an otherwise struck instrument. Unlike Curtis-Smith's design, however, Scott's invention can play quite fast passages on premarked strings.

Pianists who are actively involved in the performance of *avant-garde* works include David Tudor, David Burge, Richard Bunger, and Aloys Kontarsky. David Tudor, William Albright, and Martha Folts have been active in the performance of new music for the organ, as has Antoinette Vischer with the harpsichord. At present these experiments have been more theatrical (organ) and formal (harpsichord) than

Figure 4.12. From Richard Bunger, *The Well-Prepared Piano.* Used by permission of the author and illustrator, Richard Bunger. Second Edition. Litoral Arts Press, 350 Firefly Lane, Sebastopol, California 95472, 1981.

Figure 4.13. Conlon Nancarrow. Photo by Gordon Mumma.

real in terms of sonic exploration (note especially works by Mauricio Kagel, Gordon Mumma, Christian Wolff, and William Albright for organ and György Ligeti for harpsichord).

Unique work with the player piano has been accomplished by Conlon Nancarrow in Mexico City. His *Studies for Player Piano* (one of which was published in *New Music Quarterly* in October, 1951 with many now published by *Soundings;* see Bibliography) is a series of works, now numbering more than forty, utilizing punched piano rolls inserted in upright player pianos. The composer uses two Marshall and Wendell pianos, both with modified hammers; one set covered with leather and the other with steel straps. His extremely complex and original works vary from jazz-influenced shorter movements (especially the early studies) to mathematically proportioned canons (in the later works). The composer has spoken about his work and its relation to traditional instruments in an interview:

> I'm so tied up now with the player piano. I'd have to start thinking again: "Does the hand reach there? Can it go here?" The whole thing. No, no. You know, when I do these things for player piano, I just write music; and the notes go here, there, wherever. I don't have to think about anything else. I used to, when I was writing for instruments. It's a real luxury not to have to think about all that.[10]

Harp

Carlos Salzedo (1885–1961) developed an extremely wide range of possible effects on this versatile instrument, as well as highly original notations and names for these techniques ("gushing aeolian chords," etc.). Many have become standard for the harpist and need not be considered *avant-garde,* though they may sound like it to the uninitiated. Composers utilizing these numerous effects include Salzedo himself, Luciano Berio, and George Crumb, in particular.

The harp is indeed unique in that Salzedo, a pioneering and innovative genius, composed for it during its maturing period. He proved that (more than any other single instrument) it is capable of sounds virtually unexplored by the *avant-garde* composer. It is not much of a gamble to predict that the harp will in future years become a foremost attraction for the contemporary composer.

Ensemble Development

George Crumb's *Songs, Drones, and Refrains of Death* (1969) for baritone, electric guitar, electric contrabass, electric piano, harpsichord, and two percussionists contain a great many of the effects discussed above (see Figure 4.14). The duet here (for electric guitar and electric contrabass) is scored in seven events. Each performer is required to sing or whisper while playing his or her respective instrument in a variety of unusual ways (e.g., harmonics, glissandi, tremolo, use of metal rod, etc.). Crumb's *Black Angels* (1970) for string quartet employs amplification of the instruments both for balance and for the unique timbre alteration that electronics adds to the ensemble. This procedure, including the use of both contact and acoustic microphones, has become increasingly popular (discussed at greater length in chapter

10. Cole Cagne and Tracy Caras, *Soundpieces: Interviews with American Composers* (London: The Scarecrow Press, Inc., 1982), p. 285.

Figure 4.14. George Crumb: *Songs, Drones, and Refrains of Death*. C. F. Peters Corporation, 373 Park Avenue South. New York, NY 10016. Reprint permission granted.

8, "Analog Electronic Music"). However, even the instrumentalists often don't recognize sounds from fellow performers, posing a problem contributing to the extreme difficulty of ensemble rhythmic performance. That problem is here solved by a procedure of notating *events,* in which exact timing is not as important as exact performance of the event itself. A broad spectrum of tone colors and "noise" is thus made available to the composer as musical material.

Iannis Xenakis, long interested in preserving live and traditional instruments of the orchestra through creation of new techniques, proves convincingly in *Metastasis* (1953–54) that sixty-one traditional instruments can compete successfully with electronic sound sources.

Roman Haubenstock-Ramati was one of the first, in his *Interpolation* (1958), to utilize an unmanipulated prerecorded tape made by the performer. This enables a single instrumentalist to create a large number of ensemble effects using only a single instrument as source. His 1961 *Liaisons* for vibraphone includes provisions for a previously prepared tape to be started six to ten seconds after the performer begins. In this instance the tape serves not as an electronic device, but as a tool that enables both composer and performer to elicit more combinations of tones and effects, without losing the instrumental timbre.

George Green's *Perihelion for Concert Band* (1974) employs an incredible array of new and effective timbres often similar in nature, becoming clusters of like textures, though at times contrasted for purposes of form and direction.

David Cope's *Margins* (1972) for cello, trumpet, percussion, and two pianos emphasizes the "marginal" aspects of each instrument in a single movement structure. "The composer equally explores the contrast and developmental possibilities of dynamics and contrapuntal articulations. The tempo remains very slow throughout and the beat divides into multifold groupings of often very quick and pointillistic integrations from instrument to instrument."[11]

The previously discussed effects have also been used in combination or in conjunction with extracurricular performer activity, from finger-snapping and music stand–tapping to such dramatic effects as costumes, theatrical staging, and substitution of the original instrument with other instruments. Often composers use whispers, speaking, and shouting (as in the Crumb example, Figure 4.14) along with the performance of additional instruments such as triangles hung from music stands, maracas, and a variety of other percussion instruments.

Heinz Holliger's *Atembogen* is filled with orchestral effects, most of which involve some machination of subtle nuance or shading of breath or bow technique. Examples for winds include exhaling, inhaling, using voice, embouchure but no tone, whistle-tone; and for strings, bow with too much pressure, bow with too little pressure, bow on tailpiece, and *col legno*. Most of these are used musically and there are no hostile contraptions evident. The piece is shaped in a through-composed series of large dramatic gestures based on quasi-physical motives. For example, *Atembogen's* opening is four seconds of bowing and blowing without allowing sound to

11. From liner notes on recording: Orion ORS 75169.

occur, with strings on up-bow and winds inhaling. The work ends similarly with the conductor doing a solo while the orchestra slowly releases bows and breaths from their instruments in exhale fashion. Throughout the work there are like passages lending the "feel" of numerous episodes into deep textures and timbre explorations within the boundaries of the physical motion of bowing/breathing.

Whether in solo or chamber ensembles, the complete realization of all possible sonic events creates an entirely new performance situation with virtually endless combinational possibilities. The audience can no longer attend a string quartet performance expecting that a traditional string quartet will be heard. New orchestral and multi-orchestral combinations create almost endless possibilities equal to that of electronic production. Indeed, recordings of these works, without visual confirmation, distort beyond recognition the imagination's comprehension of the sound source. Ensembles of mixed instrumentation have contributed greatly to the development of instrument exploration. Such active groups commission, perform, and record new music and include the Contemporary Chamber Ensemble, The Aeolian Chamber Players, Die Reihe Ensemble, the Philadelphia Composers Forum, Cologne New Music Ensemble, The MW 2 Ensemble, da capo Chamber Players, the Kronos Quartet, the Arditti Quartet, the Melos Ensemble, and the ISKRA ensemble, to name but a few. There also exists a large number of school-affiliated new music ensembles made up of faculty and students possessing both a high degree of professional ability and large repertoires.

New Instruments

Enlargement and transformation of sounds on traditional instruments represents only a part of new, non-electronic sound sources for composers. Harry Partch, unlike Cage and Cowell, created new instruments rather than transforming existing ones (though his first such instrument was an adapted viola). His division of the octave into forty-three tones instead of twelve brought the need to create instruments capable of realizing his theoretical concepts (see his *Genesis of A New Music*). Except for his use of voice, almost all of his works employ original instruments, primarily percussion and struck string. Partch's *U.S. Highball: Account of Hobo Trip* (1943) and *Account of the Normandy Invasion by an American Glider Pilot* (both early works) reflect his fascination with instruments, an attempt at non-imitative music. In *Revelation in the Courthouse Square* (1961), the visual (theatrical) elements—the performers and their instruments—become an integral (in his words: *corporeal*) part of the work. *And on the Seventh Day Petals Fell in Petaluma*, a 1964 work comprising studies in the form of twenty-three duets, for *Delusion of the Fury,* a larger 1967 work, explores the possibilities of harmonic and melodic uses of microtones based on his tonal and polytonal theories of intonation (his word for major is Otonality; for minor, Utonality).

More recent compositions have extended instrumental possibilities to anything that can be beaten, blown, or bowed, with each work demanding a new instrument for realization—cars, brake drums, even a jet engine, for example. Few of these "instruments" enter any standardized orchestra, as their intrinsic theatrical value lies in their being recognized as having a direct relationship to one work or composer.

Figure 4.16. Various Partch instruments. Photos by Jonathan Glasier.

A. Gourd Tree (1964)
   Cone Gong (1965)

B. Zymo-Xyl (1963)

C. Mazda Marimba (1963)

D. Chromelodeon 1 (1945–1949)

Yoshimasa Wada has created a number of successful new wind instruments (see Figures 4.17 and 4.18) that, due to size, produce low sounds of soft dynamics often needing amplification for realistic acoustic projection. The KIVA Ensemble of the University of California at San Diego explores new instrumental resources (see Figure 4.19) often coupled with electronic amplification or modification. Arthur Frick has created a wide variety of new instruments (see Figure 4.20), many of which are mobile and often have comic implications.

George Gonzalez and Peter Richards have built a "Wave Organ" in San Francisco that amplifies the sound of energy created by ocean currents pushing and retreating in large cement pipes. The audience place their ears next to one of several

Figure 4.16. *(Continued)*

E. Bass Marimba (1951)

F. Diamond Marimba (1946)

G. Boo (1955–1957)

H. Surrogate Kithara (1953)

orifices through which both sound and air exit. Different wave and weather conditions affect the type and dynamic of the sounds produced.

Robert Rutman also creates giant instruments, often out of industrial scrap metals. His "steel 'cello," for example, is a single large piece of this substance twisted into a C-shape with a single large string strung from the top of the instrument to its bottom. His "bow chimes" have a similar shape but are held in place by a bar.

New instruments require "new" performers, with questioned virtuosity. One could hardly expect as practiced and polished a performance on an instrument created or adapted for one work alone as expected from an experienced violinist after

Figure 4.17. Instrument by Yoshimasa Wada. Photo by Seiji Kakizaki.

Figure 4.18. Instruments by Yoshimasa Wada. Photo by Seiji Kakizaki.

Figure 4.19. KIVA performance instruments. Photo by Solomon (UCSD).

intense study of a Beethoven concerto. One of two alternatives is suggested: (1) a simple but fully notated score, or (2) a freer improvisational structure whereby the performer substitutes freedom and creativity for familiarity. Douglas Leedy chooses the latter in *Usable Music I* (1968), for very small instruments with holes. This work depends almost completely on graphic representation of activities (i.e., the use of symbols to indicate such general directions as "blow" or "draw"), with less emphasis on exact rhythmic and pitch notation. Robert Moran, in *Titus* (1968), has

Figure 4.20. Instrument by Arthur Frick.

the score projected on the stage upon an automobile, showing pictorially the performers' area and amount of activity (see Figure 4.21). Each of from five to fifteen performers, using contact microphones, files, hammers, and the like, moves around and within the car, visually guided by the score.

In such works, there is an increasing necessity for performer creativity. Once the composer has admitted that the act of composition is a partially shared responsibility, it is not difficult to understand the motivation inherent in graphic or less

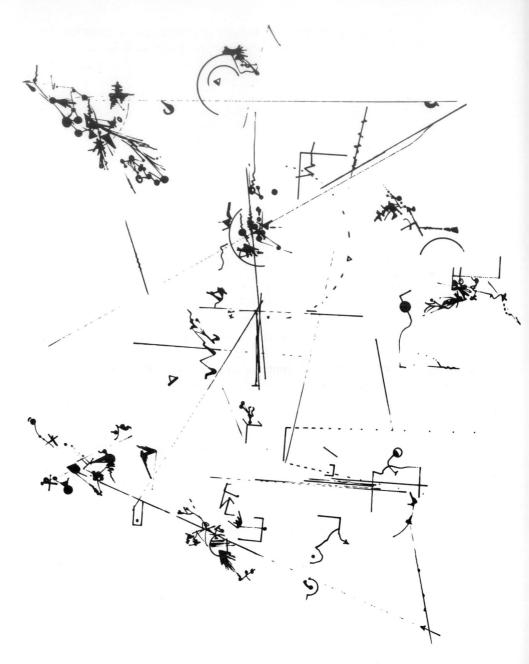

exact notational systems. New instruments and techniques have evolved from concepts of unique sounds, creating implications and philosophies of composer-
performer relationships much more significant in their ramifications than the mere
searching for different timbres.

Other composers and artists deeply involved in the creation of new musical instruments include Laurie Anderson (electronic tape-bow on violins); Christopher

Charles Banta (large marimbas); Bob Bates (mechanical instruments and music machines); Harry Bertoia (sound sculptures); Jim Burton (sound installations); Ivor Darreg (large numbers of microtonal string, wind, and electronic instruments similar in scope to those of Harry Partch); Paul De Marinis (electronic modules); Richard Dunlap (nonconventional instruments for improvisation and theater presentation); Stephen Scott (large sound sculptures); Bruce Fier (architectural sound designs); Cris Forster (notably *Chrysalis*); Ron George (original percussion instruments and ensembles); Jonathan Glasier (notably his *Harmonic Canon*); Stephen Goodman (automatic music instruments); Jim Gordon (percussion synthesizers); Jim Hobart (percussion and steel-stringed instruments); Alzek Misheff (hot-air balloons containing portable electronic instruments); Max Neuhaus (sound installations); Jim Pomeroy (music boxes); Susan Rawcliffe (wind instruments); Tom Recchion (folk instruments from found objects); Prent Rodgers (electro-acoustical instruments); Stephen von Huene (self-performing sound sculptures); Robert Wilhite (environments); and Richard Waters (notably the metal "waterphone"). More often than not, these composers/instrument builders are also the performers on their instruments, self-taught troubadours of the *avant-garde*.

The expansion of possibilities in the area of timbre modulation has proven to be a significant development resulting from instrument exploration. With the composer's increasing awareness of the subtle timbre alterations available in different registers of various instruments—muting, dynamics, attacks, and decays—comes the realization that a wealth of timbre overlap exists between instruments. Figure 4.22 shows three such overlaps with the evolving timbre changes inherent in the combinations. In the first example the piccolo is initially masked by the triangle. Its slow crescendo gradually modulates the sound to solo piccolo through the decay of the triangle sound. In the second example the trumpet (with straight mute) slowly dies away as the like-timbred oboe crescendos, and so takes over. The effect is demonstrated by the intersecting vertical dotted line. At the beginning one hears only the trumpet. At the line one begins to hear a subtle combination of the two. Terms like "obet" or "trumboe" are often employed by composers to emphasize the significance of the truly "new" sound created by the modulation. Finally one hears the oboe alone. The third example demonstrates a direct approach to dynamics with the bass drum masking the piano attack completely, but a unique effect is achieved as the piano "rings" out of the bass drum, the piano chord slowly decaying beyond the hand-stopped percussion attack. Works effectively employing timbre modulation include *Sinfonia* (1968) by Luciano Berio, *Lontano* (1967) by György Ligeti, *Ancient Voices of Children* (1970) by George Crumb, and *Apotheosis of This Earth* (1971) by Karel Husa.

Spacing and placement play an important role in the struggle for new directional sonorities from traditional instruments. A few historical examples are notable: Garbrieli's eight-and twelve-part canzonas; Mozart's *Don Giovanni;* Berlioz's *Requiem;* Berg's *Wozzeck;* Mahler's *Das Klagende Lied;* and Ives's *The Unanswered Question* (1908) for string orchestra, four flutes, and trumpet, isolated. Henry

Timbre and Spatial Modulation

Figure 4.22. Timbre-
modulations.

Brant's experiments with the vast potential of vertical, horizontal, and circular arrangements have suggested meaningful solutions to acoustic problems. In his "Space
as an Essential Aspect of Musical Composition," Brant describes many of his successful experiments in performer arrangement for optimum directional, acoustical,
and balance effectiveness.[12] The spatial composing technique of one of his examples
(*Voyage Four,* 1964) involves percussion and brass on stage, violins on one side bal-
cony, violas and 'cellos on the other, basses on floor level at the rear of the auditorium, with various woodwind instruments and a few string instruments on the two
rear balconies. Three conductors combine to direct the performers which also includes tuba, timpani, and chimes in the audience. Brant contends that, if the composer indeed intends to control his performance, each work should contain specific
instructions for performer placement. Because his works are different in both structure and instrumentation, rehearsal experimentation is necessary for exact results,
with no set schematic existing except in individual terms for each work or movement
of a work.

12. Elliot Schwartz and Barney Childs, eds., *Contemporary Composers on Contemporary Music*
(New York: Holt, Rinehart and Winston, 1967), pp. 223–42.

Henry Brant discusses his views regarding spatial performance in an interview:

> The competition, from both living and dead composers, is too great for a solo piece; it's also too great for an ensemble that doesn't use spatial separation. What would I write? A string quartet? Besides, I think that particular combination is lopsided. For thirty years I've been trying to devise a rational string quartet; it should be one violin, one viola, one instrument that doesn't exist—a tenor violin, which I'm trying to develop—and 'cello.[13]

Brant's *An American Requiem* utilizes spatial location of six different widely separated instrumental groups and four separated single players, including an optional voice. The primary ensemble is a group of sixteen woodwinds sitting on the stage in a semicircle with their backs to the audience with the conductor facing the group and the audience at centerstage. The horn, trumpet, and trombone sections contrast the individual parts of the woodwinds with unison rhythmic materials and are situated in the hall. The fifth section is made of various bells including "pipe-chimes," the construction of which is described loosely by the composer as three sets of seven pipes each, a half-inch or so different in diameter, with different pitches obtained by a two- or three-inch length differential. Two tubas join the brass in homorhythmic unison with single parts for pipe organ, voice, church bells (recorded on tape if necessary), and timpani.

An American Requiem is a long (15′) three-section work. The first section opens with the formative material of the work: a nine-note horizontal motive of a half-step cluster bordered on each end by whole steps. Each note of this line is paralleled in the same rhythm by eight other instruments, forming a mirror of the horizontal material (i.e., a vertical cluster bordered on each end by whole steps). This kind of consistency of vocabulary between melodic and harmonic content continues throughout the work. Contrasting this dissonant idea in the winds is a static organ part of triadic content (C minor, B♭ minor, etc.) characteristic of both the first and third sections. The quasi-pitched pipe-chimes add a surrealistic touch to the multileveled music. The second main section develops the polyphony of the first with contrasting sectional flutters in the brass, trills in the percussion, and the carillon in hemiola with the rest of the ensemble. The third main section returns to the organ triads and variations of the initial expository material.

Spatial modulation, aided largely by developments in timbre modulation, involves the active motion of a sound from one point to another. An extreme example of this would be a large number of violins surrounding the audience, the sound beginning with one violin then slowly moving with the same pitch to each violin in turn until the first was encountered again. Works by Henry Brant, Donald Erb (*Fanfare for Brass Ensemble and Percussion,* 1971). Cliff Crego (*Implosions,* 1971), and many others employ this technique.

Music also has elements called "combination tones." Figure 4.23 shows that when two tones, one fixed and the other gliding, occur simultaneously, combination

13. Cole Cagne and Tracy Caras, *Soundpieces: Interviews with American Composers* (London: The Scarecrow Press, Inc., 1982), p. 61.

Figure 4.23. Combination tones.

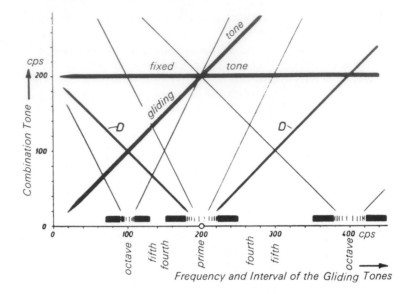

tones result. Differential (difference frequency between two pitches) and summational (sum frequency of two pitches) tones represent the two basic types of combination tones. Here the D signifies the primary difference tone, and the thickness of line the acoustical impression of roughness (loudness). Composers such as Ligeti (e.g., *Lontano*) have attempted to create and control these elements in their music. Too often, however, variations in performance or acoustics cause distortion or unsuccessful production. These tones fall generally into discussions of psychoacoustics. The *Center for New Music and Audio Technologies* (CNMAT) founded at the University of California at Berkeley (1988) has been developed to investigate matters relating to this important aspect of the musical experience. Consortiums exist between CNMAT, IRCAM (Institute for Research and Coordination of Acoustics/ Music, a part of the Georges Pompidou Center in Paris), and Stanford's CCRMA (Center for Computer Research in Music and Acoustics). Since performance is indelibly tied to the hearing process, with timbre (especially) and time greatly influencing the manner in which communication takes place, knowledge of these areas seems especially important. Figure 4.24 shows psychoacoustical characteristics in time and frequency scale in rough limits of effectiveness.

Elliott Schwartz's *Elevator Music* (1967) employs the vast acoustical, directional, and movement possibilities that a multistory building provides. Twelve floors of a building become the performing areas for twenty-four performers (stationary) while the audience rides an elevator up and down through the constantly changing environment of sound. The small spaces around the elevators make for a leakage of sound between the floors, thus providing an overlay of sound materials. There is no distinct concept of twelve individual entities except when the conductor, who is also the elevator operator, stops at a certain floor and opens the elevator doors, while the performers on *all* floors continue to play regardless of the elevator position. Dramatic change is available when the elevator stops at certain empty floors (empty in

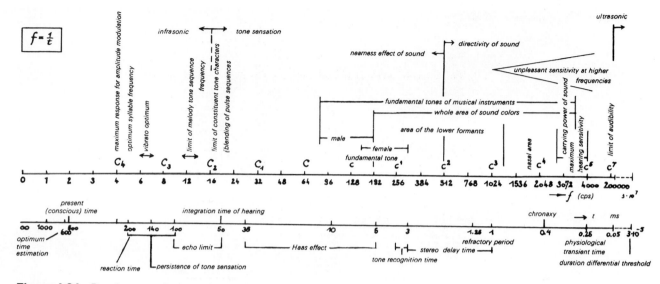

$f=\frac{1}{t}$

Figure 4.24. Psychoacoustical characteristics in terms of time and frequency.
Permission granted by Dover Publications.

the sense of visual activity, but completely filled with sound due to the above-mentioned leakage from other floors), as explicitly outlined in the score.[14] Recording of this, as well as many of Brant's works, becomes virtually impossible, as the aspects of space, movement, direction, and theater are inherent in the structure of the works.

IRCAM has developed a number of experiments to discover the variety of ways in which sound can be explored in physical spaces. Figure 4.25 is a diagrammatic exposition of the entire IRCAM installation, with Figure 4.26 a closer view of the *Espace de Projection*, a performance hall with controllable acoustic properties. Figure 4.27 shows Pierre Boulez (director of the Center) and Gerard Buquet (tubist) in the space with the variable shutters and "flats" operated by computers. The Center also includes computer and electronic music facilities.

Non-Western Influences

For centuries, composers of the mainstream Western-European traditions have borrowed both stylistic flavors and actual folk materials from music of world cultures. The list of works and composers is too long to mention here, but includes Franz Liszt (*Hungarian Rhapsodies*), Georges Bizet (*Carmen*), Edouard Lalo (*Symphonie espagnole*), Mikhail Glinka (*Spanish Overtures*), and Rimsky-Korsakov (*Capriccio on Spanish Themes*). Notable mainstream composers of this century include Claude Debussy (see chapter 1), Maurice Ravel (*Bolero*), Igor Stravinsky (use of Russian folk materials), Carlos Chavez (*Sinfonia India* using Indian and

14. For a complete description and score of this work, see *Composer* 2, no. 2 (September 1970), pp. 49–54.

Espace de Projection   Diagonal   Instruments et Voix   Electro-Acoustique   Ordinateur

Figure 4.25. IRCAM.

Mexican ideas), Heitor Villa-Lobos (*Bachianas Brasilieras*), and Silvestre Revueltas (*Cuauhnahuac* for orchestra, utilizing large numbers of Mexican and Indian musical materials).

Colin McPhee (1901–64) spent a great deal of time in the early 1930s researching and studying the music and instruments of Bali, particularly the Balinese *gamelan.* His style changed considerably as a result, and such works as *Tabuh-Tabuhan* (1936) show considerable influence of the *gamelan gong kebyar*, a twenty- to twenty-five-player ensemble and development of the older *gamelan gong*. McPhee translated the music of Bali into his own style and instrumentation (traditional Western orchestra). Alan Hovhaness (b. 1911) has been strongly influenced by the music of India as well as Armenia as exemplified by *Avak, The Healer,* 1946, and *Khaldis,* 1951. Again it is the basic style that has influenced Hovhaness's work, rather than direct quotation or instrument usage. The works of Chou Wen-Chung (Chefoo, China, b. 1923), particularly *Soliloquy of a Bhiksuni,* and Olivier Messiaen (b. 1908), with the use of Indian *talas* (repeating rhythmic patterns such as ($\frac{8}{8}$ ♩ ♩ ♩. or $\frac{7}{8}$ ♪ ♩ ♩.) in his musical ideas, have been clearly influenced by non-Western world music.

A few contemporary composers employ the use of non-Western instruments in the ensembles for performance of their music. Lou Harrison (b. 1917) has created

Figure 4.26. IRCAM *Espace de Projection.*

Figure 4.27. Pierre Boulez with Gerard Buquet in *Espace de Projection.*

Instrument Exploration

111

a wide variety of works utilizing *gamelan*-type instruments suggesting the *kempul, bonang, saron,* and *gender* of the Javanese *gamelan* as well as American folklike homemade ensembles of *gamelan*-like instruments. His *Pacifika Rondo* (1963) is for a chamber orchestra of Western and Asian instruments and *Concerto in Slendro* (1961) for violin, celesta, and percussion orchestra shows strong *gamelan* influence.

Harry Partch's instruments, discussed earlier under "New Instruments", show strong influence of Hindu, African, and folk-American crossbreeding. John Cage's prepared piano works of the thirties and forties, particularly the *Sonatas and Interludes* of 1948, show influence of the *gamelan* orchestral style.

Quotation and stylistic embodiment of non–Western traditional music are evident in the works of the author. His work includes a great deal of Navajo Indian quotation and influence, particularly *Arena* (1974), *Rituals* (1976), and *The Way* (1981), a part of the score to the former appearing later in this text. Ruth Lomon's *Five Ceremonial Masks* for piano (1980) also show Navajo influence. David Ward–Steinman's (1936) *Rituals for Dancers and Musicians* and *The Tale of Issoumbochi,* Ravi Shankar's *Concerto for Sitar and Orchestra,* Roy Travis's, *Switched–On Ashanti for Flutes, African Instruments, and Tape (1973),* and *African Sonata for Piano* (1966) are true assimilations of this type. David Fanshawe's *African Sanctus* (1975) is a hybrid of Western and non-Western music.

The styles of some composers fully depend on and develop from non-Western sources. Terry Riley's *In C* (1964), for example, compares to the *jor* section of an Indian *raga* (term derived from the Sanskrit root *ranja,* "to color, to tinge"). One hears the slow process of variation by textural overlay. Similarly, the works of Steve Reich (b. 1936), especially *Drumming* (1971) and *Four Organs* (1970), show Eastern influence, as does *Einstein on the Beach* by Philip Glass.

The "ritual" elements of some non-Western musics have influenced a number of *avant-garde* composers, including Pauline Oliveros, Jon Gibson, and Alvin Lucier. Each has developed works built on ritual-like elements taken from Indian, Zen, or Asian concepts. Lucier's *Queen of the South* (1972) takes its title from the mystical personality in alchemy known as *Sapientia Dei* connected with the south wind, an allegory for the Holy Ghost. The relationship between this work and certain ritual Navajo sand painting techniques is clear in this description of the performance:

> The performers sing into microphones or produce sound with oscillators. By means of electromagnetic transducers, large steel plates which are suspended horizontally near the floor are made to vibrate with these sounds. The vibrational patterns are made visible by sand and other granular materials which the performers sprinkle onto these plates. As they change the pitches of their sounds the granular images on the plates shift from one pattern to another. The performers, each with their own plate, are located throughout the performance space—ideally it is a gallery rather than a traditional proscenium theatre. The spectators move freely around these sonically and visually vibrating islands and choose their own degree of involvement with the ritual.[15]

15. Gordon Mumma, "Witchcraft, Cybersonics and Folkloric Virtuosity," *Darmstädter Beiträge zur Neue Musik,* 1974.

Figure 4.28. Lou Harrison teaching at USC during 1978. Photo by Betty Freeman.

Figure 4.29. Lou Harrison and William Colvig. Photo shows a number of instruments built by either or both of these builder/composers. Photo by Betty Freeman.

Vectoral Analysis: Peter Maxwell Davies: *Eight Songs for a Mad King*

(For information on vectoral analysis and procedures see chapter 1.)

1. Historical Background: Peter Maxwell Davies was born in Manchester, England, in 1934, and studied in England at the Royal College of Music and in America at Princeton University with Roger Sessions. He was one of the founders of the Fires of London (*avant-garde* chamber ensemble; formerly the Pierrot Players), who are most noted for performing Davies' works. His music often includes quotations, new instruments, new techniques on traditional instruments, and a kind of stylistic counterpoint. His better-known works include *Miss Donnithorne's Maggot* (1974), *Vesalii Icones* (1970), and *Dark Angels* (1974), all for chamber ensembles of various makeup.

    In an interview with Paul Griffiths (from *New Sounds, New Personalities*), Davies remarks:

    You can be thinking of something entirely different, and then you tune into a process that's going on somewhere. It might be a thematic idea, or a purely structural idea, with its main pivots: a big time span, with departure points and arrival points, but you don't know what's between them. I suspect that before you write down anything on paper, you've probably got, with a big work like a symphony, some small ideas and a big design. Then you start thinking through things in terms of the ideas going into the design, and then you start sketching. I'm not a perfectionist in the way that Boulez and Stockhausen are. Once a piece is done it's part of the past.[16]. . .

2. Overview: *Eight Songs for a Mad King* was first performed on April 22, 1969, in London by singer Roy Hart and the Pierrot Players conducted by

Figure 4.30. Peter Maxwell Davies. Photo by Keith McMillan. Permission by Boosey & Hawkes, Ltd., London.

16. Paul Griffiths, *New Sounds, New Personalities* (London: Faber Music Ltd., 1985).

the composer. The eight songs are based on texts created by Randolph Stow suggested by a miniature mechanical organ playing eight tunes, once the property of King George III.

One imagined the King, in his purple flannel dressing-gown and ermine night-cap, struggling to teach birds to make the music which he could so rarely torture out of his flute and harpsichord. Or trying to sing with them, in that ravaged voice, made almost inhuman by day-long soliloquies, which once murdered Handel for Fanny Burney's entertainment. There were echoes of the story of the Emperor's nightingale. But this Emperor was mad; and at times he knew it, and wept.

Each of the songs has a separate indicative title, and the texts resemble old English. Notation is metri-portional where at times the composer writes clear indications of meter and at others the bar line disappears and a free, time-proportionate-to-space notation takes over.

The forms of each of the movements are similar in that none take the usual part-form of a simple AB or ABA, but rather develop intrinsically with the text. Humorous colorations of the text and exaggerated gestures in the music of textual ideas are profuse throughout the set of songs. These gestures at times become so obvious and blatant that they tend to create a kind of reverse meaning.

3. Orchestration Techniques: Instrumentation for *Eight Songs* includes flute (doubling piccolo), clarinet, piano (doubling harpsichord and dulcimer), violin, violoncello, and a single percussionist. This latter performer plays twenty-five different instruments, including crow call, steel bars, toy bird calls, foot cymbals, railway whistle, Christmas-type jingle bells, chains, small rachet, and so on. The voluminous number of instrumental effects throughout the score includes multiphonics for voice, clarinet, and flute, tremolo in the voice, use of inside-piano techniques, and vocal effects such as breath only, glissandi, screams, harmonics, and wide vibrato. Figure 4.31 shows a number of these effects and the notation used in autograph score.

Here one can also see the proportional notation in use, notation for multiphonics, and the vertical lines that Davies uses to maintain simultaneous attacks.

Aside from unusual techniques and instruments, Davies also incorporates extreme ranges in all instruments, especially in the voice. In Figure 4.31, for example, he uses 3½ octaves in the vocal part which eventually covers over five octaves.

The work also calls for four of the performers (on flute, clarinet, violin, and 'cello) to be placed in large cages on stage, adding an element of media presentation. Figure 4.32 shows a photograph of the author's own performance of this work (note the 'cellist in a large rope cage behind the "king").

Figure 4.31. Peter Maxwell Davies. *Eight Songs for a Mad King.* Bottom system of page 2. Examples of instrument exploration. Permission granted by Boosey and Hawkes. All rights reserved.

Figure 4.32. David Cope performing *Eight Songs for a Mad King* by Peter Maxwell Davies.

Davies comments on the instrumental aspects of the piece:

The flute, clarinet, violin and cello, as well as having their usual accompanimental functions in this work, also represent on one level, the bullfinches the King was trying to teach to sing. . . . In some ways, I regard the work as a collection of musical objects borrowed from many sources, functioning as musical "stage props" around which the reciter's part weaves, lighting them from extraordinary angles, and throwing grotesque and distorted shadows from them, giving the musical objects an unexpected and sometimes sinister significance. . . . The climax of the work is the end of No. 7, where the King snatches the violin through the bars of the player's cage and breaks it. This is not just the killing of a bullfinch—it is a giving-in to insanity, and a ritual murder by the King of a part of himself, after which, at the beginning of 8, he can announce his own death.[17]

4. Basic Techniques: Davies utilizes a hybridization of various techniques embodied in a dramatic and contrasting set of songs. Neotonal (almost impressionistic at times) chromatic techniques contrast a full-blown tonality created by association with one or more of the many quotes present in the work—particularly from Handel's *Messiah* and jazz. Often the pitches chosen are so clouded by the harsh timbres as to be relatively meaningless. There is little doubt that Davies' consistent inconsistencies, such as constantly varying the basic techniques in use, are integral to his style.

5. Vertical Models: Aside from the quoted tonal material and the various "noise" sections where pitch is of little consequence, the vertical sonorities seem based on a highly chromatic set of interval explorations (the fifth and the third) not unlike triadically based sonorities. Figure 4.33A shows a chord based primarily on different fifths (perfect, augmented, diminished), while Figure 4.33B is triadically centered (G major) with an added minor ninth (G♯).

17. Randolph Stow, program notes from Introduction to the score.

Figure 4.33. Two vertical models from *8 Songs.*

A   B

6. Horizontal Models: As seen in Figure 4.31, the vocal melody is characterized by wide leaps and elements of harsh dramatic multiphonics. Most of the nonquoted material irrevocably ties to the meaning of the text.

7. Style: In *Eight Songs for a Mad King,* Davies has created a dynamic and dramatic work fashioned around a mad king whose love/hate relationships with birds abounds. Characteristically, Davies creates a "mad" style replete with quotations, bird imitations, new instrumental techniques, flexible notations, extreme dynamic and timbral contrasts, chromatic yet somewhat triadically based harmonic systems, and word-painting (i.e., the music tends to imitate a word's sound or meaning). The results are a tight fabric of associative songs highly steeped in new instrumental techniques.

This work compares favorably with the Erb vectoral analysis presented in chapter 7 and to some degree with the Glass opera *Einstein on the Beach* presented in chapter 11. The quotation and free use of pitch in terms of style and chromatic content argue directly with the works in chapters 2 and 10 where the music depends on rigorously prescribed rules of compositional structure and resource. Dramatic intent agrees favorably with the Penderecki example in the vectoral analysis of chapter 3.

Bibliography— Chapter 4[*]

Further Readings

The Futurists

Clough, Rosa Trillo. *Futurism.* New York: Philosophical Library, 1961.

Cogan, Robert, and Pozzi Escot. *Sonic Design, Practice and Problems.* Englewood Cliffs, N.J.: Prentice-Hall, 1981.

Cope, David. "Chronicles of a Cause." *Composer* 1, no. 1 (1969): pp. 35–46.

Cowell, Henry. *American Composers on American Music.* New York: Frederick Unger Publishing Co., 1933.

Garland, Peter. *Americas: Essays on American Music and Culture, 1973–80.* Santa Fe: Soundings Press, 1982.

Griffiths, Paul. *New Sounds, New Personalities, British Composers of the 1980s in Conversation.* London: Faber Music Ltd., 1985.

Payton, Rodney J. "The Music of Futurism: Concerts and Polemics." *The Musical Quarterly* 62, no. 1 (1976): pp. 25–45.

Pound, Ezra. *Antheil.* New York: Da Capo Press, 1968.

[*]Addresses for record companies, periodicals, and music publishers mentioned in this Bibliography can be found in Appendix IV.

Rossi, Nick, and Robert Choate. *Music of Our Time*. Boston: Crescendo Publishing Co., 1969.

Verkoeyen, Jos. "String Players and New Music," *Sonorum Speculum* 45 (1970): pp. 19–26.

Vinton, John, ed. *Dictionary of Contemporary Music*. New York: E. P. Dutton and Co., 1974.

Traditional Instrument Experimentation

Bartolozzi, Bruno. *New Sounds for Woodwind*. London: Oxford University Press, 1967.

Brindle, Reginald Smith. *Contemporary Percussion*. London: Oxford University Press, 1970.

Bunger, Richard. *The Well-Prepared Piano*. 2d ed. San Pedro, Calif.: Litoral Arts Press, 1981.

Cummings, Barton. *The Contemporary Tuba*. New London, Conn.: Whaling Music Publishers, 1984.

————. "A Brief Summary of New Techniques for Tuba." *Numus West* 5 (1974).

Dempster, Stuart. *The Modern Trombone: A Definition of its Idiom*. Berkeley: University of California Press, 1980.

Finkenbeinger, Gerhard, and Vera Meyer. "The Glass Harmonica: A Return from Obscurity." *Leonardo* 20, no. 2 (1987): pp. 139–42.

Heiss, John C. "For the Flute: A List of Double-stops, Triple-stops, Quadruple-stops and Shakes." *Perspectives of New Music* 5, no. 1 (1966): pp. 139–41.

————. "Some Multiple Sonorities for Flute, Oboe, Clarinet and Bassoon." *Perspectives of New Music* 7, no. 1 (1968): pp. 136–42.

Howell, Thomas. *The Avant-Garde Flute*. Berkeley: The University of California Press, 1974.

Livingston, Larry, and Frank McCarty. "Expanding Woodwind Sound Potential." *Composer* 3, no. 1 (1971): pp. 39–40.

Moore, Janet. *Understanding Music through Sound Exploration and Experiments*. New York: University Press of America, 1986.

Palm, Siegfried. "Notation for String Instruments." *Composer* 3, no. 2 (1972): pp. 63–66.

Read, Gardner. *Thesaurus of Orchestral Devices*. London: Sir Isaac Pitman and Sons, 1953.

————. *Contemporary Instrumental Techniques*. New York: Schirmer Books. 1976.

Reed, H. Owen, and Joel T. Leach. *Scoring for Percussion*. New York: Prentice-Hall, 1969.

Rehfeldt, Phillip. *New Directions for Clarinet*. Berkeley: University of California Press, 1977.

Salzedo, Carlos. "Considerations on the Piano and the Harp." *Harp News* 3, vol. 4 (1961): pp. 10–11.

————. *Modern Study of the Harp*. New York: G. Schirmer, 1921.

————. *Method for the Harp*. New York: G. Schirmer, 1929.

Steinberg, Michael. "Some Observations on the Harpsichord in Twentieth Century Music." *Perspectives of New Music* 1, no. 2 (1963): pp. 189–94.

Turetzky, Bertram. "The Bass as a Drum." *Composer* 1, no. 2 (1969): pp. 92–107.

————. "A Technique of Contemporary Writing for the Contrabass." *Composer* 1, no. 3 (1969): pp. 118–35.

————. *The Contemporary Contrabass*. Berkeley: University of California Press, 1974.

Varèse, Edgard. "New Instruments and New Music." In *Contemporary Composers on Contemporary Music*, ed. Elliott Schwartz and Barney Childs, pp. 195–208. New York: Holt, Rinehart and Winston, 1967.

Ensemble Development

Anhalt, Istvan. *Alternative Voices: Essays on Contemporary Vocal and Choral Composition.* Toronto: The University of Toronto Press, 1984.

Becker, John. "Finding a Personal Orchestral Idiom." *Musical America* 70, no. 3 (1950): pp. 126–27.

Pooler, Frank, and Brent Pierce. *New Choral Notation.* New York: Walton Music, 1973.

New Instruments

Banek, Reinhold, and Jon Scoville. *Sound Designs: A Handbook of Musical Instrument Building.* Berkeley: Ten Speed Press, 1980.

Baschet, Bernard, and F. Baschet. "Sound Sculpture: Sounds, Shapes, Public Participation, Education. *Leonardo* 20, no. 2 (1987): pp. 107–14.

Boulanger, Richard. "Toward a New Age of Performance: Reading the Book of Dreams with the Mathews Electronic Violin." *Perspectives of New Music* 24, no. 2 (1986): pp. 130–55.

Johnston, Ben. "Harry Partch." In *Dictionary of Contemporary Music,* ed. John Vinton, pp. 555–56. New York: E. P. Dutton and Co., 1974.

Partch, Harry. "And On the Seventh Day Petals Fell in Petaluma." *Source* 2, no. 1 (1968): pp. 94–113.

———. *Genesis of a New Music.* New York: Da Capo Press, 1977.

Smith, Jeff. "The Partch Reverberations: Notes on a Musical Rebel." *Soundings* 12 (1982): pp. 46–59.

Timbre and Spatial Modulation

Backus, John. *The Acoustical Foundation of Music.* New York: W. W. Norton and Co., 1969.

Bekesy, Georg von. "Musical Dynamics by Variation of Apparent Size of Sound Source." *Journal of Music Theory* 14, no. 2 (1970): pp. 141–64.

Brant, Henry. "Space as an Essential Aspect of Musical Composition." In *Contemporary Composers on Contemporary Music,* ed. Elliott Schwartz and Barney Childs, pp. 222–42. New York: Holt, Rinehart and Winston, 1967.

Cope, David. "Modulations." *Composer* 8, no. 1 (1977): pp. 25–30.

Forsyth, Michael. *Buildings for Music.* Cambridge, Mass.: MIT Press, 1985.

Junger, Miguel, and David Feit, eds. *Sound, Structures and Their Interaction.* Cambridge, Mass.: MIT Press, 1986.

Robson, Ernest. "Research of the Sounds of Literature: Formant Music and a Prosodic Notation for Performance." *Leonardo* 20, no. 2 (1987): pp. 131–38.

Schwartz, Elliott. "Elevator Music." *Composer* 2, no. 2 (1970): pp. 49–54.

Slawson, Wayne, *Sound Color.* Berkeley: University of California Press, 1985.

Winckel, Fritz. *Music, Sound and Sensation.* New York: Dover Publications, 1967.

Non-Western Influences

Chou Wen-Chung. "Asian Music and Western Composers." In *Dictionary of Contemporary Music,* ed. John Vinton, p. 141. New York: E. P. Dutton and Co., 1974.

Reck, David. *Music of the Whole Earth.* New York: Charles Scribner's Sons, 1977.

Yates, Peter. "Lou Harrison." *ACA Bulletin* 9, no. 2 (1960): pp. 2–7.

Peter Maxwell Davies

Griffith, Paul. *Peter Maxwell Davies.* London: Robson Books, 1982.
Pruslin, Stephen, ed. *Peter Maxwell Davies: Studies from Two Decades.* London: Boosey and Hawkes, 1979.

Albright, William. *Organbooks I and III* (1967). Jobert. Gother 58827.
Anderson, Laurie. *Mr. Heartbreak* (1984). Warners Records 25077.
Antheil, George. *Ballet mécanique.* Templeton.
———. *Sonatas* (3). Weintraub. Orion 73119.
———. *Symphony No. 4* (1942). Bay Cities BCD 1016.
———. *Transatlantic* (1929). Universal Edition.
Austin, Larry. *The Maze* (1965). CPE-Source.
Bamert, Matthias. *Septuria Lunaris.* London S–725.
Becker, John. *Abongo.* Autograph Editions. New World 285.
Berio, Luciano. *Sinfonia.* Universal Edition. Erato ECD 88151.
Brant, Henry. *An American Requiem* (1973). Henmar Press. Peters.
———. *Angels and Devils* (1932). Centaur CRC–2014.
———. *Fourth Millennium* (1963). MCA. Nonesuch 71222.
Cage, John. *Amores.* C. F. Peters. Bix CD–272.
———. *Bacchanale.* C. F. Peters. Columbia M2S–819.
———. *Concerto for Prepared Piano and Chamber Orchestra* (1951). C. F. Peters. Nonesuch 71202.
———. *Perilous Night, Suite for Prepared Piano.* C. F. Peters. Avant 1008.
———. *Sonatas and Interludes* (1948). C. F. Peters. Denon CD–7673.
Celli, Joseph. *Organic Oboe.* Organic Oboe records 0.0.
Chavez, Carlos. *Toccata for Percussion* (1942). Mills Music. Hungaraton HCD–12991.
Childs, Barney. *Mr. T. His Fancy.* CPE-Source.
Chou Wen-Chung. *The Willows Are New* (1957). C. F. Peters. CRI 251SD.
Cope, David. *Margins.* Carl Fischer. Orion ORS–75169.
———. *Rituals.* Folkways 33869.
———. *The Way.* Opus One Records 82.
Cowell, Henry. *The Banshee.* AMP. Folkways FX6160.
Crumb, George. *Ancient Voices of Children.* C. F. Peters. Nonesuch 9 79149–2.
———. *Black Angels.* Peters, Elektra/Nonesuch 79242–2–P.
———. *Songs, Drones, and Refrains of Death.* C. F. Peters. Desto 7155.
Crystal Rainbows: The Sounds of Harmonious Craft. Sounds Reasonable SR 7801.
Curtis-Smith, Curtis. *Rhapsodies.* Paris: Editions Salabert. CRI S–345.
Dahl, Ingolf. *Concerto for Saxophone* (1949). MCA. Brewster 1203).
Davies, Peter Maxwell. *Dark Angels.* Boosey and Hawkes. Nonesuch 71342.
———. *Eight Songs for a Mad King.* Boosey and Hawkes. Unicorn-Kanchana DKP(CD) 9052.
———. *Vesalii Icones.* Boosey and Hawkes. Nonesuch 71295.
———. *Voices* (1973). Schott. Decca HEAD 5.
Dlugoszewski, Lucia. *Space is a Diamond* (1970). Nonesuch 71275.
Druckman, Jacob. *Incenters* (1968). MCA Music. Nonesuch 71221.
Erb, Donald. *Fanfare for Brass Ensemble and Percussion.* Merion Music.
———. *The Seventh Trumpet* (1969). Merion Music. Turnabout 34433.
Fanshawe, David. *African Sanctus.* Phillips 6558001.
Foss, Lukas. *Elytres* (1964). Fischer and Schott. Turnabout 34514.

Compact Discs, Recordings, and Publishers

Gaburo, Kenneth. *Lingua II: Maledetto*. CRI 316–SD.

Gamelan Son of Lion. Gamelan in the New World. Folkways 31313.

Globokar, Vinko. *Discours 11*. C. F. Peters. DG 137005.

Harrison, Lou. *Canticle No. 3 for Ocarina, Guitar and Percussion*. Music Masters 7051–2–C.

———. *Concert in Slendro*. C. F. Peters. Desto 7144.

———. *Pacifika Rondo*. Desto 6478.

Haubenstock-Ramati, Roman. *Interpolations: a "Mobile" for Flute*. Universal Edition. RCA VICS–1312.

———. *Tableau 1* (1967). Universal Edition. Wergo 60049.

Henze, Hans Werner. *Versuch über Schweine*. Schott. DG 139456.

Holliger, Heinz. *Atembogen* (1975). Mainz: B. Schott's Söhne.

Hovhaness, Alan. *Avak: The Healer*. C. F. Peters. Crystal S–800.

———. *Khaldis*. Op. 91. C. F. Peters. Poseidon 1011.

Husa, Karel. *Apotheosis of this Earth*. AMP. Golden Crest 4134.

Johnson, Tom *Nine Bells*. India Navigation 3023.

Johnston, Ben. *Knocking Piece* (1967). CPE-Source.

Khan, Ali Akbar. *Pre-Dawn to Sunrise Ragas* (1967). Connoisseur Society CS–1967.

Korte, Karl. *Matrix*. CRI S–249.

Kraft, William. *Triangles*. MCA. Crystal S104.

Leedy, Douglas. *Usable Music I*. CPE-Source.

Ligeti, György. *Atmospheres* (1961). Universal Edition. Wergo 305.

———. *Aventures* (1962). C. F. Peters. DG 423 244–2.

———. *Lontano*. Schott. DG 429 260–2.

Lomon, Ruth. *Five Ceremonial Masks*. Published by Arsis Press. Coronet LPS3121.

Mayuzumi, Toshiro. *Concerto for Percussion*. C.F. Peters. Point 101.

McPhee, Colin. *Tabuh-Tabuhan* AMP. Mercury MG 50103.

Messiaen, Olivier. *Oiseaux exotiques* (1955). Universal Edition. CBS M2K 44762.

Meytuss, Julius. *Dnieper Dam*. Folkways FX 6160.

Moran, Robert. *Titus*. CPE-Source.

Moryl, Richard. *Chroma for Chamber Ensemble* (1972). Desto 7143.

Mossolov, Alexander. *Steel Foundry* (1928). Folkways FX 6160.

Nancarrow, Conlon. *Studies for Player Piano,* Vol. 5 (1977). Soundings, Book 4. Wergo WER 60165–50.

Norgärd, Per. *Waves* for percussion. Wilhelm Hansen. Cambridge 2824.

Other Music. *Prime Numbers*. Other Music OMJ14.

Partch, Harry. *And on the Seventh Day Petals Fell in Petaluma*. CPE-Source. CRI CD–7000.

———. *Daphne of the Dunes* (1958). Columbia MQ–31227.

———. *Delusion of the Fury*. Columbia M2–30576.

Pellman, Samuel. *Silent Night*. Alexander Broude Publishers.

Penderecki, Krzysztof. *De Natura Sonoris* for orchestra (1966). Moeck. Nonesuch 71201.

———. *Threnody for the Victims of Hiroshima*. Eulenberg. Conifer CDCF 168.

Reich, Steve. *Drumming*. Nonesuch 9 79170–2.

———. *Four Organs*. Angel S136059.

Riley, Terry. *In C*. CBS MK 7178.

Salzedo, Carlos. *Chanson dans la Nuit*. DG 139419.

Sampson, Peggy. *The Contemporary Viola de Gamba*. Music Gallery Editions. Canada, MGE 7.

Scavarda, Donald. *Matrix*. Lingua Press. Advance Records FGR–4.

Schoenberg, Arnold. *Five Pieces for Orchestra* (1909). C. F. Peters. EMI Angel CDC 49857.

Schuller, Gunther. *Seven Studies on Themes of Paul Klee.* Universal Edition. RCA LSC–2879.

Scott, Stephen. *New Music for Bowed Piano.* New Albion NAL–004.

Shankar, Ravi. *Còncerto for Sitar and Orchestra.* EMI Studio 7 69121–2.

Smith, William O. *Five Pieces for Clarinet Alone* (1959). Crystal Records 332.

Stockhausen, Karlheinz. *Gruppen.* Universal Edition. DG–137002.

——. *Zyklus* (1950). Universal Edition. Mainstream 5003.

Travis, Roy. *African Sonata.* Orion 73121.

——. *Switched-on Ashanti.* Orion 73121.

Varèse, Edgard. *Hyperprism.* G. Schirmer. Candide 31028.

——. *Intégrales* (1925). G. Schirmer. Sony Classical SK 45844.

——. *Ionisation* (1933). G. Schirmer. Nonesuch 9 79150–2.

Villa-Lobos, Heitor. *Danses Africaines.* Louisville LS–69 5.

Wada, Yoshi. *Lament for the Rise and Fall of the Elephantine Crocodile.* India Navigation IN–3025.

——. *Off the Wall.* Free Music FMP–SAJ–49.

Xenakis, Iannis. *Metastasis.* Boosey & Hawkes. Chant du Monde LDC 278368.

5. INDETERMINACY

A Brief History of Indeterminacy

William Hayes's *The Art of Composing Music by a Method Entirely New, Suited to the Meanest Capacity* (1751) describes a technique of composition using notes spattered onto staff paper by running a finger over a stiff brush dipped in ink. Mozart used dice-throwing to create music (*Musical Dice Game,* K. 294d; see chapter 10). Other such indeterminate techniques have been attempted, even as early as the eleventh and twelfth centuries, but none with the vigor and philosophical implications of endeavors since the late 1940s.

Figure 5.1 is the full score to Paul Ignace's *It Is* (1946). There are no performance instructions for interpretation as a musical composition. Obviously, two performances of *It Is* could vary to extreme degrees in instrumentation and harmonic simultaneity. However, without prior knowledge of the composer's procedure or visual access to the score, the audience can make no real decisions concerning determinacy or indeterminacy. Earle Brown's later *December 1952* is similar in nature, but more visually musical in that its short vertical and horizontal bursts of lines of varying thicknesses more easily ignite some form of rhythmic, dynamic, and pitch realization.

Beginning in the early fifties an affinity for chance techniques was developed with the *I Ching.* Christian Wolff had brought the English translation to John Cage's attention at that time, his father Kurt Wolff being founder of the publishing house, Pantheon Press, that published it. The *I Ching,* the first written book of wisdom, philosophy, and oracle (attributed to Fu Hsi, 2953–2838 B.C.), expresses directions of action as a result of six tosses of three coins (originally, the tossing of yarrow sticks). The example in Figure 5.2 shows all combinations of ▬ and ▬ ▬ with six tosses ▬ ▬ ▬ ▬ ▬ ▬ . Having asked the question, "Should I use an example of the *I Ching* in this book?" and performing the required tosses, the author received the following answer as a result: "Kun (indicates that in the case that it presupposes) there will be great progress and success, and the advantage will come from being correct and firm. (But) any movement in advance should not be (lightly) undertaken."

The Role of Improvisation

One major precursor of musical indeterminacy may be improvisation. The Baroque figured bass and classical concerto cadenzas are two predominant examples of improvisation in traditional music. The figured bass provides only the bass notes and

Figure 5.1. Paul Ignace: *It Is.*

the intervals above them in terms of short-hand numbers below the note, allowing the performer the possibility of improvising and developing rhythmic and melodic fragments and motives. The outcome, therefore, was predictable only within certain limits. Cadenzas, up to the late eighteenth century, were very rarely written out in detail, giving each performer a chance to "show off" in the manner best suited to their own particular talents or merely suggesting motives and harmonic relevance

Figure 5.2. The Hexagrams from *I Ching*. (Permission for reprint granted by University Books, Inc., New Hyde Park, New York 11040. Copyright 1964.)

THE HEXAGRAMS, in the order in which they appear in the Yî, and were arranged by king Wǎn.

| 8 | 7 | 6 | 5 | 4 | 3 | 2 | 1 |
| pî | sze | sung | hsü | mǎng | kun | khwǎn | khien |

| 16 | 15 | 14 | 13 | 12 | 11 | 10 | 9 |
| yü | khien | tâ yû | thung zǎn | phî | thâi | lî | hsiâo khû |

| 24 | 23 | 22 | 21 | 20 | 19 | 18 | 17 |
| fû | po | pî | shih ho | kwân | lin | kû | sui |

| 32 | 31 | 30 | 29 | 28 | 27 | 26 | 25 |
| hǎng | hsien | lî | khan | tâ kwo | î | tâ khû | wû wang |

| 40 | 39 | 38 | 37 | 36 | 35 | 34 | 33 |
| kieh | kien | khwei | kiâ zǎn | ming î | ȝin | tâ kwang | thun |

| 48 | 47 | 46 | 45 | 44 | 43 | 42 | 41 |
| ȝing | khwǎn | shǎng | ȝhui | kâu | kwâi | yî | sun |

| 56 | 55 | 54 | 53 | 52 | 51 | 50 | 49 |
| lü | fǎng | kwei mei | kien | kǎn | kǎn | ting | ko |

| 64 | 63 | 62 | 61 | 60 | 59 | 58 | 57 |
| wei ȝî | kî ȝî | hsiâo kwo | kung fû | kieh | hwân | tui | sun |

to the movement or the work as a whole. Donald Erb refers to the latter in remarks about his own *Concerto for Percussion and Orchestra* (1966):

> The work is cast in the traditional concerto format of three movements. The solo part is in the eighteenth and nineteenth century virtuoso tradition. The cadenzas in the second and, especially, the third movements harken back to the eighteenth century tradition of having the performer improvise much or all of the cadenza. A variation on this idea was used in the first movement, where instead of having the soloist improvise a cadenza I had the entire orchestra, other than the soloist, improvise it.[1]

1. Liner notes of the recording: Turnabout TV-S 34433 by the composer. Taken from the program notes of the first performance in 1966.

As with the Erb *Concerto* it would seem logical for the composer, rather than refusing to admit the existence of, or making as insignificant as possible, the necessary improvisational aspects of music, to use it to both their own and the performer's advantage.

The emphasis in improvisation is more *creative* than *re-creative*. Audiences are often content to quibble over inadequacies in performances of music its hundredth time around. With improvisation they can experience music for the first time, and possibly the last. Allan Bryant states that improvisation is "similar to free jazz, oriental and African music, things which are impossible to write out"[2] and "free, wild music and ideas that wouldn't come about with single composers working alone."[3] Foss adds: "Cardew is right to worry about ethics of improvisation. It needs it. *Improvisation:* one plays what one already knows."[4]

The circumstances under which more recent improvisation developed are less clear. Interest in this century may be rooted in jazz with such artists as Miles Davis (*Bitch's Brew* and beyond), the Modern Jazz Quartet, John Coltrane, Albert Ayler, Denny Zeitlin, Pharoah Sanders, Coleman Hawkins, Django Rheinhardt, and Lenny Tristano, to name just a few. A major work in *avant-garde* improvisational jazz is "Free Jazz," a 36½-minute uninterrupted "anthem" with Ornette Coleman (plastic alto saxophone) and Don Cherry (pocket trumpet). Eric Dolphy (bass clarinet), Freddie Hubbard (trumpet), Scott LaFaro (bass), Charlie Haden (bass), Billy Higgins, and Ed Blackwell (drummers) also contributed to this extraordinary landmark of the jazz *avant-garde*. Cecil Taylor (first with Steve Lacy and Buell Neidlinger, later with Bill Barron and Ted Curson) was also an important pioneer. His keyboard skills and intense energy created imaginative improvisations. More recently George Lewis, Anthony Braxton, Sun Ra, and the Art Ensemble of Chicago all have richly improvised performances and albums.

A number of contemporary composers associated with improvisation are or were actively involved in jazz, particularly composers such as Gunther Schuller. It is more plausible, however, that *contemporary* improvisation sprang from the performers' inability to realize accurately the complexities of recent music; the composer, perhaps out of frustration, perhaps because the result was the same or better, chose to allow a certain freedom in performance. Luciano Berio, for example, in his *Tempi Concertati,* requires the percussionist to hit everything as fast as possible; exact notation would be impractical or even impossible. The effect is generally predictable and effective even without a notated pitch or rhythm.

Some composers disagree that improvisation and indeterminacy share common roots. Speaking to this point William Hellermann clearly defines that distinction:

> It seems to me that there is a fundamental difference between aleatoric and
> improvisational music. Improvisation is concerned with the realization in real time of
> defined artistic goals. Aleatory, by its very nature, does not recognize the existence of
> goals. Both differ from the traditional "classic music" by leaving open to the
> performer the choice of the specific materials to be used in the piece. They are often

---

2. As quoted in "Groups," *Source: Music of the Avant-Garde,* 2, no. 1 (January 1968), p. 26.

3. Ibid., p. 24.

4. Ibid., p. 17.

lumped together for this reason and, also, because they are both thought to be "free." Actually, freedom is not really the issue. Improvisation, at its highest, seeks meaning through spontaneity. Aleatory declares meaning to be spontaneity. Both of these are very restrictive states. I find that in my own works I am increasingly concerned with improvisation, and never with anything I would call aleatory.[5]

One basic factor in improvisation is that the composer has relinquished some control over musical events to the performer. However, this is done with the full belief that the performer will play with learned skills and an integrity of context and style. In summary, the *reasons* that most composers employ improvisation are as follow:

1. Many composers (as well as performers and listeners) suggest that simply realizing notes from the printed page results in generally strained and somewhat uncreative results. Each performance is predictable and thus not as interesting as a certain amount of flexibility might make it. The "live" and fresh aspect of improvisation can provide a unique performance each time a work is played.

2. In contemporary music, improvisation often results in rhythms and patterns that would paralyze the performer if completely written out. One can note this particularly in certain jazz music, where the subtle and refined improvisatory character of syncopations before and after the beat make full and exact notation a near impossibility. Even if it were possible, would it be performable in that state and, most important, would it have the same kind of fresh musical quality that it does when improvised?

3. Many contemporary composers feel that since improvisation exists in all music to one degree or another, it is only a small step to allowing more freedom with rewards far exceeding risks.

The 1960s brought about a number of groups dedicated to improvisation: the New Music Ensemble (Larry Austin, Stanley Lunetta, John Mizelle, Arthur Woodbury, Billie Alexander, and Wayne Johnson); Sonic Arts Group (Gordon Mumma, Robert Ashley, David Behrman and Alvin Lucier); the *Musica Elettronica Viva* (Allan Bryant, Alvin Curran, Jon Phetteplace, Carol Plantamura, Frederic Rzewski, Richard Teitelbaum, and Ivan Vandor); and the University of Illinois Chamber Players, directed by Jack McKenzie. Whatever the means of producing sound, electronic or instrumental, the immediate and temporary creations were based solely on the interaction of the performers, most of whom were composers. The responsibility was with the ensemble, not a single personality. Lukas Foss remarks: "I thought I had invented a new kind of improvisation. I now know that I was merely the first not to sign my name."[6] The 1957 U.C.L.A.-based Improvisation Chamber Ensemble under the direction of Foss consisted of piano, clarinet, cello, and percussion (among the first of such groups). The ensemble worked primarily from charts indicating only initial ideas (e.g., motive, rhythm, pattern) needed to create a work.

5. Tom Everett, "Questions and Answers," *Composer* 2, no. 4 (March 1971):82.
6. As quoted in "Groups," op. cit., p. 17.

Figure 5.3. Lukas Foss. Photo permission by Carnegie Hall, 154 W. 57th St., New York, N.Y. 10019.

Many rehearsals yielded a polished result in performances that varied somewhat, but were more crystalline than live improvisation. The group also performed improvised interludes between the movements of Foss's *Time Cycle* (1960) for soprano and orchestra.

Etudes for Organ by Foss requires four different improvisational techniques, one for each movement. In the first movement, the performer varies an exactly notated motor-rhythmic single-line melody by freely repeating note groups. No more than twelve score notes should be played without returning to some group of notes of the performer's choice. In the second movement, groups of notes in the right hand are scored for which the performer may choose order, rhythm, octave, and/or number of the notes desired. Forearm clusters dominate throughout the third movement, with spontaneous choice of rhythm or white or black key clusters. The form here is more articulate, being verbally presented in four sections: ABA-Coda. The fourth movement includes performer choice of a four-part "religious or patriotic" hymn around which two secondary performers playing four-note clusters at either end of the keyboard are asked to interfere, *poco a poco,* with the hymn performance. Foss has used notes (in I, II, and IV), rhythms (in I), timbre (in III), dynamics (in II, III, and IV), each in a somewhat traditional manner, at the same time freeing another aspect of composition and performance for improvisation.

Cornelius Cardew of AMM, which also included Lou Gare, Eddie Prevost, and Keith Rowe, adds: "The past always seems intentional, but at the time it appears to be accidental."[7]

7. Ibid., p. 18.

Figure 5.4. MW 2
Ensemble of Poland.

The MW 2 Ensemble of Poland uses instruments of more traditional origin, while at the same time employing two dancers and an actor, with tapes, projection, and scenery (see Figure 5.4). Performer interaction therefore takes the form of visual as well as musical improvisation. Group improvisational situations challenge the aesthetic of a leading personality. The structure and immediate creation resulting from such groups challenges the audience's categorization of individual idols more than they philosophically or aurally alter traditional methods of creative intention.

The concept of *time* provides an essential ingredient in the contemporary composer's approach to improvisation. Morton Feldman expressed his ideas as to how objects exist *as* time, not of, in, or about time:

> . . . This was not how to make an object . . . but how this object exists *as* Time. Time regained, as Proust referred to his work. Time as an Image, as Aristotle suggested. This is the area which the visual arts later began to explore. This is the area which music, deluded that it was counting out the seconds, has neglected.
>
> I once had a conversation with Karlheinz Stockhausen, where he . . . began beating on the table and said: "A sound exists either here—or here—or here." He was convinced that he was demonstrating reality to me. That the beat, and the possible placement of sounds in relation to it, was the only thing the composer could realistically hold on to. The fact that he had reduced it to so much a square foot made him think Time was something he could handle and even parcel out, pretty much as he pleased.
>
> Frankly, this approach to Time bores me. I am not a clockmaker. I am interested in getting Time in its unstructured existence. That is, I am interested in how this wild beast lives in the jungle—not in the zoo. I am interested in how Time exists before we put our paws on it—our minds, our imaginations, into it.
>
> One would think that music more than any other art would be exploratory about Time. But is it? Timing—not Time—has been passed off as the real thing in music. . . .[8]

8. Morton Feldman, "Between Categories," *Composer* 1, no. 2 (September 1969), p. 75.

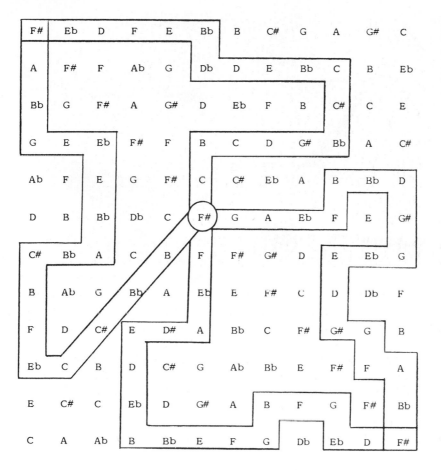

Realization of the inadequacy of traditional notation leads not only to new standards, but to the lack of notation entirely. This destroys the composer/performer relationship, a hierarchy required by most traditional audiences. Lukas Foss, in works like *Echoi* (1963), hints toward this by employing stems without noteheads though exact indications of rhythm, dynamics, and order are given.

William Duckworth's *Pitch City* (see Figure 5.5) for wind instruments instructs four performers to trace pitches from the corners to the middle. Each note's duration is equivalent to the individual performer's ability to sustain the note(s) as long as possible with breathing between notes. More notes remain unplayed (73) than played (71), while at the same time a twelve-tone row (top line, left to right) is expressed in all versions—original, retrograde (right to left), inversion (top to bottom), and inversion-retrograde (bottom to top)—and in every possible transposition. The composer's intention here is unmistakable: to prepare the complete logical and mathematical twelve-tone row structure, and then totally avoid any realization of this organization. This represents a philosophical challenge to twelve-tone rationale that must play a distinct part in any educated performer's realization of the score since

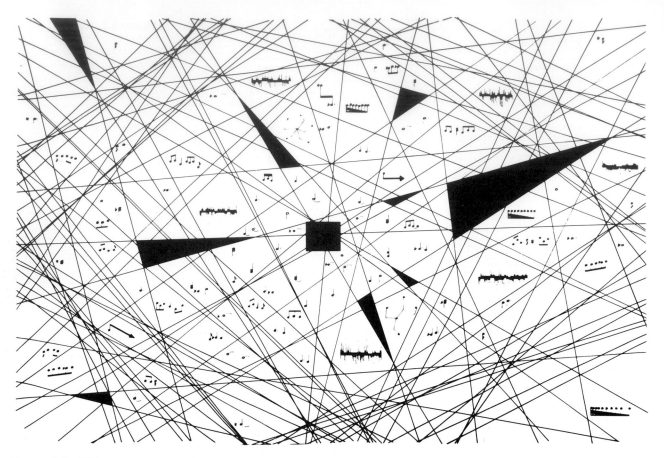

Figure 5.6. William Duckworth's *Walden Variations*. Sheet #3. Used with permission of the composer.

none of the outlined portions remotely follow twelve-tone direction. Improvisation occurs in rhythm, instrumentation, and resultant octave depending on the instrument's range.

Duckworth's *Walden Variations* (see Figure 5.6) demonstrates improvisational graphic notation. The sheet shown, the third and final score page, is a ". . . free improvisation sheet based on the design of the original sheet. The events and movements to and from events are ambiguous and can be freely interpreted. Dancers, readers, slides, movies, and/or lights may be employed as the performers feel it to be in keeping within the general spirit of the piece as they understand it."[9] Completed in 1971, *Walden Variations* is a nonstructured improvisation-based score with open instrumentation.

In the works just discussed, the composer still claims one or more compositional aspects of his work. Giuseppi Chiari's *Quel Che Volete* is probably more apropos of Morton Feldman's statement: "Down with the Masterpiece; up with art. . . ."[10]

9. From notes to the score by the composer.

10. Morton Feldman, ''Conversations without Stravinsky,'' *Source: Music of the Avant-Garde* 1, no. 2 (July 1967), p. 43.

Percussion:

Voice:

dis (appeared cleverly) world iS Slapped: with; liGhtninG !ᵘ at

Percussion:

Figure 5.7. Luciano Berio: *Circles* © Copyright 1961 by Universal Edition. Used by permission.

The piece consists entirely of verbal instructions ranging from indications suggesting materials not be played in a virtuosic manner, to exchanging instruments among performers. However vague the score may appear, close reading reveals composer intention, especially in regard to form from "you must try and play in a traditional manner" and "play as if playing was a gift" to "We must never overdo". Likewise, in *Sonant,* Mauricio Kagel employs verbal descriptions of the framework within which the performer may improvise. These often intricate instructions may be more accurate in terms of performance ease and understanding than traditional notation.

Luciano Berio's *Circles* (1960) for female voice, harp, and two percussion players includes a variety of "improvisation boxes." Figure 5.7 shows the two percussion parts (top and bottom groups of staves) with the voice in the middle. The "improvisation boxes" should not be confused with the small boxes in which the mallets are graphically shown, that is, the first small box in the two top lines from the left. The rationale behind the "improvisation" is obvious: The percussion parts would be impossible if written out, or tight and "square." Pitches and instrumentation are usually indicated in specific detail. Rhythm is left to the performer. Often Berio stacks the notes vertically in such a way that the performer can proceed in any improvised order. Occasionally the pitches are proportionally distributed within the box to indicate the approximate rhythmic placement or to introduce new "stacks" of notes. Dynamics, on the other hand, are often notated in terms of *limits* (i.e., *mf→pp*) with smooth *crescendi* and *diminuendi* indicated by dovetailing notation. The score contains no performance directions except those of placement of instruments; the composer, it seems, feels that these performance concepts are obvious. With the "boxes" occurring in only one or two parts at a time (there is little flexibility in the vocal line except its proportional non-metered notation), the composer maintains control over the direction and flow of the work, allowing the improvisation to give life to each successive performance.

Robert Erickson's *Ricercar à 5* (1966) for five trombones requires a number of improvisational techniques from the performers. This work may be performed with five trombonists or one trombonist and four prerecorded trombones on tape. The work varies from exact notation to control of only one or two elements, most often dynamics and pitch. The interplay between parts calls for sensitive and interpretative improvisatory techniques. The work was written for trombonist Stuart Dempster who speaks of these points in an interview.

> Question (Frank McCarty):   So you began to compile a body of new sounds and techniques through research, practice, and mimicry. I assume you incorporated some of these in the improvisational music that was popular among the San Francisco composers of that era.

> Answer (Stu Dempster):   Yes, those pieces gave me the first opportunity to couple my "funny sounds" with other "funny sounds" made by tapes and by other musical instruments such as Pauline's [Oliveros] accordion and Mort's [Subotnick] clarinet. I also became interested in working with composers, I did a demo for Berio in the early 1960's and asked him for a piece, never thinking he'd really do it. Later (1966), when I was working with Bob Erickson on a commission, I decided to resurrect the Berio idea. I wrote him a letter . . . and learned he was already right in the middle of the piece. The *Sequenza* (also involving improvisation techniques) was written in a way for two of us, myself and (Vinko) Globokar, who had played sketches of what became the B section. But as Berio and I worked together on the final version it became more and more my piece since he saw in me—in my performance—more and more the character of Grock, the famous European clown, about whom the piece is actually written. In the meantime, Erickson and I were spending many a Tuesday morning developing a vocabulary of sounds and sound-mixes which resulted in his composition of the *Ricercar à 5*. . . .[11]

Phil Winsor's *Orgel 1* includes a sheet of twelve basic improvisatory boxes for organ and organ recorded on tape. The verbal stylistic indications above each box (see Figure 5.8) plus the timing and overlap directions of the score, not shown, make this "free" improvisation, and not graphic indeterminacy as a quick glance might suggest.

Improvisational techniques in the last few years have created a renaissance of live performance situations. Whether as a result of, or a reaction to electronic music, the newfound creative collaboration between composers and performers cannot help but enrich the continuum and significance of all music.

11. Frank McCarty, "An Interview with Stuart Dempster," *The Instrumentalist* 28, no. 10 (May 1974), pp. 33–34. Used by permission of The Instrumentalist Co.

Indeterminacy

Experimental music, that is, actions the outcome of which are not foreseen, is more a philosophical than an audible phenomenon. Form, intended or not, is inherent in all matter and energy, and therefore subject to analysis. It is impossible, without prior knowledge of the composer or work, to distinguish the intention or nonintention of the composer, unless the sounds or actions presented are obviously from another source (intentional or unintentional). For example, John Cage's *4'33''* (1952), wherein the sounds presented are obviously nature or the audience itself, appears realizably unintentional except in concept.

It is with this latter idea, this psychoconceptual aspect, that the greatest single musical antagonism has been born. Audiences can be presented with highly organized and experimental compositions of the same general genre, instrumentation, and techniques, without reacting adversely. However, when prior knowledge exists, or when a work such as *4'33''* is played, and the audience *realizes* the unintention involved, reactions can be much more violent. One struggles with the *concept,* not the sounds. "Therefore my purpose is to remove purpose," spoke John Cage in a 1962 interview with Roger Reynolds.[12] The idea is to let sounds "happen," to free them from the composer's control. Can one learn to accept *all* sounds equally? This concept truly rejects the past twelve to fourteen centuries of Western thought; not the music itself, but the *concept of* that music. Divorcing oneself from control of

12. *Contemporary Composers on Contemporary Music,* Elliott Schwartz and Barney Childs, eds. (New York: Holt, Rinehart and Winston, 1967), p. 341.

Figure 5.9. John Cage.
Photo: Dorothy Norman.

the compositional process through chance operations continues to present philo-sophical challenges to the aesthetics, art, and ego of history. The antagonists to in-determinacy are numerous. Paul Hindemith refers to chance as "one of the ugliest modern musical diseases".[13] However, what most antagonists and some protagonists fail to realize is that one must deal with the concept of indeterminacy, not the re-sultant sounds, not the forms, not the individuals involved. If indeterminacy cannot be reckoned with in philosophical terms, then it threatens the structure, terms, and aesthetics of music and art as contemporary Western civilization has come to known them. Indeterminacy implies art as process: no beginning, no middle, no end. Each new performance, each new circumstance creates a continually variable process. As Cage has said, "If one is making an object and then proceeds in an indeterminate fashion, to let happen what will, outside of one's control, then one is simply being careless about the making of that object."[14] If art is process, however, then inde-terminacy is a viable way to proceed.

Some have argued that total indeterminacy is not possible and hence contest its philosophical consequence. Others argue that even if total indeterminacy is not possible, it is not pointless to attempt to approach it. Cage refers to his disappoint-ment and compromise arising from the knowledge that he hasn't really "done it," but merely has been ". . . going along in that general direction."[15]

In "Indeterminacy," Cage describes Bach's *Art of the Fugue* as an example of composition that is indeterminate with respect to its performance, based on lack of

13. Ibid., p. 89.
14. Ibid., p. 345.
15. Ibid.

Figure 5.10. Morton Feldman. BMI Archives. Used by permission.

directions in regard to timbre, dynamics, sequence of the "determinate" notes, and durations, making available a wide range of possible realizations.[16] This philosophy disavows the significance of the creator, emphasizing creative performing/listening; understanding being something pedagogical and within the realm of language, not aesthetics.

The terminology surrounding chance operations involves certain basic American/European divisions. The term *aleatoric*, derived by Boulez from *aléa,* French for "risk," and originally from the Latin word meaning *dice*, seems to be primarily a European concept that employs chance techniques within a controlled framework, more related to improvisation than true indeterminacy. Morton Feldman has remarked: "This is true of Boulez. This is true of Stockhausen. You can see this in the way they have approached American 'chance' music. They began by finding rationalizations for how they could incorporate chance and still keep their precious integrity."[17] After reacting to the personality behind this statement, Boulez expanded on these basic differences between aleatoric and chance techniques:

> G. W.: Feldman refers to "chance" here. Do you feel that you conceive of "chance" in the same way that, say, John Cage conceives of it?

> P. B.: No, not at all. I find that so highly unproductive, because "chance" is not an aesthetic category. "Chance" can bring something interesting only one time in a

16. John Cage, *Silence* (Cambridge, Mass.: The M.I.T. Press, paperback edition, 1961), p. 35.
17. Schwartz and Childs, p. 365.

million. . . . Most of the time you do not get that one time . . . and, if you do get it, you get it in the midst of a hundred thousand possibilities which are not interesting.

G. W.: Going to a "chance" concert, then, you feel would be like going to a baseball game, gambling for excitement?

P. B.: Yes, but even a baseball game has rules. Card games, which have much more chance, I suppose, still have rules. Can you imagine a card game with absolutely no rules?

D. C.: Like Mallarmé saying, "A throw of the dice will not abolish chance," . . . you are saying that, while nothing can be totally chance, nothing can be totally without chance.

P. B.: Exactly. With the combination of the two, you must integrate, and it is much more difficult to compose in this way, integrating on a high level than in more traditional ways. Composing by chance is not composing at all. Composing . . . means to put things together. I am interested as to what chance sounds occur on the street, but I will never take them as a musical composition. There is a big difference between unorganized sounds and those placed within complete organization.[18]

The division between American and European concepts of chance has grown deeper in recent decades. Boulez remarks: "Do you see what we are getting back to? Constantly to a refusal of choice. The first conception was purely mechanistic, automatic, fetishistic; the second is still fetishistic but one is freed from choice not by numbers but by the interpreter."[19] England's David Bedford and Brian Tilbury, however, championed the American cause of experimental work in indeterminacy, mirroring in the late sixties much the same discoveries and excitement engendered by Cage and Feldman in the early fifties. Surviving, even thriving upon, the attacks from both here and abroad, the cause for freeing sounds continues.

Indeterminacy, as a pedagogical approach to erase control over compositional elements that so many have fought to retain, must first transcend man's loss of individual ego. As such, it is merely the first step to a far-reaching eventuality: rejection of *all* human-centered creativity, and acceptance of *all* of the life around us, with the individual no longer in control, no longer the creator or destroyer of images or ideals, real or imagined.

Composer Indeterminacy

Indeterminacy involves total lack of knowledge about the outcome of an action in respect to composition, performance, or both. A number of works are *indeterminate in respect to composition but determinate in respect to performance*. This is primarily music that is predictable before performance but was composed with the use

18. Galen Wilson and David Cope, "An Interview with Pierre Boulez," *Composer* 1, no. 2 (September 1969):82–83.
19. Pierre Boulez, "Aléa," *Perspectives of New Music* 3, no. 1 (Winter 1964):42.

of some type of chance operation. Often these works come to the performer in traditional notation. Composer indeterminacy implies *determinate* performance.

In his *Music of Changes* (1951), John Cage used twenty-six large charts indicating aspects of composition (durations, tempos, dynamics), following the *I Ching* to "create" every aspect of the composition. Forty-three minutes of music and nine months later, *Music of Changes,* every aspect except conception of which was based on a huge number of coin tosses, was completed. This rigid composition technique, not unlike that of the twelve-tone school, and the dedication and care necessary for the creation of *Music of Changes,* cannot escape philosophical implications, regardless of composer intention. Possibly no other work in the history of music has been so exact in its creation, its composer having purposely attempted to destroy his own control over it. Yet it shows little trace of either the composer or the *I Ching:* it "merely" *sounds.*

R. Murray Schafer's extraordinary *The Tuning of the World,* while possibly less all-encompassing than these earlier examples, nonetheless continues the tradition of modeling music after the proportions of what he terms the "soundscape." His work covers the field from the post-industrial soundscape to acoustic designs of that soundscape. His process of listening, called "ear cleaning," has significant consequence in his view. His discussions on noise, in particular, seem applicable to the various forms and works of this chapter. From *Ear Cleaning:* ". . . take a sheet of paper and give it a sound. . . . By giving the paper a voice we have exposed its sound-soul. Every object on the earth has a sound-soul."

Magic squares (and cubes) have also been used as raw material for "formal" compositional techniques. These squares are matrices of numbers that seem to "magically" add, subtract, divide, and/or multiply to the same number regardless of the direction taken. Figure 5.11 shows a simple magic square and one possible way it might be interpreted in music values. Note that the addition of every line including the two diagonal lines is 15, and no line contains more than one of each of the numbers in use. Interpretation of this data as musical sound is completely at the discretion of the composer and may vary significantly from one work to the next.

Many wonder why such "formalistic" ends could not be achieved in more musical and less mathematical approaches, and so the enigmas around these ideas continue. Writings by and about Iannis Xenakis, for example, often contribute to these enigmas. The following is from a discussion between John Cage, Lukas Foss, and Xenakis:

Cage: I asked a Spanish lady scientist what she though about the human mind in a world of computers. She said, "Computers are always right but life isn't about being right." What do you say to that?

Xenakis: The opposite—life has reason and computers are often wrong.

Cage: You have been an architect and now you are a musician. Are you going to go to some other activity?

Xenakis: I'd like to but it is difficult.

Figure 5.11. A magic square and possible musical interpretation.

1	4	2	3	5
2	3	5	1	4
5	1	4	2	3
4	2	3	5	1
3	5	1	4	2

Pitch: (Using 0–11 ordination—beginning on C)
Line 1—Lines 2 and 1—Lines 2, 1, and 3—etc.
(Reducing numbers over 11 by 12—e.g.
C♯ E D D♯ F D♯ G G E A G♯ G♯ B etc.)
Rhythm: 1 = ♪ 2 = ♩ 3 = ♩. 4 = ♩ 5 = 𝅝
Timbre: 1 = horn   2 = flute   3 = piano   4 = violin   5 = cello

Foss: Iannis, all the music of yours that I know is built on mathematical premise, mostly probability. Is there any aspect to chance that is not mathematical, that is, not probability theory?

Xenakis: All my music is not based on mathematics—there are parts of it which use mathematics. As to chance, it is not like dice or tossing a coin, this is ignorance, as if there were impossibility of predicting. What does chance mean to you?

Foss: Anything I cannot control. You left architecture for music—why?

Xenakis: Mostly because architecture was a business and music is less business.

Foss: In order to compose you need time, solitude—what else?

Xenakis: To live in a big city.

Foss: If someone imitates you (I know of an instance) does it flatter you or make you angry or both?

Xenakis: I am angry . . . angry and depressed.

Foss: What did you want to be when you were a child?

Xenakis: An elephant.[20]

The creation of Dick Higgins's *Thousand Symphonies* involved the "machine-gunning" of one thousand pages of blank orchestral manuscript. The performance, though necessarily constituting some performer interpretation of the "holes," is basically determinate. "My machine-gunning of scores actually represents the concretization of a fantasy I had of setting the police (or armies) to composing music with their most familiar instruments—guns, machine guns. In fact . . . we actually organized an orchestral performance of the gunshot notations according to a system I worked out, and it sounded quite lovely."[21]

Mauricio Kagel's *1898,* completed in 1973 for Deutsche Grammophon's seventy-fifth anniversary, is for eleven to seventeen players with only piano and percussion as obligatory. Twenty to twenty-five children's voices also take part in the form of either taped versions or live performance. The percussion is freely orchestrated so that even "home-grown" non-pitched instruments can substitute for the indicated suggestions. Only vague hints regarding orchestration appear in the score. Further observation into the instructions of the work provide a great deal of insight:

> The purpose of these tape recordings, among others, is to demonstrate that what is needed is not 'reliable' musical education but the very opposite: an unorthodox system of changeable, ambivalent invitations to express oneself acoustically—rather than 'musically.'[22]

This is later followed by these words:

> What is the difference between proper and artificial laughter? One can almost be certain that the responses to the ambiguities inherent in this unambiguous question will produce complex aural situations.[23]

Each of these statements, and the others, seems addressed to stochastic solutions such as indeterminacy so complex that determinate results follow. Be this confusing, it is clearly more defined than the composer's own directive: "Variations of a Motive, sung increasingly wrongly."

Music that is *determinate in respect to composition but indeterminate in respect to performance* owes much of its development to the idea of "event." Such works are "composed" in terms of individual sections or fragments yet mobile in the order of appearance, creating unpredictability before and during performance.

Performer Indeterminacy

20. John Cage, Lukas Foss, and Iannis Xenakis, "Short Answers to Difficult Questions," *Composer* 2, no. 2 (September 1970), p. 40.
21. From a letter to the author.
22. Mauricio Kagel, *1898.* London: Universal (European American), 1979, p. 89.
23. Ibid.

When the timbre, structure, and dynamics of two sounds are so different as to avoid the traditional concept of melody, they become *events*. Each is equal in importance and does not necessarily build to a climax or cadence. The introduction of silence [24] as an integral part of a composition, and treated equally with sound, helps in identifying these events in time. As sounds move further and further apart, their order becomes less and less important. This reflects much the same concept as a "mobile" in art: that is, the shape, color, and design of each part is fixed, with the order and angle constantly changing.

Karlheinz Stockhausen's *Klavierstück XI, No. 7* (1957), printed on a roll 37 by 21 inches long, opens on a special wooden stand supplied with the score. It contains nineteen "events," which may be played in any order. Performer instructions require glancing at the score and performing whatever event may "catch the eye."

> At the end of the first group, he reads the tempo, dynamic and attack indications that follow, and looks at random to any other group, which he then plays in accordance with the latter indications. "Looking at random to any other group" implies that the performer will never link up expressly-chosen groups or intentionally leave out others. Each group can be joined to any of the other 18: each can thus be played at any of the six tempi and dynamic levels and with any of the six types of attack.[25]

The composer requires that when a fragment is reached for the third time the piece is concluded. This creates anywhere from three fragments or the first one randomly observed three times in succession to thirty-eight factorial or 38!—or 38 times, 37 times, 36 times, 35 . . . etc.—a truly staggering number indeed: 10! is over 3.6 million.[26] This, along with the tempo, dynamic, and attack variances, creates a work whose notes in terms of fragments are controlled by the composer, yet the resultant performance is totally unpredictable.

Figure 5.12 shows the score from measures 27 to 32 of Stockhausen's *Stop* (1965). This "Pariser Version" (the one shown in Figure 5.12—there is another version for full orchestra) is for eighteen performers in six groups of like timbres cued with the ◊ sign. This *recipe* work has determinate form through the duration lengths at the top of each "measure" yet lacks "determinate" directions for performance as "noises" is hardly a predictable notation. The composer is obviously very much aware of the outcome in general terms of form, contrast, balance, and direction (note the occasional exact notation overlapping events) but willing to allow performance unpredictability in terms of rhythm, entrance order, and pitch. This type of work, though very different from the *mobile* structures of his *Klavierstück XI, No. 7,* is still primarily composer-determined performer unpredictability.

24. Cage has often pointed out that "real" silence does not exist (see his book *Silence*). The author refers here to lack of intentional sound.

25. From the composer's directions on the score. Universal Edition No. 12654 LW.

26. "!" here is not an exclamation point but rather a factorial sign in mathematics with the number preceding the sign multiplied by stepwise diminishing numbers in turn down to 1.

Henri Pousseur's piano solo *Caractères* (1961) includes cutout windows and randomly placed score pages so that the order of the "events" is not composer-prescribed. Henry Cowell was among the first composers to provide blocks of sound with which the performer constructed the performance "form" (*Mosaic Quartet,* 1934).

Affected by the mobiles of Alex Calder, Earle Brown has developed concepts of form and order in his music derived primarily from this "event" rationale. Referring to his *Available Forms I* and *II* (1961–62), Brown writes: "The title of the work refers to the availability of many possible forms which these composed elements may assume, spontaneously directed by the conductors in the process of performing the work. The individual musical events are rehearsed, but the performances are not."[27]

In Brown's *Available Forms I* for orchestra, the score is projected on the back of the stage for the performers to read. The conductor then indicates a number that represents one of the large numerals indicated on the score. The performers read and improvise within the context of the information given in the indicated block. This risk parallels that of the Stockhausen example, though it is not so great as to imply complete lack of composer control.

27. From the program notes of the New York Philharmonic Society, February 1964.

The anti-lyrical aspects of event concepts represent one of the ideas most profoundly antagonistic to Romantic thought. Barney Childs's *Nonet* (*Source: Music of the Avant Garde* 3, no. 1 [January 1969]) includes an "event machine," a numbered acetate overlay and two rotating color-coded discs that provides the order, timing, and selection of events. In Feldman's *Intersection 3,* the duration, number, and timbre of sounds are determined by the composer while the dynamics and range (*high, middle,* and *low*) are indeterminate during performance.

John Cage's *Atlas Eclipticalis* (see Figure 5.13), first performed by the New York Philharmonic in 1962, includes the use of contact microphones placed in various locations on the instruments. Though somewhat graphic, this work provides pitch indications and directions of movement. As seen in Figure 5.14, *34'46.776" for a Pianist* (1954) is also a graphic but explicit work.

Musical "games" or "strategy" take a variety of forms (e.g., Subotnick's *Ritual;* see chapter 7). Iannis Xenakis has characterized music without in-performance "conflict" as *autonomous* (inclusive of most music to the present day) and the music of games (introducing a concept of external conflict between groups or individuals in the performance situation) as *heteronomous* music. Xenakis's *Duel* (1958–59) comprises materials like that of the mobile structure: a set of six events, each written in the score in precise manner. Unlike mobiles, however, these strategic games employ definitive *tactics* with the events of length sufficient to permit interruption, and the choice of event a direct result of an "on the spot" performer decision.

Strategie (1962), for two forty-four-member orchestras, employs Xenakis's *strategie musicale* an application to music of the mathematical *theory of games*. Seven basic sound structures have a *stochastic* basis, which was calculated with an IBM 70690 computer with 400 combinations possible between the two orchestras seated on opposite sides of the stage. An electric scoreboard is set at the end of the stage with points gained and lost by rules set by composer calculations. "At the end of a certain number of exchanges or minutes, as agreed upon by the conductors, one of the two is declared a winner and is awarded a prize."[28]

Roman Haubenstock-Ramati's *Mobile for Shakespeare*, for voice, piano, celeste, vibraphone, and three percussionists, is a prime example of "mobile" type structure indeterminacy (see Figure 5.15). Each box gives a fairly straightforward, mostly traditionally notated fragment. There are a few relatively explicit graphic symbols. The order of each box is not predetermined, and therefore while the composer has indeed "composed" each note, the performances are quite different and unpredictable.[29]

Composer and Performer Indeterminacy

Music can be *indeterminate in respect to both composition and performance.* "Chance" means produce a "chance" score: at no time is there a predictable outcome. Christian Wolff's *Duo II for Pianists* (1958), for example, involves no score and all materials are indeterminate, the only indication being areas of limitation provided by the composer: the use of pianos with no silences between performer

28. Xenakis, *Formalized Music*, p. 122.
29. See the score for fuller explanation of complete performance.

Atlas Eclipticalis, French Horn 5, Percussion 4, Cello 7, pages 245, 309, and 157

responses. The work has no designated beginning or ending, these being determined only by the situation in which performance takes place. Nam June Paik's *In Homage to John Cage* (1959) is equally indeterminate and in "happening" form. In its first performance Paik leaped offstage to Cage's seat, removed Cage's jacket and, as Tomkins puts it: "slashed his (Cage's) shirt with a wickedly long pair of scissors, cut off his necktie at the knot, poured a bottle of shampoo over his head, and then rushed out of the room."[30] Paik later telephoned the audience to let them know that the work was finished.

Cage has explored "contingency"-type indeterminacy:

> I have been writing pieces that I call "music of contingency," in which there is a rupture between cause and effect, so that the causes that are introduced don't necessarily produce effects. That's what contingency is. One piece, *Inlets,* uses conch shells, for example; if instead of blowing a conch shell, you fill it with water and tip it, it will sometimes gurgle and sometimes not. You have no control over it. Even if you try very hard to control it, it gurgles when it wishes to . . . when it's ready to. Sometimes if you rehearse with it and think that you've got it down pat, you'll discover as I do, I'm sure, that it foxes you and gurgles when it chooses.[31]

John Mizelle's *Radial Energy I* (see Figure 5.16) allows significant freedom in choice of sound sources, number of participants, location of performance, and interpretation if any. In the chart and explanation accompanying the score, the composer

---

30. Calvin Tomkins, *The Bride and the Bachelors* (New York: The Viking Press, 1965), p. 134.

31. David Cope, "An Interview with John Cage," *Composer* 10, no. 1 (1980), pp. 6–22.

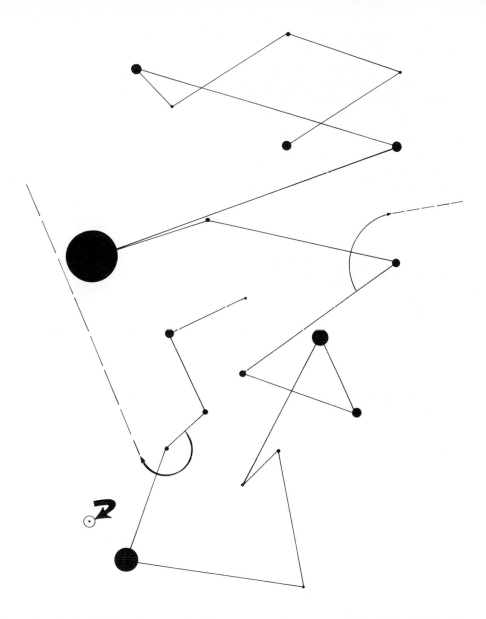

Figure 5.16. John Mizelle: *Radial Energy I.* Permission granted by *Source: Music of the Avant-garde,* Composer/Performer Edition, Davis, California.

describes in detail the silence periods between performances: 6, 7, 9, 12, 15, 17, 18, 17, 15, 12, 9, 7, and 6 *years* for the first phase of the chart, and the first point at which the piece may be concluded—that is, 150 years. Other "complete" performances may last over 382 years, depending on initial performance time, with duration of the performances between the periods of silence computed by addition, squaring, cubing, and so on, the initial performance duration (actual sound-producing performances) could last over 15 years. Likewise, the area of performance could be expanded, as the composer states, "to other planets, galaxies, etc. When all of time and space are transformed into sound, the piece (and the Universe) ends."

Barney Childs's *The Roachville Project,* a sound sculpture for four to ten performers, verbally describes a situation in which performers *and* audience create an instrument out of available materials, improvising during and after construction. Emphasis is directed *away* from sound and toward situation, theater, and total participation (see Figure 5.17).

Sylvano Bussotti's *Five Piano Pieces for David Tudor* (1959), on the other hand, reflects a totally graphic concept in which interpretation or non-interpretation is fully within the performer's realm. The artistic drawings of Bussotti are more visual than aural; the composer becomes more an inciter than controller. Graphic scores such as this represent a breach with traditional symbols. Inherent in a nonsymbolic

"The Roachville Project"

4 to 10 performers, minimum duration 30 minutes.

Provide a great deal of material, most of which should be capable of soundproduction, either immediately (wires, pipes, blocks, tubes, containers, bits and pieces of musical instruments, junk, &c.) or potentially (material which when assembled or altered or worked with can be made, maybe, to produce sound in some fashion).

The piece begins with the arrival of the performers at the material. They begin to assemble the material, as they please, any way they wish, into a "musical instrument" of sorts. The complete construction is to be a unit—that is, separate people may work for a while on separate sub-units, but these must eventually be built into the complete construction. All that is necessary for assembly, finally, is ingenuity: the *means* of assembly (nails, staples, glue, string, sticky tape, leather straps, baling wire, rivets, &c.) are up to the performers. Performers may converse together concerning problems of assembly and sound potential, but this must be done very quietly, and other conversation is to be avoided; performers may test parts they are working on for sound as they are assembling (i.e. test string tension by plucking, test resonances by tapping, &c.) but this must also be done very quietly. At a stipulated time, or when all agree that the instrument is completed, the performers improvise music on it, for any length of time. The composition is finished with the completion, at a pre-arranged time or by agreement among the performers, of this "piece-within-a-piece." All material provided need not, or perhaps will not, be used. If passing members of the audience with to become performers they may, as long as the total working number of participants never exceeds 10.

Deep Springs
April 1967

*Roachville and White Mountain City were "settlements just over the White Mountain summit from Owens Valley. . . . A writer visiting there in 1864 tells all that we know of those would-be mining centers. The 'city' from which he wrote was on Wyman Creek, on the Deep Spring slope; its rival, Roachville, was on Cottonwood Creek, and was named by its proprietor, William Roach. . . ."

W. A. Chalfant, *The Story of Inyo*

abstract representation is a concept of live creation. Bussotti's *Five Pieces* was performed in Los Angeles three times in one concert, by three different performers. More conservative members of the audience, obviously appalled by the lack of recognizable similarities among the performances in structure, length, instrumentation, or motive, reacted antagonistically to both the performers and the work. The problem seems to be rooted not in the sounds themselves, but in the categorization of who, in fact, is the creator of the order of those sounds.

In reference to these performances Halsey Stevens has pointed out the following:

> If Mr. Bussotti had wandered into the hall and didn't know what was going on, he would not have had the remotest idea that those three performances, or any one of them, might have been his own piece. They were so totally different in every respect that the only thing he could lay claim to was having designed the score, not to having composed the piece. Aleatoric music, it seems to me, as it is frequently pursued, is an amusing parlor game. . . .[32]

Had these performances been recorded and subsequently translated into traditional notation for performer "interpretation," they would have avoided the antagonism. Had the piece then been performed three times, repetition would have replaced the creative ideal of the indeterminate composer.

Figures 5.18 to 5.22 show the wide variety of notations John Cage has used, and a cross section of the types of his works. *Concert for Piano and Orchestra* (Figure 5.18, solo for piano) was written and first performed for the 1958 Cage Retrospective Concert in New York's Town Hall, with the composer conducting. The staging included a large battery of electronic equipment, with the conductor slowly bringing his hands together over his head, in clocklike fashion. This controlled the duration of the piece more than individual events which are more or less indeterminate in sequence and number.

26'1.1499'' for a String Player (1955; see Figure 5.19) is more graphic and has been "realized" by Harold Budd for Bertram Turetzky's Nonesuch recording of the work. Both *Variations I,* (1958; see Figure 5.20) and *Fontana Mix* (1958; see Figure 5.21) graphically plot areas and physical locations for performance. *Variations IV* (1963) involves laying score transparencies over a map of the performance area and determining source and direction of sounds. The recording, made in a Los Angeles art gallery, includes the various sounds of Cage at work with electronic equipment and the candid conversations of the audience-performers. One microphone was placed outside the building to catch street sounds. Cage created a final realization by splicing and selecting, evaluating, and manipulating the resultant tapes.

The score to *Fontana Mix* represents the physical areas on the instruments used (indeterminate) and intersections that could be striking areas. Since the composer has not restricted instrumentation, it is not possible to predict any real outcome of the score in performance. Moreover, since the score is randomly made by the performer by overlaying various translucent sheets, the score itself looks different in each performance. Once created, however, and the score applied to the instruments

32. David Cope, "An Interview with Halsey Stevens," *Composer* 5, no. 1 (1973) p. 30.

26'1.1499" for a String Player, pages 59 and 84

used, performers should conform to that score in some very "determined" manner
so that improvisation or reliance on past experience will not take place. The piece
cannot be predicted or predetermined by either the composer or the performer; this
implies full cooperation in indeterminacy by all participants.

    Theatre Piece, (1960; Figure 5.22), in the Cage "happening" tradition, employs
number charts significant in their graphic representation of action. *Paintings* (1965)
by Louis Andriessen (Figure 5.23), for recorder and piano, exemplifies a totally
graphic indeterminate procedure. Even with the instructions, the predictability of

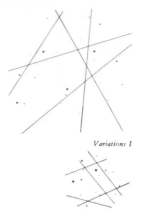

Variations I

Variations I. Extra Materials

Figure 5.20. John Cage: *Variations I.* Copyright by Henmar Press Inc., 373 Park Avenue South, New York, N.Y. 10016. International Copyright Secured. All rights reserved. Permission granted by the publisher.

Fontana Mix

Figure 5.21. John Cage: *Fontana Mix.* Copyright by Henmar Press Inc., 373 Park Avenue South, New York, N.Y. 10016. International Copyright Secured. Permission granted by the publisher.

Figure 5.22. John Cage: *Theatre Piece Part VI.* (one of eighteen unnumbered pages). Copyright by Henmar Press Inc., 373 Park Avenue South, New York, N.Y. 10016. International Copyright Secured. All rights reserved. Permission granted by the publisher.

Figure 5.23. Louis Andriessen: *Paintings.* Flötenpart, Blatt 1. Copyright © 1965 by Herman Moeck Verlag. Used with permission. All rights reserved.

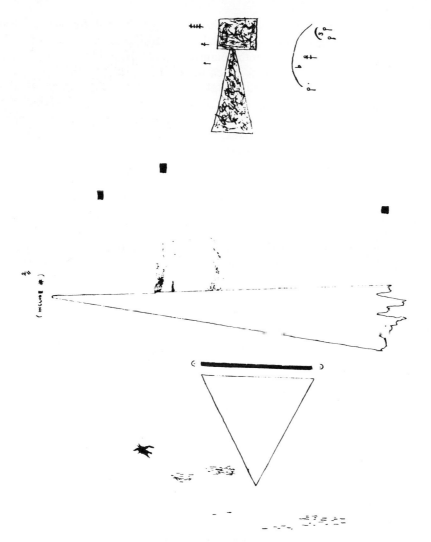

Figure 5.24. William Bland: *Speed* for organ solo.

the performance is minimal. William Bland's *Speed* (1968) for organ (see Figure 5.24) uses traditional left-to-right reading, up/down pitch level interpretation, and block-cluster chord representation, at the same time graphically encouraging non-predictable performance possibilities (e.g., center triangle with ink blur).

Other composers employ varied degrees of *graphic* notations to achieve equally varied ends. Anestis Logothetis's scores seem at first glance to be works of visual art. If one reads the instructions to his works carefully, clues appear that provide partial musical determinacy in terms of performer reaction and interpretation (e.g., *Clusters, Odyssee,* 1963, or *Ichnologia,* 1964). Robert Moran often utilizes *graphic* notations but, unlike Logothetis, gives clear indication of instrumentation and "possible" interpretation of visual symbols (see *Four Visions,* 1963, in Karkoschka's

Notation in New Music, or Bombardments No. 2, 1964, for one to five percussionists). Boguslaw Schäffer has pointed out a number of advantages of *graphic* music, at least for its usefulness to the mainstream of music. In his 1963 *Violin Concerto,* the cadenza, primarily thick black waves and twists of graphic art, is transcribed into one possible traditionally notated version. The result, based on a rather exact or literal translation, derives time in terms of left to right proportionality, pitch in terms of "up and down" relativity, and flow in terms of visual motion. This revised version is an incredibly complex, nearly unplayable, concrete structure totally foreign to the direction of the work. The plasticity of the *graphic* notation allows for a free sound, every bit as complex as the traditionally notated one, yet without the studied end result and, of course, without the "performance-to-performance" variability. In Schäffer's *Concerto* one hears the new elements, the surprises each performance offers. One does not judge a performer's mistakes or compare virtuosities in performance.

Figure 5.25 is from Roman Haubenstock-Ramati's *Jeux 2,* 1968 for two percussionists. Though mobile in structure, the graphic nature of the fragments themselves makes determinacy on the part of the composer or performer an impossibility. Note the difference here between *Jeux 2* and *Mobile for Shakespeare* (1959; Figure 5.15), the latter having composer control over the fragments, thus falling distinctly into the category of *performer-indeterminacy.* Possibly Europe's most experimental protagonist of the varieties of indeterminacy, Haubenstock-Ramati explores the areas

Figure 5.25. Roman Haubenstock-Ramati: *Jeux 2* for two percussionists. © Copyright Universal Edition, 1968. All rights reserved. Used by permission.

Figure 5.26. Robert Moran. *Sketch for a Tragic One-Act Opera.* Used by permission of the composer.

founded by John Cage, Earle Brown, and Barney Childs, unlike Stockhausen, for example, who now works with *conceptual music, antimusic,* and so on, each new area as it comes into view.

Figure 5.26, Robert Moran's *Sketch for a Tragic One-Act Opera* is in colors that cannot be reproduced here. The graphic nature of the score, even though instrumentation is traditional in left margin contributes to composer-performer indeterminacy. The indications here, since this is only a "sketch," define texture and dynamics more than pitch or exact rhythms.

Other composers involved with indeterminate techniques include Folke Rabe, Bo Nilsson, Cornelius Cardew (though it should be noted that Cardew later disowned his former style to compose "political-reformation" music), Roland Kayn, Allan Bryant, Joseph Byrd, Richard Maxfield, Philip Corner, Douglas Leedy, Robert Ashley, and James Fulkerson.

Vectoral Analysis: John Cage: *Cartridge Music*

(For information on vectoral analysis and procedures, see chapter 1.)

1. Historical Background: John Cage (b. 1912, Los Angeles, California) began his studies with Henry Cowell and Arnold Schoenberg with whom he studied counterpoint. Regarding the latter, Cage remarks:

My composition arises out of asking questions. I am reminded of an early story about a class with Schoenberg. He had us go to the blackboard to solve a particular problem in counterpoint (though it was a class in harmony). He said: "When you have a solution, turn around and let me see it." I did that. He then said: "Now another solution, please." I gave another and another until finally, having made seven or eight, I reflected a moment and then said with some certainty: "There aren't any more solutions." He said: "O.K. What is the principle underlying all of the solutions?" I couldn't answer his question; but I had always worshipped the man, and at that point I did even more. He ascended, so to speak. I spent the rest of my life, until recently, hearing him ask that question over and over. And then it occurred to me through the direction that my work has taken, which is renunciation of choices and the substitution of asking questions, that the principle underlying all of the solutions that I had given him was the question that he had asked, because they certainly didn't come from any other point. He would have accepted that answer, I think. The answers have the question in common. Therefore the question underlies the answers. I'm sure that he would have found my answer interesting; though he was very brilliant—he may have been thinking of something else.[33]

Cage's music through the mid-thirties developed chromatic concepts and used tone-row fragments, often with set rhythmic patterns. His *Sonata for Clarinet* (1933) is a good example of his work at this time. The work contains no effects whatsoever, but rather develops a kind of free twelve-tone procedure with definite rows but little working out of systematic serial techniques.

A second period developed in the mid- to late 1930s concentrating on wide diversities of timbral resources and an aesthetic about "noise." The prepared piano, developed in 1938, increased his interest in percussion instruments. The *First Construction in Metal* (1939) and important contributions to electronic music, particularly the *Imaginary Landscape* series begun in 1939, are all characteristic of Cage's imaginative leap into new sonic and timbral realms (Figure 5.27).

A third period developed early in the 1950s when Cage began to infuse indeterminacy into his works. The *Concerto for Prepared Piano and Orchestra* (1951), *4′33″* a blank score in which extraneous sounds to the performance become the work itself; (1952), and *Fontana Mix* (1958; for tape) represent his work at this time.

Throughout his career, Cage has actively referenced his work to the other arts in collaboration with Merce Cunningham, dance; Robert

33. David Cope, "An Interview with John Cage," *Composer* 10, no. 1 (1980), pp. 6–22.

Figure 5.27. John Cage (standing at left) conducting a recording session of a percussion work by Lou Harrison (white shirt, far right) about 1940. Accidental overlay of two photos (superimposition) created the music in upper center and bass drum.

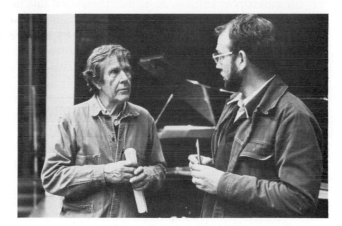

Figure 5.28. John Cage and David Cope during preparation of a *Cartridge Music* performance. Photo by Carol Foote (1980).

Rauschenberg, art; and Jasper Johns, sculpture as well as philosophy (e.g., Buckminster Fuller). His concept of and search for the "possibility of saying nothing" has influenced numerous composers, artists, and writers; few doubt that the present-day evolution of music would not exist without his vast input and contributions.

2. Overview: *Cartridge Music* was completed in 1960. The "score" consists of four transparent sheets described as follows: sheet one—nineteen ⅛-inch black dots arranged randomly; sheet two—ten ¼-inch circles arranged randomly; sheet three—a single two-inch-diameter circle numbered as a clock in five-second increments (0 to 60); sheet four—a very long curved dotted line with a ¼-inch circle at one end.

The score also contains twenty numbered nontransparent sheets having various shapes inscribed with the number of shapes corresponding to the number of the sheet. Each performer makes his or her own score from these materials. First, a nontransparent sheet is chosen with its number corresponding to the number of cartridges available to that performer (*cartridge* here referring to a contact mike or record player needle cartridge). The performer then places the transparent sheets randomly over the numbered nontransparent sheet with the curved dotted line arranged so that the circle at the end of the dotted line contains a point outside a shape and so that the dotted line intersects at least one point within one of the shapes. Figure 5.29 shows how the score might look (only one of nearly limitless possibilities). Note that the dotted line in the upper left terminates in a "filled" circle and that it intersects a point *inside* one of the shapes (i.e., intersects a point inside the large shape, lower right-hand side of the score). One then "reads" the dotted line from one end to the other in either direction, making note of intersections with lines, circles, and dots. Each of these intersections correlates with specific actions given in the performance notes. For example, "intersection of the dotted line with a point within a shape" indicates a sound produced in any manner on the object inserted in the cartridge corresponding to that shape.

Timing of the work is gauged by the circle (stopwatch), here located in the upper center of Figure 5.29. First, the arrangement shown exists for only one moment of the work, with total duration being fully at the will of the performers. Second, actions during that minute take place only over periods created by intersections of the dotted line with the time circle in this case, since the circle has not been intersected, no specific times are given.

The performer should prepare such arrangements for each minute of the scheduled performance prior to the first rehearsal. Exact schedules of actions should be made with clear indications of what procedures are necessary in exact timing sequence. Each part should be prepared separately from any other performer's part, Instruments to be used in performance (i.e., on which the contact microphones are to be used) are at the performer's discretion. "All events, ordinarily thought to be undesirable, such as feedback, humming, howling, etc. are to be accepted in this situation." Cage refers to a performance of the work in an interview with the author:

D. C.   Did you in the process of recording the piece listen to what you were doing?

J. C.   We did, so to speak, what we had to do. You are usually a bit too busy to listen. And the idea is that the players confound one another. That's one of the ideas of the piece. So that if you do listen to what you're doing, you're apt to get the wrong attitude toward the piece. What you have to develop is an indifference to whether your work is effective or ineffective; let happen what will. In my mind it arises from the experience that is so frequent in American life, of traffic congestion, and how to take it with what I call a sober and quiet mind, how to remain susceptible to divine influences.[34]

3. Orchestration Techniques: The choice of timbres involved is up to the performer except that the sound will be initiated by the cartridge. In a 1980 performance, the author utilized the insides of a piano, connecting and performing with the contact mikes directly on the strings and the sounding board. Other performers chose percussion instruments, primarily bass drum and tamtam respectively. Springs, wind-up toys, and a variety of other smaller "instruments" were also employed with effective results. Cage remarks further:

I can't recognize *Cartridge Music* from one performance to the next. Somewhere I tell that story of going into a house . . . and the hostess to be nice had put *Cartridge Music* on in another room. . . . I turned to her and asked, "What is that music?" And she said, "You can't be serious." I said, "It's very interesting; what is it?" And then she told me. I was pleased that I couldn't recognize it. . . . I don't hear it, you see. I performed it . . . with David Tudor, and we made a recording when Earle Brown was in charge of Time Records. Earle asked David and me if . . . we wanted to hear the end result. Neither one of us wanted to hear it.[35]

4. Basic Techniques: The basic scoring of *Cartridge Music* is experimental in nature (actions for which the final result is not foreseen). Composer indeterminacy is nearly complete, with Cage having no predictable way to foresee the sounds in any given performance situation. The performer's making of the score is indeterminate in the first step (creation of the sequences of actions from the graphs), but rehearsed carefully in the second step (carrying out of those prescribed actions).

D. C. In a performance of *Cartridge Music,* does it cross your mind that this is a good performance, a bad performance, or enjoyable . . . ?

J. C. If I think that way then I won't hear very well. The only time that I think that things are good or bad is when some other intentions than are proper to the piece take over. That happens so frequently with orchestral music, where the players don't do what they're supposed to do. Then I don't think that it's good or bad, but has moved out of the realm of music into the world of society and becomes a theatrical situation that was not intended at all.[36]

34. Ibid.
35. Ibid.
36. Ibid.

5, 6. Vertical and Horizontal Models: Since any and all possible timbres and textures can occur in this piece, no model can exist.

7. Style: *Cartridge Music* is representative of Cage's developed indeterminacy. He has carefully, through obviously involved processes, divorced himself from the process of creative control over the elements of this work. This separation is intricate, some say as intricate as that of trying to put one's personal creative process *into* a composition. *Cartridge Music* demonstrates mature Cage philosophies in full boom. Relationships with Zen, a complex fusion of Western and Eastern ideas, deserving far more space than is available here are significant, with Cage standing as antithetical to the general flow of Western musical traditions.

This Cage analysis demonstrates an indeterminate approach to composition where even the composer will be unaware of the outcome. This closely resembles the stochastic concepts espoused by Iannis Xenakis in chapter 10. In both cases, rigorous constructs are set in place, the rules of which set composition into motion. The results of both are at least specifically unpredictable, with both composers rigidly adhering to them regardless of any additions or subtractions they (based on hearing) might like to put in place. The Oliveros Vectoral Analysis in the next chapter reveals similar characteristics, but the indeterminacy is left to the particular performance situation. All these examples compare favorably with the serial concepts found in chapter 2, but not with the "lyricism" expressed by the works found in chapters 1, 4, 8, 9, 11, and 12.

Bibliography— Chapter 5*

Further Readings

A Brief History of Indeterminacy

Boulez, Pierre. "Alea." *Perspectives of New Music* 3, no. 1 (1964): pp. 42–53.
Cage, John. "History of Experimental Music in the United States." In *Silence: Lectures and Writings*. Cambridge, Mass.: The M.I.T. Press, 1966.
Copland, Aaron. "The Music of Chance." In *Our New Music*. New York: W. W. Norton and Co., 1968.
Kayn, Roland. "Random or not Random." *Horyzonty muzyki*. Cracow, 1966.
MacKenzie, I. A. "The Critique." *Composer* 2, no. 4 (1971): p. 92.
O'Grady, T. J. "Aesthetic Values in Indeterminate Music." *Musical Quarterly* 67, no. 3 (1981): pp. 366–81.
Shattuck, Roger. *The Banquet Years*. New York: Vintage Books, 1968.
Tomkins, Calvin. *The Bride and the Bachelors*. New York: Viking Press, 1965.
Yates, Peter. *Twentieth Century Music*. New York: Pantheon Books, 1967.

The Role of Improvisation

Brinkman, R., ed. *Improvisation Und Neue Musik*. Mainz: B. Schott, 1979.
Foss, Lukas. "The Changing Composer-Performer Relationship: A Monologue and a Dialogue." *Perspectives of New Music* 1, no. 2 (1963): pp. 45–53.

*Addresses for record companies, periodicals, and music publishers mentioned in this Bibliography can be found in Appendix IV.

———. "Work-Notes for Echoi." *Perspectives of New Music* 3, no. 1 (1964): pp. 54–61.

Hibbard, William. "Some Aspects of Serial Improvisation." *American Guild of Organists Quarterly* (1966).

Logan, Wendell. "The Case of Mr. John Coltrane: A Compositional View." *Numus West* 8 (1975): pp. 40–45.

Schuller, Gunther. *Early Jazz: Its Roots and Development.* New York: Oxford University Press, 1968.

Indeterminacy

Cage, John. *I-VI: Method Structure Intention . . .* Cambridge, Mass.: Harvard University Press, 1990.

Charles, Daniel. "Entr'acte: 'Formal' or 'Informal' Music." *Musical Quarterly* (1965): pp. 144–65.

Childs, Barney. "Indeterminacy and Theory: Some Notes." *Composer* 1, no. 1 (1969): pp. 15–34.

Higgins, Dick. *Postface.* New York: Something Else Press, 1964.

Schafer, R. Murray. *The Tuning of the World.* New York: Alfred A. Knopf, 1977.

Young, La Monte, and Jackson Mac Low, eds. *An Anthology of Chance Operations.* New York: La Monte Young and Jackson Mac Low, 1963.

Young, La Monte, and Marian Zazeela. *Selected Writings.* Munich: Heiner Friedrich, 1969.

Xenakis, Iannis. *Formalized Music.* Bloomington: Indiana University Press, 1971.

Composer Indeterminacy

Behrman, David. "What Indeterminate Notation Determines." *Perspectives of New Music* 3, no. 2 (1964): pp. 58–73.

Brown, Earle. "Form in New Music." *Source* 1, no. 1 (1967).

Cage, John. *Empty Words: Writings '73–'78.* Middletown, Conn.: Wesleyan University Press, 1979.

———. *M: Writings '67–'72.* Middletown, Conn.: Wesleyan University Press, 1973.

———. *Silence: Lectures and Writings.* Cambridge, Mass.: The M.I.T. Press, 1966.

———. *Writings Through Finnegans Wake.* New York: Printed Editions, 1979.

Cope, David. "An Interview with John Cage." *Composer* 10, no. 1 (1980): pp. 6–22.

Feldman, Morton. "Predetermined/Indetermined." *Composer* (England) (1966): pp. 3–4.

———. "Between Categories." *Composer* 1, no. 2 (1969): pp. 73–77.

Olson, Harry F., and Herbert Belar. "Aid to Composition Employing a Random Probability System." *Journal of the Acoustical Society of America* 33, no. 9 (1961).

Reynolds, Roger. "It(')s Time." *Electronic Music Review* 7 (1968): pp. 12–17.

———. "Indeterminacy: Some Considerations." *Perspectives of New Music* 4, no. 1 (1965): pp. 136–40.

———. *Mind Models.* New York: Praeger Books, 1976.

Xenakis, Iannis. *Formalized Music.* Bloomington, Indiana University Press, 1971.

Performer Indeterminacy

Cage, John. *Notations.* New York: Something Else Press, 1969.

Cardew, Cornelius, ed. *Scratch Music.* Cambridge, Mass.: The MIT Press, 1974.

Reynolds, Roger. "Happenings in Japan and Elsewhere." *Arts in Society* 5, no. 1 (1968): pp. 90–101.

Composer and Performer Indeterminacy

Cage, John. *Notations*. New York: Something Else Press, 1969.

———. *Pour les Oiseaux*. Paris: Pierre Belford, 1976.

———. *A Year from Monday*. Middletown, Conn.: Wesleyan University Press, 1967.

Layton, Billy Jim. "The New Liberalism." *Perspectives of New Music* 3, no. 2 (1964): pp. 137–42.

Sumner, Melody, ed. *The Guests Go In To Supper*. New York: Burning Books, 1986.

Young, La Monte, and Jackson Mac Low, eds. *An Anthology of Chance Operations*. New York: La Monte Young and Jackson Mac Low, 1963.

John Cage

Cage, John. *The John Cage Catalog*. New York: C. F. Peters Co., 1962.

———. *A Year from Monday*. Middletown, Conn.: Wesleyan University Press, 1967.

Kostelanetz, Richard. *John Cage*. New York: Praeger, 1970.

———. *Master Minds*. New York: Macmillan, 1969.

Metzger, Heinz-Klaus, and Rainer Riehn, eds. *A Book about John Cage and his Music*. New York: C. F. Peters, 1981.

Pritchett, James. "From Choice to Chance: John Cage's *Concerto for Prepared Piano*." *Perspectives of New Music* 26, no. 1 (1988): pp. 50–81.

Compact Discs, Recordings, and Publishers

Andriessen, Louis. *Ittrospezione 11* (1963). Donemus.

———. *Paintings*. Belwin-Mills.

Ashley, Robert. *in memoriam Crazy Horse* (1963). Advance 5.

———. *Wolfman* (1964). CPE-Source IV.

Austin, Larry. *Accidents* (1967). CPE-Source.

———. *Piano Variations* (1964). Advance S–10.

———. *Improvisations for Orchestra and Jazz Soloists* (1961). Columbia MS–6733.

Ayler, Albert. *Music is the Healing Force*. Impulse 9191.

Berio, Luciano. *Circles*. Universal Edition. Candide 31027.

Boucourechliev, Andre. *Archipel I*. (1972). Angel S–36655.

———. *Archipel IV* (for solo piano) (1972). Finnadar 9021.

Boulez, Pierre. *Improvisations sur Mallarmé* (1957). Universal Edition. Hungaraton 11385–2.

———. *Structures II* (1952). Universal Edition. Erato ECD 88074.

Brown, Earle. *Available Forms I* and *II*. AMP. RCA Vics1239.

———. *December 1952*. C. F. Peters. CRI S–330.

———. *Du* (1951). Boelke-Bomart. Son Nova 1.

———. *Four Systems*. (1954). Columbia MS–7 139.

———. *Hodograph I*. (1959). Mainstream 5007.

———. *Music for Violoncello and Pianoforte* (1952). Mainstream 5007.

———. *Quartet*. (1965). Mainstream 5009.

Bussotti, Sylvano. *Coeur pour Batteur-Positively Yes*. Universal Edition. Columbia MS–7139.

————. *Five Pieces for David Tudor.* Universal Edition. CP2 3–5.

————. *Frammento.* Ricordi (1967). Mainstream 5005.

————. *Per tre sul piano* (1959). Universal. EMI EMSP 55.

Cage, John. *Amores for Prepared Piano and Percussion.* (1943). Peters. Bis CD272.

————. *Aria with Fontana Mix* (1958). C. F. Peters. Virgin VC 7 90704–2.

————. *Atlas Eclipticalis.* Peters DG–137009.

————. *Cartridge Music.* C. F. Peters. Mainstream 5015.

————. *Concert for Piano and Orchestra.* C. F. Peters.

————. *HPSCHD* (1969). C. F. Peters. Nonesuch 71224.

————. *Fontana Mix.* C. F. Peters. Columbia MS–7139.

————. *4'33".* C. F. Peters. Hungaraton HCD–12991.

————. *Music of Changes.* C. F. Peters. Wergo Wer 60099–50.

————. *Solo for Voice 2* (1960). C. F. Peters. Odyssey 32–160156.

————. *Theatre Piece.* C. F. Peters.

————. *34' 46.776" for a Pianist.* C. F. Peters.

————. *26'1.1499" for a String Player.* C. F. Peters. Nonesuch 71237.

————. *Variations I*(1958). C. F. Peters. Wergo 60033.

————. *Variations II* (1961). C. F. Peters. Columbia MS–7051.

————. *Variations III* (1963). C. F. Peters. DG–139442.

————. *Variations IV.* C. F. Peters. Everest 3132.

Chiari, Giuseppe. *Quel Che Volete* (1965). CPE-Source.

Coltrane, John. The Mastery of John Coltrane (1983). Impulse IZ–9 345–46–60–61.

Davis, Miles, *Bitch's Brew* (1969). Columbia PG–26.

Douglas, Bill. *Improvisations III* (1969). Orion 73125.

Duckworth, William. *Pitch City.* CAP.

Erb, Donald. *Concerto for Percussion and Orchestra.* Merion Music. Turnabout TV-S 34433.

Feldman, Morton. *Chorus and Instruments.* (1963). C. F. Peters. Odyssey 321601 56.

————. *Christian Wolff in Cambridge* (1963). C. F. Peters. Odyssey 32–160156.

————. *Durations* (1962). C. F. Peters. Mainstream 5007.

————. *False Relationships and the Extended Ending* (1968). C. F. Peters. CRI S276.

————. *In Search of an Orchestration* (1967). C. F. Peters.

————. *Intersection 3* (1953). C. F. Peters. DG–I 39442.

————. *King of Denmark* (1965). C. F. Peters. Columbia MS–7139.

————. *Out of "Last Pieces"* (1962). C. F. Peters. Columbia MS–6733.

————. *Viola in my Life* (1972). C. F. Peters. CRI S–276.

Foss, Lukas. *Echoi.* Helidon 2549001.

————. *Etudes for Organ* (1967). CPE-Source.

————. *Fragments of Archilocos* (1965). Helidon 2549001.

————. *Music for Clarinet, Percussion and Piano* (1961). RCA LSC–2558.

————. *Time Cycle.* CRS 8219.

Haubenstock-Ramati, Roman. *Interpolation: a "Mobile" for Flute* (1,2,3). (1958). Universal Edition. RCA Vics–1312.

————. *Mobile for Shakespeare.* Universal Edition.

————. *Ohne Titel.* Universal Edition. Wergo Wer 60119–50.

Higgins, Dick. *Thousand Symphonies* (1969). CPE-Source.

Hykes, David. *Harmonic Meetings.* CHCEL–013/014.

Kagel, Mauricio. *1898.* London: Universal Edition.

————. *Improvisation ajoutée* (1962). C. F. Peters. Odyssey 32–160158.

————. *Rrrrrrr.* . . . . (1980–81). Aulos Pre 66004.

Kayn, Roland. *Calaxis* (1962). Moeck.

Logothetis, Anestis. *Ichnologia*.

————. *Kulmination.* (1961). Edition Modern/Munich. Wergo 60057.

————. *Labyrinthos* (1965). Universal Edition.

————. *Odyssee.* Universal Edition.

Lutoslawski, Witold. *Livre Pour Orchestra.* (1968). J. & W. Chester Ltd. Ades 14122–2.

————. *Trois Poèmes d'Henri Michaux* (1963). PWM. MUZA PNCD–041.

Maderna, Bruno. *Viola* (1971). Finnadar 9007.

Mizelle, John. *Radial Energy* (1967). CPE-Source.

Moran, Robert. *Bombardments No. 2.* C. F. Peters.

————. *Four Visions.* Universal Edition.

Mumma, Gordon. *Mesa for Cybersonic Bandoneon* (1965). Odyssey 32–160158.

Nilsson, Bo. *Reaktionen* (1960). Universal Edition.

Oliveros, Pauline. *Outline for flute, percussion, and string bass: An improvisation chart* (1963). Nonesuch 71237.

Pousseur, Henri. *Caractères.* Universal Edition.

————. *Phonémes pour Cathy* (1973). Universal Edition. Virgin VC 90704–2.

————. *Sound Patterns* (1964). Odyssey 32–160156.

Rabe, Folke. *Piece* (1961). W. Hansen.

Schäffer, Boguslaw. *S'alto* (1963). PWM.

————. *Violin Concerto.* PWM.

Schuller, Gunther. *Concertino for Jazz Quartet and Orchestra* (1959). Atlantic S–1359.

————. *Conversations* (1959). Atlantic S–1345.

————. *Seven Studies on Themes of Paul Klee* (1959). Universal Edition. RCA LSC–2879.

————. *Transformation.* Columbia WL–127.

Stockhausen, Karlheinz. *Klavierstück XI.* Universal Edition. HCD 12569–2.

————. *STOP.* Universal Edition.

Winsor, Phil. *Orgel.* Carl Fischer.

Wolff, Christian. *Duo, Duet and Summer* (1961). Mainstream 5015.

————. *Duo II for Pianists.* C. F. Peters.

————. *Edges* (1968). CPE-Source.

————. *For 1, 2 or 3 People* (1964). C. F. Peters. Odyssey 32–160158.

————. *Trio 2* (1961). C. F. Peters.

Xenakis, Iannis. *Akrata* (1968). Boosey and Hawkes. Nonesuch 71201.

————. *Duel.* Boosey and Hawkes.

Zeitlin, Denny. *Expansions.* 1750 Arch Records 1758.

EXPERIMENTALISM

6

Experimentalism is, for the purposes of this text, a redefining of the boundaries of a given art form. "Art as life" or "art as everything" both qualify. The scope of this book does not permit fully detailed coverage of the cross-disciplinary aspects of the arts in general, and the added stimulus that the visual arts in particular have given to new music. However, the impetus generated by artists such as Marcel Duchamp, Man Ray, Robert Rauschenberg, Wassily Kandinsky, and many others has been profound. In the mainstream of music one finds composers like Arnold Schoenberg, who was himself an expressionist painter of repute, and Igor Stravinsky influenced by Expressionism and painters like Pablo Picasso (see chapter 1). In the *avant-garde* one encounters cross-relationships particularly between composers and artists such as Erik Satie (Man Ray), John Cage (Robert Rauschenberg), and Earle Brown (Alexander Calder).

If one were to trace the roots of experimentalism, the music of Erik Satie, particularly in works like *Vexations* (1893?), a twenty-four-hour hour marathon work for piano, was among the first to clearly demonstrate experimental tendencies. The *Musical Sculpture* (undated) by Marcel Duchamp is also noteworthy, showing a direct relationship with current concept music. His early work *The Bride Stripped Bare by Her Bachelors, Even* is especially provocative. Duchamp's *Erratum Musical* (1913) is a work of numbers with notes for each number, Petr Kotik has made two realizations, one for two pianos, the other for five instruments. The dada artists and later the antiart, concept art, and minimal art movements have all preceded parallel activities in music.

Paul Nougé, who was active in the surrealistic movement, in his *Music is Dangerous* (1929), points out that most known "uses" of music such as relaxation, forgetting, and pleasure are but subtle facades for its emotional dangers, drawing proofs from the ancient modal theories wherein each mode provoked distinct emotions (phrygian: excitement; lydian: calming; etc.)[1] His "iatric" music (medicinal music: noting that a great many medical terms end in "iatric" such as pediatric, etc.) further postulates music's profound remedial capabilities in the sense that a witch doctor has therapeutic powers, predating our current fascination with music therapy. Most

Chronology and Fundamentals

---

1. Paul Nougé, *Music is Dangerous*, trans. Felix Giovanelli from *View* magazine. Reprinted in book form by *Soundings* (1973).

important, however, Nougé proposes that the audience is not separate from or even "safe" from musical performance: "Our answer is that the concept of *spectator,* which seems to play so important a role in certain minds, is one of the grossest imaginable."[2] It is doubtful that Nougé's writings have had a direct influence over the new experimentation of our present era; however, it is most noteworthy that such expressions as ". . . how we may defend ourselves against music. . . . Evidently, the easiest way is to refuse once and for all to have anything to do with it . . ." are not new or light divertissement as might be supposed.[3]

Questions regarding the most fundamental ideas, often more about the composer's relationship with sound than with the sounds themselves, inevitably arise from these concepts. The continual expansion of the definition of music to include all sound, regardless of origin or "beauty," may eventually annul the experimental designation used here. The primary motive behind this philosophy, however, would remain: to destroy the concept of an "immaculate" art separate from life.

Robert Rauschenberg, possibly more than any other artist aside from Jackson Pollock and Marcel Duchamp, has sustained a creative "antiart" movement that has substantially affected a number of composers. His *Erased de Kooning Drawing* is exactly that: a de Kooning drawing he obtained directly from the artist himself erased as completely as possible using a special selection of erasers collected by Rauschenberg. The act of "decomposing" the work of art becomes, in this instance, the "act" of creation of a white sheet of paper only barely showing hints of lines, or even less—slight depressions in the paper where the original drawing once existed. If one can deal with art as *change,* beauty as totally *relative,* any *act* as plausibly artistic, then Rauschenberg's erasure presents a work as significant as the original drawing. Whether one deals with it as such or not is of little consequence: it is antiart.

Robert Rauschenberg's *Black Painting* of 1952 demonstrates both the conceptual nature of his work and the extraordinary complexity of shading provided the right lighting. The painting itself is entirely black. What the painter has accomplished is to successfully distill a single sculptural feature of painting (reflection). The application of the principle reveals the complex refinement of the concept when applied rigorously.

One composer has come close to this approach in music, but in an entirely different way. He has substituted an entire work of the past *verbatim* for his own. Paul Ignace indicates some of the rationale behind such actions in a letter to the author.

> When I was first asked to compose a piece for orchestra I had no idea what they wanted, except an experience of some kind. I wrote and asked for a complete list of the other works included in concerts of the series, and when I discovered that the concert preceding the night of my premiere included Berlioz's *Symphonie Fantastique,* I made up my mind. I insisted that my work be unrehearsed (there wouldn't have been much anyway, as those things go) and that I would bring score and parts the night of the concert. Imagine the shock when the conductor and players opened their music to find the work that they had performed the night before . . . but

2. Ibid., p. 17.
3. Ibid., p. 24.

they performed it, much to the anger and horror of the audience and reviewers. They were angry, of course, not at the sounds but at my plagiarism (legal, according to copyright laws) but few realized they listened to the sounds in an entirely new way— something very good, very creative, in my way of thinking. No, I did not receive money for my endeavor!

(The work, by the way, was titled *Symphonie Fantastique No. 2.*)[4]

Yehuda Yannay's *Houdini's Ninth* (1970) is experimental theater quite apropos of this genre. Bernard Jacobson characterizes one performance in this excerpt from his article in *Stereo Review.*

> A man cycled onto the stage, put a record of the (Beethoven) *Choral* Symphony finale on a phonograph, and proceeded to mix some kind of culinary concoction onto the surface of the actual disc, with bizarre effects on the sound. This was interwoven with an episode involving a double-bass player in a sort of straitjacket, and dominating the proceedings was a projection of an incredibly stupid poem published in *Dwight's Journal of Music,* Boston, on December 17, 1870. It was in honor of Beethoven's centenary, and took a very encouraging view of his affliction of deafness: "A price how small," it cheerily informed him, "for privilege how great,/ When thy locked sense groped upward and there/ The shining ladder reaching through the air."[5]

Encouraged by the words of social philosophers Marshall McLuhan and R. Buckminster Fuller, and his own studies with Eastern philosopher D. T. Suzuki, John Cage developed a unique personal philosophy. His sweeping statement: "Everything we do is music" has engendered many reactions. Luciano Berio has countered, ". . . music is everything that one listens to with the intention of listening to music."[6] Cage's works encompass most of the aspects of the new concepts of the last sixty years: electronic music, improvisation, indeterminacy, multimedia, and experimentalism. From his work in the thirties, when he originated the prepared piano, to his extension of multimedia "happenings," he has remained the remarkable enigma. His ideas and works amuse, startle, antagonize, and somehow also encourage the worlds of music, dance, and art. If change, not idolatry, be the mark of greatness, then John Cage has surely reached this pinnacle. Nothing can or will be the same after him.

Aside from Cage, no other composer has achieved the shock value of, and relevance to, antiart, except perhaps La Monte Young. In particular, his *Composition 1960 #3,* where the duration of the piece is announced and the audience told to do whatever they wish for the remainder of the composition, and *Composition 1960 #6,* where the performers stare and react exactly as if they were the audience are excellent examples of the "anti" aspect at work.[7]

---

4. From a letter to the author.

5. Available on film from the composer: 4044 N. Downer Ave., Milwaukee, WI. 53211 (as of December 1974).

6. From Luciano Berio: Two Interviews (with Rossana Dalmonte and Bálint András Varga). London: Marion Boyars, 1985, p. 19.

7. Barney Childs discusses these works and others in an excellent article, "Indeterminacy and Theory: Some Notes," *Composer* 1, no. 1 (June 1969), pp. 15–34.

Critics of these and other experimentalists address themselves to the "dead end" and "pointless" philosophies implied. To these, I. A. MacKenzie has replied:

> Art is imitation, repetition, memory, or rejection of life. Nothing is created by man, just recreated: a storeroom to collect the bits and pieces of the whole he feels worthy of saving, to be brought to life again whenever the need occurs, but never as good as the original. Art exists only as a refuge against new experience, un-recreated experience with reality: second-hand living. The terms "musician," "painter," "writer," merely break these limitations down further for easier construction, assimilation and comfort. I am none of these. I am not an artist. I do not imitate, or need of developing *[sic]* a memory with art for a thousand million possibilities of the present confront me, and I don't want that number diminished by one.
>
> I am a mapmaker, a suggester of possible routes for those interested in experiences with what has already been created—everything. I am similar to the "artist" in that I do not create, dissimilar with him in that I do not pretend to.
>
> Untouched by style, convenience, or tradition, the elements I observe (not manipulate) I discovered, but only for myself and my discovery has style, convenience just as yours.
>
> I do nothing that anyone else could not do easily and do not pretend to. I only give directions when someone wishes them and would be happy to stop anytime. . . .
>
> Everything exists: why should I mechanically alter one thing into another, one thought into another? All exist—it is much more—to find the original.[8]

With the basic concepts presented in this chapter, a new transcendental form of expression emerges. These new experiments are necessary and important and contribute to musical values rather than being detrimental. Understanding these new experiments, however, is often difficult, and audiences question the creative rationale as to why these works exist. Their antagonism, however, is often more philosophical than musical. Cage speaks of this in *A Year from Monday:* "Art's in process of coming into its own: life"[9] and "We used to have the artist up on a pedestal. Now he's no more extraordinary than we are."[10] Tzara states: "Art is not the most precious manifestation of life. Art has not the celestial and universal value that people like to attribute to it. Life is far more interesting."[11]

These directions extend to include those sounds that attempt to distort the mind (*danger music*), that don't exist (*conceptualism*), and that come about without the hand of man (*biomusic* and *soundscapes*).

Danger Music

The history of *danger music* is long indeed, and if one follows Paul Nougé's thinking in *Music is Dangerous,*[12] all music has such potential. While, as he points out, we may use it for "relaxation." "forgetting" or "pleasure," it . . . "probably entails

8. I. A MacKenzie, as paraphrased by David Cope in *Notes in Discontinuum* (Los Angeles: Discant Music, 1970), p. 2.

9. John Cage, *A Year from Monday* (Middletown, Conn.: Wesleyan University Press ,1967), p. 6.

10. Ibid., p. 50.

11. Robert Motherwell, *The Dada Painters and Poets: An Anthology* (New York: Wittenborn, Schultz, Inc., 1951), p. 248.

12. Nougé, op. cit.

Figure 6.1. Nam June Paik during a 1962 *Fluxus* performance.

serious consequences."[13] This fascinating book describes a number of accounts of man's unfortunate encounters with the dangers of music:

> Sometimes we find peculiar stories in a newspaper. A few weeks ago, a young American went home after coming out of a performance of *Tannhauser,* and killed himself; not without having first written a note in which he explained that where Tannhäuser had weakened, he, yes he, would set a better example of courage and grandeur.[14]

Most danger music involves a more direct attack on the performer or spectator. Nam June Paik's *Danger Music for Dick Higgins* has the score reading: "Creep into the Vagina of a living Whale."[15] Figure 6.1 shows Paik during a 1962 *Fluxus* performance.

The visual arts have certainly had direct influence on danger music. Ayo, for example, has created a number of finger boxes, each containing a substance unknown to the "spectator." One experiences the art by placing their fingers into their small creations, some of which contain felt, fur, and similar "pleasantries." Some, however, contain razor blades, broken glass, and pocket knives. "Chance" has a new dimension here as one must weigh the odds of pain against pleasure.

Though blood (and even death) are not unknown to danger music, these seldom occur as a direct result of composer notation. "Accidents" are welcomed, however. Such was the case of two happenings in 1962: the first involved a somewhat "bloodied" Robert Whitman at Bennington College; the second involved a woman

13. Ibid., p. 11

14. Ibid.

15. See John Cage's *Notations* (New York: Something Else Press, 1969), unpaged, for a copy of the score in full.

Figure 6.2. Robert Ashley.

spectator/performer at an Al Hansen happening falling from a window down a number of stories and eventually through a glass roof.

The environment around us provides another source of danger: sound pollution. While discussed in more depth later in this chapter under "Soundscapes," the aural dangers of even the average household cannot escape the artist's cognizance. Robert Ashley's *Wolfman* (1964) exemplifies *danger music*. Through use of a prerecorded tape and a voice "screaming" through a microphone involving electronic feedback, all turned to extremely loud levels, the work easily reaches decibel counts above danger level. The recording of this work, with instructions "to be played at the highest possible volume level" indeed constitutes ear annihilation to the uninitiated in a small "live" room.[16]

Phil Corner's adaptation of his own *Prelude* from *4 Suits* creates interesting danger music:

> I threw out a rifle and then slowly picked it up and pointed it at the audience (no one bolted for the doors, by the way) . . . counterpointed by a woman who slowly picked up a bouquet of roses—there was a countdown . . . at the end of which she threw the flowers into the audience, all over, with great love and joy, while I silently let fall the rifle and slunk offstage. Yet this was apparently not the right message for some, as I was accosted afterwards by one of the *Up Against The Wall Motherfucker* crowd, and yelled at: "Next time a real rifle!"[17]

Corner's *"One antipersonnel-type CBU bomb will be thrown into the audience"* is another example of danger music used to express antiwar political views. Corner speaks of this work:

> I tried to push the concert situation to a point where those present would *have* to feel the immediacy of the situation—*their* situation, since this had to be something in which those present shared a complicity. Failure! Could I have been that naive? For

16. *Wolfman* is published in *Source: Music of the Avant-Garde* 2, no. 2 (July 1968). Both the score and the recording are available.
17. From a letter to the author.

the audience reaction is *not* predictable. I discovered that right then and there. For that reason the thing was not even ever done. The defenses against identifying with the victims, with putting ourselves in their places, is too strong. Guilt is covered up by a selfish fear. A self-serving, even dishonest one, I might add. I felt it then and still do. The idea that that would really be acted on, that a real terrorist act would be announced so and carried out in this way seems to be incredible. Finally though, the "performance" would have been to announce the cancellation of the performance.[18]

Danger music is often philosophy more than sound. Performances merge with reality. Danger music denotes war with music, war with the sanctity of sensual isolation. Daniel Lentz's comments in the Coda of his *Skeletons Don't Say Peek*[19] explicitly attack the hierarchy of traditional concert and instrumental performance routine:

I too am sad. In fact, I am very sad. Men are still fighting wars and playing music. Some are guerilla wars, and some are guerilla compositions. But they are, nevertheless, war and music. They are fought with weapons and instruments. There is so little difference. One type is used for the defense of an army or nation; the other, for the defense of a vestigial culture. Do we need the protection of generals and composers? Do we need their incredibly scary anti ballistic missile systems and synthesizers? Shouldn't we attempt their destruction, before they destroy us? From whom are they protecting us? From the Russians? The Princetonians? What, in the late-middle 20th century does weaponry have to do with music? Can we eliminate one without first eliminating the other? Won't the metaphor be too powerful until it is taken away? Has there ever been an instrument built which wasn't used? Couldn't the players you saw in action tonight just as well have been aggressive soldiers of war? Did you watch closely their gestures? Is there a real difference between them and the Special Forces? Are they not identical mentalities? They are out to kill us and you sit there waiting. Are you all crazy? Can't you see, nor hear? But wait . . . don't blame the players. We are only cogs in the great hierarchy. We follow directions. The artistic generals tell us what to do and when to do it and the manner in which it is to be done. They are not even specific. Aren't they kind, as they destroy us? We are like you: just poor citizens caught up in the immense musical-industrial complex. Sure, if you threaten us or our friends, we will play for you. We have no recourse but to protect our "raison d'être."

Prior to this final "performer" announcement, all the instruments have been taken from the performers, placed in front of the piano, and *saluted*. The act of not playing, the drama of attacking the performance situation, eliminates all vestige of traditional and, for that matter, nontraditional equipment, instruments, and concepts.

Daniel Lentz's works are often antiwar as well. *Anti Bass Music,* for example (see Figure 6.3), employs a number of notations relating the concert situation to the battlefield. The work, supplied with four optional endings which may be performed

18. Ibid.

19. Part of Harold Budd's *California 99* (1969), the movements of which were composed by Bertram Turetzky, Pauline Oliveros, Larry Austin, Barney Childs, Stanley Lunetta, John Mizelle, and David Sherr as well as Lentz.

Figure 6.3. Daniel Lentz: *Anti Bass Music,* page 11.

in multiples; that is, more than one ending may be employed, includes a reading of a list of American composers not killed in Viet Nam, and the use of twenty-five to one hundred laughing machines.

Conceptualism

Minimal art is the closest "art" relative to *conceptualism.* Works such as Robert Rauschenberg's *White Paintings,* canvases covered as evenly as possible with white paint, are parallel to such conceptual works as John Cage's classic *4'33".*

4'33" received its first performance in August, 1952, at Woodstock, New York by pianist David Tudor. Using a stopwatch, he covered the piano keyboard at the beginning of each movement, playing nothing, but timing the silences of each period marked by Cage in the otherwise blank score. Unfortunately, the brilliance of Tudor's dramatic performance had the adverse effect of limiting this work to piano since the score mentions no instrumentation. The instruction "for any instrument or combination of instruments" makes realization practical on any instrument. Virtually anything with a total duration of four minutes and thirty-three seconds and movements of one minute, forty seconds; two minutes, twenty-three seconds; and thirty seconds respectively, could successfully serve as a realization of the score, from thinking-in-a-bathtub to silence by a symphony orchestra.[20] Cage has clarified the concept behind such works:

> . . . where it is realized that sounds occur whether intended or not, one turns in the direction of those he does not intend. The turning is psychological and seems at first to be a giving up of everything that belongs to humanity—for a musician, the giving up of music. This psychological turning leads to the world of nature, where, gradually or suddenly, one sees that humanity and nature, not separate, are in this world together; that nothing was lost when everything was given away. In fact, everything is gained.[21]

Rauschenberg's *White Paintings* link further with *4'33"* when one realizes that in the former the shadows of spectators, variance of lights, reflections, and so on,

20. This work is published in *Source: Music of the Avant-Garde* 1, no. 2 (July 1967):46 ff.
21. John Cage, *Silence* (Cambridge, Mass.: The M.I.T. Press, paperback edition, 1961), p. 8.

turn the seemingly blank canvas into a veritable mass of visual activity. In the latter, the coughs, laughter, and other audible movements of the audience as well as the extraneous sounds from without the performance area become, in fact, the work. In both cases the act of the creator is minimal *and* conceptual.

Minimal music, most often minimal in materials and not duration, as will be seen, is also clearly defined in the works of La Monte Young. His *Composition 1960 #7* contains only the notes B and F♯ with the instructions to be held for a "long time." *Composition 1960 #10* requests the performer to "draw a straight line and follow it."[22] In 1960, at Berkeley, he presented a composition that consisted of turning loose a jar full of butterflies that made a sound however inaudible.[23]

Other works by Young of that same year include his infamous "line piece":

> My "Composition 1960 No. 9" consists of a straight line drawn on a piece of paper. It is to be performed and comes with no instructions. The night I met Jackson MacLow we went down to my apartment and he read some of his poems for us. Later when he was going home, he said he'd write out directions to get to his place so we could come and visit him sometime. He happened to pick up "Composition No. 9" and said, "Can I write it here?" I said, "No, wait, that's a piece. Don't write on that." He said, "Whadaya mean a piece? That's just a line."[24]

Karlheinz Stockhausen's *Mikrophonie I* (1964) uses only one sound source, a tam-tam, six feet in diameter upon which the performers manipulate the various verbal instructions of the score, "scraping, trumpeting," and so on.

Concept music, though often overlapping many of the aforementioned works, is also extremist and more powerful and often more interesting in premise than in the performance situation—if there is one. Eric Andersen's *Opus 48 "Which turns anonymous when the instruction is carried out"* is sent through the mail on a piece of cardboard that states in total: "Place the chosen tautology." This is concept music or implication of music not being present. Tom Johnson, in his book *Imaginary Music,* includes a number of nonplayable concept pieces.[25] His *Celestial Music for Imaginary Trumpets* (see Figure 6.4) is clearly concept music, as performance is impossible; one is able to only "conceptualize" or imagine the work. Robert Moran's *Composition for Piano with Pianist* states: "A pianist comes onto the stage and goes directly to the concert grand piano. He climbs into the piano, and sits on the strings. The piano plays him."[26] This conceptual *message* is more important than any "real" sounds.

Concept philosophy is often implied only in the score and is not "real" to the audience. *"Accidents"* (1967) by Larry Austin, for example, contains instructions

22. A great deal of material on and by LaMonte Young is found in *Selected Writings* by La Monte Young and Marian Zazeela (Munich: Heiner Friedrich, 1969).

23. Richard Kostelanetz, *The Theatre of Mixed Means* (New York: Dial Press, 1968), from the article (first page) on La Monte Young.

24. Young and Zazeela, *Selected Writings,* unpaged (from the Lecture 1960, copyright 1965 by the Tulane Drama Review).

25. Tom Johnson, *Imaginary Music.* New York: Two-Eighteen Press (P.O. Box 218, Village Station, New York, N.Y. 10014), 1974.

26. Published in *Soundings* 1, p. 44.

Figure 6.4. Tom Johnson: *Celestial Music for Imaginary Trumpets.* © Copyright 1974 by Tom Johnson. All rights reserved. Used by permission. From *Imaginary Music* by Tom Johnson, Two Eighteen Press, N.Y.C.

in which the pianist performs while avoiding actual sounds. The speed of performance makes accidents unavoidable. As if repenting sins, the performer must return to each gesture in which an accident occurred (i.e., a sound made) and repeat it until error-free (i.e., no sound occurring).

The German-originated but often New York-based movement Fluxus, which included Paik, Young, Dick Higgins, Eric Andersen, Thomas Schmidt, Jackson MacLow, and George Brecht, represented the basic directions in concept music for a number of years, finally becoming a publisher of art objects. Blank structures provide objectives in the experiments of these composers, poets, and artists. Often these works do not contain the slightest hint as to what action is intended or what materials are to be used.[27] Figure 6.5 provides a George Maciunas view of what the Fluxus art movement means. The references to "Spikes (sic) Jones" and Marcel Duchamp suggest the levity that many members of the various group felt about their projects. Figures 6.6 and 6.7 provide photo documentation of some of the members of Fluxus. Other individuals involved, but not shown here, included Jonas Mekas, Bob Watts, Ben Patterson, and Joe Jones.

Text sound music is based on the *textljud kompositioner* of two Swedish composers, Lars-Gunnar Bodin and Bengt-Emil Johnson. Termed sound poetry, speech music, and even lexical music, its origins extend back to the Futurists in Italy just after the turn of the century. Works in this genre expand reading and speaking concepts, utilizing onomatopoeia and other intricate textural mechanics to produce rhythmic and contrapuntal structures. Often these incorporate long repetitions of words in solo or ensemble situations, with changing and developing emphasis, accents, and meaning. Frequently these works are altered through electronic processes.

Composers aware of this form early in this century include Hugo Ball, Tristan Tzara, and Kurt Schwitters in the twenties; Marcel Duchamp in the thirties and forties; and John Cage in the fifties and sixties. Composers currently interested in the genre include John Giorno, Aram Saroyan, Brion Gysin, Beth Anderson, Robert Ashley, Anthony Gnazzo, Tim Bell, Stephen Ruppenthal, and Charles Amirkhanian. Amirkhanian has produced a large number of text sound works, including *Seatbelt Seatbelt* (1973), *Mugic* (1973), *Mahogany Ballpark* (1976), and *Dutiful Ducks* (1977).

27. *Fluxus* movements have also arisen in other countries, including Japan (Takehisa Kosugi, Chieko Shiomi) and Germany.

ART	FLUXUS ART-AMUSEMENT

To justify artist's professional, parasitic and elite status in society,
he must demonstrate
    artist's indispensability and exclusiveness,
he must demonstrate
    the dependability of audience upon him,
he must demonstrate
    that no one but the artist can do art.
	To establish artist's nonprofessional status in society,
	he must demonstrate
	    artist's dispensability and inclusiveness,
	he must demonstrate
	    the selfsufficiency of the audience,
	he must demonstrate
	    that anything can be art and anyone can do it.

Therefore, art must appear to be complex, pretentious, profound, serious, intellectual, inspired, skillfull, significant, theatrical, it must appear to be valuable as commodity so as to provide the artist with an income.
 	
To raise its value (artist's income and patrons profit), art is made to appear rare, limited in quantity and therefore obtainable and accessible only to the social elite and institutions.
	Therefore, art-amusement must be simple, amusing, unpretentious, concerned with insignificances, require no skill or countless rehearsals, have no commodity or institutional value.
	The value of art-amusement must be lowered by marking it unlimited, massproduced, obtainable by all and eventually produced by all.
	Fluxus art-amusement is the rear-guard without any pretention or urge to participate in the competition of ,,one-upmanship'' with the avant-garde. It strives for the monostructural and nontheatrical qualities of simple natural event, a game or a gag. It is the fusion of Spikes Jones, Vaudeville, gag, children's games and Duchamp.
	
	George Maciunas
	
	from: Happening & Fluxus
	       Materials put together by H. Sohm
	       Kölnischer Kunstverein 1970

Figure 6.5. "Fluxus" by George Maciunas from Happening and Fluxus, materials put together by H. Sohm, Kölnischer Kunstverein, 1970.

Figure 6.6. Mieko Shiomi and Alison Knowles during a performance of *"Disappearing Music for Face"* (smile-no smile) at the Washington Square (New York City) gallery on October 30, 1964.

Figure 6.7. Fluxus members (left to right): Emmett Williams, Robert Filliou, George Brecht, Eric Andersen, Thomas Schmit, Robin Page, and Ben Vautier at the exhibition of Happening and Fluxus at the Kölnischer Kunstverein in Cologne, Germany. Photo by Ad Petersen.

Biomusic

Biomusic, or music created by natural functions rather than by necessarily conscious attempts at composition, has taken some interesting turns in recent years. A number of composers have become interested in "brain-wave" music. Human and, for that matter, other advanced animals' brains function with bits of electric currents. Amplifying such energy produces enough current to serve as control voltages on synthesizer functions utilizing normal electronic music gear such as oscillators, filters, and so on. The brain directly controls sonic output.

"Brain-wave" experiments have created conflicting reports. Stockhausen notes:

> . . . I attended a concert in which David Tudor, together with a composer at Davis, California, where I taught for six months, were performing a piece with "brain waves." The performance, in the beginning, seemed to be very magic-like, a table lifting society, and it seemed to promise quite a lot because of the way they were watching and looking at each other. The speakers' cardboard membranes were pushing the air, and these pulsations—a kind of colored low noise—were produced by the performer's brain waves. It's the same effect as if air were being pumped into a tire. So what? There's a certain periodicity which becomes more or less irregular, maybe interesting for doctors.[28]

Composer David Rosenboom has developed procedures far more sophisticated than those described by Stockhausen.[29] Success, of course, remains in the "heads" of the *performers* and their necessarily practiced art of controlling *alpha* waves.

Possibly one of the most fascinating areas of biomusic is the sound of the humpback whale.

> Quite apart from any esthetic judgment one might make about them, the sounds produced by Humpback whales can properly be called songs because they occur in complete sequences that are repeated. . . . Humpback whale songs are far longer than bird songs. The shortest Humpback song recorded lasts six minutes and the longest is more than thirty minutes.[30]

Not only have recordings and tapes of the "songs" of the humpback whale become popular in and of themselves, but they have equally impressed composers. George Crumb's *Voice of the Whale* (*Vox Balaenae,* 1971) ". . . was inspired by the singing of the humpback whale, a tape recording of which I had heard two or three years previously."[31] Likewise, composers like Allen Strange and Priscilla McLean have completed works influenced by this most highly developed species of water mammals.

28. Jonathan Cott, *Stockhausen* (New York: Simon and Schuster, 1973), p. 43.

29. Prevalent in performances such as on the David Frost television show and others on NET (early 1970s).

30. Liner notes on Columbia ST–620, "Songs of the Humpback Whale."

31. Liner notes on Columbia M–32739.

Works involving a "rediscovery" of bioenvironmental sounds include Pauline Oliveros's *Sonic Meditation XIII.* Yehuda Yannay's *Bugpiece* involves yet another life form in a slightly different manner, but is definitely biomusic. The work uses "live notation" in the form of

> . . . one beetle, one centipede, and five or six ants. These insects were in a real sense the "composers" and conductors, even if Yannay did set up the parameters as to how the chance operations would work. All the lights in the auditorium were turned off, the overhead projector was turned on so the audience and performers (with their backs to the audience) could see the bugs running around in a plastic box set on the projector. Different areas of the "playing field" represented varieties of loud and soft. Green, yellow, and blue gels represented high and low pitches. The ants did most of the running, even one was maimed. The beetle stayed around the sides, but did make one mad dash across the field. To spark things up, the centipede was a late entry, and he chased the beetle.[32]

An even later entry into the "bio" scene, *plant-created music,* is described vividly in an article from *Rolling Stone:*

> It could be said they were singing, but that is too anthropomorphic a way to describe the sounds the plants were emitting: strange electronic garglings, ethereal chirpings and shriekings to a mysterious nonlinear rhythm that reveals the secret life-pulse of the vegetable kingdom. Then something very strange happened. A spectator gently held a knife to one of the stalks and addressed the plant. "Hey you! Perk up or you get it." The words plunged the room into sudden silence. The plants stopped singing. Coleuses may be pretty but they certainly aren't dumb. Somehow the threatened plant conveyed a warning of danger to its pot-mates, and they responded by entering a sort of suspended animation . . . discovery of an early-warning system among plants is just one of the revelations that have come to three electronic music specialists at Sounds Reasonable, Inc., a recording studio in Washington, D.C. There Ed Barnett, Norman Lederman and Gary Burge have been experimenting with ways to create music from the silent vibes of plants. So far their efforts have yielded a single, called *"Stereofernic Orchidstra"* . . . the record is a studio mix of four plants, an Indian azalea, a philodendron, a Boston fern and an amaryllis, recorded at the National Botanical Gardens. The first side features the raw plant "voices" tuned to different pitches on an oscillator. It sounds like a demonic, atonal violin section in electro-frenzy. On the second side the plants control the changes on an ARP music synthesizer. The result is more musical, but no less bizarre.[33]

John Cage speaks of his work in related areas:

> I've had for a long time the desire to hear the mushroom itself, and that could be done with very fine technology, because they are dropping spores and those spores are hitting surfaces. There certainly is sound taking place. . . . It leads, of course, to the

32. Clifford Barnes, "Music: Melody sent into exile," *Cincinnati Post,* November 15, 1972.

33. Jim Wiggins, "Lily Sings the Blues," *Rolling Stone,* September 12, 1975, p. 12. © 1975 by Straight Arrow Publishers Inc. All Rights Reserved. Reprinted by Permission.

thought about hearing anything in the world since we know that everything is in a state of vibration, so that not only mushrooms, but also chairs and tables, for instance, could be heard . . . I have a project . . . to amplify a city park for children. It was to be done at Ivrea near Turino. . . . There is a marvelous hill in the center of the city that is high and has a beautiful view of the Alps and is isolated enough from the traffic sounds so that you hear the sounds of the plants. . . . I was spoiled by that marvelous situation in Ivrea where the silence—when you weren't playing the plants—was very audible and beautiful; you could hear it as if you were in a concert hall. In other words, I wanted the silence of the mountain to be heard by the children after they had heard the sounds that they themselves had made by playing the plants. . . . Every now and then the plants were going to become unplayable, and the children would be obliged to hear the silence.[34]

Biomusic, while in and of itself representing some of the oldest forms of organized sound on earth, is still, as with most of the music described within this chapter, primarily natural *artifact* becoming *art in fact*.

Soundscapes

Many composers articulate aural expression in terms of natural sound quite apart from biomusic. Among these are many of Pauline Oliveros's *Sonic Meditations*.[35]

V:
Take a walk at night. Walk so silently that the bottoms of your feet become ears.

and

XVII:
Ear Ly
(For Kenneth Gaburo's NMCE)
1. Enhance or paraphrase the auditory environment so perfectly that a listener cannot distinguish between the real sounds of the environment and the performed sounds.
2. Become performers by not performing.

The latter work combines all available sounds of the organic and inorganic environments.

Other composers, such as I. A. MacKenzie, verbally express actions, or concepts that often contain written directions toward action, but without any reference to sound other than that inherent in the environment of the situation (Figures 6.8, 6.9). His "wind sound sculptures" (1930s) involve the principle of instruments played by wind (later, he also produced water and fire sculptures) and need neither performer nor audience (see Figure 6.10). The wish, before he died, of having these placed in places where humans would not be able to hear them, has been carried out, bearing close resemblance to the self-destructing sculptures of Jean Tinguely.

34. David Cope, "An Interview with John Cage," *Composer* 10, no. 1 (1980), pp. 6–22.
35. Copyright 1974 by Smith Publications. All Rights Reserved

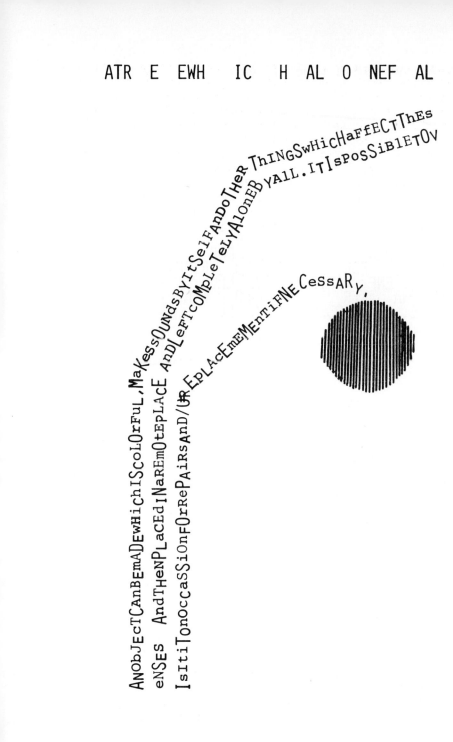

ATR E EWH IC H AL O NEF AL LS...

Figure 6.8. I. A. MacKenzie: *Environment.* Copyright by Discant Music, Los Angeles, California.

Figure 6.9. I. A. MacKenzie: *Environment*. Copyright by Discant Music, Los Angeles, California.

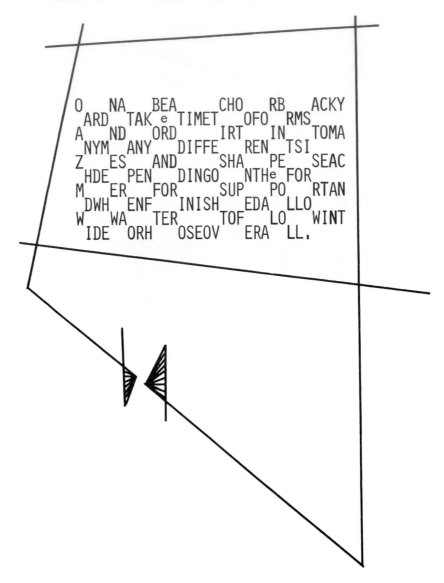

FEWeR LoVEs THaN tImE ALLoWS,...

The following excerpts from an interview between the author and MacKenzie in 1968, just three months before his death, represent his direction toward anti-ego in art. He considered the concert stage the archvillain of true equality of sounds.

I. A. M.: Basically, I was curious about the fundamental concept of whether I, or mankind for that matter, was really important in the functioning of music. . . . I still followed traditional notation . . . but demanded less and less skill from the performer since it was not to be had anyway . . . my preoccupation seemed to be

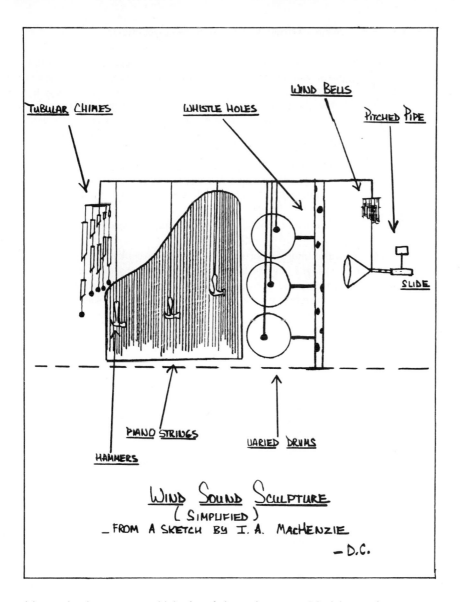

Figure 6.10. From *The Composer*, Vol. I, no. 1 (June 1969). Copyright by *Composer Magazine*, 1969.

with creating instruments which played themselves. . . . Musicians and composers . . . seem to delight in creating codes and systems that will separate them more from the common man and, I'm afraid, their audiences. . . .

D. C.: Was publication possible?

I. A. M.: Out of the question. By 1927 my music had become so involved in new instruments of my own invention, the publisher would have had to publish the instrument with the music. By 1930, I abandoned the written music completely anyway, believing that I should be more interested in sound than codes. . . .

D. C.:   . . . What was your . . . reaction (to universities)?

I. A. M.:   My reaction was harsh. . . . The teachers were very dull; more interested in talking *about* sound than *in* sound; mostly more interested in themselves. Many times I would hear visiting composers lecture on their works . . . only to find that the lecturer was just flesh and blood, not a god. . . . I found quickly that for me, at least, the university and its intellect and pomposity was creatively bankrupt: it offered nothing but security . . . and the same old traditional claptrap. . . . As long as people continue to raise gods, not people, the situation won't change. As long as so-called "great" performers are regarded as towering musical figures, instead of rather grotesque finger gymnasts, the situation won't change. The university has contributed to this as well, creating a caste system. . . .

D. C.:   . . . you say that around 1930 you began just creating instruments.

I. A. M.:   Yes. But, more important, instruments without human performers. By 1934, early spring, I had created my first wind-sound sculpture . . . an elaboration of the old Chinese wind chimes . . . in fact, that's where I got the idea. . . . I used to listen to storms approach through their sound and somehow felt I was "tuning in" on nature (nature being something I have always felt to be more impressive and profound than man or myself, to be exact). . . .

D. C.:   What do you consider yourself?

I. A. M.:   I don't. Categorizing, defining and such limit creativity. . . . Whether one thing is a work of art, and another not, is unimportant. This is cataloguing, not problem-solving. Problems are: God, beauty, nature; creating with or without them, or to them or from them. Creating is solving; cataloguing is avoiding. . . . I don't dislike systems or codes any more than money; but, as before, if these are used by someone to catalogue their own or someone else's work, they have become destructive rather than helpful. . . . I create what I like, in hopes that God, nature, and people (in that order) may like some or all of them. . . .

   . . . My sketches are, I suppose, my musical notation. However . . . when I create the work, I let it go its own way, and I sort of follow along. Problems of balance and so forth are worked out as I go along; intonation is achieved through experimentation until I have what I want. . . . I am in complete control of pitch, timbre, and . . . length. . . . I hope the sculpture will last forever, though forever is a long time (I think).

D. C.:   How do you regard the partially controlled aspects?

I. A. M.:   With joy. Certainly rhythm is partially controlled . . . and the same with harmony and melody, which are the least controlled.

D. C.:   Does it disturb you when, leaving the instrument alone, it is performing without human audience?

I. A. M.: Human audience? That's up to humans. It's never without an audience.
. . . I have been moving toward something, not away from something. I have never
maintained that I am right or even important; I am just doing what I think I can
do best. . . . I have learned two very important things about sound: (1) it exists,
period. No more, no less. There is no good or bad except in individual terms . . .
and (2) music (sound) communicates nothing. If I were to define (not categorize)
Art, I would have to say it is that which communicates nothing. Rather, it incites
or creates something new in each of us (I can say "Hello" and you can reply
"Hello." This is communication, bad as it is, but it is not Art. Art's beauty and
importance is that it does not communicate!) . . . *Sounds* hold an interest for me;
I don't give a damn how one produces them. . . .

One last thing: if one should consider the nightingale and its music and inspect
closely the battery of technique in use, he might reconsider his own bloated self-
view: certainly music is sound (the existence of the former term owes to social
implications only) and man, or even his life, has contributed little enough to
expand its vocabulary.[36]

Other artists have worked in similar areas. The German sculptor Hans Haacke,
a member of *Atelier 17* in Paris and a founder, along with Pene, Mack, and Vecker
of *Group Zero*, a group dedicated to breaking ties with the past of nonobjective art,
creates wind and water sculptures, as did Harry Bertoia. Japanese environmental
artist Shinoda creates elaborate metal sculptures with sound as a by-product. Composer Jon Hassell has recently explored acoustical environments and objects, and
large-scale outdoor sound-sculpture events, especially *Nadam,* a "sound-space" work.
His *Landmusic Series* (1969–72) is a combination of minimal music and soundscapes. Some are like the Oliveros *Sonic Meditations,* being but brief suggestions:
"Underground thunder spreading across an open field." Another in the series calls
for compact battery-powered speaker, microphone, and amplifier combinations to
be planted in trees to produce subtle sound amplifications of "wind, leaves, birds,
and squirrels who come near. . . ."[37] Terry Allen's three lead-covered eucalyptus
trees (1986) installed in San Diego are equipped with specially designed loudspeakers that gently call to passersby with Navajo chants, Aztec poems, and Thai
bands. The trees are inconspicuously hidden in a forest of eucalyptus on the campus
of the University of California, San Diego.

The struggle, gaining intensity in the late sixties, for the safety and revital-
ization of the environment holds close ties with the antiart movement. Besides the
creation of works that incorporate the environment without artistic distortion, the
direction implies an immaculate concept of nature, with distrust of man's creations
and re-creations in what appears to be their inherent destructiveness. Sound pollution, the aural by-product of twentieth-century convenience living such as the noise
of freeways, airways, refrigeration, has exponentially compounded the situation. The
need for *intensity* of sound to compensate for the increased level of accepted background noise subsequently leads to a battle over dominance between organized and
unorganized sound.

36. David Cope, "Chronicles of a Cause: I. A. MacKenzie," *Composer* 1, no. 1 (June 1969), pp. 35–
    42.
37. Tom Johnson, "New Music," *Musical America* 24, no. 11 (November 1974), p. MA–14.

The *World Soundscape Project* was designed to explore and note trends in man's relation to his sonic environment. Based in Canada near Vancouver, and directed by R. Murray Schafer, the project attempted to bring together research on the scientific, sociological, and aesthetic aspects of the environment and has five significant documents to date:

1. *The Book of Noise;*

2. *Okeanos* (a ninety-minute quadraphonic tape composition by Bruce Davis, Brian Fawcett, and R. Murray Schafer dealing with the symbolism of the ocean);

3. *The Music of the Environment* (an article on the concept of the World Soundscape; the first treatment of the acoustic environment as a macro-cultural composition);

4. *A Survey of Community Noise By-Laws in Canada;* and

5. *The Vancouver Soundscape* (a combination two-record set and booklet detailing a sonic study of the city of Vancouver and its environs, and concluding with two most significant chapters dealing in turn with "Noise Pollution Problems" and "Toward Acoustic Design").[38]

The records of this latter document include a variety of sounds, from surf to suburban baseball games. Most remarkable are the extremes of everyday sounds pinpointed in this collection; sounds that ". . . too often people ignore (or think they ignore). . . ."[39] The thrust of these concepts is focused in these comments taken from an open letter called "a brief introduction. . . .":

> Acoustics as a design study has been limited to closed environments: concert halls, sound-proof rooms and the like. It is time that acoustic design be applied to the environment as a great macro-cultural composition, of which man and nature are the composers/performers. To disguise an acoustic ambience with background music or masking noise, to block it out with ear muffs, cocoon-like sound-proof rooms or automobiles is not, in our view, a satisfactory solution to the problem of noise nor is it a creative approach to acoustic design.[40]

Within the framework of "Moozak at the Oakridge Shopping Mall" and "A Ventilator at Eaton's Department Store," one can hardly escape the immediate intimacy and beauty of "Full Surf . . . on a Gusty March Afternoon" or "Children's Voices, Recorded on the Playground of Seymour School. . . ."

38. Available from Sonic Research Studio, Communication Studies, Simon Fraser University, Burnaby 2, British Columbia, Canada.

39. From "A Brief Introduction to the World Soundscape Project": open letter by R. Murray Schafer, Peter Huse, Bruce Davis, Howard Broomfield, Hildegarde Westerkamp, Barry Truax, and Adam Woog, Vancouver, 1973.

40. Ibid.

Though quite a few years must pass before the trials of many of the experimental concepts and works included in this chapter expose their real contribution, their vitality and originality cannot be overlooked, regardless of their inherent threats to tradition.

1. Historical Background: Pauline Oliveros was born in Houston, Texas, on May 30, 1932, and studied composition at the University of Houston (1949–52) with Paul Koepe. She received her B.A. degree from San Francisco State College. She studied with Robert Erickson from 1954–60 and was co-director with Ramon Sender and Morton Subotnick of the San Francisco Tape Center from 1961 to 1965 and first-year director of the Mills Tape Music Center in 1966. In 1967 she became Professor of Music at the University of California at San Diego where she taught until 1981 when she retired to become a consulting director of the Creative Music Foundation at West Hurley in New York State. She currently resides in New York City and operates a foundation bearing her name. This organization dedicates its efforts to encouraging the creative efforts of other artists and especially collaborative and educational projects in the arts.

    Vectoral Analysis: Pauline Oliveros: Sonic Meditation XIII

    Oliveros is a professional accordionist who has added significant literature to that medium, including *The Wanderer,* with the twenty-two-piece Springfield Accordion Orchestra, and *Horse Sings from Cloud* (accordion and voice). Her work ranges from musique concrète to conceptual pieces. She explores the furthest edge of experimentalism without imitating others in the field. She has been an outspoken proponent of women's rights in a world of new music dominated by male composers.

2. Overview: The work of Pauline Oliveros, especially that of her conceptual period, requires serious analysis and direct involvement for a true understanding of intent and impact. Having been a performer under the composer's direction of this particular work in April, 1978, the author has realized in a very special way the focus and implications of the series of works titled *Sonic Meditations*. Figure 6.12 provides the entire score to *Meditation XIII.*

    Gone is the entire traditional assemblage of musical notations and directions. Here the composer merely assists the performers (read "audience") as a "horse to water." In performance, the group in which the author participated focused on a series of breathing exercises for relaxation while incense burned in the four corners of the concert hall. Then, lying on their backs in a feet-first circle, all explicitly followed the directions provided in the score. The "cycle" referred to in Figure 6.12 originated from the ensemble as a whole rather than any individual with such egocentric utterances or "solos" being implicitly destructive in the mind of the composer. Since loud sounds would disrupt the otherwise introspective posture of the experience, sounds from the performers invariably were as soft

Figure 6.11. "Training of musical consciousness is a large order." Composer Pauline Oliveros. Photo credit: Becky Cohen, Del Mar, Calif.

Figure 6.12. Pauline Oliveros: *Sonic Meditation XIII.*

Listen to the environment as a drone. Establish contact mentally with all of the continuous external sounds and include all of your own continuous internal sounds, such as blood pressure, heart beat, and nervous system. When you feel prepared, or when you are triggered by a random or intermittent sound from the external or internal environment, make any sound you like in one breath, or a cycle of sounds. When a sound or a cycle of sounds is completed re-establish mental connection with the drone, which you first established before making another sound or cycle of like sounds.

as those from the environment of the performance space, creating a cushion of sounds having little direction or impact. With the performance lasting twenty or more minutes, one could find no real beginning, and the ending seemed fashioned more by the exhaustion of the quiet and disarming fear of interruption rather than by a planned or composed sequence of events during the work.

3. Orchestration Techniques: With the environmental references in *Meditation XIII* one assumes that natural sounds, ones made by the voice or body, best serve the composer's wishes. These then follow the prescription of "listening" to the droning aspects of the performance area. Oliveros's use of the term "continuous" here voids most of the sounds one ordinarily finds in a daily environment. Natural drones are, in fact, difficult to find at all. Birds, dogs, and the like all take staccato and quasi-random forms, obviously not what she wishes us to contemplate. In the 1978 performance, a steady hum of the hall's heating system combined with a sixty-cycle hum from the electric lighting system provided the necessary drone elements. Internal sounds, such

as heartbeats or blood flow, were difficult to perceive. In fact, careful listening produced the hallucinatory effect that the aforementioned drones were, in fact, growing to a deafening roar. All participants used self-chosen humming variants in "breath"-length phrases on pitches matching as closely as possible those of the perceived drones. The resultant work was subtle and effete, not only minimal but fragile. Its consistency and dynamics created a suspension of the ordinary performance situation and, when the work seemed complete, the audience, mesmerized by the exhaustion of listening, did not applaud for minutes, providing a special magic to the concert.

4. Basic Techniques: This kind of prose format has been used successfully by a number of minimal composers. Critics suggest that these brief and poetic models contain no technique. Once in rehearsal, however, the predictability of the final outcome becomes obvious. Clearly, no two performances will be exactly alike. However, if the instructions are followed to the letter (critically important here), broad and lengthy vocalized pitches reinforcing the existing sounds in the performance space will be the rule. Since such is relatively predictable, at least in proscenium situations, one can reasonably expect similar results from one performance to the next.

5. Vertical Models: In five different run-throughs during rehearsals for the 1978 performance, and with three different sets of personnel, these consisted of one- to four-voice soft textures with hairpin articulations at the beginning and ending of each voice. The tuning is naturally based on the extant pitches of the drones encountered in the performance arena.

6. Horizontal Models: In the 1978 performance, a melody resulted in the entrance patterns of the four different voices. This varied depending on the various breath lengths of the individuals in the ensemble. Since so little happens during the performance, this becomes a very important feature of the work.

7. Style: Pauline Oliveros's *Sonic Meditation XIII* is a minimal work notated in prose English. If the instructions are followed exactly, a subtle work emerges through very soft and slow modulations of environment-reinforcing drones. This, and the other works in this series, are aptly named.

The Oliveros vectoral analysis points out similarities with Cage's *Cartridge Music* presented in the last chapter. Only general constraints are placed on performers who are within the guidelines laid out by the score free to explore a variety of possibilities. Surprisingly favorable comparisons can be made with the strictness in chapter 2, if one realizes the rigor of performance here compared to the rigor of compositional process in Webern's *Symphonie*. The lack of perceivable lyric qualities (in the traditional sense) argues with the works presented in the vectoral analyses in chapters 1, 3, 11, and 12 in particular.

Bibliography— Chapter 6*

Further Readings

Chronology and Fundamentals

Ahlstrom, David. "Footnotes for Mr. T." *Composer* 2, no. 1 (1970): pp. 25–31.

Austin, Larry. "Music is Dead, Long Live Music." *New York Times,* July 6, 1969.

Brindle, Reginald Smith. *The New Music: The Avant Garde since 1945.* 2d ed. New York: Oxford Press, 1988.

Brown, Anthony. "An Introduction to the Music of Morton Feldman." **asterisk* 1, no. 1 (1974).

———. "An Interview with John Cage." **asterisk* 1, no. 1 (1974).

Byron, Michael, ed. *Pieces: An Anthology.* Vancouver. A.R.C., 1975.

Cage, John. *Notations.* New York: Something Else Press, 1969.

———. *Themes and Variations.* New York: Station Hill Press, 1982.

———. *Empty Words.* Middletown: Wesleyan University Press, 1973.

Everett, Tom. "Five Questions: 35 Answers." *Composer* 2, no. 4 (1971): pp. 79–88.

Griffiths, Paul. *Modern Music: "The avant garde since 1945."* New York: George Brazillen, 1981.

Higgins, Dick. *A Dialectic of Centuries: Notes Towards a Theory of the New Arts.* 2d ed. West Glover, Vt.: Printed Editions, 1979.

Kostelanetz, Richard. *John Cage.* New York: Praeger, 1970.

———. *Conversing with Cage.* New York: Praeger, 1988.

———. *The Theatre of Mixed Means.* New York: Dial Press, 1968.

———. *Music of Today.* New York: Time-Life Books, 1967.

Motherwell, Robert. *The Dada Painters and Poets.* An Anthology. New York: Wittenborn, Schultz, 1951.

Palmer, Robert. "A Father Figure for the Avant Garde." *Atlantic Monthly,* May 1981, pp. 48–56.

Partch, Harry. "Show Horses in the Concert Ring." *Soundings* 1, no. 1 (1973).

Schafer, R. Murray. *Ear Cleaning.* Vancouver: BMI Canada Ltd., 1974.

Shattuck, Roger. *The Banquet Years.* New York: Vintage Books, 1968.

Danger Music

Higgins, Dick. "Boredom and Danger." *Source* 3, no. 1 (1966): pp. 14–17.

Johnson, Roger. *Scores: An Anthology of New Music.* New York: Schirmer Books, 1980.

Lentz, Daniel. "Music Lib." *Composer* 4, no. 1 (1972): pp. 6–16.

MacLow, Jackson. *An Anthology.* New York: Heiner Friedrich, 1970.

Nouge, Paul. "Music is Dangerous." *Soundings* 1, no. 1 (1973).

Conceptualism

Gaburo, Kenneth. *Collection of Works.* San Diego: Lingua Press, 1975.

Johnson, Roger. *Scores: An Anthology of New Music.* New York: Schirmer Books, 1980.

Johnson, Tom. *Imaginary Music.* New York: Two-Eighteen Press, 1974.

Knowles, Alison. *More by Alison Knowles.* New York: Printed Editions, 1976.

Moore, Carmen. "The Sound of Mind." *Village Voice,* December 24, 1970.

Nyman, Michael. *Experimental Music.* New York: Schirmer Books, 1974.

*Addresses for record companies, periodicals, and music publishers mentioned in this Bibliography can be found in Appendix IV.

Osterreich, Norbert. "Music with Roots in the Aether." *Perspectives of New Music* 16, no. 1 (1977): pp. 214–28.
Zimmerman, Walter. *Desert Plants.* Vancouver: A.R.C., 1976.

Biomusic

Henahan, Donal, "Music Draws Strains Direct from Brains." *New York Times,* November 25, 1970.
Huff, Jay. "An Interview with David Behrman." *Composer* 4, no. 1 (1972): pp. 29–32.
Johnson, Roger. *Scores: An Anthology of New Music.* New York: Schirmer Books, 1980.
Moore, Carmen. "The Sound of Mind." *Village Voice,* December 24, 1970.
Rosenboom, David, ed. *Biofeedback and the Arts: Results of Early Experimentation.* Vancouver: A.R.C., 1976.

Soundscapes

Comte, Pierre, "Leonardo in Orbit: Satellite Art." *Leonardo* 20, no. 1 (1987): pp. 17–21.
Corner, Philip. *I can walk through the World as Music.* New York: Printed Editions, 1982.
Davis, Bob, and Rich Gold. *Break Glass in Case of Fire.* Oakland: Mills College, Center for Contemporary Music, 1986.
Fontana, Bill. "The Relocation of Ambient Sound: Urban Sound Sculpture." *Leonardo* 20, no. 2 (1987): pp. 143–47.
Grayson, John. *Sound Sculpture.* Vancouver: A.R.C., 1977.
———. *Environments of Musical Sculpture You Can Build.* Vancouver: A.R.C. 1977.
Johnson, Roger. *Scores: An Anthology of New Music.* New York: Schirmer Books, 1980.
Oliveros, Pauline. "Many Strands." *Numus West* 3 (1973).
Osterreich, Norbert. "Music with Roots in the Aether." *Perspectives of New Music* 16, no. 1 (1977): pp. 214–28.

Pauline Oliveros

Oliveros, Pauline. *Software for People.* New York: Printed Editions, 1982.
Oliveros, Pauline, and Becky Cohen. *Initiation Dream.* Los Angeles: Astro Arts, 1982.

Compact Discs, Recordings, and Publishers

10 + 2:12 American Text Sound Pieces. 1750 Arch Records 1752.
Amirkhanian, Charles. *Lexical Music* (1973–77). 1750 Arch Street S–1779.
Anderson, Laurie. *Mister Heartbreak* (1984). Warner Brothers 25077–2.
Ashley, Robert. *Private Parts* (1979). Lovely Music LML–1001.
———. *Wolfman.* CPE-Source 2, no. 2. Source Records 4.
Austin, Larry. *Accidents.* CPE-Source 2, no. 2.
Budd, Harold. *Coeur D'Orr* (1969). Advance 16.
———. *Oak of Golden Dreams* (1970). Advance 16.
Cage, John. *Variations IV* (1963). Everest 3132.
Corner, Philip. *Ear Journeys: Water* (1977). Printed Editions.
———. *Rounds.* Soundings 3, no. 4:92.

Crumb, George. *Voice of the Whale.* C. F. Peters. New World NW–357–2.

Duchamp, Marcel. *The Bride Stripped Bare by Her Bachelors, Even, Erratum Musical.* Finnidar 9017.

Gibson, Jon. *Visitations* (1968–72). Chatham Square CS–LP–12.

Glass, Philip. *Einstein on the Beach* (1976). CBS M4K38875.

———. *Music in Fifths.* Chatham Square CS–LP–1003.

———. *Music in Similar Motion* (1969). Chatham Square CS–LP–1003.

———. *Music in 12 Parts* (1974). Virgin 91311–2.

———. *Music with Changing Parts* (1971). Chatham Square CS–LP–1001/2.

Hassell, Jon. *Vernal Equinox* (1978). Lovely Music LML 1021.

Leedy, Douglas. *Entropical Paradise* (1971). Seraphim S–6060.

Monk, Meredith. *Key* (1977). Lovely Music LML 1051.

Moran, Robert. *Four Visions* (1964). Universal Edition.

Oliveros, Pauline. *Accordion and Voice.* Lovely Music 1901.

———. *Sonic Meditations* (1974). Smith Publications.

Pearson, Tina, and Hildegard Westerkamp, eds. *Women Voicing.* Musicworks 31.

Reich, Steve. *Drumming* (1971). Nonesuch 9 79170–2.

———. *Four Organs* (1970). Angel S–36059.

———. *It's gonna Rain.* Columbia MS–7265.

———. *Music for 18 Musicians* (1976). ECM 1129–2.

———. *The Desert Music* (1984). Nonesuch 979101–2.

Riley, Terry. *A Rainbow in Curved Air* (1969). CBS MK–7315.

———. *In C* (1967). Celestial Harmonies 13026–2.

———. *Poppy Nogood and the Phantom Band* (1969). CBS MK–7315.

Rosenboom, David. *Portable Gold and Philosopher's Stones* (for brains in fours) (1972). A.R.C. ST–1002.

Rzewski, Frederick. *Coming Together* (1971). Soundings 3, no. 4. Hungaroton HCD 12545.

Satie, Erik. *Vexations.* Salabert.

Songs of the Humpback Whale. Columbia ST–620.

The Sounds of Sound Sculpture. A.R.C. ST–1001.

Stockhausen, Karlheinz. *aus dem Sieben Tagen* (1968). Universal Edition.

———. *Mikrophonie I.* Universal Edition. Columbia MS–7355.

The Vancouver Soundscape (1973). Sonic Research Studio, Canada. EPM 186.

Winsor, Phil. *Melted Ears* (1967). Carl Fischer. Advance S–14.

Young, La Monte. *Dream House* (1968–). Shandar 83.510.

EXTENDED MEDIA RESOURCES

7

Media forms involving music are the rational extension of composite forms such as ballet and opera. Many multimedia forms grew from experiments with "chance" relationships between simultaneously produced art forms (e.g., *happenings*).

Alexander Scriabin's *Prometheus—The Poem of Fire* (1910) is one of the first examples of mixed-media compositions with origins not directly related to opera or ballet. The scoring calls for large orchestra, chorus, piano, organ, and *clavier à lumières,* an instrument with a keyboard-controlled lighting console. The part for the *clavier à lumières* employs traditional musical notation, and each key is associated with a color. Scriabin directly ascribed tonal regions with colors as in *f* is blue, *the color of reason;* F, *the blood red of hell;* D, *the sunny key;* and so on. With *Prometheus* he envisioned far more than a superfluous "light-show." His concepts embodied a deeply philosophical and religious symbolism with beams and "clouds" of light moving throughout the hall. The chorus was to be draped in white robes and vocalize on vowel sounds. Unfortunately, *Prometheus* (which was completed in early 1910) was premiered in 1911 without the *clavier à lumières*—without any lighting at all, in fact. It waited until March 20, 1915, just five weeks before the composer's death, to receive any mixed-media complement at all. Even then only weak color projections moved on a small screen, falling considerably short of the composer's intentions.

Schoenberg's *Die glückliche Hand* (Op. 18, 1910–13) also required lighting effects, which proved technologically unfeasible. The resulting presentation was a poor realization of the composer's intent. *Prometheus,* at least, has had a media "revival" in the past few years, with numerous attempts made at fulfilling the composer's wishes. Unfortunately, most of the results seem diluted by the architecture of the concert hall's interior, or by the lack of real musical translation of sound into light.

The Dadaists and those who worked in the Bauhaus were among the first to openly confront media concepts; that is, try to *integrate* all the art forms available. While certainly one can trace other attempts through Wagner's *gesamtkunstwerk* back to Greek concepts, to do so would go beyond the scope of this book and thereby neglect unique attributes of the "audience participation" aspects of today's media

Background and Aesthetics

forms.[1] Aside from early commercial "shows" that employed perfumes (*The Song of Solomon* was performed in Paris in 1891 with sound, light, and perfumes, for example) and Scriabin's aforementioned *Poem of Fire,* which was not truly realized, Erik Satie's *Relâche* (1924) was one of the first landmarks in media forms. René Clair's film, also a landmark in cinematography for 1924, the understated Satie music, the ballet, the surrealistic scenery—all combined to create a vessel of often interplaying, often contradicting images.

Theatrical elements in new music seem to have closer historical ties with the ballet than with opera or oratorio. Though many mainstream composers, notably William Schuman and Aaron Copland, have created ballets for dance groups (especially for Martha Graham), it was John Cage and the Merce Cunningham dance group that injected theater into the combination of art forms, with each surviving by its dependence upon the other.

These directions, combined with the television-cinema age, and the need in electronic music for auxiliary visual material, have contributed largely to the contemporary revival of the *gesamtkunstwerk* concept in the form of "happenings." Richard Maxfield writes: "I view as irrelevant the repetitious sawing on strings and baton-wielding spectacle we focus our eyes upon during a conventional concert. Much more sensible either no visual counterpart or one more imaginatively selected such as lighting, cinema, choreography, fireworks, trees. . . ."[2] The sophistication of equipment and techniques of lighting and still and moving projections have made many new multimedia possibilities available to the twentieth-century artist-composer. Like all other facets of twentieth-century life, the new forms of art must inevitably share responsibility with the electromechanical environment in which they develop.

The aesthetics of media forms remain targets at which many an active as well as passive participant or bystander seem to take special aim. Coming to grips with the definitions and categorization of varieties of intentions involved may help in the conciliation of some antagonists. Two composers, Robert Ceely and Paul Goldstaub, tend to sum up the points of view quite succinctly:

Ceely: . . . it [multimedia] is most interesting in that it usually fails.

Goldstaub: The first time I conducted [Toshiro] Mayazumi's *Metamusic* (certainly a multimedia work of classic stature) it brought home the simple truth that people have overlooked for centuries: concert going is partially a visual and social experience, as well as musical. If composers can *use* this to enrich the quality of the experience of their music, everyone gains.[3]

---

1. The Bauhaus, founded by Walter Gropius in 1919, included very basic interdisciplinary media such as art, architecture, and design. Though short-lived (until 1933) it served as an example in the arts that has founded very solid ground for media studies in the American university.

2. As quoted in *An Anthology of Chance Operations,* La Monte Young and Jackson Mac Low, eds. (New York: 1963). No page numbers.

3. Tom Everett, "Questions and Answers," *Composer Magazine* 4, no. 1 (Fall-Winter 1972): pp. 20–21.

Multimedia is often used synonymously with a number of terms, most often *inter-media* and *mixed media*. Adding to the confusion are the terms *theatre pieces, merged-medium, environmental works, happenings,* and so forth. To avoid continuing this terminology explosion, the author defines three major categories of *media forms:*

1. Multimedia: This form is a loose structure in which the various media do not depend on each other for meaning. *Happenings* are excellent examples of multimedia events, in that each element is significant and structured in such a way that it could stand on its own merits.

2. Mixed media: This form tends toward equalization of elements, though any hierarchial order is possible. *Environments* more often than not fit this media form in that, though the elements are dependent on each other, "they are mixed, but not truly integrated."[4]

3. Intermedia: This form has all of its elements in equal balance and integrated to the fullest degree. *Merged-medium* fits this category well in that ". . . all elements are equal and integrated."[5]

A number of terms fall within these three main categories (some in more than one category as they may or may not attain balance or integration):

Multimedia	*Mixed media*	*Intermedia*
(loosely knit composite forms)	(more integrated with varying degrees of importance of elements)	(very integrated, each element depending on the others for the work to hold together)
Happenings	Opera	Merged-medium
Collage	Film and TV	Environments
Theatre pieces	Kinetic theatre	Films
Ballet		Meditations
Light-show		

4. Stanley Gibb, "Understanding Terminology and Concepts Related to Media Art Forms," *The American Music Teacher* (April–May 1973), pp. 23–25. This is possibly the most well thought out and formulated writing on this subject and is highly recommended to those seeking real insight into media art forms.
5. Ibid.

Two important factors must be considered carefully in observing the above listings:

1. Composers have been very flexible in their use of the preceding terms. Indeed, their use of certain terminologies may not fit the above chart. The author's own *Deadliest Angel Revision,* 1971, is a good example: it is billed as *multimedia* or a *theatre piece* when in fact it is *intermedia.* Therefore one cannot always accurately judge the composition by its "nomer."

2. None of the preceding classifications implies a quality judgment. Each is merely a starting point from which one can discuss the forms with some degree of consistency. Important works exist in each of the categories.

With this in mind it is necessary to note that the author has attempted to choose works that emphasize in particular each of the preceding categories.

Multimedia The summer of 1952 marked some of the first multimedia "happenings" when John Cage, David Tudor, Robert Rauschenberg, and Merce Cunningham teamed to play records, read lectures from stepladders, dance, use projections, and display "white paintings" at Black Mountain College, an interdisciplinary college that flourished in North Carolina from 1933 to 1957. The concept was a random sequence of nonrandom materials; that is, the order and combinations were chance, but the lectures, projections, and paintings in themselves were not. The resultant "theater" of events allowed each art form to remain isolated, contributing to the whole only as each performer reacted to another's event or personality.

April 17, 1958 introduced *Poème électronique* by Edgard Varèse at the Brussels World's Fair (see chapter 8). This multimedia presentation by Varèse, in collaboration with architect Le Corbusier, took place within a pavilion that was shaped externally like a three-peaked circus tent and internally like a cow's stomach. The composition, 480 seconds in length, was accompanied by projected images of paintings, written script, and montages. Neither of the artists made attempts at correlation between visual and aural images. The result produced occasional simultaneities of rhythm or spatial relationships, but more often separation of concepts. The intense organization of each artist's approach to his own material, however, was so apparent that correlation seemed almost inappropriate. The performance, attended by nearly three million people, remains as the most culturally significant representation of multimedia in history.

An important experimental media contribution developed during the late fifties and early sixties with the ONCE group in Ann Arbor, Michigan. Composers, artists, filmmakers, and architects focused their activities into the ONCE festival of contemporary music, the Space Theatre of Milton Cohen, the Cooperative Studio for Electronic Music of Robert Ashley and Gordon Mumma, and the Ann Arbor Film Festival of George Manupeli. Mumma's *Music from the Venezia Space Theatre* (1964), composed for Cohen's Space Theatre, was ". . . an hour long program of light projection, film, sculpture, modern dance and electronic music, and (first) performed by an ensemble of the ONCE group. The projected images of the Space

Theatre, which evolved continuously between the realistic and the abstract, were as diverse as the sound sources, and moved through the entire space surrounding the audience."[6]

Multimedia, as an offshoot of the American experimental school, has also developed along lines more indeterminate than structured. The thread of separation lies in the area of "theater": the necessity of partial indeterminacy for a play to "happen." Roger Reynolds's *Ping* (1968), based on a text by Samuel Beckett, is an excellent example of a somewhat improvisatory work that explores "theatrical" possibilities. Three performers (flute, piano, harmonium, bowed cymbal, and bowed tam-tam) create the "live" situation, augmented by a twenty-five-minute tape. The instruments are amplified using contact microphones. A twenty-two-minute film and 160 slides projected alternately to the left and right add visual material. Effects in and around the performance area are created by matrixed mirrors projecting secondary images, blurs, and colors: a cohesive factor enjoining sight and sound experience. The score[7], explicit as to materials, duration, pitches for the most part, and dynamics, allows improvisation from *all* performers, including the projectionists. For example, the projectionists may, within certain limitations, alter images through the use of such devices as filters and prisms. Reynolds's *The Emperor of Ice Cream* (1962) includes the projection of the score (both graphic and traditional in notation) for the eight singers, piano, percussion, and bass. Each projection, or score page, represents twenty seconds of time, and the position, movement, and "choreography" of each performer is indicated by dotted lines and the positioning of sound-symbols. Theatrical effects are written on the score in words, some as performance cues and others spoken, with performers becoming actors and dancers as well as musicians.

Morton Subotnick's *Ritual Electronic Chamber Music* involves four performers at "game boards" or lighted buttons for channel or amplitude of the electronic tape or one of four projections. Each performer's choice of which button to press sets up choices for other "players." In the center, a "High Priestess" moves about, playing lights on her body and moving the sound throughout the room. The work may be performed without an audience or in a very small chamber group of interested persons.

"Relevant action is theatrical (music [imaginary separation of hearing from the other senses] does not exist) . . ."[8] speaks John Cage of, among other things, the audience's ability to see and hear other sounds outside the performance area. Feelings, smells, and even tastes seem somehow neglected by most composers in the superficially imposed restriction of their creativity to sound alone. More often than not, Cage's approach to multimedia is philosophical: accept *all* sounds, sights, and other sensory experiences that occur in and around a performance situation, *equally,* regardless of their origin. This would include such things as car noises and coughs. Some of his works involve "stage" multimedia. *Water Walk,* for example, which

6. Gordon Mumma, Program notes on Lovely Music, VR 1091.

7. Roger Reynolds, *Ping,* as published in *Source: Music of the Avant-Garde* (Composer/Performer Edition) 3, no. 2 (July 1969): pp.70–86.

8. John Cage, *Silence* (Cambridge, Mass.: The M.I.T. Press, paperback edition, 1961), p. 15.

Figure 7.1. Morton Subotnick.

was first performed over Milan television in 1958 by Cage, who was a quiz show contestant, includes banging a rubber fish inside a piano on the strings, Cage watering a vase of roses, and a pressure cooker spurting steam, among other "props."

Whether initiated by determinate or indeterminate procedures, multimedia is the result of a natural concern by the composer and artist alike to allow and/or control *all* the aspects of the human sensory system within the framework of the performance situation. Peter Maxwell Davies's *Eight Songs for a Mad King* (see analysis, chapter 4) requires that the flute, clarinet, violin, and 'cello players sit in cages "representing, on one level, the bullfinches the King (George III) was trying to teach to sing . . . the percussion player . . . the King's brutal keeper, who plays him off stage at the end, beating a bass drum with a cat-o'-nine-tails."[9] While the visual forms of drama and setting contribute to live performance intensity, the significance of this highly acclaimed work is caught aurally on the recording. The media form is born in the listener's mind via program notes, while they listen to the record.

Boguslaw Schäffer is an active composer of theatre music and happenings. His *Audiences No. 1–5* (1964; see Figure 7.2) is "music for actors" with the texts by the composer, and involves projections, drama, and musical events. His happenings include *Non-stop* (1960) for piano, with a duration varying from 6 to 480 hours, and *Incident* (1966) for an "ensemble" of *audience* which lasts 4 hours.

George Crumb's *Voice of the Whale (Vox Balaenae)* (1971), like the Davies work, has multimedia aspects that are related to live performance only and that in no real way detract from the music by their absence when the music is recorded. The composer requests that the performers wear black visors and the stage be bathed in deep blue light. Clearly, the music can easily stand alone, and the visual aspects, though interesting in performance, are by no means absolutely essential to the work. The music retains its artistic identity without the visual complement.

Multimedia techniques have invaded *rock* idioms, with extraordinary results. The Velvet Underground, for example, toured America as a part of Andy Warhol's

9. Liner notes on the recording (Nonesuch H-71285) by Peter Maxwell Davies.

Figure 7.2. Boguslaw
Schäffer: *Audiences No. 4.*

mixed-media show *The Exploding Plastic Inevitable* in the mid-sixties. Pink Floyd's 1980 performance of *The Wall,* an extensive light show, proved influential in commercial circles. The group played in front of and behind a huge wall (seventy-feet high) that was both constructed and destroyed during performance. Multidirectional speaker setups, along with complicated lighting and projections, contributed to the ambitious multimedia event. Led Zeppelin's laser shows and Funkadelic have since developed extensive media programs. Visual theatrics seemed almost a requisite for rock performances in the 1980s, with Devo and other *new wave* groups equally preoccupied with visuals and sound effects. Kiss, Ted Nugent, Black Sabbath, Alice Cooper, and Ozzy Ozborne all contributed to a diverse popular multimedia and theatrical culture.

Work by Nam June Paik and James Searight in the area of video feedback (camera focused directly into the screen to which it feeds; i.e., looping) create interesting potential for the multimedia composer. Allan Kaprow catalogs some of his basic concepts for multimedia categories in the following ways:

a. The line between art and life should be kept as fluid, and perhaps indistinct, as possible. . . .
b. Therefore, the source of themes, materials, actions, and the relationships between them are to be derived from any place or period *except* from the arts, their derivatives and their milieu. . . .
c. The performance of a Happening should take place over several widely spaced, sometimes moving and changing locales. . . .
d. Time, which follows closely on space consideration, should be variable and discontinuous. . . .
e. Happenings should be performed once only. . . .
f. It follows that audiences should be eliminated entirely.[10]

10. Allan Kaprow, Assemblage, Environments & Happenings (New York: Abrams, 1966), unpaged.

Clearly these techniques revoke the basic tenets of Western-world artistic heritage and begin important contributions to the experimental arts. Other composers and artists involved in these techniques include Jean-Jacques Lebel, Wolf Vostell, George Brecht, and Kenneth Dewey.

Mixed and Intermedia

When superficially imposed definitions of art exist psychologically within audiences, domination of one art form over another can exist. Projected scores or performer-interpreted projections share equally the difficulty of misinterpretation; "music seen" or "paintings as sound" represent displacement of traditional dogmatic categorization of the arts. Daniel Lentz's *Sermon* (1970) for string quartet modified by electronic filters, reverberation, ring modulation, and gate device involves score projection. Once a score is visible to the audience it becomes obvious that it must be made visually interesting and artistic. Lentz has solved this problem by creating an artistic score in color: red = played, blue = sung, green = hummed, yellow = whistled, violet = spoken, brown = whispered, with an orange line surrounding the score page referring to time one half-inch representing one second. The result is greater visual excitement *and* more meaningful notation for the performers.

Allen Strange's *No Dead Horses on the Moon* requires seven 16mm projectors to surround the audience with visual images (see Figure 7.3). The recorded sound, projected from the four corners of the room, surrounds the audience. Correlation between visual and aural materials is obtained by written instructions to the performers (in this case the projectionists). In No. 6, for example, the projectionist is instructed to move a projector. The films are created by scraping the emulsion from 16mm black leader film and then constructing loops, creating a sevenfold visual ostinato (see example). The resulting flashing dots, lines, and "strobe" effects, along with the sound, engulf the audience in an imaginative "light show."

At the same time, these concepts alter a basic concert ritual of audience-performer separation. Robert Ashley's *Public Opinion Descends Upon the Demonstrators* (1961) embraces the ideal of "total theater." Specific prerecorded sounds are produced by a single performer on electronic playback equipment only when a member of the audience acts or reacts in a certain manner by speaking, glancing, looking about, gesturing, looking toward a loudspeaker, or leaving. Whether or not performance precludes knowledge on the part of the audience of the compositional concept, it soon becomes obvious that all participants, including the composer, performer, and audience, share equal responsibility in creating the work.

Barton McLean's *Identity* series of compositions deal directly with man's relationship with his surroundings, perception of a work in a complete environmental setting, and audience control over sounds. More complete and detailed than Stockhausen's *Musik für ein Haus* or Sigmund Krauze's experiments with environmental

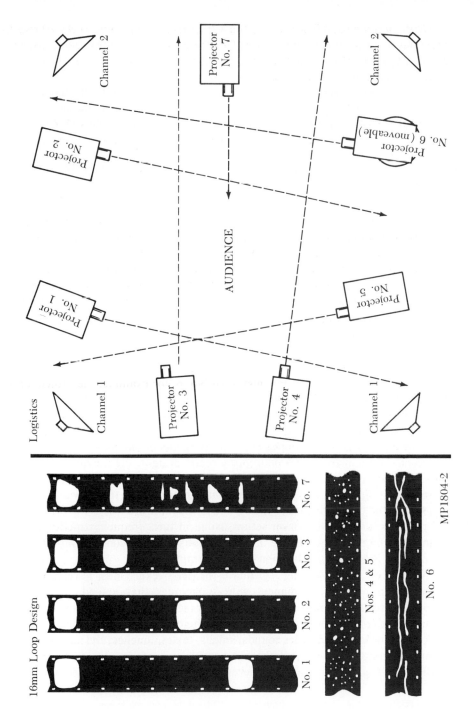

Figure 7.3. Allen Strange: *No Dead Horses on the Moon.* (Copyright Media Press, Champaign, Ill., 1969. Used by permission. All rights reserved.)

music in Germany and Poland, McLean's *Identity* series includes works for specific buildings and situations. One of these (for the Cultural Center in South Bend, Indiana) is, in the composer's words:

> . . . a true environmental experience in that the hearer who walks through it reacts to the sounds both passively and actively. This latter aspect, perhaps the most unique in its conception, although allowing for the overall direction and control of the work to remain in the hands of the composer, nevertheless provides to the listener the opportunity to participate in smaller, but highly meaningful choices. Thus, the hearer, in exercising creative choices of his own which shape the smaller details of the work, enters into the actual creative experience. Furthermore, no musical training is necessary for this interaction, since it is set up so that all choices made by the hearer on this smaller structural level are equally valid. On the other hand, for those who have more time and intuitive ability, it is possible to grow with the work and, upon repeated hearings, to exercise intelligent choices on gradually higher and higher planes.[11]

The building is controlled in terms of lighting, speaker activity, and so on by the audience motion that triggers a wide variety of sounds. By movement and by the audience's discovery of the planned placement of photoelectric cells, microphones, and various visual control devices, the building becomes a self-contained environment.

Figures 7.4 and 7.5 show the extent to which media techniques have become sophisticated during the past few years. These diagrams represent two of the media aspects of the Learning Resources Center at Middle Tennessee State University in Murfreesboro. The figures demonstrate the potential of media in education, the sciences, and communications, as well as in the arts.[12]

Ron Pellegrino has developed laser scanning and projection systems that extend electronic music instrumentation into the realm of light. Figure 7.6 shows a simple laser scanning system. Sound from a synthesizer, computer, or collection of function generators, controls a power amplifier that in turn uses the galvanometer and "chopper" for the projection of a single laser beam into three components. Figure 7.7 presents three possible laser setups using, in turn, frequency modulation (first example); frequency, amplitude, and ring modulation (second example); and frequency and amplitude modulation (third example).

Composers, often lacking legitimate theater backgrounds, have consequently allowed improvised performances with techniques that extend beyond "time-honored" Greek concepts. Paul Ignace's *Feast* (1964) is a good example of just such a mixed-media work. The audience is given choices of sensual experiences based on a provided menu that includes sounds, smells, tastes, touches, and sights. The composer does not evoke *certain* responses but evokes as many different responses as possible. In *Feast* mixed media achieves the ideal philosophy implied and inherent

---

11. The quote from the composer is from materials about the work made available to the author.

12. More information on this most interesting media center is available from the Director of the Learning Resources Center at Middle Tennessee State University.

environmental simulation
equipment that will provide
a controllable temperature
range of 30°-100°F
and a humidity range of 20%-90%

domed ceiling capable
of having images
projected onto it

projectors provide
360° screen coverage

upper level catwalk

Astro-Turf

Control Center

ELECTRONIC MEDIA
THEATRE

LEARNING RESOURCES CENTER
MIDDLE TENNESSEE STATE UNIVERSITY

Figure 7.4. Electronic media theatre. Permission granted by the Learning Resources Center, Dr. Marshall Gunselman, Director; Middle Tennessee State University.

LIGHTING   THREE COLORS,
CONTINUOUSLY VARIABLE INTENSITY

TEMP. WIND HUM. EXHST.   RAIN   ODOR

OUTPUT DEVICES

OUTPUT MODIFIERS

LOGIC LEVELS

POWER LEVELS

DIGITAL
CONTROL
CONSOLE

REMOTE DEVICES

(Diagram does not denote number of devices. See specs.)

Figure 7.5. Remote devices. Permission granted by the Learning Resources Center, Dr. Marshall Gunselman, Director; Middle Tennessee State University.

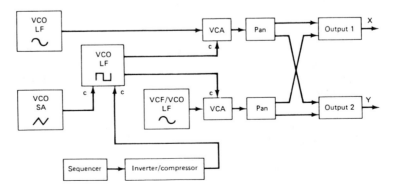

Chapter 7

within its thesis: no action (relevant or not) can be considered unimportant to the totality of a work. The distinctions between "theater" and "reality" eventually fall away.

Figure 7.8 shows two views (the first exploded) of *Pavilion,* completed in 1969 in Japan. This extraordinary building was the site for many mixed-media compositions, some of which included theater and dynamic effects such as enshrouding the building in fog, mirroring the internal ceiling, and so on. A wide range of stylistically different composers have used the facility for exploration and performance.

Mauricio Kagel's *Match* (for two violoncelli and percussion) is a dramatic game that unfolded in full-blown detail to the composer in a dream. Characterized by visual humor, which met with immediate applause at its premiere in Berlin in October of 1965, it is strikingly serious music, leading to what the composer has called a "shaking concert of derision" at the end of the first live performance.[13] The intense and dramatic music, when fused with the visual wittiness, results in a complicated collage of constantly varying grades of emotional polarities. Regarding a portion of *Match* the composer has noted:

> During the first rehearsal of these uncertain measures I was told by the interpreters that the passage in question reminded them of the most memorable of the *circene* scenes: the death leap. Such an appreciation was already known to me; the similarity between this situation with what was dreamed a few weeks previously left no room for doubt: both musicians were suspended in mid-air with their cellos on top of their heads and by means of slow pirouettes they produced very sharp, brilliant sounds. The roll of the drum, that from some point in space resounded over the entire environment, maintained the spectators in pure tension until leading to an aggressive attack on the cymbal. Thus was overcome the first of the mortal leap with good fortune.[14]

Possibly one of the most prolific and well-known mixed-media composers is Robert Moran. His *Hallelujah* for twenty marching bands, forty church choirs and organs, carillons, rock groups, a gospel group, and the entire city of Bethlehem, Pennsylvania was first performed in 1971 and is truly a landmark in mixed-media performance. His earlier *39 Minutes for 39 Autos* for thirty-nine amplified auto horns, auto lights, Moog synthesizer, thirty skyscrapers, radio stations, a television station, dancers, and others, first performed on August 29, 1969 in San Francisco, provides further example of equally staggering proportions. Of these the composer has remarked:

> In my work, *39 Minutes for 39 Autos,* I attempted to make everyone a musician. One hundred thousand persons participated in the premiere. My *Hallelujah,* commissioned by Lehigh University, used hundreds of musicians . . . in this composition I tried to make every musician a human being.[15]

13. Mauricio Kagel, "On Match for Three Performers," *Composer* 3, no. 2 (Spring 1972); translated from *Sonda #3* (Juventudes Musicales, Madrid) June 1968, pp. 70–78.
14. Ibid., p. 73.
15. Robert Moran in a letter to the author.

Figure 7.8. Schematic drawings of the main building of *Pavilion* in Japan, 1969.

Figure 7.9. Mauricio Kagel.

Moran's works embrace an incredible variety of mixed-media explorations. *Divertissement No. 1* (1967) for popcorn, electric frying pan, and any instrumental soloist, for example, requires the performer to read popping corn as noteheads on five-lined white-staved dark sunglasses. *Bombardments No. 4* (1968) for trombone and tape, commissioned by Stu Dempster, requests that the trombonist, wrapped in a sack, become a visual analog gargoyle with legs, slide arms, and body movements all sharing in the vision of struggling shape, lit dimly from both sides, and its aural counterpart.

In general, film music does not qualify as a particular significant exploration of media forms. There are, however, a number of exceptions that should be noted. Aside from *Relâche* (1924) by René Clair mentioned previously, work by composer John Whitney and his brother James is particularly significant. Beginning in 1940 they began their experiments with abstract film and infrasonics, a series of pendulums mechanically connected to a wedge-shaped aperture and influencing an optical sound track producing sine wave oscillations with a frequency range of a little more than four octaves. Like the sound track notations of Norman McLaren (discussed in chapter 8), the Whitney experiments have provided a vast new source of media materials. John Whitney speaks to this point:

> It is hoped that the partnership of sound and picture will attract the attention it deserves in artistic circles. The problem that confronts the individual consists of a number of difficulties whose acquaintance he may already have made in the course of his experiences in modern music or painting. Whether the necessary technical apparatus will always be placed at the disposal of the artist is a question that touches on an elementary problem, whose solution lies hidden in the darkness of the future.[16]

16. John Whitney, "Moving Pictures and Electronic Music," *Die Reihe* 7 (1960): p. 71.

Salvatore Martirano's *L'sGA* (1968) is a massive and intense mixed-media work overloading the senses with dramatic, visual, and aural messages. *L'sGA,* in the composer's words, is

> Lincoln's *Gettysburg Address* for actor, tape, and film, using a helium "bomb" which the actor breathes from at the end of the piece so that his voice goes up a couple of octaves . . . all you need to do is catch a few words now and then to understand what the meaning is. You hear "government" and you hear "people." And thus I would hope that the person watching would create the framework of specific and exact meaning according to how he sees things. Because I'm not forcing him to catch on to a sequence of events in which each one has to be understood for the next one to make sense. It's almost kind of throwing it in all different places and gradually, I would hope, the conception is built up in the audience.[17]

Groups devoted to mixed-media performance include ZAJ (pronounced *thack;* a Mexican Theater of the Absurd); THE; Harkins and Larson (formed in 1975 at CME in San Diego); and individual performers such as Stuart Dempster whose performance of Robert Erickson's *General Speech for Trombone,* 1969, is most notable.

Figure 7.10 is from *Metabiosis V: A Light, Sound and Audience Environment* (1972) by Ronald Pellegrino. The total environment system is explored in this world[18] with the incorporation of the given space and natural variables an intrinsic part of the design. Merrill Ellis's *Mutations* for brass choir, electronic tape, and light projections is a dramatic and integrated approach to intermedia. The work begins with a standard concert setting. Suddenly the hall is plunged into darkness, the players leave the stage making vocal and other unusual sounds and, with the electronic tape becoming the main aural source, projections in the form of films, lights, and so on, flash on the ceiling and walls, engulfing the audience in a "sea" of visual activity. *Mutating* the ABA form, the players return to the rear of the hall and perform again under a dim flashing light. The work concludes in total darkness and silence.

Landscape Journey (1963) by Donald Scavarda, for clarinet, piano, and film, reflects the contrasting elements of aural and visual materials. Sections of sound alone interplay with soundless projections to create an obvious alternating formal structure. The abstract fast-moving shapes and colors on two screens balance the contrast and dependence of the two instruments in use.

Scavarda speaks of the intermedia implications in his work:

> . . . these sounds (are synthesized) with abstract color film to create a filmic extension of the instrumental timbres. The plasticity of the slowly shifting instrumental timbre is further "pushed" by the use of dramatic silences and contrasts with the rapidly moving film which is gradually introduced as the work evolves. . . . Here the film does not have a notational function but rather is an intrinsic part of the structure of the piece. Thus, timbre is perceived visually as well as aurally. The two projectors, placed immediately in back of the piano bench, are "performed" by the pianist, who also operates a rheostat controlling a single lamp (which lights the scores) in an otherwise darkened hall.[19]

17. Panel Discussion: *ASUC Proceedings* 3 (1968): p. 43.

18. *Thinking for the Electronic Music Synthesizer* (chapter 6) as outlined in *ASUC Proceedings* 7, no. 8 (1972–73), pp. 52–59.

19. From a letter to the author.

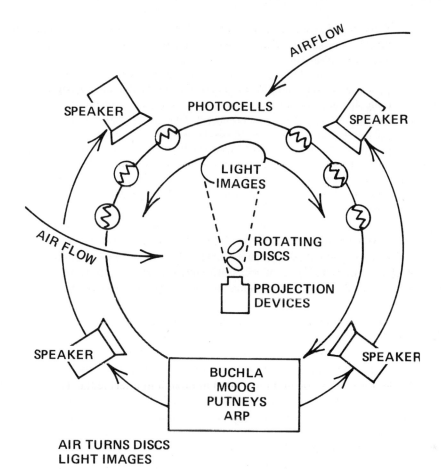

SPEAKER

AIRFLOW

PHOTOCELLS

SPEAKER

LIGHT IMAGES

AIR FLOW

ROTATING DISCS

PROJECTION DEVICES

SPEAKER

SPEAKER

BUCHLA
MOOG
PUTNEYS
ARP

AIR TURNS DISCS
LIGHT IMAGES

Figure 7.10. *Metabiosis V: A Light, Sound, and Audience Environment* by Ron Pellegrino. Used by permission of *Proceedings* of the American Society of University Composers 7/8 (72–73) © ASUC, Inc., c/o American Music Center, 210 Broadway, Suite 15–79, New York, N.Y. 10023.

Figure 7.11. Merrill Ellis (photo by Ron Bray: North Texas State University, Electronic Music Center, Denton, Texas).

Videos

> The TV extension of our nerves in hirsute pattern possesses the power to evoke a flood of related imagery in clothing, hairdo, walk and gesture. All this adds up to the compressional implosion—the return to nonspecialized forms of clothes and spaces, the seeking of multi-uses for rooms and things and objects in a single word—the iconic. In music, poetry and painting, the tactile implosion means the insistence on qualities that are close to casual speech. Thus Schoenberg and Stravinsky and Carl Orff and Bartók, far from being advanced seekers of esoteric effects, seem now to have brought music very close to the condition of ordinary human speech . . . the great explosion of the Renaissance that split musical instruments off from song and speech and gave them specialist functions is now being played backward in our age of electronic implosion.—Marshall McLuhan from *Understanding Media*

In music videos, composers have the opportunity to correlate their rhythmic and timbral techniques with the visual arts, roaming freely (because of the advent of sophisticated digital editing machines) between reality and the abstract. Monitor screen size and the home videocassette machine allow for intimate viewing and possibilities of a nonlinear experience in the ability to freeze-frame, fast-forward, and otherwise create your own version of the video. In certain styles of music (predominantly rock) the music video has become a staple of the medium, more secure in some ways than the more traditional aural-only performance of records, compact discs, and tapes. While slower to develop in the *avant-garde,* certain composers and idioms have found themselves immediately successful in this format.

In the 1960s, Nam June Paik began to study the television (video) medium seriously. Experiments with video feedback and loops as well as other abstract techniques proved seminal in the history of the medium as an art form. More recently, Robert Ashley has used videos as a part of the theater he creates. As these pioneers have developed significant alternatives to its naive and often commercial use, other composers have turned to the medium that may have the single biggest technological impact in the music world; note the incredible success of *MTV.*

To date, experimentation in music videos relevant to this book has been somewhat limited to five areas or styles: (1) *avant-garde* jazz, (2) New Age music, (3) performance art, (4) minimalism, and (5) experimental rock. Each of these seems especially well suited to the medium with each able to have real-world equivalents to their form. For example, the nightclub performance tradition of jazz fits the visual experience of the video format. In performance art, seeing has equal impact to hearing. New Age music, discussed more thoroughly in chapter 11, has ambient overtones that metaphorically suggest real-world equivalents such as waves, meadows, waterfalls, and so on, and minimalism, with its lack of material, seems only heightened by the hallucinatory music video. It is clear that all work with video will not be limited to these five styles; however, for the reasons presented, it is most useful to direct our attention to them in particular.

Aside from the standard video camera recording of jazz group performances, the following stand out as examples of good work in both the visual and aural fields. The video by The Art Ensemble of Chicago (1982 University of Illinois performance—fifty-two minutes), called "Live from the Jazz Showcase," creates a surreal blend of dance, costume, and music. The performers wear masks and body paint and dance while the music fuses American jazz with African traditional music. Directed by William Mahin, the video is a collection of long shots and close-ups that artfully capture the extraordinary nature of the performance. Likewise, "The New Music" (1985, directed by Peter Bull and Alex Gibney), by Bobby Bradford and John Carter, represents an Ornette Coleman–derived free-jazz experimentation. This is a brief portrait of the performers during an *avant-garde* performance using a variety of instrumental exploration techniques. Elvin Jones's "Different Drummer" (1984, directed by Edward Gray) is an explosive documentary of the drummer's life and unbridled performance techniques. In contrast, the Weather Report video titled "The Evolutionary Spiral" (1984, directed by Larry Lachman) is an abstract work that strives to "travel from the birth of the universe, through ancient cultures and the high tech world of today, then on to a vision of art in the future . . ." (from the cover of the cassette).

New Age videos represent the work of composers like Mark Isham, William Ackerman, George Winston, and Alex De Grassi. Most notable of their recent issues is "Autumn Portrait" (1985, directed by Stanley Dorfman). The soft ambient music mirrors the autumnal New England that washes across the screen. No apparent correlation is made from image to sound; however, the tempo seems linked to the speed of camera motion. The various works each blend into the next with no distinction save their different instrumentation. Brian Eno's "Thursday Afternoon," directed by Eno in 1986, creates an extremely slow moving abstract portrait of Christine Alicino with a backdrop of very soft ambient music by the composer.

With the advent of composer/performers such as Laurie Anderson and many others, video provides the perfect medium for melding their visual-physical actions with their music. Yoko Ono's "Then and Now," directed by Barbara Braustark in 1984, attests remarkably to these possibilities in the *then* part of the video—for example, many "happenings" and "bag art performances" of the 1960s are relived with John Lennon. The *now* portion reveals Ono through a series of intimate interviews and reflections on those performances.

In the minimalistic school of video, Philip Glass's *Koyaanisqatsi* stands out. Directed by Godfrey Reggio, this work, originally a film made in 1984, uses only image and music in a tapestry of natural and unnatural scenes with slow and fast camera speeds mirrored in the tempi of the music. There is no narrative here or need of one; it is beautifully photographed by Ron Fricke and mesmerizing in effect.

Most rock video follows the formulaic traditions of television and media in general and warrants little but social commentary. A few performers, works, and visuals, however, have significant merit when viewed separately from the onslaught of other types in the stream that rails from various cable TV stations. "The Mothership Connection Live from Houston," for example, by George Clinton and the Parliament-Funkadelic (1986), directed by Archie Ivey, Peter Conn, and Wayne Isham, represents what some have called the "post-hippie funk-rock traveling circus." This video has an assortment of live performances and shorter video clips, one of which, "Atomic Dog," is a classic music video with computer animation and appropriate musical accompaniment. "Danspak," directed by Merrill Aldighieri and Joe Tripician (1983), represents rock music from a number of *avant-garde* underground artists of New York City. The group Devo, visually interesting in live performance, makes the natural transition to music videos in their "The Men Who Make Music" (1979, directed by Charles Statler and Gerald Casale) and "We're All Devo" (1983, directed by Gerald Casale). The former was, by some accounts, the first rock video ever made. The latter is technically professional and conceptually masterful. It also includes "Worried Man" by Neil Young, a work from his never-released "Human Highway." Laurie Anderson's *Home of the Brave* is a fascinating filmic work with political overtones. Pink Floyd's video of "The Wall," while it does not do justice to the live performance, has nonetheless classic footage of this amorphous rock quasi-opera. "Gimme Shelter" (1981, directed by David Maysles, Albert Maysles, and Charlotte Zwerin) is a video-verité of the 1969 Altamont Speedway concert of the Rolling Stones. The video includes the murder of Meredith Hunter in what must be the most horrifying moments on tape. Except for this, however, the classic action of the veteran and venerable group is classic. The chaotic camera work only heightens the effect of being in this nightmarish scene.

The art of video making has had immense impact on motion photography. The opportunity of immediate playback with built-in replay monitors, for example, as well as the inexpensive nature of videotape (as opposed to film) have added to the extraordinary popularity of the medium. Large-scale video projectors have likewise expanded the potential for theater presentation. Thus video is *the* future of film and hence the future for those composers and performers interested in the extended media applications of their work. When digital editing equipment prices fall into the general market range, the tendency for most performance-oriented musicians, even traditional concert hall performers, will be to tape their performances, if only for personal uses. These will be archived, becoming the next in a series of technological tools begun with the work of Edison on the cylinder tape recorder in the nineteenth century.

As with laser beams, videos may also have direct audio control of imaging through MIDI interface mechanisms. Very Vivid of Toronto has created such an instrument called *Mandala*. Video animation effects may be generated directly from a composition in virtually hundreds of combinations. Since digitized music and digitized visual images represent the same kind of data, they may be mixed, controlled, generated, and edited in a wide variety of ways, allowing composers to interrelate directly with visual imagery and vice versa.

Vectoral Analysis: Donald Erb: *Souvenir* (1970)

(For information on vectoral analysis and procedures, see chapter 1).

1. Historical Background: Donald Erb was born in Youngstown, Ohio, in 1927. After early years as a jazz trumpeter, he studied composition formally with, among others, Bernard Heiden at Indiana University and Nadia Boulanger. His major works include *Symphony of Overtures* (1964)

Figure 7.12. Donald Erb.

and *The Seventh Trumpet* (1969) for orchestra, *Harold's Trip to the Sky* (1972) for chamber ensemble, and *Concerto for Percussion and Orchestra* (1966).

Souvenir, for dancers, instrumental ensemble, electronic tape, projections, and props, was completed early in 1970 and first performed in February of that year at Oberlin College. Laurence Berger (dance) and Royce Dendler (sculpture) premiered the work and created subsequent performances in northern Ohio.

2. Overview: *Souvenir* is an eight-and-a-half-minute work of driving intensity. The sonic form of the work derives from the skeletal scoring for the twelve to twenty wind and percussion players, who surround the audience in the dark, and the electronic tape created from electronic sources in the Cleveland Institute of Music electronic laboratory. The tape portion exists throughout the work and consists of a slightly out-of-tune "perfect" fifth interval (B—F♯), which acts as a continual drone. The live performers begin during the second minute signaled by the conductor, whose primary job is to flash a light cue at the end of each minute during the performance. All play *pianissimo* using either long tones within a minor second of either of the tape pitches or short pointillistic effects on their respective instruments. These slowly and consistently grow throughout the piece until the *crescendo* reaches *fortissimo* at around seven-and-a-half minutes. The parts are written in English and are easy to memorize, which is almost a necessity, since the piece is performed in the dark.

Elements are added according to the following schematic:

Minutes:		Action:
0–1		Nothing; just tape
1–2		Players quietly begin to play
2–3		Slide projections begin
3–4		Dancers enter
4–5		Weather balloons are added
5–6		Silly string is sprayed
6–7½		Continue
7–8½		(or end) Conductor strikes gong, signaling ping-pong balls to be "dumped"

The hall is filled with "black light" which is nonvisible light that excites certain luminescent paints. The dancers, covered with luminescent tape, bring small props (i.e., sponge rubber balls of various sizes) also covered with luminescent paints of various colors, all of which glow in the dark. The projections (optional) are of the performers' choice, but fit in with the joyous, positive nature of the work and not so bright as to nullify the effect of the black lights. The weather balloons, eight to twelve feet in diameter war surplus balloons, are also covered with luminescent paints and bounced into the hall, whereupon the audience usually begins to participate. Luminescent "silly string" is sprayed into the whole auditorium, inundating the performers and audience. The ping-pong balls (about 5,000) have been painted with luminescent paint and fall into the audience becoming "souvenirs" of the performance. The activity clearly accelerates in correspondence with the sounds: a singular and direct *crescendo* from beginning to end.

3. Orchestration Techniques: The taped perfect-fifth drone is created by sawtooth waves drawn through low pass filters. These in turn are slowly adjusted so that the timbre is continually altering during performance. The slight "beating" of the inharmonic fifth also contributes to the perception of change.

   The live performance ensemble is free enough so that exact sounds are unpredictable. It is interesting to note, however, that the long tones, in the interval of seconds with the tape, create subtle shifts in motion and dissonant threads against which the pointillistic events are superimposed. All these occur spatially within the concert space.

4. Basic Techniques: Erb has employed a quasi-improvisatory verbal score that clearly defines limits in performance. The sensual overload that slowly

occurs with aural, visual, and tactile elements gradually develops a counterpoint inherent in the "play-by-play" scoring.

5, 6. Vertical and Horizontal Models: Pitch content is limited in the non-effect material to seconds surrounding the taped fifth (i.e., B♭—C and F—G). These contribute to a dissonant yet static quality lacking the tension suggested by their "cluster" content. The stretto of effects (both aural and visual) add to the momentum of intensity that ensues during the performance.

7. Style: The style of *Souvenir* is possibly best summed up in the composer's own words: "One reason that it works (is that) it is an outgoing and happy work; non-neurotic."[20] The style is intermedia. Audiences, at least those observed by this author, become first mesmerized by the visual material and then, with growing anticipation, actively involved with pushing balloons in the air, dodging silly string, and throwing ping-pong balls during the near cataclysm of sound and energy surrounding them.

This work, while outwardly expressing a disdain for the seriousness with which most of the composers in this book take their work, also shows a distinct relationship with a number of other examples presented in vectoral analysis: particularly those of chapter 4 (sets, costume, dramatics, etc.) and chapter 11 (staging, costumes, special lighting, etc.). Its extreme "direction" toward climax and explosion contradict the formal structures of many works lacking such a compositional device such as the works found in the vectoral analyses of chapters 2, 5, 6, and 10.

Background and Aesthetics

Ashley, Robert. "Notes for Public Opinion Descends Upon the Demonstrators." *Asterisk* 1, no. 1 (1961).

Austin, Larry. "SYCOM—Systems Complex for the Studio and Performing Arts." *Numus West* 5 (1974).

Goddard, Don. *Sound/Art Exhibition Catalog.* New York: SoundArt Foundation, 1983.

Hansen, Al. *A Primer of Happenings and Time-Space Art.* New York: Something Else Press, 1968.

Higgins, Dick. *FOEW&OMBWHNW.* New York: Something Else Press, 1969.

———. *Postface.* New York: Something Else Press, 1964.

McLuhan, Marshall. *Understanding Media. The Extensions of Man.* New York: New American Library, 1964.

Rossi, Nick, and Robert Choate. *Music of Our Time.* Boston: Crescendo, 1969.

Salzman, Eric. "Mixed Media." In *Dictionary of Contemporary Music,* ed. John Vinton, pp. 489–92. New York: E. P. Dutton and Co., 1974.

**Bibliography—
Chapter 7***

Further Readings

20. From a telephone interview with the author.

*Addresses for record companies, periodicals, and music publishers mentioned in this Bibliography can be found in Appendix IV.

Tomkins, Calvin. *The Bride and the Bachelors*. New York: Viking Press, 1965.

Yates, Peter. *Twentieth Century Music*. New York: Pantheon Books, 1967.

Young, La Monte, and Marian Zazeela. *Selected Writings*. Munich: Heiner Friedrich, 1969.

Basic Definitions

Dallin, Leon. *Techniques of Twentieth Century Composition*. 3d ed. Dubuque: Wm. C. Brown Publishers, 1974.

Gibb, Stanley. "Understanding Terminology and Concepts Related to Media Art Forms." *The American Music Teacher* 22, no. 5 (1973): pp. 23–25.

Higgins, Dick. *Postface*. New York: Something Else Press, 1964.

———. *A Dialectic of Centuries: Notes Towards a Theory of the New Arts*. 2d ed. New York: Printed Editions, 1979.

Kirby, Michael. *The Art of Time*. New York: E. P. Dutton and Co., 1969.

Nyman, Michael. *Experimental Music*. London: Macmillan Ltd., 1974.

Subotnick, Morton. "Extending the Stuff Music Is Made of." *Music Educators Journal* 55, no. 3 (1968): pp. 109–10.

Multimedia

Becker, Jurgen, and Wolf Vostell, eds. *Happenings*. Hamburg: Rowohlt, 1965.

Cage, John. *M. Writings '67–'72*. Middletown, Conn.: Wesleyan University Press, 1973.

———. *Silence*. Middletown, Conn.: Wesleyan University Press, 1961.

———. *A Year from Monday*. Middletown, Conn.: Wesleyan University Press, 1967.

Chase, Gilbert. "Toward a Total Musical Theatre." *Arts in Society* 1969.

Cross, Lowell. "David Tudor." In *Dictionary of Contemporary Music,* ed. John Vinton, pp. 768–69. New York: E. P. Dutton and Co., 1974.

Cunningham, Merce. *Changes: Notes on Choreography,* ed. Frances Starr. New York: Something Else Press, 1969.

Hansen, Al. *A Primer of Happenings and Time-Space Art*. New York: Something Else Press, 1968.

Hiller, Lejaren. "HPSCHD." *Source* 2, no. 2 (1968): pp. 10–19.

Hoffman, Paul. "An Interview with Robert Moran." *Composer* 4, no. 2 (1973): pp. 46–48.

Kagel, Mauricio. "Uber das instrumentale Theater." *Neue Musik* (1961).

Kaprow, Allan. *Assemblage, Environments and Happenings*. New York: Abrams, 1966.

Kirby, Michael. *Happenings*. New York: E. P. Dutton and Co., 1965.

Kostelanetz, Richard. *The Theatre of Mixed Means*. New York: Dial, 1968.

———, ed. *John Cage*. New York: Praeger Publishers, 1970.

MacLow, Jackson. *The Pronouns: A Collection of Forty Dances for the Dancer's Station*. Barrytown, N.Y.: Station Hill Press, 1980.

Mumma, Gordon. "Four Sound Environments for Modern Dance." *Impulse, the Annual of Contemporary Dance* (1967).

Nyman, Michael. *Experimental Music*. London: Macmillan Ltd., 1974.

Pellegrino, Ronald. *The Electronic Arts of Sound and Light*. New York: Van Nostrand Reinhold Company, 1983.

Penn, William. "The Celluloid Image and Mixed Media." *Composer* 1, no. 4 (1970): p. 179.

Zahler, Noel. "Isomorphism, Computers and the Multi-media Work." *Proceedings of the 1987 International Computer Music Conference*. San Francisco: Computer Music Association, 1987.

Mixed and Intermedia

Beckwith, John, and Udo Kasemets, eds. *The Modern Composer and His World*. Toronto: University of Toronto Press, 1961.

Doubravova, J. "Music and Visual Art: Their Relation as a Topical Problem of Contemporary Music in Czechoslovakia." *International Review of the Aesthetics and Sociology of Music* 11, no. 2 (1980): pp. 219–28.

Evans, Brian. "Integration of Music and Graphics through Algorithmic Congruence." *Proceedings of the 1987 International Computer Music Conference*. San Francisco: Computer Music Association, 1987.

Kagel, Mauricio. "On Match for Three Performers." *Composer* 3, no. 2 (1972): pp. 70–81.

Kirby, E. T. *Total Theatre*. New York: E. P. Dutton and Co., 1969.

Klüver, Billy, Julic Martin, and Barbara Rose. *Pavilion*. New York: Dutton, 1972.

Nyman, Michael. *Experimental Music*. London: Macmillan Ltd., 1974.

Salzman, Eric. "Mixed Media." In *Dictionary of Contemporary Music,* ed. John Vinton, pp. 489–92. New York: E. P. Dutton and Co., 1974.

Videos

DeWitt, Tom. "Visual Music: Searching for an Aesthetic." *Leonardo* 20.2 (1987): pp. 115–22.

Khatchadourian, Haig. *Music, Film and Art*. New York: Gordon and Breach, 1985.

Muscutt, Keith. "Projected Kinetic Displays and Photomicrographs based on the use of Polarized Light." *Leonardo* 11, no. 2 (1976): pp. 97–102.

McLuhan, Marshall. *Understanding Media. The Extensions of Man*. New York: New American Library, 1964.

Shore, Michael. *Music Video: A Consumers Guide*. New York: Ballantine, 1987.

Sondheim, Alan, ed. *Individuals. (Post-movement Art in America)*. New York: Dutton, 1977.

Whitney, John. "Moving Pictures and Electronic Music." *Die Reihe* 7 (1965): pp. 61–71.

———. *Digital Harmony*. Peterborough, N.H.: Byte Books, 1980.

Youngblood, Gene. *Expanded Cinema*. New York: Dutton, 1970.

Donald Erb

Machlis, Joseph. *Introduction to Contemporary Music*. 2d ed. New York: W. W. Norton and Company, 1979.

Compact Discs, Recordings, and Publishers

Ashley, Robert. *Public Opinion Descends Upon the Demonstrators*.

Austin, Larry. *Bass* (1967). CPE-Source.

———. *Sinfonia Concertante*. Centaur CRC–2029.

———. *The Maze* (1965).

Beerman, Burton. *Mixtures*. Media Press.

Berio, Luciano. *Laborintus II* (1965). Universal Edition. Harmonia Mundi HMA 190764.

Cage, John. *Theatre Piece* (1960). Peters.

———. *Variations III* (1963). Peters. DG–139442.

———. *Water Music* (1952).

Cage, John, and Lejaren Hiller. *HPSCHD* (1969). Peters. Nonesuch H–71224.

Colgrass, Michael. *As Quiet As* (1966). MCA. (RCA LSC–3001).

Cope, David. *BTRB* (1970). Brass Press.

————. *Cradle Falling* (1985).

————. *Deadliest Angel Revision* (1971). Seesaw Music Corp.

Crumb, George. *Ancient Voices of Children* (1970). Peters. Nonesuch 979149–2.

————. *Black Angels* (1970). Peters. Elektra/Nonesuch 79242–2–P.

————. *Voice of the Whale (Vox Balaenae)*. Peters. New World NW–357–2.

Davies, Peter Maxwell. *8 Songs for a Mad King*. Boosey & Hawkes. Unicorn-Kanchana DKPCD–9052.

Erb, Donald. *Souvenir*. Merion Music.

Erickson, Robert. *General Speech,* (1969). New World 254.

Foss, Lukas. *Baroque Variations* (1967). Carl Fischer. Nonesuch 71202.

Ives, Charles. *Central Park in the Dark* (1906). AMP. DG 423243–2.

Kagel, Mauricio. *Die Himmelsmechanik* (1965).

————. *Kommentart und Extempore* (1967).

————. *Ludwig Van* (1970). DG–2530014.

————. *Match* (1966). Universal Edition. DG–137006.

————. *Variaktionen* (1967). Universal Edition.

Kasemets, Udo. (1968). *It: Tribute to Buckminster Fuller, Marshall McLuhan and John Cage.*

Knowles, Alison. (1980). *Natural Assemblages and the True Crow*. New York: Printed Editions, 1980.

Kraft, William. *Contextures: Riots—Decade '60* (1971). London 6613.

Martirano, Salvatore. *L'sGA*. MCA. Polidor 245001.

————. *Underworld* (1959). MCA.

Moran, Robert. *39 Minutes for 39 Autos* (1969).

Oliveira, Jocy de. *Probabilistic Theatre 1* (1967).

Reck, David. *Blues and Screamer* (1966). CPE-Source.

Reynolds, Roger. *Emperor of Ice Cream*. Peters.

————. *Ping*. CPE-Source. CRI–285.

Rochberg, George. *Music for the Magic Theatre* (1972). Theodore Presser. Desto DC–6444.

Satie, Erik. *Relâche*. Salabert. Vanguard VECD 7527.

Schäffer, Boguslaw. *Audiences No. 1–5*. PWM.

————. *Incident*. PWM.

————. *Non-Stop*. PWM.

Scriabin, Alexander. *Poem of Fire* (Symphony No. 5). Balawe Publishers. London 417252–2.

Somers, Harry. *Improvisation* (1968).

Stockhausen, Karlheinz. *Momente* (1963). Nonesuch 71157.

————. *Opus 1970*. DG–139461.

Strange, Allan. *No Dead Horses on the Moon*. Media Press.

————. *Vanity Faire* (1970).

Subotnick, Morton. *A Ritual Game Room* (1970). MCA.

————. *Mandolin* (1960). MCA.

————. *Play* (1962). MCA.

Analog Electronic Music

8

Electronic music,[1] or that music composed with or altered by electronic apparatus, has a long and involved history. Early experimental instruments include the "Clavecin Electrique" or "Electric Harpsichord" of Delaborde in Paris, 1761, and Elisha Gray's "Electroharmonic Piano" in Chicago, 1876.[2] Some composers typically utilized these instruments to imitate styles and materials of their times. Many composers, however, attempted to develop a unique aesthetic wherein *all* sounds could act as material for compositions. E. T. A. Hoffman's *The Automaton* in the early nineteenth century, and *The Art of Noises,* 1913, by the Italian futurist Luigi Russolo, evidence these attempts. From 1920 to 1940, experiments with electronic instruments began to take place with composers such as Otto Luening, Norman McLaren, Pierre Schaeffer, Leon Theremin (who in 1923 invented the Theremin), Friederich Trautwein, Paul Hindemith, Ernst Toch, and many others contributing significantly to the new sound resources.

The following series of photographs represents a brief synopsis of the evolution of electronic music in the twentieth century. The telharmonium, devised by Thaddeus Cahill around the turn of the century (his first patent for an "electric music" machine was filed on February 4, 1896), began auspiciously in 1906 with its installation in "Telharmonic Hall" in New York City. The largest of these instruments is shown in Figure 8.1. Figure 8.2 shows the telharmonium in performance on its multiple keyboards.

Around 1920, Leon Theremin invented the Theremin, which was originally called the "Etherophone" and "Thereminovox." One performed the Theremin by moving

Origins and Evolutions

---

1. It must be made abundantly clear that the author does not seek to imply, by the use of the term *electronic music,* any stylistic or material similarity among composers who employ this medium. The term as used here does not connote an inherent style, something that is in fact nonexistent. In a lecture given in Los Angeles, Milton Babbitt argued that a recording of a Tschaikovsky symphony is actually electronic music, in that all the sound actually heard is electronically produced. The term as used by the author here refers *only* to that music composed from or altered by electronic apparatus, and as such is as limitless stylistically as music for string quartet or symphony orchestra.
2. For more detailed history, see Otto Luening, "Some Random Remarks on Electronic Music," *Journal of Music Theory* 8, no. 1 (Spring 1964), pp. 89–98.

Figure 8.1. Thaddeus Cahill's *Telharmonium* in 1906. Located in the basement of "Telharmonic Hall," it utilized twelve cogged metal wheels that, when contacting a metal brush, created an electric current. (Smithsonian Institution photo number #77494)

Figure 8.2. Performing the telharmonium.

their hands in its vicinity, creating pitches and (importantly) glissandi between pitches caused by "heterodyning." Figure 8.3 shows Theremin in a performance for two Theremins and traditional instruments.

Joerg Mager created his *Klaviatur-Spaerophon* in 1925. This instrument, using inductance capacitance principles and audio-frequency generators, voided the glissando effects of the *Theremin*. Performing classical masterworks, Mager was supported by both the Heinrich Hertz Institute and the German Telegraph-Technical Office. Figure 8.4 shows both the instrument builder performing and the triple-keyboard performance technique.

Concurrently with Mager's creations in Germany, John Hays Hammond, father of the Hammond organ, began experimenting with electrical sound production in the United States. His first major effort, called the "breathing piano," involved the use of reflective slats within a soundproof case that opened by the use of an extra pedal. While not explicitly electronic, the concept parallels that of regenerative procedures in radio. Figure 8.5 shows a working model of the instrument.

By 1929, Edouard Coupleaux and Joseph Givelet had created the automatic synthesizer that they exhibited at the Paris Exposition. Their "Automatically Operating Musical Instrument of the Electric Oscillation Type" (AOMIEOT) utilized

Figure 8.3. Leon Theremin (left) in a performance with his namesake instrument. (Smithsonian Institution photo number #77461)

Figure 8.4. Joerg Mager performing on the *Klaviatur-Spaerophon* around 1925.

Figure 8.5. Hammond's "Breathing Piano."

oscillators performed much the way player pianos operate (paper roll). However, both timbre and pitch bending could be affected with the potentials far exceeding its counterpart in the non-electronic world. Figure 8.6 is a photo of the AOMIEOT.

One year later, Emerick Spielmann created the *Superpiano,* an instrument that utilized "light-choppers," interrupting light on photoelectric cells that in turn generated alternating currents for pitch. Figure 8.7 and Figure 8.8 provide examples of performance techniques and of the tone wheels built into the machine.

One of the most successful pioneering electronic musical instruments prior to the present-day analog and digital synthesizers was the *ondes Martenot*. The instrument was created by Maurice Martenot around 1928 but not fully discovered until the mid-thirties when it received a solo performance at the premiere of Dimitri

Figure 8.6. Edouard Coupleaux and Joseph Givelet with their "automatic synthesizer."

Figure 8.7. The *Superpiano* in performance.

Figure 8.8. The *Superpiano* construction.

Figure 8.9. The *ondes Martenot* (1977 construction).

Levidis's *Symphonic Poem*. Looking like a clavichord, it followed the same basic principles of the Theremin but with a much more traditional look and touch. Monophonic in nature, its pitch was controlled by a lateral movement of a finger ring attached to a metal ribbon. Using an intriguing silencing device, the performer could cover up the glissandi so obvious when using the *Theremin*. Figure 8.9 shows a performance model of the *ondes Martenot*.

Many composers, including Olivier Messiaen, Darius Milhaud, Arthur Honegger, and Edgard Varèse, have effectively used the *ondes Martenot* in their works. In 1936, Edgard Varèse said: "I am sure that the time will come when the composer, after he has graphically realized his score, will see this score automatically put on a machine that will faithfully transmit the musical content to the listener. . . ."[3] A year later, John Cage remarked: "To make music . . . will continue to increase until we reach a music produced through the aid of electrical instruments."[4]

French composers Pierre Schaeffer and Pierre Henry developed *musique concrète* by rerecording "natural" sounds at various speeds and splicing in composer-controlled rhythms. In Germany (until 1956) composers tended to shun *concrète*, using only electronic sources, often only sine waves. In America, the pioneering work of composers like Percy Grainger, whose *Free Music* of 1935 used four Theremins, explored electronic resources. Along with Burnett Cross, Grainger later created a "free music" machine using various oscillators. The works of John Cage, Vladimir Ussachevsky, and Otto Luening brought attention to these new sound sources, all during the five-year period 1948 to 1952—the years of real discovery and experimentation. The "Tapesichordists," as Luening and Ussachevsky were termed in a *Time* magazine review of their renowned Museum of Modern Art concert of October 28, 1952, while not taken seriously until the early sixties, steadfastly and consistently improved their working conditions, equipment, and technical knowledge.

One of the most important philosophical concepts that became suspect at the dawn of the electronic music age was that of timbral continuity. Heretofore, composers had been constrained to traditional or nontraditional instruments that limit

---

3. From a lecture given at Mary Austin House, Santa Fe, New Mexico, 1936.
4. John Cage, *Silence* (Cambridge, Mass.: The M.I.T. Press, 1961), p. 3.

Figure 8.10. Pierre Henry.

their human performers in range, timbre, performability of complex rhythmic gestures, and so on. With electronic music, however, composers may realize a tremendous expansion of these sonic possibilities. In fact, virtually *any* timbre is possible. Audiences not prepared for the demands placed on their ears have often been antagonized by the exercise of such freedom. Composers no longer need to make decisions that previously automatically limited their timbre potential by the mere selection of a traditional instrument or group of instruments. More interestingly, each sound in electronic music can become an instrument played as little as "once" during a composition, creating thousands of virtual "performers." Hence the extreme focus on "moment" and "moment forms" in composition since the 1960s.

New sounds, however, become old quickly. New control, where the composer becomes a performer capable of literally any microcosm of controllable elements in time was equally available to those preferring lack of control. This latter point is strikingly evidenced by such contrasting works as Milton Babbitt's *Vision and Prayer* (1961) and Karlheinz Stockhausen's *Mikrophonie I* (1965). The former is composed of pure electronic sounds (with "live" voice) carefully notated by the composer, while the latter involves two performers acting on one six-foot gong with a score composed primarily of verbal descriptions of how the sounds should affect the listener, such as "grating," "scraping," and the like. Two other performers control directional microphones, filters, and potentiometers controlling electronic timbre and volume control, respectively.

Certainly the creation of new, nonequal-tempered scales combined with nearly limitless rhythmic possibilities (no longer restricted to the ten fingers of the pianist or the thousand of an orchestra) present opportunities that many composers cannot resist. Few, however, would agree with "New Music for an Old World Dr. Thaddeus Cahill's Dynamophone An Extraordinary Electrical Invention for Producing Scientifically Perfect Music," titling a *McClures' Magazine* article of July 1906,[5] or

5. Elliott Schwartz, *Electronic Music: A Listener's Guide* (New York: Praeger Publishers, 1973), p. 241 (from Otto Luening's remarks).

Casio's 1981 claim that one can ". . . become an instant musician . . . easily, without the long years of training necessary for mastering a regular instrument."

Nourished by the 1948 invention of the long-playing record, electronic music became accessible to every listener's living room despite the singular neglect shown it by "concert music" radio stations in the United States. Moreover, electronic music's lack of visual interest in the concert hall has helped spawn a whole genre of interesting combinations of "live electronics"—tape with "live" performers—and has contributed greatly to the refinement and growth of media forms.

With the advent of tape recorders and unlimited resources of sound and rhythm, such concepts as "noise," "consonance-dissonance," and "live performance" have become increasingly difficult to define. Synthesizers enable composers to control all the elements of production (dynamics, envelope, duration, etc.) except performance acoustics and audience receptivity. This has not gained a universal acceptance. Igor Stravinsky remarked:

> What about the much publicized "infinity of possibilities" in connection with the new art material of electronically produced sound? With few exceptions "infinite possibilities" has meant collages of organ burbling, rubber suction (indecent, this), machine-gunning, and other—this is curious—representational and associative noises more appropriate to Mr. Disney's musical mimicries.[6]

Ernst Krěnek seems almost to answer Stravinsky's objection in his article "A Glance over the Shoulders of the Young":

> To the superficial observer, it appears that the phenomena demonstrated so far in electronic music: levels of colour, texture, density, consistency and mass of sound material, are of a considerably lower intellectual level of musical consciousness than the aspirations which were associated with the demanding music of the past. Perhaps this only represents a beginning; history cites us many examples of the way in which creative energy has been expended on the achievement of progress of one dimension while temporarily impoverishing the other dimensions of the subject.[7]

Inexperienced electronic music composers can very often be "hypnotized" by the time required to make the exact sound needed. Other composers have noted that, up until the era of mechanical music, a composer/performer needed a certain physical energy to produce a *forte,* an energy corresponding in some ways, at least, to the energy of the sound itself. It is possible for one to lose that perspective when a small flick of a finger can create huge volumes of sound, or the same flick can quiet the flow to nothing. Obviously a very different quality of action/reaction is present

Aesthetic Challenges

---

6. Igor Stravinsky and Robert Craft, *Dialogues and A Diary* (Garden City, N.Y.: Doubleday & Co., Inc., 1963), p. 25.
7. Ernst Krěnek, "A Glance over the Shoulders of the Young," *Die Reihe I* (Bryn Mawr, Pennsylvania: Theodore Presser Co., in association with Universal Edition, c. 1958), p. 16.

in electronic music, comparable only to pipe organs and certain mechanical instruments of the past. *Psychoacoustics,* the study of listener discrimination and receptivity of these complexities, has become a real and vital tool of the composer attempting to communicate.[8] Luciano Berio has commented:

> When someone hears electronic music it doesn't reverberate to other levels of his experience, as instrumental music has and does. Up to now I feel electronic music has been developing, evolving as a bridge between what we know and what we don't know yet. It is not without reason that the best musical works that have been produced up until now (from the early 50s to the present) are those that try to make this connection.[9]

Fundamental Concepts

Two basic sound sources exist: electronic and *musique concrète* (e.g., instrumental sounds, sounds of nature). There seems to have been, at least in the early fifties, a definite desire by composers to make a choice between one or the other with France dedicated to the *concrète* and Germany to the electronic. However, by 1960, especially in Stockhausen's *Gesang der Jünglinge,* both sources were considered of equal potential. Experimentation with tape loops continuous lengths of tape looped so as to pass and repass the playback head, creating rhythmic ostinati or continuous sound flow, and with gluing bits of recorded magnetic tape to white leader tape resulted in either a very controlled and measurable (in fractions of inches) rhythmic base or a random flux of sounds.

After sound materials are chosen as shown in Figure 8.11, an extremely simplified schematic, manipulation becomes important. At this point, material can be altered by combining sounds with mixers, and ring modulators, eliminating certain sounds through the use of various filters such as low-pass, high-pass, band-pass, and band reject and filter banks—see Figure 8.12, or distorting sounds by reverberation and/or various types of modulations; frequency, amplitude, and ring; along with speed changes of the tape recorder, and so on.

Amplitude modulation (AM), or continuously changing dynamics (also known as *tremolo*), and frequency modulation (FM), or continuously changing pitch (also known as *vibrato*), have brought about an important concept known as *voltage control.* When, for example, a composer wishes to "warm" a sound with vibrato, quick hand manipulation of the frequency control by repeatedly turning it back and forth creates the desired effect. Assigning such repetitions to another module (i.e., the sine wave output of another oscillator at the proper frequency), however, is more efficient. The capacity of one oscillator, or for that matter any electronic instrument, to manipulate another oscillator is termed voltage control.

8. See especially Fritz Winckel, "The Psycho-Acoustical Analysis of Structure as Applied to Electronic Music," *Journal of Music Theory* 7, no. 2, p. 194; and Milton Babbitt, "An Introduction to the R.C.A. Synthesizer," *Journal of Music Theory* 8, no. 2, p. 251.
9. David Felder, "An Interview with Luciano Berio," *Composer* 7, no. 1 (1976), p. 11.

Figure 8.11. Electronic music diagram: from source to playback.

Synchronization (sequencing), or the placing of all events into a composed order by means of such devices as splicing, rerecording, mixing, and speed alteration, readies the tape for playback. *Classic* studios utilize previously recorded sounds or short groups of sounds and splicing techniques. While most electronic music involves a certain amount of splicing, classic electronic music evolves *all* timing, order, and so on, by splicing. This classic approach was used, for example, in the *Poème électronique* (1958) by Edgard Varèse. A number of composers, including Mario Davidovsky and Vladimir Ussachevsky, have used this technique since that time. Prolongation of this tedious and time-consuming approach means one constantly

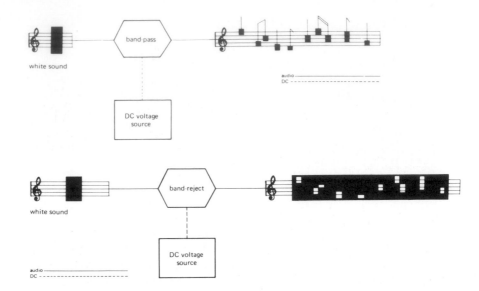

Figure 8.12. Band-pass and band-reject filtering. From *Electronic Music,* by Allen Strange. © Copyright 1972. Wm. C. Brown Company Publishers, Dubuque, Iowa. Permission granted.

confronts the splicing block for each new sound. The introduction of keyboards, sequencers, and so on, and multitrack recorders, making "live" production on tape of as many consecutive sounds as the composer wishes without splicing, has eliminated many such classical approaches. While keyboards, sequencers, and the like make near "real-time" performance possible, some feel this leads to sonic masturbation rather than to great music. No doubt, classic and "live" electronic means can *both* serve the talented composer well, each having its share of advantages and drawbacks.

The playback stage cannot be underestimated in importance. The viability of a majority of compositions on tape requires specific placement of loudspeakers. Some composers have even "composed" proper placement of the tape machine itself for theatrical or dramatic effect. In *Musik für ein Haus* (1968) by Karlheinz Stockhausen, exact locations of all electronic materials in a two-story house are inherent to the "real" performance of the tape work. Acoustical considerations likewise become extremely important for the composer and/or performer in the placement of loudspeakers. Stockhausen discusses this:

> . . . I should like to explain . . . just how loudspeakers are properly placed in an auditorium (a procedure which is becoming better and better known to me and which demands the greatest care in the particular place in question, as well as often up to four hours of time from me and several other collaborators sitting in various parts of the hall; in Madrid, for example, Kontarsky, Fritsch, Gehlhaar, Alings, Boje, and I took several hours to set the loudspeakers up; some of them were even lying on their backs up in the balcony, and others were on stands on the stage, and we had put pieces of wood under the front edge of each speaker so that they were pointed up at the ceiling and the sound was only reflected into the house at an angle at a greater distance; we set up two loudspeakers contrary to the usual way with their diaphragm sides at an acute angle directly toward the wooden walls in order to prevent hiss and to enable the people sitting right in front of these loudspeakers—at a distance of about 5–7 meters (16½ to 23 feet)—to hear the loudspeakers standing on the opposite

Figure 8.13. The SYNTHI 100 of Electronic Music Studios (London) Limited, 277 Putney Bridge Road, London SW 15 2 pt, England. By permission.

side, as well as those which were diagonally opposite; in principle we try to send the sound of the loudspeakers, particularly when instrumentalists are playing at the same time, as *high* as possible into the house to achieve a smooth acoustic match, especially in four-track reproduction).[10]

Pierre Boulez, in an interview with the author, offered the following observations:

Early Studios

I think that you cannot do good work in this area until you have teams working together. You must have composer and technician alike. Four things, really: composer, technician, good equipment, and a company or factory with money to back the operation, as well as performers in some cases, and as long as these elements cannot work together you will have small laboratories without any outstanding results.[11]

Highly sophisticated studios do exist, among them the Institute of Sonology at Utrecht State University in Holland which contains four studios, six scientific staff members, four technical staff members, and two secretaries, with computer, classic, "live" and DC/AC patch panels and combination availabilities;[12] the EMS studio in Putney, England (see Figure 8.13) and a host of advanced studios based at American universities, including the aforementioned Columbia-Princeton Laboratory, studios at the University of Illinois, North Texas State University, University of

10. Karlheinz Stockhausen, "Not A Special Day," *Composer* 1, no. 2 (September 1969), pp. 65–66.
11. Galen Wilson and David Cope, "An Interview with Pierre Boulez," *Composer* 1, no. 2 (September 1969), pp. 84–85.
12. For a more detailed and complete description of the Institute of Sonology with photos and block diagrams see *Sonorum Speculum #52* (Donemus, 51 Jacob Obrechstraat, Amsterdam, Netherlands).

Figure 8.14. Karlheinz Stockhausen. (Copyright: Werner Scholz)

California at San Diego, the Cleveland Institute of Music, and many others. The RCA Mark II Synthesizer, located at the Columbia-Princeton Center since 1959, has served as the source of a large number of important compositions by Babbitt, Ussachevsky, and Luening—especially the first totally synthesized extended work, *Composition for Synthesizer* (1961) by Milton Babbitt.[13]

Experiments in 1940 by Norman McLaren with film sound tracks have created a unique and less expensive approach to electronic "notation." By cutting notches in the film, and by scratching and painting on the sound track portion of the film, McLaren produced a wide variety of "electronic" sounds from the projector (the performer). Lejaren Hiller, who with Leonard Isaacson wrote *Experimental Music* (McGraw-Hill, 1959), describes situations in which the composer, with a pen filled with magnetic dyes, could sit at his desk and compose on unmagnetized tape without the aid of any electronic equipment, excepting a tape recorder for experimentation and synchronization.

Examples of *Concrète* and Synthesized Music

One of the most popular of early tape pieces, Stockhausen's *Gesang der Jünglinge* (1955–56), combines singing with electronically produced sounds. *Musique concrète* manipulation produces variable comprehensibility of the text (Daniel 3, "Song of the Men in the Fiery Furnace"). The score calls for five groups of loudspeakers to surround the audience. Stockhausen uses the spatial direction and movement of the sounds to create form, avoiding the traditional melodic or timbre repetitions.

Stockhausen's numerous other electronic works, especially *Kontakte* (1960), *Telemusik* (1966), and *Hymnen* (1969)—the latter a collage of electronically altered hymns and *concrète* sounds—has made him one of the most widely known of Europe's electronic composers.

Luciano Berio's *Thema: Omaggio à Joyce* (1958) uses voice (completely *concrète*), first recognizably and then slowly transformed into a fantastic array of sounds

13. Unlike the *analog* synthesizers previously mentioned, the RCA Mark II used punched paper tape relatively the size of a player-piano roll instead of a keyboard. Though computerlike in appearance (with the *digital* input), the Mark II is not a computer: for computer information see the next chapter.

Figure 8.15. Vladimir Ussachevsky. BMI Archives. Used by permission.

by means of splicing and tape speed variation, exploring an absolute minimum of materials. His *Visage* (1961) is a "classic" of electronic music; an imaginative vocal-electronic treatment in a strikingly dramatic form originally composed as a radio program. A voice (that of Cathy Berberian) speaks only one word (*parole*; Italian for "words"), but through intense crying, whispering, laughing, and such, evokes an emotional gamut virtually without peer in the history of music.

John Cage was among the first of the Americans to employ tape techniques. His *Imaginary Landscape No. 5* (1951–52) uses a prepared score for making a recording on tape. All of Cage's works must, however, be studied in the light of his *indeterminate concepts* of musical technique (see chapter 5) and as such must be considered for the most part a cooperative effort between himself and the performer. Therefore, the bulk of his electronic music is found scattered throughout this book, especially under the subject headings of chapters 5 and 6.

A large percentage of Vladimir Ussachevsky's early works from 1951 to 1954, including *Sonic Contours, Transposition, Reverberation,* and *Composition* (all on Folkways FX 6160), were experiments only, principally based on sounds of piano and flute. His *A Piece for Tape Recorder* (1955) is less of an experiment, yet obvious enough in construction to serve well as a good educational or introductory tool in electronic music. His longtime associates Otto Luening and Milton Babbitt have produced, especially at the Columbia-Princeton Electronic Music Center, a large number of works, particularly tape in combination with live instruments. Ussachevsky's *Of Wood and Brass* (1965) is a unique work employing tape loops of varying lengths on which are recorded *concrète* sounds "of wood and brass" fed through a ring modulator that collects the sidebands and nullifies the original inputs, creating neoelectronic effects. This and others of Ussachevsky's later works are highly sophisticated examples of electronic music—quite individualistic and advanced in comparison with the early embryonic years.

Figure 8.16. Mario Davidovsky.

Mario Davidovsky's *Study No. II* (1966) for tape is a truly incredible creation in that each of the extremely quick-moving electronic sounds was placed in order by splicing (classic electronic music). The straightforward ABA form and the use of more or less "pure" electronic material (sine and square waves) marks another unusual feature of this work. The "limitless possibilities" are almost completely unexplored and, except for the obvious performance limitations, one could easily imagine the work as a string quartet.

More recently, Morton Subotnick (one of the founders of the San Francisco Tape Center) achieved much success with *Silver Apples of the Moon* (1967), commissioned to fit the two sides of an LP recording, and *The Wild Bull* (1968). Both works employ contrasts in texture and timbre as organizational principles, and the composer has distinctly abandoned the "pure" electronic sounds for more instrumental- and natural-like sounds. More recent works (in the 1970s) in this genre by Subotnick include *Touch, Sidewinder,* and *4 Butterflies.*

Milton Babbitt's *Ensembles for Synthesizer* (1961–63) concentrates on compact rhythmic textures and formal aspects of the tape medium, avoiding timbral displays. Charles Wuorinen's *Time's Encomium* (1968–69), also realized on the RCA Mark II Synthesizer at the Columbia-Princeton Center, evidences instrumental style in both its clear composer control (often twelve-tone) and its extremely complicated rhythmic passages. The work contrasts what the composer calls "synthesized sound" (clarity of pitch) with "processed synthesized sound" (utilizing reverberation).

A number of rock groups have employed electronic sound materials in their music. The Beatles (especially in *Sgt. Pepper's Lonely Hearts Club Band*), Jimi Hendrix Experience, and The United States of America (see Bibliography) used electronically produced or altered sound, but for the most part these were only experiments, exploiting such sounds for shock or text emphasis rather than actual musical development. Rock and pop groups have used portable synthesizers and various effects modules as standard instruments of their ensembles. Notable among

Figure 8.18. Charles Wuorinen.

Figure 8.17. Milton Babbitt. By permission.

these groups are The Grateful Dead ("Dark Star"), Soft Machine ("Joy of a Toy"), Mothers of Invention ("Penguin in Bondage"), Todd Rundgren ("Born to Synthesize"), King Crimson ("Pictures of a City"), Yes ("Close to the Edge"), Weather Report ("Nubian Sundance"), Tangerine Dream ("Rubycon"), and Frank Zappa ("Roxy and Elsewhere," "Lumpy Gravy," and "Uncle Meat"). The Who's Pete Townshend employs feedback effectively in "My Generation," a work that was quite influential in the creation of "punk" rock. Devo (described by *Rolling Stone* as "a group of Captain Beefheart-influenced dadaists") includes massive electronic instrumentation. Even the singers' voices are continually modified by electronic devices. As rock enters the 1990s it is difficult to find a group not "plugged in" in some way. Most groups have an entourage of "roadies" who control mixer consoles that feed giant sets of speakers with electronically synthesized samples, modified, or amplified sound.

More recently, "industrial music" has brought many elements of the *avant-garde* (minimalism, new instrumental sounds from "industrial" sources, and especially electronic techniques) to popular music. Groups such as Throbbing Gristle and Einsterzende Neubäuten have used electronically recorded and often electronically distorted sounds of saws, crowbars, and other unusual "musical" instruments to their music. As well, since the late 1980s "rap" groups have contributed significantly to the dispersion of electronic music. Groups like Public Enemy and Ice T, in particular, have creatively explored the electronic and minimalistic uses of subtly shifting "rap" patterns. Possibly less classifiable, but nonetheless important, are groups such as the Butt Hole Surfers and Sonic Youth, as well as performers Kramer and Holger Czukay. Each performs an *avant-garde* rock, that is often as startling and revolutionary as the more or less traditional *avant-garde* composers mentioned for the most part herein.

Walter Carlos (now Wendy Carlos), on the other hand, developed electronic "orchestrations" of works by Bach (e.g., *Switched-on Bach* and *The Well-Tempered Synthesizer*) that represent an interesting application of the early Moog instrument. These works demonstrate levels of speed and accuracy far beyond human capability. Isao Tomita's realizations of Stravinsky's *Firebird,* Holst's *Planets,* and Mussorgsky's *Pictures at an Exhibition* demonstrate the synthesizer's ability both to imitate acoustic timbres as well as to orchestrate quasi-real sounds in novel and striking ways. These records have provided the stimulus for some of the ever-increasing manifestations of the popularity of electronic sounds among the general public.

Electronic music has also flourished in Latin America with composers working in a variety of private and institutional studios. Important composers represented on recording include Joaquin Orellana (b. Guatemala, 1939; particularly *Humanofonía I,* 1971); Oscar Bazán (b. Argentina, 1936; particularly *Parca,* 1974); Jacqueline Nova (b. Belgium, 1936, d. Columbia, 1975; especially *Creación de la Tierra,* 1972); Graciela Paraskevaidís (b. Buenos Aires, 1940; especially *Huauqui,* 1975); and Coriún Aharonián (b. Montevideo, 1940; particularly *Homenaje a la Flecha Clavada en el Pecho de Don Juan Diáz de Solís,* 1975).

Performance Considerations

The obvious loss to the audience of more or less theatrical or visual activity during performance of works on tape has inspired three alternatives: (1) combination of live performer with tape; (2) live electronic music; from the Synket (a complex, compact live electronic instrument invented and developed by Paul Ketoff in 1963) to extremely complex situations involving recording and playback in numerous arrangements in concert, and performers or audience intercepting light beams to set off oscillators; and (3) tape used in conjunction with projections and/or theatrical events. In fact, the need for auxiliary action in electronic music performance played a large part in the need for developing mixed-media presentations.

Works for live performer(s) and tape have been popular over the past few decades. Henri Pousseur (b. 1929), for example, in *Rimes pour Différentes Sources Sonores* (1959), treats orchestra and tape as antiphonal bodies, contrasting the available materials of each. The speakers are placed on stage in "live" performance, in such a way as to visually accentuate the contrast. Otto Luening (b. 1900) and Vladimir Ussachevsky, who worked together on *Rhapsodic Variations for Tape Recorder and Orchestra* (1954), were among the first in America to realize and experiment with live and prerecorded sound sources. Bruno Maderna (in *Musica su due Dimensioni*) began studies in this area in 1952 at the NW German Radio in Cologne. These early examples extended the contrast possibilities of live and recorded sources.

One of the most dynamic works written for tape and orchestra is *Collages* (1960, Symphony No. 3) by Roberto Gerhard. This large seven-section work employs a *concrète*/electronic tape not unlike that used by Varèse in *Déserts*, contrasting a dramatically pointillistic orchestral score.

Mario Davidovsky has composed a number of *Synchronisms* for a variety of traditional instruments and tape. The first, third, and sixth of these are for solo instruments and tape (flute, 'cello, and piano respectively, the latter winning a Pulitzer Prize). These intense compositions require a great deal of "synchronized" rhythmic interchange from "live" to recorded source (all the *Synchronisms* are recorded; see chapter Bibliography for record numbers).

Kenneth Gaburo's 1962 work *Antiphony III (Pearl-white Moments)* combines sixteen soloists in four groups performing live with tape through two speaker systems, incorporating antiphonal interplay between live and tape sounds both acoustically and visually. *Antiphony III's* tape materials include both purely electronic sound sources and those more imitative of the live performers, expanding the echo and reiterative effects inherently restricted in totally live performances.

Donald Erb (b. 1927), in *In No Strange Land* (1968) for trombone, double bass, and tape, reflects more complementary possibilities of electronic and instrumental sounds. Imitative techniques involve instruments in neoelectronic sound effects, thus minimizing the musical and sonic disparities between electronic and instrumental materials. Composers like Robert Erickson have used prerecorded instrumental sounds with live performance. In *Ricercar à 3* (1967), Erickson employs two prerecorded contrabasses with one live contrabass, allowing the performer to play with and against the tape, a source of unusual combinative effects.

The author's *Arena* (1974; 'cello and tape), is a *classical* studio composition that reflects both a dialogue between live instrument and tape, and contrasting cohesion. Figure 8.21 shows a passage in which the tape "takes over" each pitch begun by the 'cello, in turn creating vertical sonorities from the horizontal line. The rhythm

Figure 8.21. David Cope: *Arena* ('cello and tape), page 7. © Copyright 1974 by David Cope. All rights reserved.

Figure 8.21. *(Continued)*

and pitch of the 'cello must be precisely synchronized for the passage to work (including the quarter-tone inflection indicated by the arrows attached to the accidentals). The bottom staff reflects more interplay—the harmonics on the tape are only symbolically represented—answered by the artificial harmonics on the 'cello. This score reflects the often necessary, exact, and graphic notations used by composers for tape with "live" instruments.

Richard Felciano has written many works for a wide variety of combinations of traditional instruments and tape. *God of the Expanding Universe* and *Litany* are excellent examples of works for organ and tape. His *Crasis* and *Lamentations for Jani Christou* represent examples of chamber music with tape.

John Watts's *WARP* (1972) includes ARP-created electronic sounds on tape with brass quintet. The four-channel quadraphonic speaker setup heightens both the balance and the effective humor and drama of this work. Combinations of large ensembles with tape occupy an increasing bulk of tape music composition. Works for tape and band include Donald Erb's *Reticulation* (1965) and Herbert Bielawa's *Spectrum.* Vladimir Ussachevsky's *Creation-Prologue* (1961) is for tape and choir.[14]

John Eaton combines the compact "live performance" *Synket* and full orchestra in his *Concert Piece for Synket and Symphony Orchestra* which effectively utilizes visual "concerto" performance techniques with specially designed electronic equipment. Merrill Ellis included soprano, live synthesizer, and orchestra in his *Kaleidoscope.* These last two works concentrate on the "live" performability of synthesizers or live-electronic music.

Live-Electronic Music

John Cage was the first to employ entirely live-electronic techniques in his *Imaginary Landscape No. 4* (c. 1949, first performed in 1951) in which twelve radios are performed by two performers each (twenty-four performers in all). His *Imaginary Landscape No. 1* (1939) uses recordings of constant and variable pitch frequencies in combination with more conventional percussion instruments.

In *Reconnaissance* (1967) Donald Erb employs a Moog synthesizer performed live with a group of other live instrumentalists (viola, piano, bass, percussion), achieving both the visual complement of "live" performance and the available sonic resources of electronic equipment. The work also utilizes a Moog polyphonic instrument—a keyboard instrument of four octaves each divided into forty-three tones capable of producing polyphony in a live performance situation (the synthesizer in use here can only produce chords of the same ratio in live performance).

The "Chapman Stick" is a live-performed electronic instrument resembling an enlarged guitar without an associated resonator. Because the instrument can amplify very small touches on the string surface, the performer need not strum the strings. Hence, it is possible, even promoted, for one to use both hands to "finger" the instrument. This allows for vastly increased potential for chords and counterpoint. With the appropriate straps for support, one can even use thumbs to produce

14. For a more complete listing, see *Music Educators Journal* 55, no. 3 (November 1968), p. 73. Also consult publishers' listings.

Figure 8.22. Richard Felciano. Photo © Michelle Vignes. By permission.

ten pitches simultaneously. Max Mathews has also created an electronic violin. Similar percussion and wind instruments have been created but usually employ contact microphone enhancement rather than a completely new form of construction.

A number of groups dedicated to the live performance of electronic music (most now disbanded) were formed in the sixties: The Sonic Arts Union (formed in 1966), with Gordon Mumma, Robert Ashley, Alvin Lucier, and David Behrman; *Musica Elettronica Viva* (1967, in Italy), with Frederic Rzewski, Allan Bryant, and Alvin Curran; and the Once Group (Michigan), with Robert Ashley, Gordon Mumma, and others. Festivals of live-electronic music occurred at Davis, California (1967), Buffalo (1968), and Los Angeles (1968 and 1969), among others. A live-electronics group, "It takes a year one earth to go around the sun," formed in 1970 by David Rosenboom (originator and director of New York's Electric Circus until 1969), with Jon Hassell, Gerald Shapiro, and Terry Riley, spent the summer of that year performing on electronic instruments designed by the members themselves, on "mesas in Wyoming, ghost towns in Death Valley, and lava caves in New Mexico." The works, performed by the composer/performers, are extremely loose in construction, serving as "launching pads" for the performers' rehearsed interplay.

Figure 8.23. Alvin Lucier.
Photo by Mary Lucier.

Alvin Lucier's *North American Time Capsule* (1967) involves a vocoder (Sylvania design), an instrument designed to encode speech sounds into digital information. The speech of the performers acts as the electronic source material in "live" performance. Gordon Mumma's *Mesa* (1966) uses electronic sound modification as well. He uses a Bandoneon (an accordion-like instrument) instead of voices. Work with tape-delay techniques for echoes and canons have been used in live performance by Pauline Oliveros (*I of IV,* 1966, and *Lightpiece for David Tudor,* 1965).[15] By separation of record and playback heads and cross-coupling, a large number of reiterative compositional techniques can be employed.

Several composers in the sixties explored the possibilities of interactive electroacoustical, process-oriented composition. Representative works of this time include David Behrman's *Wavetrain* (1964), John Cage's *Variations V* (1965), Gordon Mumma's *Hornpipe* (1967), and Alvin Lucier's *Queen of the South* (1972). Behrman's *Wavetrain* involves the acoustical resonances of grand pianos or zithers. Cage's *Variations V* uses the movements of dancers on the stage translated by photoelectric cells and capacitance sensors into electronic articulations for the accompanying sound. Lucier's *Queen of the South* (which is discussed in chapter 4), employs large plate surfaces, which are resonated with special loudspeakerlike transducers.

Mumma's *Hornpipe* is described in detail by the composer himself:

Hornpipe is an interactive live-electronic work for solo hornist, cybersonic[16] console, and a performance space. The hornist performs with various techniques on a valveless waldhorn and a standard "French horn." These techniques include a traditional embouchure, and the production of multiphonics with special double-reeds.

The cybersonic console, attached to the hornist's belt, has microphones with which it "hears" the sounds made by the hornist and the acoustical resonances of the space. The electronic circuitry of the console analyzes the acoustical resonances of the

15. See Pauline Oliveros, "Tape Delay Techniques for Electronic Music Composition," *Composer* 1, no. 3 (December 1969), pp.135–42.
16. A term coined by Mumma; refers to sound-control procedures in which the controls are automatically derived from the sounds being controlled.

Figure 8.24. Gordon Mumma performing *Hornpipe* (1967). Photo by Narrye Caldwell, 1974.

space, and responds interactively with the hornist. The console is connected by an umbilical cable to a stereophonic sound system, so that its responses are heard from loudspeakers. [See Figure 8.24.]

The cybersonic console has several functions. First, it makes an electronic map of the acoustical resonances of the space. This is achieved during the first few minutes of the performance by eight electronically resonant circuits that become automatically tuned to the acoustical resonances of the space. Second, each circuit has a memory that accumulates information about its resonant condition.

Technically, this condition is determined from the frequency (F) and the resonant efficiency (Q) of the circuit. [See Figure 8.25.] Third, when sufficient information is obtained, a VCA (voltage controlled amplifier) for each circuit is gated on, sending its electronically resonant response through the umbilical to the loudspeakers. Because each of the eight resonant circuits is somewhat independent, and has different memory and gating characteristics, these responses can occur in many different combinations.

A performance of *Hornpipe* begins as a solo, without electronic sound. When the responses of the cybersonic console are heard from the loudspeakers, the hornist can then interact with the electronic map of the cybersonic console. By playing sounds which reinforce the electronic map, the hornist can increase the responses of the

Figure 8.25. Functional diagram, Gordon Mumma's *Hornpipe* (1967).

cybersonic console. By playing sounds which are anti-resonant (opposed) to the resonances of the electronic map, the hornist can decrease the responses of the cybersonic console.

The performer's choice of anti-resonant sounds strongly influences the continuity of a performance. Without the reinforcement of its original electronic map, the cybersonic console gradually makes a new map representing the hornist's anti-resonant sounds. In other words, having interacted with the responses of the cybersonic console, and learned the electronic map of the acoustical resonances of the space, the hornist can choose sounds which deceive the console into thinking it is in a different performance space. After the cybersonic console has developed a new map

Figure 8.26. *Music of DOD* by Allen Strange (1977).

(of the hornist's anti-resonant sounds), it no longer responds to the natural acoustical resonances of the space. The performance of *Hornpipe* has evolved from an introductory solo, through an ensemble between hornist, cybersonic console and performance space, to a concluding solo section for horn.[17]

The score to Allen Strange's *Music of DOD* (1977), for virtuoso instrument and one player, lays out the design for an electronic instrument with a short performance note regarding dissonance and resolution (see Figure 8.26).

Figure 8.27 is from Stockhausen's *Studie II* (1956, Universal Edition). The lower portion indicates dynamics (envelope). The upper portion denotes pitch (100 to 17,200 Hertz, or cycles per second) based on a scale of 81 steps "equal-tempered" at a constant interval ratio of $\sqrt[25]{5}$ (piano at $\sqrt[5]{2}$) and timbre. The middle portion indicates centimeters of tape at 76.2 centimeters per second. This score represents less than seven seconds of performing time.

17. Gordon Mumma, performance notes for *Hornpipe*.

Figure 8.27. Karlheinz Stockhausen: *Studie II.* (Reprinted by permission of Universal Edition; as it appeared in the English edition of *Die Reihe* No. 1, copyright 1958 by Theodore Presser Company, Bryn Mawr, Pa.)

**Vectoral Analysis:
Edgard Varèse:
*Poème électronique***

(For information on vectoral analysis and procedures, see chapter 1.)

For background information on Varèse, see chapter 1.

1. Historical Background: *Poème électronique* (1956–58) was composed at the Philips Studio at Eindhaven, having been commissioned for performance in the Philips Pavilion at the 1958 Brussels Worlds Fair. The pavilion was designed by the French architect Le Corbusier who was assisted, interestingly enough, by then-architect Iannis Xenakis. The design of the pavilion included 400 or more loudspeakers, most of which were hidden in the walls or above the ceilings. David Ernst speaks of the elaborate setup:

   The taped sounds were distributed by telephone relays among various combinations of loudspeakers. These "sound paths" were determined by a fifteen channel control tape, each track of which contained twelve separate signals. Therefore 180 (15 × 12) control signals were available to regulate the sound routes, lighting effects and a variety of light sources which consisted of film projectors and projection lanterns, spotlights, ultraviolet lamps, bulbs, and fluorescent lamps of various colors.[18]

18. David Ernst, *The Evolution of Electronic Music* (New York: Schirmer Books, 1977), p. 42.

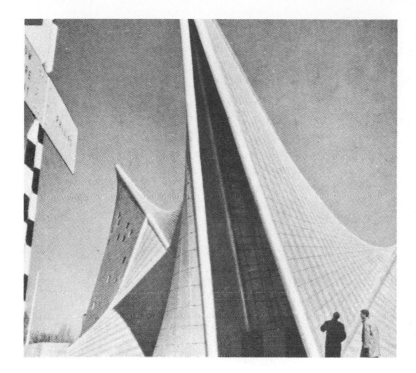

Figure 8.28. The Philips Pavilion at the Brussels Exposition (World's Fair) built by Le Corbusier where *Poème électronique* was first performed in 1958.

Nearly 16,000 people each day for six months provided an audience for the performance of this work of purely taped sounds with both *musique concrète* and electronic sources. The projected images, various photographs of paintings, script, or other montages, were not synchronized with the sound in any particular manner. The projections were chosen by Le Corbusier to fit the elaborate and complex internal design of the pavilion.

2. Overview: Varèse often referred to his work as "organized sound" rather than traditional composition. Clearly *Poème électronique* is very highly organized sound. One method of analyzing electronic music visually "keys" certain sounds so that "paper" analysis becomes possible. Figure 8.29 shows one possible such "keying."

While there are obviously more than seven different sound sources and variants present in this piece, one can clearly identify the ones shown here as basic to its structure. The visual identities are drawn to resemble in some way the aural image presented or in some cases the instruments suggested by the sounds.

Figure 8.30 shows how these symbols can be organized to represent a timeline of the piece (left to right, top to bottom). Occasional numbers within a diagram represent repetitions of a sound. Assorted "doodlings" between connections represent important but nonformal materials. When one symbol becomes an offshoot of another symbol, it represents a counterpoint, with the first stated material being more significant.

Figure 8.29. Key to diagrams used in Figure 8.30.

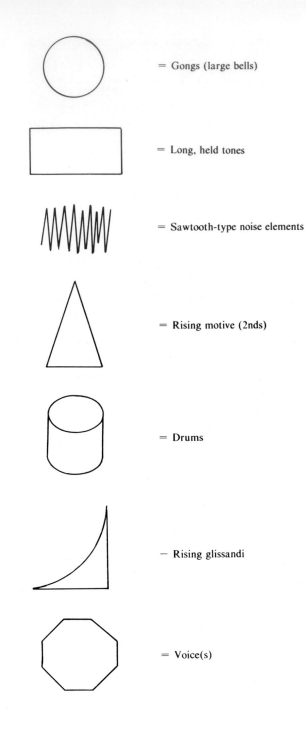

= Gongs (large bells)

= Long, held tones

= Sawtooth-type noise elements

= Rising motive (2nds)

= Drums

— Rising glissandi

= Voice(s)

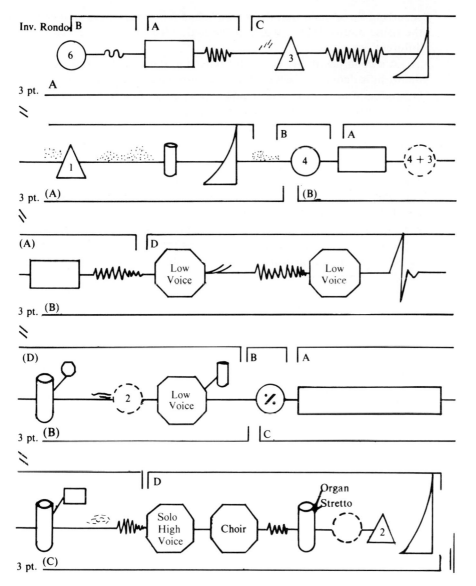

Figure 8.30. Diagrammatic formal analysis of Varèse's *Poème électronique.*

Occasional reference to subjects represented by words (e.g., "low voice solo") clearly identify important characteristics that are varied in the context of the work.

The form of the piece takes two distinct shapes. First, one perceives a characteristic rondo (return) quality even on first hearing. One such interpretation is shown above the symbols: the "inverted rondo," meaning that the main repeating sequence appears second rather than first. Note that the "A" portion repeats twice in the body of the work between sections of other materials, some of which, like "B," also repeat. At least two other rondo possibilities exist here: one, with the opening gongs being "A" and occurring three main times with two "shadow" occurrences; and two, with the rising motive (the triangle) as the main idea (A) occurring on three different occasions.

A second possibility is shown (under the symbols) as "three-part." Here the form is defined as sectional in three large parts, with each part beginning in nearly the same manner (i.e., gongs followed by long held notes). This separate and distinct (from the rondo interpretation just discussed) formal possibility should not be ignored even though it is less audible on first hearing.

3. Orchestration Techniques: Varèse uses two basic sound materials: *concrète* and electronic. Within each of those categories are two main divisions: *concrète*—instrumental and vocal; electronic—sine-type tones (simple resonances) and complex (nearly noise) elements. His techniques of variation within these timbres are extremely subtle. A good example of this is the way in which he varies the initial six attacks of the gong-type motive at the beginning of the work. The sixth sound is filtered so that it sounds nearly an octave lower in pitch. The reverberation characteristic as well as timbre of each of the bells is clearly different in the succeeding appearances of the motivic structure.

4. Basic Techniques: Most techniques presented here are a by-product of *classical* tape composition discussed earlier in this chapter. Most notable in *Poème électronique* are the tape speed changes (N.B.: the solo female entrance where her range is extended beyond human potential), envelope control (cutoffs on the opening long note section, for example, show strong hints of editing executions), synchronization (e.g., the fast switching between drums and organ in the final stretto), and other techniques typical of this period of electronic composition.

5, 6. Vertical and Horizontal Models: Neither of these categories is particularly important in a work whose sonorities are determinates of chosen percussive materials. However, the final "long note" section before the entrance of the low-voice solo clearly defines the harmonic context of the piece. The horizontal materials that most noticeably represent clear identities suggest either seconds, minor or major, or widely leaping pointillism.

7. Style: *Poème électronique* represents an important work (along with Stockhausen's *Gesang der Jünglinge;* 1954) in the hybridization of electronic principles that are highly organized and defined. The recognizable sounds (jet airplane, drums, temple bells, human voices, for example) represent an interesting layer of separate identities, which, along with the often humorous "squeaks and squawks," present a dynamic and linear design not unlike the composer's instrumental works of earlier vintage.

This classic of the electronic music genre compares favorably in concept and stylistic approach to both the works presented in the vectoral analyses of chapter 9 (Risset) and chapter 3 (Penderecki). In the former case, the centricity of interest in timbre and the electronic medium resemble one another. In the latter case, even though Penderecki's work does not employ electronics of any kind, there are abstract sonorities that create new resonances and hence a vertical sense of depth. While the technology of Varèse's use of electronic sounds suggests a very different kind of music than appeared in his earlier *Density 21.5* (see vectoral analysis of chapter 1), one finds much of the same lyrical and phrase structure present.

Bibliography— Chapter 8*

Further Readings

Origins and Evolutions

Appleton, Jon, and Ronald Perera, eds. *The Development and Practice of Electronic Music.* Englewood Cliffs, N.J.: Prentice-Hall, 1974.

Chavez, Carlos. *Toward a New Music: Music and Electricity.* New York: W. W. Norton, 1937.

Eimert, Herbert, and Karlheinz Stockhausen, eds. *Die Reihe* 1 (1965).

Ernst, David. *The Evolution of Electronic Music.* New York: Schirmer Books, 1977.

Griffiths, Paul. *A Guide to Electronic Music.* London: Thane and Hudson, 1979.

Kondracki, M., et al. *International Electronic Music Discography.* Mainz. B. Schott, 1979.

Luening, Otto. "Some Random Remarks about Electronic Music." *Journal of Music Theory* 8 (1964): pp. 89–98.

———. "An Unfinished History of Electronic Music." *Music Educators Journal* 55 (1968): pp. 42–49.

———. *The Odyssey of An American Composer: The Autobiography of Otto Luening.* New York: C. F. Peters, 1981.

Maconie, Robin. "Stockhausen's Mikrophonie 1." *Perspectives of New Music* 10, no. 2 (1971): pp. 92–101.

Russcol, Herbert. *The Liberation of Sound.* Englewood Cliffs, N.J.: Prentice-Hall, 1972.

Schrader, Barry. *Introduction to Electro-Acoustic Music.* Englewood Cliffs, N.J.: Prentice-Hall, Inc., 1982.

Stockhausen, Karlheinz. "The Concept of Unity in Electronic Music." In *Perspectives on Contemporary Music Theory,* ed. Benjamin Boretz and Edward T. Cone. New York: W. W. Norton and Co., 1972.

Trythall, Gilbert. *Electronic Music.* New York: Grosset and Dunlap, 1973.

Aesthetic Challenges

Appleton, Jon, and Ronald Perera, eds. *The Development and Practice of Electronic Music.* Englewood Cliffs, N.J.: Prentice-Hall, 1974.

Cage, John. *Silence.* Cambridge, Mass.: The M.I.T. Press, 1961.

Ceely, Robert. "Thoughts about Electronic Music." *Composer* 5, no. 1 (1973): pp. 11–14.

Ernst, David. *The Evolution of Electronic Music.* New York: Schirmer Books, 1977.

Griffiths, Paul. *A Guide to Electronic Music.* London: Thane and Hudson, 1979.

Manning, Peter. *Electronic and Computer Music.* Oxford, England: Clarendon Press, 1985.

*Addresses for record companies, periodicals, and music publishers mentioned in this Bibliography can be found in Appendix IV.

Oram, Daphne. *An Individual Note.* London: Galliard Ltd., 1972.

Pousseur, Henri. "Calculation and Imagination in Electronic Music." *Electronic Music Review* 5 (1968): pp. 21–29.

Prieberg, F. K. *Musica ex Machina.* Berlin: Verlag Ullstein, 1960.

Stockhausen, Karlheinz. "The Concept of Unity in Electronic Music." In *Perspectives on Contemporary Music Theory,* ed. Benjamin Boretz and Edward T. Cone. New York: W. W. Norton and Co., 1972.

Stroh, W. M. *Zur Sociologie der elektronischen Musik.* Zurich: Amadeus, 1980.

Trythall, Gilbert. *Electronic Music.* New York: Grosset and Dunlap, 1973.

de la Vega, Aurelio. "Electronic Music, Tool of Creativity." *Music Journal* 23 (1965): p. 52.

Wells, Thomas, and Eric Vogel. *The Technique of Electronic Music.* Austin, Tex.: University Stores, 1974.

Fundamental Concepts

Appleton, Jon, and Ronald Perera, eds. *The Development and Practice of Electronic Music.* Englewood Cliffs, N.J.: Prentice-Hall, 1974.

Babbitt, Milton. "An Introduction to the RCA Synthesizer." *Journal of Music Theory* 8 (1964): pp. 251–65.

Beckwith, John, and Udo Kasmets, eds. *The Modern Composer and His World.* Toronto: University of Toronto Press, 1961.

Berio, Luciano. "The Studio di Fonologia Musicale of the Milan Radio." Score 15 (1956): p. 89.

Cope, David. "A View on Electronic Music." *db: The Sound Engineering Magazine,* August 1975, pp. 30–32.

———. "An Approach to Electronic Music Composition." *Composer* 6, no. 1 (1975): pp. 14–16.

Emmerson, Simon. *The Language of Electromagnetic Music.* London: Macmillan Press, 1986.

Ernst, David. *The Evolution of Electronic Music.* New York: Schirmer Books, 1977.

Everett, Tom. "Five Questions: Forty Answers." *Composer* 3, no. 1 (1971): pp. 30–38.

Manning, Peter. *Electronic and Computer Music.* Oxford, England: Clarendon Press, 1985.

Meyers, Robert G. "Technical Basis of Electronic Music." *Journal of Music Theory* 8 (1964): pp. 2–52.

Oliveros, Pauline. "Tape Delay Techniques for Electronic Music." *Composer* 1, no. 3 (1969): pp.135–43.

Olsen, Harry F. *Music, Physics and Engineering.* New York: Dover, 1967.

Schrader, Barry. *Introduction to Electro-Acoustic Music.* Englewood Cliffs, N.J.: Prentice-Hall, 1982.

Stockhausen, Karlheinz. "The Concept of Unity in Electronic Music." In *Perspectives on Contemporary Music Theory,* ed. Benjamin Boretz and Edward T. Cone. New York: W. W. Norton and Co., 1972.

Strange, Allen. *Electronic Music.* 2d ed. Dubuque, Iowa: Wm. C. Brown Publishers, 1982.

Weinland, John David. "An Electronic Music Primer." *Journal of Music Theory* 13, no. 1 (1969): pp. 250–75.

Wells, Thomas, and Eric Vogel. *The Technique of Electronic Music.* Austin, Tex.: University Stores, 1974.

Early Studios

Cott, Jonathan. *Stockhausen.* New York: Simon and Schuster, 1973.

Cross, Lowell M., ed. *A Bibliography of Electronic Music.* Toronto: University of Toronto Press, 1967.

Douglas, Alan. *Electronic Music Production.* London: Pitman Publishing, 1973.

———. *Electronic Music Instrument Manual.* 4th ed. London: Pitman, 1972.

Ernst, David. *The Evolution of Electronic Music.* New York: Schirmer Books, 1977.

Henry, Thomas. *Build a Better Music Synthesizer.* Blue Ridge Summit, Pa.: Tab Books, 1987.

Holmes, Thomas B. *Electronic and Experimental Music.* New York: Charles Scribner's Sons, 1985.

Horn, Delton. *Music Synthesizers, A Manual of Design and Construction.* Blue Ridge Summit, Pa.: Tab Books, 1984.

Judd, F. C. *Electronic Music and Musique Concrète.* London: Neville Spearman, 1961.

———. *Electronics in Music.* London: Neville Spearman, 1972.

Manning, Peter. *Electronic and Computer Music.* Oxford, England: Clarendon Press, 1985.

Naumann, J., and James Wagner. *Analog Electronic Music Technologies and Voltage Controlled Synthesizer Studios.* New York: Schirmer Books, 1986.

Pellegrino, Ronald. "Some Thoughts on Thinking for the Electronic Music Synthesizer." *Proceedings* (American Society of University Composers) 7, no. 8 (1972): pp. 47–55.

Rossi, Nick, and Robert Choate, eds. *Music of Our Time.* Boston: Crescendo Publishing Co., 1969.

Schwartz, Elliott. *Electronic Music: A Listener's Guide.* New York: Praeger Publishers, 1972.

Strange, Allen. *Electronic Music.* 2d ed. Dubuque, Iowa: Wm. C. Brown Publishers, 1982.

Examples of Concrète and Synthesized Music

Appleton, Jon, and Ronald Perera, eds. *The Development and Practice of Electronic Music.* Englewood Cliffs, N.J.: Prentice-Hall, 1974.

Coker, Cecil, Peter Denes, and Elliot Pinson. *Speech/Synthesis.* Farmingdale, N.Y.: Comspace Corp., 1963.

Cross, Lowell M., ed. *A Bibliography of Electronic Music.* Toronto: University of Toronto Press, 1967.

Dallin, Leon. *Techniques of Twentieth Century Composition.* 3d ed. Dubuque, Iowa: Wm. C. Brown Publishers, 1974.

Davies, Hugh. "A Discography of Electronic Music and Musique Concrète." *Recorded Sound* 14 (1964): pp. 205–24.

———, ed. *International Electronic Music Catalog.* Cambridge, Mass.: M.I.T. Press, 1968.

Ellis, Merrill. "Musique Concrète at Home." *Music Educators Journal* 55, no. 3 (1968): pp. 94–96.

Maconie, Robin. "Stockhausen's Mikrophonie 1." *Perspectives of New Music* 10, no. 2 (1971): pp. 92–101.

Schaeffer, Pierre. *A la Recherche d'une Musique Concrète.* Paris: Editions du Seuil, 1952.

Strange, Allen. "Tape Piece." *Composer* 2, no. 1 (1970): pp. 12–16.

Ussachevsky, Vladimir. "Sound Materials in the Experimental Media of Musique Concrète, Tape Music and Electronic Music." *Journal of the Acoustical Society of America* 29.

Wörner, Karl. *Stockhausen, Life and Work.* Translated by Bill Hopkins. Berkeley: University of California Press, 1973.

Performance Considerations

Dockstader, Tod. "Inside-Out: Electronic Rock." *Electronic Music Review* 5 (1968): pp. 15–20.

Leitner, Gerhard. *Sound: Space.* New York: New York University Press, 1978.

Schwartz, Elliott. *Electronic Music: A Listener's Guide.* New York: Praeger Publishers, 1972.

Ussachevsky, Vladimir. "Note on a Piece for Tape Recorder." In *Problems of Modern Music,* ed. Paul Henry Lang, pp. 64–71. New York: W. W. Norton and Co., 1960.

Vercoe, Barry. "Electronic Sounds and the Sensitive Performer." *Music Educators Journal* 55, no. 3 (1968): pp. 104–7.

Live-Electronic Music

Appleton, Jon, and Ronald Perera, eds. *The Development and Practice of Electronic Music.* Englewood Cliffs, N.J.: Prentice-Hall, 1974.

Mumma, Gordon. "Creative Aspects of Live Electronic Music Technology." *Audio Engineering Society Reprint* No. 550.

———. "The ONCE Festival and How it Happened." *Arts in Society* 4, no. 2 (1967): pp. 381–98.

Nyman, Michael. *Experimental Music.* London: Studio Vista, 1974.

Schwartz, Elliott. *Electronic Music: A Listener's Guide.* New York: Praeger Publishers, 1972.

Edgard Varèse

Schuller, Gunther. "Conversation with Varèse." *Perspectives of New Music* 3, no. 2 (1964): pp. 32–37.

Varèse, Louise Norton. *A Looking Glass Diary.* New York: W. W. Norton, 1972.

Vinton, John, ed. *Dictionary of Contemporary Music.* New York: E. P. Dutton and Co., 1974.

Wen-chung, Chou. The Liberation of Sound. In *Contemporary Composers on Contemporary Music,* eds. Barney Childs and Elliott Schwartz, pp. 308–15. New York: Holt, Rinehart and Winston, 1967.

———. "Varèse: A Sketch of the Man and His Music." *Musical Quarterly* 52, 1966.

Compact Discs, Recordings, and Publishers

Albright, William. *Organbook I, III* (1967; 1977–78). Jobert. Gothic 58627.

Anderson, Ruth. *Points* (1973–74). 1750 Arch Records S–1765.

Babbitt, Milton. *Composition for Synthesizer.* Columbia MS–6566.

———. *Ensembles for Synthesizer* (1967). Periodic Music PE–1632.

Beatles, The. *Sgt. Pepper's Lonely Hearts Club Band.* Capitol MAS–2653.

Beerman, Burton. *Sensations for Clarinet and Tape* (1972). ACA. Advance Recordings FGR 15S.

Berio, Luciano. *Thema: Omaggio à Joyce.* Zerboni Editions. Turnabout 34177.

———. *Visage.* Turnabout 34046.

Beyer, Johanna. *Music of the Spheres* (1938). 1760 Arch St. S–1765.

Bielawa, Herbert. *Spectrum* (1967). Cornell University Wind Ensemble CUWE–1.

Blacher, Boris. *Electronic Impulses* (1965). Mace S–9097.

Bolcom, William. *Black Host* (1967). Nonesuch 71260.

Borden, David. *Variations on America By Charles Ives* (1970). Cornell University Wind Ensemble CUWE–7.

Cage, John. *Aria with Fontana Mix* (1958). Mainstream 5005.

————. *Imaginary Landscape No. 4.* C. F. Peters.

————. *Imaginary Landscape No. 5.* C. F. Peters.

————. *Variations IV.* Everest 3230.

Ceely, Robert. *Elegia* (1963–64). CRI–328.

Chadabe, Joel. *Street Scene* (1967). Opus One 16.

Cope, David. *Arena.* Carl Fischer. Orion IRS–75169.

Davidovsky, Mario. *Synchronisms 1, 2, and 3* (1963; 1964; 1965). Edward B. Marks Corp. CRI S–204.

————. *Synchronisms 4, 5, and 6* (1967; 1968; 1969). Edward B. Marks Corp. Turnabout 34487.

————. *Electronic Study No. 2* (1962). Finnadar 9010.

Dockstader, Tod. *Quartermass* (1964). Owl 6.

Druckman, Jacob. *Animas II* (1969). MCA Music. CRI S–255.

————. *Animas III* (1969). MCA Music. Nonesuch 71253.

Duckworth, William. *Gambit* (1967). Capra 1201.

Eaton, John. *Concert Piece for Synket and Orchestra* (1966). Turnabout 34428.

Electronic Music: *The Pioneers.* CRI ACS 6010.

Erb, Donald. *In No Strange Land.* Merion Music. Nonesuch 71223.

————. *Reconnaissance.* Nonesuch 71223.

————. *Reticulation.* Merion Music.

Felciano, Richard. *"and from the abyss"* (1976). E. C. Schirmer. Opus One 19.

————. *Crasis* (1976). E. C. Schirmer. CRI S–349.

————. *God of the Expanding Universe* (1971). E. C. Schirmer.

————. *Lamentations for Jani Christou* (1970). E. C. Schirmer.

Gaburo, Kenneth. *Antiphony III* (Pearl White Moments). Nonesuch 71199.

Gerhard, Roberto. *Collages* (Symphony #3). Angel S–36558.

Hendrix, Jimi. *Jimi Hendrix Experience* (1968). Reprise 6261.

Henry, Pierre. *Apocalypse de Jean* (1968). Philips 6521 002.

Henry, Pierre, and Pierre Schaeffer. *Symphonie pour un Homme seul* (1950). Adès 14.122–2.

Hiller, Lejaren. *Machine Music* (1964). Presser. Turnabout 34536.

————. *Malta* (for tuba and tape, 1975). CAPRA Records 1206.

Ichiyanagi, Toshi. *Life Music* (for tape and orchestra, 1966). Varèse Sarabande 81060.

Kagel, Mauricio. *Acoustica* (1970). DG–2707059.

Korte, Karl. *Remembrances* (1971). Nonesuch 71289.

Kupferman, Meyer. *Superflute* (1972). Nonesuch 71289.

Ligeti, György. *Articulation* (1958). Wergo 60059.

Lockwood, Annea. *World Rhythms* (1975). 1750 Arch Records S–1765.

Lucier, Alvin. *Music on a Long Thin Wire* (1977). Lovely Music 1011/2.

————. *North American Time Capsule* (1967). Recorded on Odyssey 32–160156.

————. *Vespers* (1968). Recorded on Mainstream Records 5010.

Luening, Otto. *Synthesis* (1960). Peters. CRI S–219.

MacInnis, Donald. *Collide-a-Scope* (1968). Golden Crest S–4085.

Marshall, Ingram. *Fragility Cycles* (1976). IBU Records.

McLean, Barton. *Genesis* (1973). Orion ORS 75192.

————. *Song of the Nahuatl* (1977). Folkways FTS 33450.

McLean, Priscilla. *Dance of Dawn* (1974). CRI SD 335.

————. *Invisible Chariots* (1977). Folkways Records FTS 33450.

Messiaen, Olivier. *Trois petites liturgies de la présence divine* (1945). Forlane UCD 16504/05.

Miller, Edward. *Piece for Clarinet and Tape* (1967). Advance FGR 17S.

Mimarogiu, Ilhan. *Wings of the Delirious Demon* (1972). Finnadar 9001.

Mumma, Gordon. *Hornpipe.* Mainstream 5010.

————. *Megaton for Wm. Burroughs* (1963). Lovely Music LML/VR–1091.

————. *Mesa.* Odyssey 32–160158.

Oliveros, Pauline. *Bye Bye Butterfly* (1965). 1750 Arch Records S–1765.

————. *I of IV.* Odyssey 32–160160.

Ross, Eric. *Electronic études* (Op. 18). Doria Records ER–103.

Souster, Tim. *Spectral* (1972). Transatlantic Records TRAG 343.

Stockhausen, Karlheinz. *Gesang der Jünglinge.* DG–138811.

————. *Hymnen.* Universal Edition. DG–2707039.

————. *Kontakte.* Universal Edition. DG–138811.

————. *Stimmung* (1968). Universal Edition. Hyperion CDA66115.

————. *Telemusik.* Universal Edition. DG–17012.

Strange, Allen. *Two × Two* (1968). Capra 1210.

Subotnick, Morton. *After the Butterfly* (1980). Nonesuch N–78001.

————. *4 Butterflies* (1973). Columbia M–32741.

————. *Sidewinder* (1970). Columbia M–30683.

————. *Silver Apples of the Moon.* Nonesuch 71174.

————. *The Wild Bull.* Nonesuch 71208.

Thome, Diane. *Anais.* CRI S–437.

Truax, Barry. *Solar Eclipse* (1985). Cambridge Street Records CSR 8501.

United States of America. *United States of America.* Columbia CS–9614.

Ussachevsky, Vladimir. *A Piece for Tape Recorder.* CRI–122.

————. *Creation-Prologue.* Columbia MS–6566.

————. *Of Wood and Brass.* CRI S–227.

Ussachevsky, Vladimir, and Otto Luening. *Concerted Piece for Tape Recorder and Orchestra.* CRI 227–SD.

————. *A Poem in Cycles and Bells for Tape Recorder and Orchestra* (1954).

Varèse, Edgard. *Déserts* (1954). G. Schirmer. Angel S–36786.

————. *Poème électronique.* Columbia MS–6146.

Wilson, Galen. *Applications* (1968). Capra 1201.

Wilson, George Blach. *Exigencies.* CRI S–271.

Wuorinen, Charles. *Times Encomium.* Nonesuch 71225.

Digital Electronic Music

Computer music differentiates between the terms *analog* and *digital.* The electronic music discussed in chapter 8 is *analog:* continuous, noninterrupted magnetic information. Sound, such as singing, breathing, and so on; most of the activities of life, is analog. *Digital,* on the other hand, refers to information stated in numbers; that is, discrete, noncontinuous digits, or bits of information. Unlike analog synthesizers, computers are digital in nature, working only with numbers.

The *digits* that *digital* refers to in computers are binary, or containing two states. The binary system incorporates only the symbols "0" and "1." These occur in columns referencing the more traditional decimal (or base 10) system, and are listed right to left in exponential order:

etc.	32	16	8	4	2	1	Decimal columns
	0	0	0	1	0	0	Binary digits

A "1" "trips" the column into existence, while a "0' signals that the column is Ø. In the preceding example, the number generated is 4. Typically, the exponential listing is taken for granted. These binary numbers can exist in traditional mathematical operations with one example shown below:

$$
\begin{array}{cccc}
0 & 0 & 0 & 1 \\
1 & 0 & 0 & 0 \\
\hline
1 & 0 & 0 & 1 \\
\end{array}
$$

Note that addition exists in much the same way it does in decimal mathematics (i.e., $0 + 0 = 0$; $1 + 0 = 1$, etc.). Here the number 1 was added to the number 8, with the result (adding all "tripped" digits) equaling 9.

Understanding binary mathematics is important to one's understanding of computers and consequently of computer music. The fact that numbers of any amount can be represented by two digits (0 and 1) makes computers possible. Doors (opened/closed), mousetraps (set/unset), or even directions (up/down) all present real-world binary equivalents. More importantly, magnetic fields (positive/negative) or electric current (on/off) represent ways in which computers can operate using binary concepts. Since objects require only two states of existence, the operations can be less than a trillionth of a second and take little space (some designers are now talking in terms of "molecular" operations). It is the concept that computers can operate with extreme speed and take little space that makes the "digital" nature of computers important. In contrast, computers can lose some of their mystique; the complicated innards are often merely rows upon rows of millions of devices housing smaller devices whose only job is to be on/off, open/closed, or the equivalent.

Since sound is analog and computers digital, composers interested in the use of computers have found inherent contradictions in the compositional possibilities of the instrument. The speed at which computers operate, however, and the mass of material and control they offer are important attractions for composers exploring new compositional techniques. Composers (primarily in the early and mid-sixties) such as Lejaren Hiller, Max Matthews, James Tenney, J. K. Randall, and Hubert Howe were among the first to become dedicated to the problems and advantages of computer music. Work at the Bell Laboratories beginning in 1959 proved enlightening and led to the first MUSIC series of programs discussed later in the chapter. Figure 9.1 provides a demonstration of the process. Sound is first produced as numerical amplitude values. These are then smoothed, allowing each of the differences between samples in memory to be transformed into analog sound. The process may also be reversed as will be discussed in detail later in this chapter.

Significant to these early experiments was the exploration of an instrument called the *digital to analog converter,* often called the DAC. It is conceptually similar to motion pictures. If one looks at film it is quickly apparent that material present is "digital" (i.e., "fixed" images of discrete material); there is no analog motion. However, when these digital elements are shown through a projector at the typical speed

Figure 9.1. How analog sounds are computed and used to create waveforms.

These values are stored in digital memory . . .

. . . and are used to recreate the original analog waveform.

Chapter 9

of twenty-four per second, a "feel" of analog motion occurs. The same is possible with computers and sound. If one takes enough numbers representing waveforms and "projects" them through alternations in voltage, the analog impression of sound results. Though this concept is a simplified one, it does give the basic essence of the converter concept.

Typically, between 20,000 and 55,000 numbers (termed *samples*) must be produced for quality sound. These numbers are then converted into voltages that are smoothed and filtered in order to cancel the "rate" numbers themselves, which can sometimes be read as an extra frequency, an effect called *aliasing*. This then produces the "electronic" sound through a high-fidelity system.

With the parameters of sound existing (in the initial state) in numbers, composers can control extremely small and often very precise data. Editing, for example, can be accomplished by the extracting of "numbers," avoiding the complicated necessity of splicing common to "classical" electronic music. Careful control of tuning (previously relegated to hand manipulation of knobs) and dynamics is easily feasible. In these ways, the computer offers the composer *more* control and precision in the compositional process.

Analog to digital (A/D) aspects of computer operation often prove as valuable as DAC. Here the composer or experimenter replaces speakers with microphones, and the computer acts as an analytical midwife. Instead of sound being initiated in terms of numbers, it is first analog and then translated into numbers for storage (digital recording), editing (manipulation), or composition (*musique concrète*). Live acoustical events can be recorded via digital mechanics and carefully categorized according to a wide variety of different available techniques for timbral data, spatial content, and reference to compositional potential.

The author has divided composer use of computers into two basic categories: (1) computer-generated sound, wherein the composer has precise control possibilities over musical materials and parameters; and (2) hybrid operations, wherein the computer controls synthesizer functions. In addition to the discussion of these that follows, computer applications in notation and teaching will also be examined.

Early Developments

Computer-generated sound (sometimes referred to as "computer sound synthesis") began at the Bell Telephone Laboratories in 1959 with Max Matthews and James Tenney. J. K. Randall and Hubert Howe, among others at Princeton, collaborated with the Bell Laboratories to produce the first effective computer program for sound generation: MUSIC IVB. This program, as well as the host of programs designed since, allows the composer extensive control over all the elements of composition. MUSIC IVB was a culmination of MUSIC IV designed by Matthews using the IBM 7090 computer; it eventually became MUSIC V for the GE 645 computer.

Other programs include the Music Simulator-Interpreter for Compositional Procedure (Musicomp) developed for the IBM 7090 by Lejaren Hiller and Robert Baker, MUSIGOL developed by Donald MacInnis for the Burroughs 5500, and the Transformational Electronic Music Process Organizer (TEMPO) developed by John

Figure 9.2. John Chowning. Photo courtesy of the Stanford University News and Publications Service.

Clough at Oberlin College. All of these programs deal explicitly with composer control of all the available parameters of sound and use the computer (with digital input) as a high-speed "performer" to achieve a magnetic tape recording of their works as output (analog voltage on tape).

Research into computer-generated sound continues at many locations, most notably at the Center for Computer Research in Music and Acoustics (CCRMA) at Stanford University. There John Chowning and Leland Smith study digital recording techniques, digital signal processing, psychoacoustical information, advanced synthesis techniques, and the automatic production of musical manuscripts. The Center for New Music and Audio Technologies (CNMAT) founded at the University of California at Berkeley (1988) has been developed to investigate matters relating to this important aspect of the musical experience. Consortiums exist between it, IRCAM in Paris, and Stanford as well as the Media Laboratory at M.I.T.

John Chowning's research and composition have received considerable acclaim. His early work centered on sound production and basic modulation procedures. Early MUSIC V techniques called for instrument definition in terms of building complex tones called Fourier or additive synthesis, with each overtone added separately—a tedious and time-consuming process, though the results are often highly controllable. Chowning has worked primarily with concepts of frequency modulation, developing techniques using program and carrier waves. These produce highly complex tones including "inharmonic" materials and frequently sound like "bell tones." This procedure became so important to the development of certain computer programs for music that *Chowning FM* is the term often used to designate the technique. As well, his research of musical *space* using computer techniques and discoveries correlating reverberation as well as dynamics, direction, and doppler to spatial modulation have contributed greatly to the development of new programs and works. Both space and FM principles are apparent in his *Turenas* (1972) and *Stria* (1977), both computer-generated quadraphonic tape compositions.

He speaks of the former work in an interview:

> In *Turenas,* I used only the FM technique for generating the tones, I used it in both a harmonic series mode and a noisy inharmonic series mode, with transformations between the two. One of the compositional uses of FM was in timbral transformation. This was often coupled with spatial manipulation. As the sounds crossed the space they underwent a timbral transformation.[1]

Chowning's *Phoné,* completed in 1981, forms elegant vocal effects derived from the use of vibrato in a quasi-random formant structure.

Excellent examples of current computer uses with computer-generated sound are described in *Proceedings* 7, no. 8, American Society of University Composers. A complete recording of the works referred to by their respective composers or programmers includes Hubert S. Howe, Jr.: *Freeze;* David Cohen: seven examples including a Bach fugue, original studies, and computer-generated fragments; John Melby: *Forandrer;* and Donald MacInnis: *Quadrilith.* These, with their verbal annotations, prove invaluable to the uninitiated as well as to the experienced. Computer-generated sound has proven to be a most prolific and fertile resource for composers.

Dreamsong, a highly regarded computer composition (1977/1978 at Stanford Center for Computer Research in Music and Acoustics) by Michael McNabb, integrates sets of synthesized sounds and digitally recorded natural sounds. The title derives from the fact that many of the sounds presented are vaguely recognizable (as in a dream) while others shift in and out of recognition. This work, unlike most in the genre, is relatively simple in harmonic and melodic structure in order to enable the composer and hence the audience to focus on the more important elements of texture and timbre usually in transition or modulating. Figure 9.3 shows the two modes from which most of the pitch material in *Dreamsong* was derived. This work, considered by many a classic of the field, has revitalized a sense of the lyric even in the world of electronic abstractions.

Figure 9.3. Modes used in Michael McNabb's *Dreamsong* with synthesized and digitally recorded sounds.

Hybrid Composition

Research and composition in the area of direct computer control over synthesizer modules (oscillators, filters, etc.) has become very impressive in the past few years. In a sense, the sequencer referred to in chapter 8 is a mini-analog computer. With various potentiometer settings (usually three to five per note) on a sequence of notes variable which is depending on the make and model of the sequencer one can "program" a *series* of notes rather than one or two at a time.

1. Curtis Roads, *Composers and the Computer* (Los Altos, Calif.: William Kaufmann, Inc., 1985), p. 21.

Newer developments include the Synthi 100's Digital Sequencer 256 (E.M.S.), with solid-state storage capacity of 10,240 bits of information. It is capable of precisely controlling six different simultaneous parameters over a sequence of 256 successive events. Through several modes of operation, any or all of the 256 stored items and their time relationships can be retrieved and even varied without difficulty. The Sequencer 256 is indeed a small special-purpose digital computer, complete with analog-to-digital and digital-to-analog converters. Surprisingly compact about the length of a five-octave piano keyboard, but one-third its depth and width, the 256 provides high-speed operation and full information retrieval. Buchla's late seventies *Music Easel* has full analog retrieval and is especially designed for storage of traditional instrument sounds. More recently, Buchla's *300 Series Music Box* combines microprocessing units with an analog synthesizer. The two instruments function in a truly symbiotic relationship with "hands-on" capabilities in both analog and digital spheres.

Salvatore Martirano's *Sal-Mar Construction* (1973) is a semiportable "live-performance" computer with retrieval and storage capabilities. His performances and tours with this instrument have brought much attention to the "live" potential of the computer-synthesizer combination. MUSYS, developed by Peter Zinovieff, Peter Grogono, and David Cockerell, uses PDP8/L and PDP8/S computers to control special-purpose electronic equipment.

Many composers have begun to research and utilize the potential for microprocessors (small microcomputers) to be used in live performance situations. David Behrman has worked extensively in this area. His *On the Other Ocean* (1977), for example, involves flute, bassoon, and the Kim-1 microcomputer-controlled polyphonic analog synthesizer (hybrid microprocessor utilization). The live performers choose their pitches according to the synthesizer's accompaniment, and the synthesizer chooses its accompaniment according to the live performers' pitches, producing a kind of "live-looping" compositional process. Composers continue to explore new concepts and applications of the computer. Visual input is an increasingly viable

Figure 9.4. David Behrman. Photo by Mary Lucier.

source for future experimentation. One method is to *draw* (using a special light pen) graph representations of waveforms directly on a cathode-ray tube (CRT; television-like computer input). The computer then translates these to digital information, processes, and, through a D/A converter, produces an electromagnetic force on tape (and/or "live" through studio speakers as the composer may wish). Printed graphs can also be assimilated by computer functions through Graphos I.

Notation Software

Computer recognition of traditionally notated scores creates the potential for actual performances of extremely difficult music without the composer having any knowledge of computer languages. It presents composers with an incredible experimental laboratory: immediate performance of works with any degree of complexity for experimentation, revision, and/or reorchestration.

Leland Smith at Stanford's Artificial Intelligence Laboratory uses a large PDP 10 computer to create exacting traditional music notation. The computer using light-sensitive paper similar to Xerox "prints" music according to data fed into the terminal. Figure 9.5 is an example of this notation. Advantages of this kind of notation/copying are as follows:

1. Speed: The computer can produce copies rapidly once the information is stored internally.

Figure 9.5. *Intermezzo and Capriccio for Piano* by Leland Smith. Example of computer notation. System designed by Leland Smith at Stanford's CCRMA. Computer Music Graphics, San Andreas Press, 3732 Laguna Ave., Palo Alto, CA 94306.

2. Editing: Since the storage is digital, simple computations can create quick transpositions (for transposing instruments) and corrections.

3. Flexibility: With data in numbers, it is easy to rearrange measure distribution for part-page turns as well as score layout.

4. Extractions: Once a score is in the computer, parts can be extracted in seconds (in transposition if necessary).

5. Versatility: Pages can be rearranged quickly in a variety of ways for determination of best readability.

Smith's program, Score, also follows the IBM PC computer interface. The elegance of his notation techniques translates beautifully from mainframe to mini. With such programs, digital processes have brought engraving-quality music printing

to everyone with such a need. And, with the advent of laser printers, the output
quality rivals the very best of traditional copyists. Symbols are added to staves in
one of three ways: from the standard typing keyboard, by use of the mouse, or by
use of a synthesizer keyboard. In the first two modes, the user indicates which of
the symbols shown in Figure 9.6 should be added to the staff where a blinking cursor
has been set to the correct pitch. This screendump is from the program Professional
Composer, one of the first such program readily available. Clicking on the appropriate box causes the object to be added to the current location of the cursor. Other
menu items such as tempo signs, meter, and so on, exist in this powerful program.
Figure 9.7 shows one of these (tuplet), which allows any number of pitches to exist
within a beat or division of the beat and adds the appropriate number above or below
the set, whichever makes the most sense.

Here five eighth notes will be set into the place reserved for four. Appropriate
vertical alignment is automatic in this program. Figure 9.8 shows the "symbols"
menu pulled down and how items such as clefs are added to and/or subtracted from
the screen area. Here, clefs are being removed from the open window. In Figure 9.9
(again from Professional Composer), a grace note is being added by a selection from
the "groupings" menu. The music may be varied at any time and performed through
the computer's speaker or a stereo system.

The third manner of using Professional Composer requires a separate software
package called Professional Performer. The user simply plays the material to be
notated on a synthesizer connected through a MIDI interface (see later section) to
the computer. Once the file is stored it can be translated into notation by having
Professional Performer communicate its data to Professional Composer.

One immediate and typical result from this process is that, if no rounding-off
subprogram is used, the resulting manuscript is fraught with 128th notes, syncopations, and rests since human performers are not very accurate in even the best of

circumstances and with the best of training. Hence programs use "resolving" programs to diminish the number of mistakes in interpretation. In Professional Composer one uses a *quantizing* approach. This involves rounding off pitches to a certain level (typically 8th notes) to get a more accurate representation of the performance in Performer and then adding legitimate 16th and 128th notes as needed.

Other programs, especially the one by Leland Smith called Score, effectively employ the same general techniques as Composer/Performer except that they are written for the IBM PC or compatible (Composer uses the Macintosh as does Finale). In all of these instances, users are able at sometimes five times the speed of ordinary pen-and-paper copying to create engraved-quality music printing using microcomputers and laser printers. All can handle part-extraction, transposition of parts, and so forth. Clearly these procedures are significant tools for composers, even those who are not interested in computers for sonic applications and composition.

Controllers, Synthesizers, and Samplers

Figure 9.10 shows a drawing of the Yamaha Disklavier, a computer-controlled piano. The "control wagon" is shown as it "performs" the keys and pedals of an otherwise traditional grand piano through a cable. This instrument may be used for playback and/or recording. In the latter case it exactly matches in playback the notes, rhythms, dynamics, and articulation of that which it has recorded. This can be quite useful for teachers, performers, accompanists, and composers. The process of communication (i.e., control unit to the piano) is by a computer through a Musical Instrument Digital Interface (*MIDI,* to be discussed later in this chapter).

With the advent of inexpensive personal computers, classroom applications have increased. MIDI has allowed digital synthesizers to connect to personal computers to create inroads and potential. Theorists and teachers, such as Arthur Hunkins (University of North Carolina), Dorothy Gross (University of Minnesota), Fred Hofstetter (University of Delaware), Rosemary Killam (North Texas State University), Gary Wittlich (Indiana University), Wolfgang Kuhn (Stanford), Paul Lorton (University of San Francisco), and Herb Bielawa (San Francisco State), have all developed sight-singing and/or ear-training programs. The advantages that the computer offers include (1) immediate feedback, (2) storage and retrieval of scoring, (3) timbre versatility, (4) notation speed, and (5) long-term correlation of instructional viability of materials used. Recent programs such as Listen, Perceive, and Practica Musica have made computer music theory affordable for the layperson and music student alike.

Figure 9.10. Yamaha's Disklavier.

Hammer Sensor Unit

Sensor Board

Key Sensor Unit

Key Driver Unit

Pedal Driver Unit

Control Wagon

Cable

Figure 9.11. Synclavier II. New England Digital Corp.

Digital instruments such as the Synclavier II (see Figure 9.11) have made computers as viable a resource for composers as the synthesizer became in the early sixties.

The table shown in Figure 9.12 provides a list of digital music equipment (a fraction of the actual number available). Rough retail costs are provided in column 3. The comments refer to whether the equipment is a synthesizer (creates sound from oscillators), sampler (to be discussed in some detail later), both of these ("DIGI/SYN"), drum machine, or MIDI-PIANO. In some cases, special synthesis (additive or *Fourier*) has been added to further identify the type in use. Lists of MIDI data for performance may be stored in associated computer memory or in MIDI sequencers in resident RAM and/or associated tape decks or disk drives.

With the exception of New England Digital Corporation's entry, the elegant *Synclavier,* synthesizers have obviously entered the arena of anyone interested in music produced digitally. Since these machines in no way influence the *style* of music performed on them, the business of creating and selling them has also become widespread in the popular music industry. Hence, competition has become vigorous, and new developments are reviewed by a stream of new monthly magazines devoted to electronic music (see Appendix IV).

A new digital guitar contains metal touch-plates and plucking bars instead of frets and strings. Built by Oncor Sound of Salt Lake City, it was adapted (by Cal Gold of New England Digital Corporation) for use with the Synclavier computerized synthesizer. Jazz artist Pat Metheny was one of the first professionals to use the instrument.

PRODUCER	PRODUCT	PRICE	COMMENTS	
ALESIS	MMT-8	$299	SE	
ANETEK	POCKET SEQ.	$199	SE	
ATARI	STACY	?	MUS COM	
BACHMANN	WS 400	$5,000	DP	
BROTHER	MIDI 30/40	$259/$299	SE	
BROTHER	PDC-100	$399	SE	
CASIO	CELVIANO AP-7	$3,750	DP	
CASIO	MT-750	$399	KB	
DIGIDESIGN	SAMPLE CELL	$2,995	MAC CARD	
DYNACORD	ADS-K	$6,185	SA/MO	
EMU	EIII	$10,000?	SA/MO	
EMU	PROTEUS II	$1,195	SA/MO	
ENSONIQ	EPS-16	$5,000	SA/KB	
ENSONIQ	VFX	$1,595	SY/KB	
GIBSON	MATRIX 12	$6,399	SY/KB	
KAWAI	K1R	$595	SY/MO	
KAWAI	K4R	$995	SY/MO	
KAWAI	Q-80	$795	SE	
KORG	C-7000	$3,150	DP	
KORG	M3R	$995	SY/MO	
KORG	T1	$5,699	SA/SY/KB	
KORG	T2	$4,169	SY/KB	
KORG	T3	$3,749	SY/KB	
KORG	WS	$2,399	SY/KB	
KORG M1	M1	$1,395	SY/KB	
KURZWEIL	250	$10,715	SA/KB	
KURZWEIL	EGM IV	$4,000	DP	
KURZWEIL	K1200	$3,195	SA/KB	
NEW ENG. DIGITAL	SYNCLAVIER	$72,000	SY/SA/KB	
PEAVY	DPM SP	$649	SY/MO	
ROLAND	D70	$1,800	SY/KB	
ROLAND	HP-3700	$4,000	DP	
ROLAND	JX-1	$749	C/KB	
ROLAND	MC-50	$895	SE	
ROLAND	PC 200	$299	C/KB	
ROLAND	SC-55	$695	MO	
ROLAND	U-20	$1,395	SA/KB	
ROLAND	U-220	$795	SA/MO	
TECHNICS	SX-PX66	$4,199	DP	
YAMAHA	C1	?	MUS COM	
YAMAHA	CLP-560	$2,995	DP	
YAMAHA	DISKLAVIER	$10-20,000	CCP	
YAMAHA	QX5FD	$1,095	SE	
YAMAHA	SY77	$2,200	SY/SA/KB	
YAMAHA	TG33	$499	SY/MO	
YAMAHA	TG55	$795	SY/SA/MO	

Figure 9.12. Table of synthesizers/samplers with manufacturers and approximate costs listed. Symbols: SE = sequencer; Mus Com = dedicated music computer; Dp = digital piano; Kb = keyboard; Mac Card = Macintosh card; Sa = sampler; Mo = module; Sy = synthesizer; C = controller; CCP = computer-controlled piano. These charts represent but a fraction of the software and hardware available. Addresses for the companies listed here are provided in Appendix IV. Prices represent those found in actual catalogs rather than those provided by manufacturers.

Casio Chord Switch
Accompaniment Select Switch
Memory Switch
Octave Shift Switch
Accompaniment Sound Set Switch
Electronic Sound Effect Buttons
Rhythm Selector Buttons
Select Switch
Start/Stop Switch
Tempo Control Knob
Tempo Indicator Lamp
Balance Control Knob
Synchro Start Switch
Sound Selector Buttons
Select Switch
Sustain Switch
Vibrato Switches
MS Button
Memory Play Button
Program Buttons
Memory Step Display
Program Indicator Lamps
Volume Control Knob
Function Switches
One Key Play Keys
Built-in Speaker

Power Indication Lamp
Power Switch
Fill-in Switch
Chord Indicators
Melody Guide Indicators
Headphone Jack
Line Out HIGH
Line Out LOW
Foot Volume Jack
Sustain Jack
Foot Switch Jack
Pitch Control Knob
MS Jack
AC Power Socket

(Rear panel)

Figure 9.13. The Casiotone 701 (Casio Inc., 15 Gardner Road, Fairfield, NJ 07006).

Constant emphasis on miniaturization has increased accessibility. Casio, for example, has created a number of fairly inexpensive digital instruments capable of a wide range of functions. Figure 9.13 shows one of their larger models. Note the multitude of options, memory, and especially the encoding reading device storage function (coiled wire and nozzle attached to the rear of the Casiotone 701). This equipment can "read" music from a coded sheet (see Figure 9.14) that can then be played back at various speeds and with different timbres. This $5'' \times 13'' \times 37''$ computer has more options than many electronic organs of a decade past, yet is but a fraction of their size. Yamaha's PS-20 exemplifies the competitive nature of the industry (see Figure 9.15).

Figure 9.14. The Casiotone's MS memory function "reading" an encoded score.

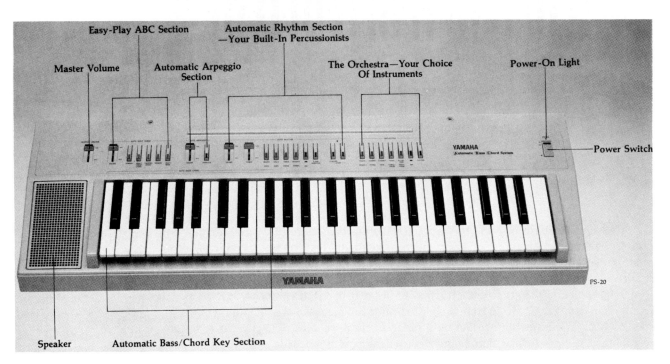

Figure 9.15. The Yamaha PS-20 (Yamaha; Nippon Gakki Co., Ltd., Hamamatsu, Japan).

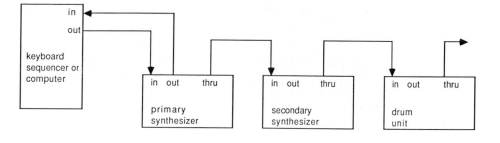

Figure 9.16. A "MIDI-chained" network of synthesizers and drum unit.

MIDI (acronym for Musical Instrument Digital Interface) is the industry standard for communication between synthesizers, drum machines, and other digital equipment. It was intended to create a cooperative standard for what had become, by the middle 1980s, a nightmare of different equipment with almost no opportunity to develop compatible "systems." Figure 9.16 shows a typical MIDI-chained network of synthesizers. Allowing the different brands of synthesizers to "talk" to one another enables composers to mix the sound qualities and various advantages of one unit over another during composition without having to create completely separate and highly redundant setups. Figure 9.17 provides a summary of MIDI commands.

MIDI: The Default Standard

MIDI Command Summary

Figure 9.17. A summary of MIDI commands.

Code: c = channel; k = key number (middle C is 60); v = velocity (0 is slow and 127 is fast); p = pressure or p = patch (depending on circumstance); d = device number; h = pitch wheel change.

```
1001cccc      = note "on" event
0kkkkkkk
0vvvvvvv

1000cccc      = note "off" event
0kkkkkkk
0vvvvvvv

1010cccc      = note "pressure" update
0kkkkkkk
0ppppppp

1101cccc      = "channel pressure" update
0ppppppp

1011cccc      = control change
0ddddddd
0vvvvvvv

1110cccc      = pitch wheel change
0hhhhhhh
01111111

1100cccc      = patch change
0ppppppp
```

Note how the first four digits (binary code) determine how the remaining code will be translated in each case.

The command bytes follow the description that begins this chapter and allow for 128 different states of descriptive elements about note-on and note-off states. The approach is very simple. It avoids, however, any control of timbre, turning this over to the synthesizer or sampler being addressed. This has alienated many composers who wish to analyze and digitally dictate timbre between machines. However, as the title of this section suggests, the MIDI standard is just that. As of this writing, virtually all major manufacturers of synthesizers and related equipment have adopted this procedure for transmission of keystroke information. As well, many minicomputer companies have added MIDI ports to their lines of personal computers so that one can use available software to create music by hooking up computers to synthesizers. As well, MIDI equipment may be added to device outputs if none has been provided with the original instrument. In each case, the actual transmission of MIDI code takes place through a special MIDI cord with two XLR type connectors.

The implications of MIDI include (1) a central (digital) control of many "instruments" simultaneously, (2) a virtually limitless ability to add to one's equipment assemblage, (3) creation of a "tapeless" recording facility since works can be saved on floppy disks, (4) greater cost-efficiency since add-on synthesizers do not require keyboards and other redundant modules, and (5) less obsolescence in that new equipment may simply be included in the system since whole new "installations" are not required.

Two important organizations, the International MIDI Association and the MIDI Manufacturers Association (see Appendix IV), are charged with updating and extending the MIDI code. The former includes users as well as manufacturers. However, the manufacturers of digital musical equipment exert tremendous influence over the available directions of new music. As well, the wide acceptability of MIDI as the industry standard suggests that composers in the last decade of this century will not be required to be electronics experts as has often been the case during the past two decades. The consequences of this may be extraordinary. In the past, the presentation of less-than-perfect equipment or synthesizers without user-demanded features was not well received by the generally electronically wise community capable of building their own equipment if not satisfied. The "new" digital electroacoustic composer, on the other hand, may be so unversed in the electrical and digital aspects as to exist at the mercy of the economics of the largely untrained business moguls.

SMPTE (Society of Motion Picture and Television Engineers) time code is the industry standard for linking multitrack digital recording and video together. Several MIDI/SMPTE synchronizers now exist. These operate by translating SMPTE time code into the number of MIDI elapsed beats. Since video production has made inexpensive what was, with film, an extremely costly process, the impact of these synchronizers should be profound for both popular and nonpopular forms of contemporary music.

Digital software has proliferated abundantly in the past few years as evidenced by the table in Figure 9.18. The prices are average consumer costs based on retail encouraged by the company.

PRODUCER	PRODUCT	PRICE	COMMENTS	
ALTECH	MIDI BASIC	$79	MAC/IBM (L)	
ALTECH	MIDI PASCAL	$63	MAC (L)	
ARS NOVA	PRACTICA MUSICA	$79	MAC (E)	
BRODERBUND	JAM SESSION	$29	MAC (SE)	
BRODERBUND	MAC DRUMS	$33	MAC (SE)	
C-LAB	CREATOR	$335	ATARI ST (SE)	
C-LAB	NOTATOR	$529	ATARI ST (N)	
CODA	FINALE	$549	MAC/IBM (N)	
CODA	MUSIC PROSE	$249	MAC (N)	
CODA	PERCEIVE	$79	MAC (E)	
DIGIDESIGN	AUTO MEDIA	$699	MAC (R)	
DIGIDESIGN	SOFT SYNTH	$295	MAC (ED)	
DIGIDESIGN	SOUND DESIGNER	$495	MAC (ED)	
DOCTOR T	BEYOND	$149	MAC (SE)	
DOCTOR T	COPYIST PRO	$195	ATARI ST (N)	
ELECTRONIC ARTS	DELUXE MUSIC	$99	MAC (N)	
ELECTRONIC ARTS	DELUXE RECORDER	$109	MAC (R)	
FARRALON	MAC RECORDER	$195	MAC (R)	
HIP SOFTWARE	HARMONY GRID	$69	MAC (I)	
IBIS	PLAY IT BY EAR	$79	IBM (I)	
INTELLIGENT MUSIC	M	$99	MAC (I)	
MARK OF UNICORN	COMPOSER	$359	MAC (N)	
MARK OF UNICORN	PERFORMER	$359	MAC (SE)	
MUSICATOR A/S	MUSICATOR	$369	IBM (SE)	
OPCODE	EZ VISION	$120	MAC (SE)	
OPCODE	MAX	$395	MAC (L)	
OPCODE	STUDIO VISION	$699	MAC (SE)	
OPCODE	VISION	$339	MAC (SE)	
P & G	BAND IN A BOX	$59	MAC/IBM/ATARI (I)	
PASSPORT DESIGN	ALCHEMY	$459	MAC (ED)	
PASSPORT DESIGN	ENCORE	$375	ATARI ST (N)	
PASSPORT DESIGN	ENCORE	$375	MAC (N)	
PASSPORT DESIGN	MASTER TRACKS	$329	MAC (SE)	
PASSPORT DESIGN	TRAX	$79	ATARI ST (SE)	
PASSPORT DESIGNS	SCORE	$695	IBM (N)	
PERSONAL COMPOS	PERSONAL COMPOS	$595	IBM (N)	
RESONATE	LISTEN	$75	MAC (E)	
RHAPSODY	PERSONAL COMPOS	$225	MAC (SE)	
TEMPORAL ACUITY	MUSIC PRINTER	$595	IBM (N)	
THOUGHT PROCESS	NOTE PROCESSOR	$389	IBM (N)	
TWELVE TONE	CAKEWALK	$95	IBM (SE)	
VOYETRA	MPC	$289	IBM (I)	
VOYETRA	SEQUENCER PLUS	$129	IBM (SE)	

Figure 9.18. Table showing software programs for developing synthesizer/sequencing music. The Symbols: N = notation program; L = language; Se = sequencer; R = recorder; E = education software; I = interactive application; Ed = editor. These charts represent but a fraction of the software and hardware available. Addresses for the companies listed here are provided in Appendix IV. Prices represent those found in actual catalogs rather than those provided by manufacturers.

Digital electronics information flow is inherently cleaner than its analog counterpart. The latter suffers generation noise as added machine hum during copying, line impedence, and circuit static that multiplies significantly as modules are added to the system. Digital information, however, proceeds through editing as discrete bits of information (the on/off states described at the beginning of this chapter). Hence, even when an analog system is "noisy," the digital information flows without distortion or added gains of unwanted and distracting frequencies or glitches.

CDs (compact discs) provide a good example of this. The immediate popularity of this digital approach to recording rests with the fact that the laser that reads the data from the disc reads only the digitized bumps that grace the grooves of the recording. Dust and other potentially distorting material are ignored. There is no system interference. The results are excellent playback with an almost infinite lifetime. CDs show virtually no sign of wear since there is no contact involved.

Figure 9.19 presents a straightforward comparison of compact discs and long-playing records. The advantages of the CD appear distinctly obvious in the areas of signal-to-noise ratio and life expectancy. The CD-ROM, while it does not allow recording, presents up to 1,400 prerecorded sounds for use in composition.

Figure 9.19. A comparison of CDs versus LPs.

	Compact Disc	LP Record
Disc diameter (mm)	120	300
Disc thickness (mm)	1·2	1·5 2·3
Disc playing time (min)	60	50~ 60
Rotation speed (rpm)	200-500	33⅓ or 45
Scanning velocity (m/s)	1·2 - 1·4	0·4 approx.
Width of grooves or tracks (μm)	1·6	100 approx.
Diameter of center hole (mm)	15	7·24
Number of channels	2	2
Frequency range (Hz)	20-20,000 (±0·5dB)	30-20,000 (±2dB)
Typical dynamic range (dB)	90	55
Signal-to-noise ratio (dB)	90	60
Channel separation (dB)	90	25-35
Total harmonic distortion	0·005%	0·2%
Wow-and-flutter	Quartz accuracy	0·03%
Disc material	Transparent PVC with aluminum reflective coating and lacquer protective layer	Black vinyl
Life expectancy (disc)	Indefinite (no physical contact)	100 playings approx.
Life expectancy (laser/ stylus)	5,000 hours	400 – 800 hours
Effect of dust, scratches, and static charges	Largely ignored by the laser beam	Causes increasing background noise and mistracking

Digital recording, the other end of the process, has also experienced important changes due to the current technology. DAT (or "digital audio tape") has added one more digital component to the recording process. While DAT technology suffers the same lack of random access that analog cassettes do, they nonetheless provide inexpensive routes to high-quality low-noise recording. The optimum system envisaged by most computer music composers and recording engineers would be one that has the sound represented digitally as long as possible with only two processes involving a change in the form of the data: analog to digital (A/D) and digital to analog (D/A). This, combined with access to the information (editing and splicing), creates the perfect environment for composition and processing. Recent advances now make this package possible. Some of these systems are listed in the hardware chart provided in the previous section (listed as "samplers" in Figure 9.12.).

Synthesis techniques have long been digitized from their inception to final analogization. Recording has only recently had this advantage. Called by many the "sampling" approach to mark the contrast to "synthesize," this process makes the potentials of *musique concrète* real. Most new synthesizers have sampling as a built-in option or feature. Figure 9.20 demonstrates the sampling process.

Here an instant of a percussive voice is represented first by a waveform and then by a series of vertical lines each representing a sample. Note how the last example accurately reflects the middle snapshot. Figure 9.21 shows the makeup of a

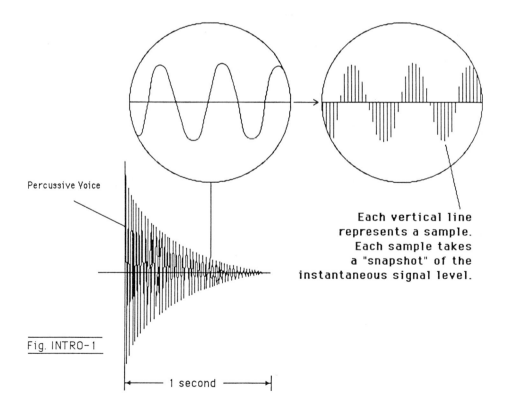

Figure 9.20. A demonstration of how sampling takes place in the EMAX (from the EMAX Manual). Permission granted by E-mu, Inc. All rights reserved.

Percussive Voice

Fig. INTRO-1

|← 1 second →|

Each vertical line represents a sample. Each sample takes a "snapshot" of the instantaneous signal level.

Figure 9.21. Example of a simple "sampling" system.

complete "sampling" system. In this example, only one of many possibilities, the live analog sound is converted to a digital imprint. It is then committed to RAM (Random Access Memory). Editing (discussed at a later point in this section) is then possible. At some point, the music is converted to disc or tape which may be necessary immediately if the sound sampling requires more RAM than available. When completed, the digital information is then stored on a CD for ultimate performance over a traditional system. Two major problems exist with this model:

1. As indicated earlier in this chapter, sampling requires an immense amount of memory, typically 1 megabyte for every 21 seconds, depending on sampling rate (rates vary with 48k/sec standard). Storing this data and retaining random access (ability to get to any point quickly and directly and not have to rewind/fast-forward as with tape) requires immense hard disc capacity.

2. Editing processes must be clean or free of inadvertent noise addition to the music. The user must be able to access each harmonic in the sound being processed and must be able to add or subtract energy anywhere in the spectrum.

As the end of the century approaches, both problems appear to be solved by a wealth of new products, principally for the mini- and the microcomputer markets. In the first instance, hard disks have become more available in significantly large sizes. A number of manufacturers have created (in some instances particularly *for* the music industry) 800-megabyte disks that hold between thirty and fifty minutes of digitally sampled music. As well, laser disks allow massive storage of sampled sounds and even complete works of great complexity. While their use is limited (the laser initially "burns" in the information onto a blank disk and once done the process cannot be repeated on that disk), current technology has also created open-architecture instruments that have expandable RAM up to one hundred and sixty four megabytes in some minicomputers at this writing. Thus, the storage and access problems are beginning to be solved. Figure 9.22 shows a more elaborate sampling system that includes CD-ROM interface to an Emulator II with SMPTE Time Code synchronization for video combinations and editing.

Problems of editing have been addressed by the advent of a series of software programs that provide user control of the various harmonics of a given instant of time. Figure 9.23 shows a typical screen in Sound Designer's program with the

Figure 9.23. Visual diagram of the amplitude characteristics of various harmonics of a sampled sound on the EMAX using Sound Designer. Permission granted by Digidesign, Inc.

EMAX sampling device (discussed later in this chapter). Here the figure represents 110 milliseconds of time and shows a sound heavy in harmonics between 0 and 55 kHz in frequency. It also shows their envelopes. The display on the left allows various applications including "playback" (the speaker icon), "select" (inverted sine wave with white box), and so on. The menus on the top (e.g., "File, Edit," etc.) may all be pulled down by the mouse for a host of other possible choices. The sound may also be viewed as a waveform. Figure 9.24 shows how sine waves may be stretched over both amplitude and time using various built-in features of this particular system.

Figure 9.25 shows Sound Designer's mechanics for editing a section of a sound by capturing a repeating loop. Here the recording of a D on the piano has been selected as source material. Note the single millisecond clicks at the bottom of the window. One moves within the sound by scrolling through it (Figure 9.25b, c, d). By using the mouse and controlling the pointer, one can alter and invent envelopes

Figure 9.24. Various scaling box adjustments including normal scaling (top), amplitude axis stretched (middle), and time axis stretched (bottom).

for many different time elements. Figure 9.26 shows filter and amplitude envelopes. By grabbing any black segment or line with the pointer arrow, holding down the mouse's button, and pulling, one creates a new node.

Larger (and more musical) editing potential exists at higher levels. Figure 9.27, for example, shows how the tempo for a segment of music can be altered, rhythm varied, and so forth. With a single acoustic sound sampled and edited, digital samplers like the EMAX can take the digital information and manipulate it in many ways. For example, a single sung human voice can be duplicated and set at different pitch levels so that it can be turned into a complete choir. This can then be assigned to a keyboard, for example, and the composer may create an entire choral composition that is in reality a "real" choir constructed from one voice.

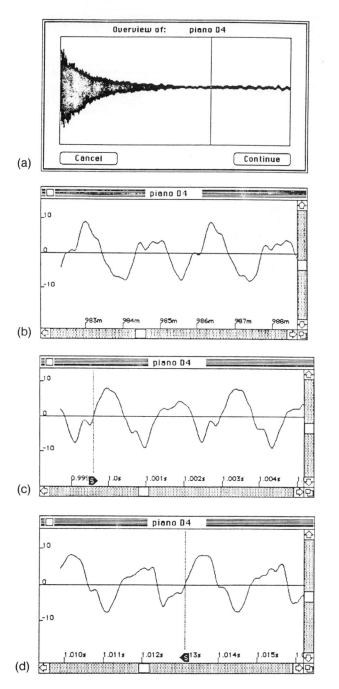

Figure 9.25. These screens demonstrate how to make a digital sound loop using Sound Designer software. (a) An overview provides location of stable sustain area; (b) scaling the waveform displays one or two periods; (c) placing a loop marker begins the loop; (d) placing loop end marker at zero crossing ends the loop. Permission granted by Digidesign, Inc. All rights reserved.

Figure 9.26. Filter and amplifier envelope-adjusting process using the EMAX and Sound Designer software. Permission granted by Digidesign, Inc. All rights reserved.

Figure 9.27. The arpeggiator module of Sound Designer's software. Permission granted by Digidesign, Inc. All rights reserved.

Music thus created may then be reedited and varied. One option provided by Professional Performer allows the composer to view the operation from the perspective of a traditional tape recorder. Figure 9.28 shows a screen dump of a typical setup. Here, screen buttons accessed via the button on the mouse allow standard applications of rewind, stop, play, and so on, while measures, beats, and counter ticks are counted. The object to the lower left, partially hidden by the "counter," allows mouse control over tempo. Tracks may be added, deleted, or independently edited.

The system allows for step-recording and editing as seen in the two examples of Figures 9.29 and 9.30. This provides more traditional musical editing as one proceeds, not by instants of time, but by notes. The second example also demonstrates a non-mouse option: use of the main keyboard's keypad. Digidesign, manufacturer of Sound Designer and Softsynth, also shows waveforms in real time (optional), emulating as oscilloscope. Remembering that such instruments have scientific as well as artistic uses suggests that many new editors applicable to the world of digital recording will be made available from the technological community. Many of these will have applications outside music such as speech synthesis, voice analysis (voice-print checkers for security are now a reality), and speech pathology, to name just

Figure 9.30. The Macintosh keypad for use with Professional Performer software. Permission granted by Mark of the Unicorn. All rights reserved.

a few. These should also be of use to recording engineers. MacADIOS (GW Instruments of Cambridge, Mass.) performs mathematical spectral analysis based on the Fast Fourier Transform (FFT) in characterizing any given signal by way of measuring the component harmonics.

Looping live sounds allows for experimentation on the effects and/or differences in acoustical situations. For example, capturing the acoustics of a room at different temperatures or with different placements of furniture or speakers would allow for careful "tuning" of concert halls for different ensembles. It would also allow almost immediate replication of any given environment. Such programs should have significant effect in the world of acoustic engineering in the next few years.

Certainly the hardware and software of sampling represents the future of digital editing and recording. It also marks the first occasion in history when composers may have the opportunity to master their electronic medium technologically. Many composers, dissatisfied with the electronic purity of synthesized imitations of real world sounds while concomitantly unable to retain traditional performances of their music, will no doubt turn to this substitute. Since the composer will probably do the performance, it will retain, in turn, an importance beyond simple rendition, and likewise the real performance, if it ever then occurs, will be well informed.

Vectoral Analysis: Jean-Claude Risset: *Inharmonic Soundscapes*

(For information on vectoral analysis and procedures, see chapter 1).

1. Historical Background: Jean-Claude Risset (b. 1936, France) is the head of computer research at CNRS in Marseilles, France. He studied piano with Robert Trimaille and composition with Suzanne Demarquez and André Jolivet. He earned the *Doctorates-Sciences Physiques* in 1967 at the *Ecole Normale Superieure*. He spent three years working with Max Matthews at the Bell Laboratories in the early sixties researching sound synthesis, imitation of real timbres, and pitch paradoxes. He published a catalog of computer-synthesized sounds in 1969 and set up a computer music installation in Orsay, France, in 1971.

Inharmonic Soundscapes is a reduction for tape of a larger work titled *Inharmonique* for soprano and tape first performed in April, 1977, at IRCAM. All of the computer synthesis for the work was done at IRCAM with a basic MUSIC V type program. Some sections were digitally mixed with the Stanford program titled MIXSND.

2. Overview: *Inharmonic Soundscapes* falls cleanly into a cyclic arrangement of three main sections preceded by an introduction and followed by a brief coda (both of similar material). If one assigns basic block symbols to the sounds as in Figure 9.31, then a formal layout would look like that shown in Figure 9.32.

   The quote (three-fourths of the way through line one) indicates a timbral and pitch reference to the work analyzed in a previous chapter—*Poème électronique* by Edgard Varèse. Though possibly not intentional, it is certainly and immediately observable when one is familiar with both works. The two transitions, overlapped symbols at the end of the first A and the end of the second A, integrate the basic sound materials.

3. Orchestration Techniques: The bell-like sonorities of both basic materials (the bowed glass of "A" and the rung bells of "B") are the direct result of the "inharmonicity" described by the work's title. The spectrum of these types of sounds characteristically includes partials that do not conform exactly to the tuning specifications of the overtone series. This, combined with bell-like envelopes provides the basic consistency for the entire work. There is very little material present here, as well as only slight alterations and variants to that material. Yet the resulting diversity in terms of color is extraordinary.

   Risset speaks of his timbral studies in an interview:

   Instrument-like tones can be transformed in subtle ways. For example, it is possible to construct an inharmonic bell-like tone with a more or less distinct pitch in a fashion similar to building up a chord. That is, the amplitudes of selected frequency components all follow the same amplitude envelope (for example, an abrupt attack and a long decay). However, in contrast to a standard chord, the amplitude envelope of each component is given a different duration. Then one can take the same frequency components and apply a different amplitude envelope—one that builds slowly. As a result, the character of the tones changes. Because of the different lengths of the components, they do not swell in synchrony. Hence, instead of fusing into a bell-like sound, the components are diffracted, although the underlying harmony remains the same. Thus, by changing a single function in the score, one can change the internal structure of a sound.[2]

4. Basic Techniques: The most notable technique, aside from the timbral resources, is rhythmic diversity. A random quality, edged with a directional (climax) touch, suggests computer control within parameters guided subtly by the composer.

---

2. Ibid.

Figure 9.31. Symbology for analysis of Risset's *Inharmonic Soundscapes*.

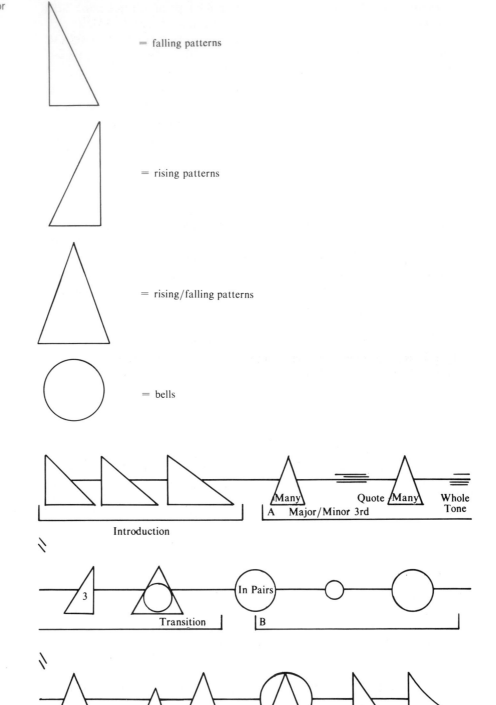

= falling patterns

= rising patterns

= rising/falling patterns

= bells

Figure 9.32. Symbolic analysis of Risset's *Inharmonic Soundscapes*.

Figure 9.33. Jean-Claude Risset. Photo by Rozenn Risset. Permission granted.

5, 6. Vertical and Horizontal Models: For the most part, the harmonic sonorities of this piece result from the extended durations of the melodic attacks. Note that there are suggestions of pitch content, at two points in the top line in Figure 9.32. In the first instance, a major/minor third is heard in varying guises (e.g., E♭, E♮, C) while in the second appearance, a whole-tone scale is implied (i.e., E, D, C, B♭, with a G below). Both of these are typical materials and suggest a relatively consonant vocabulary with tuning logically derived from the inharmonic materials.

7. Style: Risset has created a consistent vocabulary of inharmonic timbral material in *Inharmonic Soundscapes*. The form, while simple, supplies balance and direction to a work constructed from subtle variations of glass and bell-like timbres. The composer speaks of his use of the computer:

> The computer, a powerful tool, makes new sound sources available. However, it is necessary to learn how to use these new possibilities to produce the desired results . . . in order to take full advantage of the vast potential of direct digital synthesis of sound, one needs a deep understanding of the nature of sounds and of the correlations between the physical parameters and the aural effects of sound: this psychoacoustic science is still in its infancy, but its present growth is promising.[3]

This work exemplifies some of the major technological developments of the past thirty years and yet, strangely, very few of the new paradigms for compositional approaches; in short, it is exploratory by instrumentation but traditional by design. It therefore resembles the works presented in vectoral analyses in chapters 4 and 11 very closely, with ties to those analyzed in chapters 3 and 7. It contrasts the Webern of chapter 2 (though influenced by it in some very real ways [pointillism]) and the Xenakis of chapter 10. It bears little relation to Glass's *Einstein on the Beach* (chapter 11).

3. From IRCAM (31 Rue Saint-Merri F-75004, Paris); "document paru" or introductory booklet.

Bibliography— Chapter 9*

Further Readings

Definitions

Bateman, Wayne. *Introduction to Computer Music*. New York: John Wiley and Sons, 1980.

Darter, Tom. *The Art of Electronic Music*. New York: Quill, 1984.

Davis, Deta. *Computer Applications in Music: A Bibliography*. Madison, Wis.: A-R Editions, 1988.

Foerster, Heinz von, and James W. Beauchamp, eds. *Music by Computers*. New York: John Wiley and Sons, 1969.

Hiller, Lejaren, and Leonard Isaacson. *Experimental Music*. New York: McGraw-Hill, 1959.

Lincoln, Harry. *The Computer and Music*. Ithaca, N.Y.: Cornell University Press, 1970.

Loy, Gareth. "The Composer Seduced into Programming." *Perspectives of New Music* 19, no. 1 (1981): pp. 184–98.

Mathews, Max. *The Technology of Computer Music*. Cambridge, Mass.: M.I.T. Press, 1969.

Moore, F. R. "The Futures of Music." *Perspectives of New Music* 19, no. 1 (1981): pp. 212–26.

Moorer, James. "Music and Computer Composition." *Communications of the ACM* 15, no. 2 (1972): pp. 104–13.

———. "Musical Composition with the Computer." *Journal of the Acoustical Society of America* 34, no. 6 (1964).

Roads, Curtis. *Composers and the Computer*. Madison, Wis.: A-R Editions, 1985.

Early Developments

Abbott, Curtis. "Machine Tongues II." *Computer Music Journal* 2, no. 2 (1978): pp. 4–6.

Alles, H. G. "A Portable Digital Sound Synthesis System." *Computer Music Journal* 1, no. 4 (1977): pp. 5–6.

Bayer, Douglas. "Real-Time Software for a Digital Music Synthesizer." *Computer Music Journal* 1, no. 4 (1977): pp. 22–23.

Chadabe, Joel, and Roger Meyers. "An Introduction to the Play Program." *Computer Music Journal* 2, no. 1 (1978): pp. 12–18.

Chowning, John. "The Simulation of Moving Sound Sources." *Journal of the Audio Engineering Society* 2 (1971): pp. 2–6.

———. "The Synthesis of Complex Audio Spectra by Means of Frequency Modulation." *Journal of the Audio Engineering Society* 21 (1973): pp. 526–34.

Crombie, David. *The Complete Synthesizer*. London: Omnibus Press, 1982.

Crombie, David, and Paul Wiffen. *The Casio CZ Book*. New York: Amsco, 1986.

Darter, Tom, ed. *The Whole Synthesizer Catalog*. Milwaukee, Hal Leonard Publishing, 1985.

Davis, Deta. *Computer Applications in Music: A Bibliography*. Madison, Wis.: A-R Editions, 1988.

DeFurio, Steve. *The Secrets of Analog and Digital Synthesis*. New York: Ferro, 1985.

De Poli, Giovanni. "A Tutorial on Digital Sound Synthesis Techniques." *Computer Music Journal* 7, no. 4 (1983): pp. 8–26.

*Addresses for record companies, periodicals, and music publishers mentioned in this Bibliography can be found in Appendix IV.

Divilbiss, J. L. "Real-time Generation of Music with a Digital Computer." *Journal of Music Theory* 8 (1964): pp. 99–111.

Dodge, C., and T. A. Jerse. *Computer Music Synthesis, Composition and Performance.* New York: Schirmer Books, 1985.

Fukuda, Yasuhiko. *DX7.* New York: Amsco, 1984.

Garnett, Guy. "Modeling Piano Sound using Waveguide Digital Filtering Techniques." In *Proceedings of the International Computer Music Conference,* comp. James Beauchamp, pp. 89–95. San Francisco: Computer Music Association, 1987.

Gordon, John, and John Grey. "Perception of Spectral Modifications on Orchestral Instrument Tones." *Computer Music Journal* 2, no. 1 (1978): pp. 24–31.

Howe, Hubert S., Jr. "Electronic Music and Microcomputers." *Perspectives of New Music* 18, no. 1 (1977): pp. 70–84.

———. *Electronic Music Synthesis.* New York: W. W. Norton and Co., 1975.

Lawson, James, and Max Mathews. "Computer Program to Control a Digital Real-Time Sound Synthesizer." *Computer Music Journal* 1, no. 4 (1977): pp. 16–21.

Le Brun, Marc. "Digital Waveshaping Synthesis." *Journal of the Audio Engineering Society* 27, no. 4 (1979).

Longton, M. "SAM: Priorities in the Design of a Microprocessor-based Music Program." *Interface* 10/1 (1981).

Massey, Howard. *The Complete DX7.* New York: Amsco, 1986.

Moore, F. R. "An Introduction to the Mathematics of Digital Signal Processing." *Computer Music Journal* 2, no. 1 (1978): pp. 38–47.

Moorer, James. "Signal Processing Aspects of Computer Music—A Survey." *Proceedings of the IEEE* 65, no. 8 (1977).

Pohlmann, Ken C. *Principles of Digital Audio.* Indianapolis: Howard W. Sams Company, 1985.

Robinson, Charlie Q. "Real Time Synthesis of Bowed String Timbres." In *Proceedings of the International Computer Music Conference,* comp. James Beauchamp, pp. 125–29. San Francisco: Computer Music Association, 1987.

Slawson, Wayne. "A Speech-Oriented Synthesizer of Computer Music." *Journal of Music Theory* 13, no. 1 (1969): pp. 94–127.

Truax, Barry. "Organizational Techniques for C:M Ratios in Frequency Modulation." *Computer Music Journal* 1, no. 4 (1977): pp. 39–45.

———. "Real-time Granulation of Sampled Sound with the DMX–1000." In *Proceedings of the International Computer Music Conference,* comp. James Beauchamp, pp. 138–45. San Francisco: Computer Music Association, 1987.

Vercoe, Barry. "The Music 360 Languages for Sound Synthesis." *Computer Music Newsletter* 2 (1971).

Wessel, David, David Bristow, and Zack Settel. "Control of Phrasing and Articulation in Synthesis." In *Proceedings of the International Computer Music Conference,* comp. James Beauchamp, pp. 108–16. San Francisco: Computer Music Association, 1987.

Hybrid Composition

Colbeck, Julian. *KEYFAX Complete Guide to Electronic Keyboards.* New York: Amsco, 1985.

Davis, Deta. *Computer Applications in Music: A Bibliography.* Madison, Wis.: A-R Editions, 1988.

Friedman, Dean. *The Complete Guide to Synthesizers, Sequencers, and Drum Machines.* New York: Amsco, 1985.

Laske, Otto. "Toward a Theory of Interfaces for Computer Music Systems." *Computer Music Journal* 1, no. 4 (1977): pp. 53–59.

Mathews, Max, and John Pierce, eds. *Current Directions in Computer Music Research.* Cambridge, Mass.: The MIT Press, 1989.

Shortess, George K. "Interactive Sound Installations Using Microcomputers." *Leonardo* 20, no. 2 (1987): pp. 149–53.

Notation Software

David, Deta. *Computer Applications in Music: A Bibliography.* Madison, Wis.: A-R Editions, 1988.

Smith, L. C. "Score, A Musician's Approach to Computer Music." *Journal of the Audio Engineering Society* 20, no. 1 (1972): pp. 7–14.

————. "Editing and Printing Music by Computers." *Journal of Music Theory* 17, no. 2 (1973): pp. 292–309.

Controllers, Synthesizers, and Samplers

Chamberlain, Hal. *Musical Applications of Microprocessors.* 2d ed. Berkeley, Calif.: Hayden Book Company, 1986.

Davis, Deta. *Computer Applications in Music: A Bibliography.* Madison, Wis.: A-R Editions, 1988.

Friedman, Dean. *The Complete Guide to Synthesizers, Sequencers, and Drum Machines.* New York: Amsco, 1985.

Vilordi, Frank, and Steve Tarshis. *Electronic Drums.* New York: Amsco, 1985.

MIDI: The Default Standard

Anderton, Craig. *MIDI for Musicians.* New York: Amsco, 1986.

————. *Digital Delay Handbook.* New York: Amsco, 1985.

Baird, Jock. *Understanding MIDI.* New York: Amsco, 1986.

Boom, Michael. *Music Through MIDI.* Redmond, Wash.: Microsoft Press, 1987.

DeFurio, Steve, and Joe Scacciaferro. *The MIDI Implementation Book.* Pompton Lakes, N.J.: Ferro Technologies, 1986.

Francois, Jean-Charles, Xavier Chabot, and John Silber. "MIDI Synthesizers in Performance: Realtime Dynamic Timbre Production." In *Proceedings of the International Computer Music Conference,* comp. James Beauchamp, pp. 238–40. San Francisco: Computer Music Association, 1987.

Loy, Gareth. "Musicians Make a Standard: The MIDI Phenomenon." *Computer Music Journal* 9, no. 4 (1985): pp. 8–26.

Moore, F. R. "The Dysfunctions of MIDI." In *Proceedings of the International Computer Music Conference,* comp. James Beauchamp, pp. 256–63. San Francisco: Computer Music Association, 1987.

Otsuka, Akira, and Akihiko Nakajima. *MIDI Basics.* New York: Amsco, 1987.

Sampling and Digital Recording

Davis, Deta. *Computer Applications in Music: A Bibliography.* Madison, Wis.: A-R Editions, 1988.

Grey, John. "An Exploration of Musical Timbre." *Center for Computer Research in Music and Acoustics Report.* Stanford, Calif.: Stanford University Report STAN-M-2, 1975.

————. "Multidimensional Perceptual Scaling of Musical Timbres." *Journal of the Acoustical Society of America* (1977).

Loy, Gareth. "On the Scheduling of Multiple Parallel Processors Executing Synchronously." In *Proceedings of the International Computer Music Conference,* comp. James Beauchamp, pp. 117–24. San Francisco: Computer Music Association, 1987.

Massey, Howard. *The Complete Guide to MIDI Software.* New York: Amsco, 1987.

McNabb, Michael. "Dreamsong: The Composition." *Computer Music Journal* 5, no. 4 (1981): pp. 36–53.

Morgan, Christopher. *The BYTE Book of Computer Music.* New York: BYTE, 1980.

Pohlmann, Ken. *The Compact Disc.* Madison, Wis.: A-R Editions, 1989.

Strawn, John, ed. *Digital Audio Signal Processing.* Madison, Wis.: A-R Editions, 1985.

————. *Digital Audio Engineering.* Madison, Wis.: A-R Editions, 1985.

Jean-Claude Risset

Risset, Jean-Claude. "Computer Music Experiments 1964–" *Computer Music Journal* 9, no. 1 (1985): pp. 11–18.

Alvarez, Javier. *Papaloti* (1987). Chant du Monde LDC–278044/45.

Appleton, Jon. *Four Fantasies for Synclavier* (1982). Folkways FTS 37461.

————. *Georganne's Farewell.* Folkways 33442.

————. *In Deserto* (1977). Folkways 33445.

Austin, Larry. *Sonata Concertante* (1988). Centaur CRC–2029.

Baitz, Rick. *Kaleidocycles for Synclavier* (1985). Centaur CRC–2039.

Berger, Jonathan. *Meteora* (1987). Chant du Monde LDC–278044/45.

Behrman, David. *On the Other Ocean.* Lovely Music Records LWL–1041.

Boulez, Pierre. *Respons* (1982). IRCAM–0001.

Bresnick, Martin. *Lady Nells Dumpe* (1987). Centaur CRC–2039.

Brün, Herbert. *I toLD You so!* (1981). Centaur CRC–2045.

Chowning, John. *Stria.* IRCAM–0001.

————. *Turenas.* Wergo WER 2012–50.

Computer Music from CCRMA (in three volumes). Acoustics Digital Recordings 3.

Cope, David. *Glassworks* (1979). Folkways FTS–33452.

Dartmouth Digital Synthesizer. Folkways FTS–33442.

Dashow, James. *Effetti Collaterali* (1976). Dawsonville. Tulstar Productions, New Directions in Music.

d'Escrivan, Julio. *Sin ti por el alma adentro* (1987). Chant du Monde LDC–278044/45.

Dodge, Charles. *Earth's Magnetic Field* (1970). Nonesuch 71250.

————. *Speech Songs* (1973). CRI S–348.

Ghent, Emmanuel. *Brazen* (1975). Tulstar Productions, New Directions in Music.

Greesel, Joel. *Crossings* (1976). CRI 393–SD.

Guttman, Ben. *Different Attitudes* (1987). Chant du Monde LDC–278044/45.

Harvey, Jonathan. *Mortuos Plango, Vivos Voco.* IRCAM–0001.

Hiller, Lejaren, and Robert Baker. *Computer Cantata* (1963). CRI 310–SD.

Hiller, Lejaren, and John Cage. *HPSCHD* (1968). Peters. Nonesuch H–71224.

Hoffmann, Richard. *In Memoriam Patris* (1976). CRI 393–SD.

Hunt, Jerry. *Fluud for dual Synclaviers* (1988). Centaur CRC–2029.

Compact Discs, Recordings, and Publishers

Jaffe, Stephen. *Silicon Valley Breakdown* (1982). The Stanford Center for Computer Research in Music and Acoustics Digital Recordings Number 1.

Jones, David Evan. *Still Life in Wood and Metal* (1991). Centaur CRC 2052.

———. *Scritto for Computer Tape* (1986). Werge WER 2024–50.

———. *Tibiae* (1983). CRI 581.

———. *Still Voices* (1982). CRS 8840.

Kaegi, Werner. *Ritournelles* (1987). Chant du Monde LDC–278044/45.

Karpen, Richard. *Exchange* (1987). Chant du Monde LDC–278044/45.

Kermogard, Henri. *Hapsis* (1987). Chant du Monde LDC–278044/45.

Levine, Josh. *Tel* (1987). Chant du Monde LDC–278044/45.

Lindroff, Scott. *Syntax for Synclavier* (1985). Centaur CRC–2039.

Machover, Tod. *Soft Morning, City!* IRCAM–0001.

Martirano, Salvatore. *Everything Goes When the Whistle Blows* (1985). Centaur CRC–2045.

McKee, William. *Episodes I* and *II* (1978). Tulstar Productions, New Directions in Music.

McNabb, Michael. *Dreamsong.* The Stanford Center for Computer Research in Music and Acoustics Digital Recordings, no. 2.

Melby, John. *Chor der Waisen* (1985). Centaur CRC–2045.

———. *Concerto for Violin and Computer-Synthesized Tape.* New World NW–333.

———. *91 Plus 5 for Brass Quintet and Computer.* CRI SD–310.

Morrill, Dexter. *Six Dark Questions for Soprano and Computer* (1979). Redwood ES–10.

———. *Studies for Trumpet and Computer.* Golden Crest Records RE–7068.

Olive, Joseph. *Mar-ri-ia-a* (1973). Tulstar Productions, New Directions in Music.

Peterson, Tracy. *Voices* (1976). Tulstar Productions, New Directions in Music.

Randall, J. K. *Lyric Variations for Violin and Computer* (1967). Vanguard C–10057.

———. *Quartets in Pairs* (1964). Nonesuch 71245.

Rimmer, John. *Fleeting Images* (1987). Chant de Monde LDC–278044/45.

Risset, Jean-Claude. *Inharmonic Soundscapes* (1977). Tulstar, New Directions in Music.

———. *Sud* (1985). Wergo WER 2013–50.

Rolnick, Neil B. *What Is the Use?* (1985). Centaur CRC–2039.

Teitelbaum, Richard. *Golem 1* (1987). Centaur CRC–2039.

Thome, Diane. *Los Nombres* (1974). Tulstar, New Directions in Music.

Tipei, Sever. *Cuniculi* (1986). Centaur 2045.

Truax, Barry. *Digital Soundscapes* (1979). Wergo WER–2017–50.

———. *Sonic Landscapes.* Melbourne SMLP 4033.

Vercoe, Barry. *Synapse for Viola and Computer* (1976). CRI S–393.

Wallraff, Dean. *Dance* (1978). Dawsonville. Tulstar, New Directions in Music.

Winham, Godfrey. *NP* (Two Pieces for Computer-Synthesized Sound). CRI 39 3–SD.

Winsor, Phil. *Dulcimer Dream* (1988). Centaur CRC–2029.

Wyatt, Scott. *Still Hidden Laughs* (1988). Centaur CRC–2045.

AUTOMATED MUSIC

Since most automated music composed during the past forty years has been accomplished with the use of computers, it is important to differentiate between this type of use and computer-generated synthesis, the subject of the preceding chapter. The work covered in this chapter does not relate to the manner in which sound is actually produced, edited, or broadcast. It is rather related to the ordering of sounds in a composition. Some have distinguished the latter by using the term *computer assisted composition* (CAC).

In a generic sense, automated music has a rich and varied tradition. Aeolian harps (stringed instruments played by the wind), for example, date back to ancient China. Musical clocks and boxes enjoyed popularity in the fourteenth century as did barrel organs, musical chimes, and self-playing carillons. As mentioned in chapter 5, automatic composition occurred in history as early as the eighteenth century. Mozart incorporated dice throwing to allow creation of his K. 516f, a *Musikalisches Würfelspiel,* or "musical dice game," which is a musically sophisticated game used to compose viable music in his style. It consists of two eight-by-eleven matrices containing the numbers 1 through 176 (2 × 8 × 11). The number 8 represents the number of eight-bar phrases (traditional to classical period forms), and the number 11 represents all possible outcomes of the throws of two dice. These numbers are then keyed to 176 measures of music. Throwing the dice eight times produces the first 8 measures of a new work, which are then repeated. The second matrix creates a contrasting second theme. This type of music, referred to as *ars combinatoria,* was also practiced by Haydn and other classical composers. E. T. A. Hoffman and Luigi Russolo also had visions of approaches that in one way or another automated their compositional processes.

Figure 10.1 shows the first one of two selection boxes for Mozart's K. 516f. The dice, which can have sums of from two to twelve (here as the left-hand column), are thrown, producing corresponding numbers in the selected boxes. These are then keyed to music such as that shown in Figure 10.2. Figure 10.3 shows one of the 46 thousand-billion possible correct combinations (according to $N = D^r$, where R = rank and D = vertical dimension of the 172 measures) resulting from the playing of this game. The keyed numbers for this result are 96, 6, 158, 85, 80, 68, 21, 94

Figure 10.1. A table of measure numbers from Mozart's *Musikalisches Würfelspiel*, K. 516f.

	I	II	III	IV	V	VI	VII	VIII
2	70	121	26	9	112	49	109	14
3	117	39	126	56	174	18	116	83
4	66	139	15	132	73	58	145	79
5	90	176	7	34	67	160	52	170
6	25	143	64	125	76	136	1	93
7	138	71	150	29	101	162	23	151
8	16	155	57	175	43	168	89	172
9	120	88	48	166	51	115	72	111
10	65	77	19	82	137	38	149	8
11	102	4	31	164	144	59	173	78
12	35	20	108	92	12	124	44	131

Figure 10.2. Measures of music from Mozart's *Musikalisches Würfelspiel*.

Figure 10.3. A random example of music from Mozart's K. 516f.

(which contains both first and second endings for the repeat), 35, 4, 19, 166, 43, 162, 1, and 170. Though the boxes are fixed in almost random order, the results are not, and the harmonic changes remain the same no matter what the various choices are per vertical column. Such machinations match well with what computers do best, and *Musikalisches Würfelspiels* have been the subject of at least two software programs: *Mozart* by Jon Appleton and the author's own *Wulfy.*

Joseph Schillinger, a mathematician, created designs for composition of new works by machines. Leon Theremin in fact built Schillinger's Rhythmicon, which performed rhythmic patterns, and also his Musamaton (Schillinger's name for automatic instruments that varied previously composed music). Both of these instruments are good examples of complex mathematical models intended for the untrained musician.

One of the first true composing machines, built by H. F. Olson and H. Belar (1951), included two random number generators and a real sound-generating system. Pitch and rhythm were controlled by weighted probabilities during the composition process. Sawtooth wave outputs completed the device, which predates synthesizers. Some of Olson and Belar's first attempts involved biasing composition toward the musical language of Stephen Foster melodies through first-, second-, and third-order frequency counts. "Order" here refers to the number of parameters that affect note choice (i.e., first order could mean just those conditions constrained by preceding notes, etc.).

The first serious automated music to take place was by Lejaren Hiller and Leonard Iasaacson in the creation of the *Illiac Suite for String Quartet* (1956). Their studies (primarily in 1955–56) began at the University of Illinois with the Illiac high-speed digital computer and involved the programming of data and stylistic parameters. Their program was limited to choices it could make within number systems coded by input to musical note tables. The results of their work, the *Illiac Suite for String Quartet,* was published in the April 1957 edition of *New Music Quarterly.* It was composed automatically but written in traditional musical notation by researchers for "live" nonelectronic performance. The score of this work and a chronicle of the research that led to its composition are described in Hiller and Isaacson's *Experimental Music.*

Also in 1956, Martin Klein and Douglas Bolito of Burroughs, Inc. used a DATATRON computer to create a popular tune called *Push Button Bertha.* An anonymous Burroughs publication describes the compositional process as follows: "The operator inspires DATATRON by first keying in a ten-digit random number. This causes the machine to generate and store 1,000 single digits, each representing one of the eight diatonic notes in the scale with two allowable accidentals. The program then motivates DATATRON to pick notes at random, testing each for melodic acceptability as it goes along" (from "Syncopation by Automation," *Data from ElectroData,* August 1956, Pasadena, Calif., ElectroData Division of Burroughs, Inc.). The work, while musically trivial, is important as one of the first totally machine-composed pieces of music.

At about this same time, Iannis Xenakis began work based on stochastic (probability) techniques and developed programs that utilized mathematical processes (see the vectoral analysis of this chapter). Using the FORTRAN programming language on the IBM-7090, he produced his free *stochastic music* detailed in his book *Formalized Music.* Works such as *Metastasis* (1954), *Pithoprakta* (1956), and *Achoripsis* (1957) were based on such calculations.

In 1960, Pierre Barbaud began studying the potential of automated composition. He worked principally with random permutational methods applied to traditional harmonies and twelve-tone processes. In the late 1960s he developed an aesthetic that compared automated music with music composed by humans. "It [automated music] is 'human' inasmuch as it is the product of rational beings" see his "Algorithmic Music" under Expert Systems in the Bibliography. Barbaud and Roger Blanchard worked as well during this period, completing a number of important papers on the subject.

Gottfried Michael Koenig's work at the Institute of Sonology in Utrecht has since 1964 focused on automated composition. His work *PROJECT 2* (1969) demonstrates an effective use of statistical procedures that fit together in combinations. His *Ubung fur Klavier* (Study for Piano), written in 1970, uses this program as well. Other experiments during this time included computer generation of hymn tunes based on the statistical analysis of thirty-seven hymns up to the eighth-order approximation (see definition in previous description of work by Belar and Olson). These experiments were carried out by F. Brooks, A. Hopkins, P. Neumann, and W. Wright.

Robert Baker's *CSX-1 Study* employed the MUSICOMP (MUsic Simulator Interpreter for COMPositional Procedures) at the University of Illinois. Baker and Hiller then collaborated in the creation of *Computer Cantata,* completed in 1963 and one of the most interesting of the early pioneering works in automated composition. This highly serialized work includes various tempered tuning systems of from nine to fifteen notes per octave.

In the same year, Herbert Brün completed *Sonoriferous Loops* for instrumental ensemble and tape using MUSICOMP. This work and his *Nonsequitur VI* (1966, for tape and ensemble) are based on probability distributions, one of the most popular of early processes for automated composition and analysis of style. These two works stand alongside the *Illiac Suite* of Hiller and Isaacson as preeminent early computer compositions.

Cage and Hiller's dynamic *HPSCHD* (1969) utilizes a subroutine of MUSICOMP called *ICHING*. Through the use of computer printout sheets of "highly sophisticated random numbers," they created the first recording with published indeterminate performance instructions. The listener controls the record player knobs using printout sheets containing a different set of numbers for loudness and treble/bass control for each speaker. With both Xenakis and Cage, the computer serves, though to different ends, to bring about results otherwise difficult to achieve. In neither case has the computer actually produced the resultant sound; it has only aided the composer by virtue of its high-speed computations.

Hiller speaks of his work with automated music in an interview:

Nowadays I think that my computer pieces possess more expressive content than I would have first guessed. In other words, I hear in the pieces more of a reflection of my general approach to music than I would have supposed at the beginning. I don't find even the *Illiac Suite* that far disjunct from the other things I do. I suppose that my programming contains biases that are subjective.

More recently, Hiller has completed a set of three *Algorithms* (I, 1968; II, 1972; and III, 1981) that employ various stochastic and random elements.

James Tenney's work at Bell Laboratories produced a number of important works involving automated composition, including *Four Stochastic Studies* (1962), *Stochastic String Quartet* (1963), and *Dialogue* (1963). The results Tenney obtained are significant not only in their inherent musical worth but also in how they contrast with those works produced stochastically by Xenakis. Harriet Padberg (1964) assigned notes to letters of the alphabet and created meaningful phrases in English using computer programs to transform the results into music. She also employed transformations of group theory. The *Canon and Free Fugue* that resulted from her labors has proven integrally bound to its title in melody and rhythm.

John Myhill composed his *Scherzo a tre Voice* in 1965. This work is based in part on the previously described techniques of Joseph Schillinger. Composing the *Scherzo a tre Voice* involved his program following graphically depicted sinusoidal waveforms to create three simultaneously sounding voices or melodies operating in counterpoint.

Since these initial experiments, many other individuals have been directly involved with automated music. They include, among others, Barry Truax, William Buxton, Thomas DeLio, Scot Gresham-Lancaster, Allen Strange, Larry Austin, Petr Kotik, Denis Lorrain, Horacio Vaggione, David Zacarelli, Clarence Barlow, Charles Dodge, Peter Gena, Kevin Jones, and Laura Tedeschini Lalli. Programs by many of these and other individuals are included in the last section of this chapter under "Current Programs."

Expert Systems

Expert systems, as contrasted to neural networks (to be described later in this chapter), provide straightforward methods for creating automated music. They operate within constraints created by if/then/else clauses. Each time a decision by the machine is required, a fork is created whereby "if" some action is required, "then" that action takes place, "else" an alternate action takes place. Expert systems can be used to enable machines to create random (i.e., stochastic or probablistic) compositions.

Figure 10.5 shows a simple program for computer creation of twelve-tone rows. It is written in the BASIC computer langauge. This figure gives a good example of "if/then/else" clauses. Line 80 here can be read as "IF I = 1, THEN go to line 130, else continue (go to line 90)." This program is not particularly complex as an expert system. It simply produces random twelve-tone rows. However, complexity and sophisticated results are more a matter of creating further rules in much this same manner than of creating distinctly different programs. It is easy to see how, for example, this program could next form a matrix (see chapter 2) or compose music following strict twelve-tone procedures.

Expert systems can also be used to define protocols such as those found in tonal music. These often take the reverse form of hierarchial analysis. For example, one

```
0 RANDOMIZE
10 DIM N(12), M(12), N$(12)
20 DIM A(12, 12)
30 N$(1)="C ": N$(2)="C# ": N$(3)="D ": N$(4)="D# "
40 N$(5)="E ": N$(6)="F ": N$(7)="F# ": N$(8)="G "
50 N$(9)="G# ": N$(10)="A ": N$(11)="A# ": N$(12)="B "
60 FOR I = 1 TO 12
70 N(I) = INT (1 + (12 * RND))
80 IF I = 1 THEN 130
90 I1 = I - 1
100 FOR J = 1 TO I1
110 IF N(I) = N(J) THEN 70
120 NEXT J
130 NEXT I
140 FOR K = 1 TO 12
150 IF K = 1 THEN M(1) = N(1)
160 IF K = 1 THEN 230
170 Q = K - 1
180 P = N(K) - N(Q)
190 R = M(Q) - P
200 IF R < 1 THEN R = R + 12
210 IF R > 12 THEN R = R - 12
220 M(K) = R
230 NEXT K
240 FOR A = 1 TO 12
250 G = N(A)
255 PRINT N$(G)" "
260 NEXT A
390 END
```

Figure 10.5. A program written in the computer language BASIC for creating random twelve-tone rows.

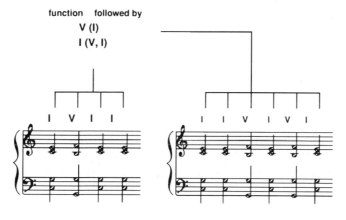

Figure 10.6. Generating new progressions from succession rules created by parsing extant music.

can create new realizations of the chord protocols found in Figure 10.6 by first analyzing, or parsing, music (upward progression in the figure to the left) and determining the explicit protocols or succession rules in the music. These protocols could then initiate machine composition at some point in the resultant analysis (downward progression in the figure to the right).

Again, the example is a simple one and the results trivial. However, the *process* used is obviously logical and ultimately useful. Complex results can be had by the addition of more sophisticated elements to the program. Lerdahl and Jackendoff, for example, call their analytic approach a "generative grammar for tonal music" that incorporates a number of linguistically associated approaches to certain musical styles. Figure 10.7 presents their "well-formedness" rules based on musical

Figure 10.7. Fred Lerdahl and Ray Jackendoff's block diagram of their surface and depth approach to musical analysis using musical linguistics. From *A Generative Theory of Tonal Music* by Fred Lerdahl and Ray Jackendoff. Printed by the MIT Press (1983). Permission granted. All rights reserved.

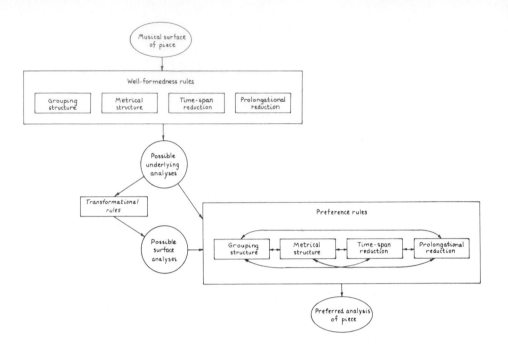

surface features, and possible underlying analyses based on linguistic principles. Figure 10.8 demonstrates their hierarchial approach to Beethoven's "Tempest" Sonata, Op. 31, No. 2. Here only the most important and critical material survives to the last (bottom) layer of the analysis. Primary material is shown in the top-level parsing as initial splinters from main lines, while secondary and tertiary material is represented by angular lines.

Now, imagining a replacement of this latter example in the left-hand area of Figure 10.6 and building a similar one parallel to the right-hand side of that same figure, one can derive a sophisticated expert system for generating tonal music. The system could include the hierarchy of the Lerdahl and Jackendoff approach directly in the generation of new examples of tonal music.

Expert systems have also proven useful in terms of pattern matching. Since musical motives or patterns are found in many styles both tonal and nontonal, pattern matching lists of notes and durations for motive recurrences and their variations can contribute to convincing iterations of new music in established styles. In the author's work with EMI (Experiments in Musical Intelligence, discussed more fully under "Current Programs" in this chapter), these are called signatures. A signature is a motive that is used by a composer in more than one work. In some composers these are ostinati such as the Alberti-bass, walking bass, um-pah-pah, and so on, which usually help to reference a period but not a particular composer. In many composers' works there are more subtle patterns that the ear uses to recognize a composer's style but that cannot be so easily defined. These include cadences, melodic patterns, and ornaments that repeat in various guises but always remind the listener of that composer. Signatures can also include unique control of textures, timbres, dynamics, and so forth.

Figure 10.8. Fred Lerdahl and Ray Jackendoff's analysis of Beethoven's "Tempest" Sonata, Op. 31, No. 2. From *A Generative Theory of Tonal Music* by Fred Lerdahl and Ray Jackendoff. Printed by the MIT Press (1983). Permission granted. All rights reserved.

Figure 10.9 shows a pitch and duration pattern found in both upper and lower voices in Mozart. The first excerpt presents the basic structure—the leap of an octave upward followed by a chromatic correction a half-step down, with repetitions of the pattern finally widening to a major second. The second example differs from it by the use of eighth notes and the immediate statement of the lowered chromatic major second. The third example delays the move from minor to major by many repetitions but still represents an example of the same signature being used. The fourth example is expressed without the downbeat octave but is nonetheless recognizable as a variant. The fifth example does not resolve to the major second at all, but eludes it. The last example does not resolve either, and has less embellishment. The dates of the compositions from which the fragments shown in Figure 10.9 were drawn

Figure 10.9. From Mozarts (1) Sonata 10, measure 131, movement 3, 1778; (2) Sonata 13, measure 24, movement 3, 1778; (3) Piano Concerto 23, movement 1, 1786; (4) Sonata 16, movement 1, 1778; (5) Sonata 6, measure 90, movement 1, 1775; (6) Sonata 5, movement 3, 1774.

span fourteen years. The fragments of 1774–75 (the last two) show less clarity than those of 1778, and the examples from the later 1780s are elusive variants.

Motives vary from one another, yet the ear is able to pick them up as a match. There are also virtually thousands of ways of varying motives. Relatively few methods, however, are both used by composers and apparent to the ear. Extended retrogrades, for example, don't occur, and if they did they would not be heard. Successful pattern matching is based only on those forms of variation that can be heard.

Figure 10.10 presents an algorithm of one possible expert system used for music composition based on the two kinds of models thus far presented: succession rules and pattern matching. Note how melody and harmony are treated separately according to their different roles. The succession rules section to the right of the figure could be eliminated if the actual data of the originally analyzed music were to accompany the functions as they moved down the right-hand side of the algorithm. However, this would create a complex *Musikalisches Würfelspiel,* which may or may not be the intent of such a program.

Modeling analytical and compositional processes in these ways creates better understanding of the musical intelligence required to replicate reasonable facsimiles of given styles or to create wholly new styles based on mathematical formulas, statistics, and/or random processes. Expert systems may be thusly applied in a wide variety of implementations.

An Example Program

The following program presents pattern-matching code that will be used for discovering a Mozart signature such as those discussed in the previous section. It could also be used as an engine for the left-hand side of Figure 10.10. This program is based on one of the major components of the EMI (Experiments in Musical Intelligence, to be discussed later in this chapter) system. The code is self-sufficient. The only requirement is that the reader use CommonLISP. For those who know LISP, these functions are meant to demonstrate basic pattern matching. For those who do not know LISP but wish to, the code may be useful if used concomitantly with a LISP text. For those interested only in the output, accurately typing in this code to a CommonLISP file, loading it, and then typing "(pattern-match X Y)" where "X

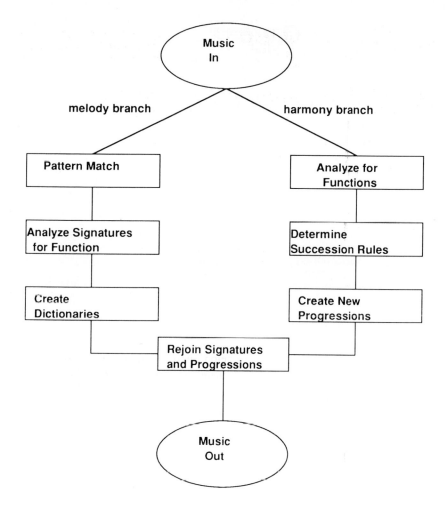

Figure 10.10. An algorithm for automated music composition.

and Y" are coded works such as those shown in Figure 10.11, followed by a carriage return ($<$cr$>$), will produce the desired results.

This model is presented top-down—that is, one begins describing the point of the code, which then breaks into smaller and smaller elements until no further subdivision is possible. However, since music is most often composed in exactly the same way (i.e., placing notes one after another on a microscopic scale), a bottom-up approach may also be useful. This program assumes that (1) pattern matching is a powerful technique to use in attempting to discover some of the reasons that composers' styles sound as they do, (2) patterns judged as alike that occur in different works of a composer are valuable and constitute what the author will call signatures, and (3) reusing such signatures in music composed following standard chord protocols and voice leading can lead to replications in the style of a composer.

Data here will take the form of numerical representations for notes, with 60 being middle C, 61 being C#, and so forth. Figure 10.11 shows three short excerpts

Figure 10.11. Three excerpts from Mozart sonatas to be used for pattern matching.

;This is bars 20 - 22 of the first movement of Sonata K. 533.
(setf (get 'mozart-K.533 'notes) '(72 77 76 75 73 74 70 67 65 64 65))

;This is bars 25 - 26 of the first movement of Sonata K. 280.
(setf (get 'mozart-K.280 'notes) '(82 79 78 79 74 73 74 70 67 65 64))

;This is bars 4 - 6 from the end of the last movement of Sonata K.333.
(setf (get 'mozart-K.333 'notes) '(79 77 75 74 72 70 69 75 69 70 -0 74 77 75 72 69 70))

from three different Mozart sonatas with the pitch representations for each excerpt below each one. Rests are entered as zero. Obviously, using just pitch in the process here has significant limitations. Missing are all of the inflections of timbre, duration, articulation, place within the bar, relation to beat, and so on. However, one can factor these into the pattern-matching process by adding code at strategic places. As well, the examples are also small and not randomly chosen, so the brief experiment is seriously biased. However, randomly choosing examples that will not prove the point is hardly useful within the space limitations of this book.

By ear, one can quickly recognize the signature present beginning on the sixth note of the second example and the fifth note of the first example. The pattern continues until the last note of the second example and the second-to-last note of the first example. The pattern matcher described here will have to be able to find this figure. The match between the second and third examples is not so clear in that the last six notes of the third example, while resembling those of the first two examples, is not an exact match. The pattern matcher, since the author does hear this as a variant, will also have to be able to catch this pattern.

There are four program variables, which are shown in Figure 10.12. The first is a location into which the results of the pattern-matching process will be stored. It is the place where we will find the patterns that have matched between two works

Figure 10.12. Setting the global variables of the program.

```
(defvar *signatures* nil)

(defvar *range-tolerance* 1)
(defvar *error-tolerance* 0)
(defvar *pattern-size* 5)
```

given as arguments to the top-level function. The other three are numbers that allow alteration of the process without having to rewrite code. The first, *range-tolerance*, indicates the allowance for a possible matching interval to be out of range. The default, as shown, is 1, or a minor second. This variable will allow, for example, major, and minor versions of the same interval to match. The second variable, *error-tolerance*, indicates the number of intervals that can be completely wrong and still match. The default of 0 is a good one since it allows a lot of play with *range-tolerance* before having to turn to *error-tolerance*. This will also be helpful in factoring rests that are problematic for matchers.

Obviously, using high numbers in either or both of these variables will cause noise, so alterations will be in the range of 0 to 5 or so. The last variable declaration, *pattern-size*, determines the size of motive that the program uses in trying to find matches. It should be noted that the default size here does not indicate any preference of the author. Setting this particular variable is extremely important in the matching process. Amounts can range from 2 to whatever size depending on the size of the note lists being compared. Large sizes with small note lists will yield little if any results.

The top level of the program shown in Figure 10.13 is iterative. It operates the more powerful matching functions by feeding them data that equates to the works

```
(defun pattern-match (work-1 work-2)
  (setq *signatures*
    (signify-matches
      (match (decide-patterns (define-as-intervals work-1))
             (decide-patterns (define-as-intervals work-2))))))
```

Figure 10.13. The top-level LISP function of the pattern matcher described in the text.

turned into intervals ("define-as-intervals") and lists of patterns (according to the variable *pattern-size*). The function "signify-matches" counts the number of times a motive occurs in the resultant list and removes all of the occurrences other than the first. As will be seen, this matcher uses and returns intervals instead of note representations, since intervals are not pitch-level sensitive (i.e., a minor second down followed by a major second up is the same whether its actual value is C-B-D or D-C#-E). This means that sequence and transpositions will be caught in the process of matching.

The function "define-as-intervals" shown in Figure 10.14 turns the data given as its arguments into a list of intervals. By subtracting the second note from the

```
;(define-as-intervals '(66 67 69 70 69 66)) = (1 2 1 -1 -3)

(defun define-as-intervals (note-lists)
  (if (null (second note-lists)) nil
    (cons (- (second note-lists)(first note-lists))
          (define-as-intervals (rest note-lists)))))
```

Figure 10.14. The function "define-as-intervals" that was used by "pattern match."

first, the program translates the note numbers into intervals. It stops one before the end of the list "(null (second note-lists))" because it cannot figure an interval between the last note of the list and an empty list.

The function "decide-patterns" shown in Figure 10.15 takes *pattern-size* and turns the note lists into successive lists of *pattern-size* sublists. Note that it recurses one step at a time while taking *pattern-size* amounts of data from the first

Figure 10.15. The function "decide-patterns."

```
:(decide-patterns '(14 23 22 1 2 3 4 5 6 7)) = ((14 23 22) (23 22 1)
:(22 1 2) (1 2 3) (2 3 4) (3 4 5) (4 5 6) (5 6 7))


(defun decide-patterns (work)
   (if (< (length work) *pattern-size*) nil
      (cons (butlast work (- (length work) *pattern-size*))
            (decide-patterns (rest work)))))
```

part of the list. Hence, sublists represent all possible *pattern-size* (here set to 3)-length patterns in the argument. While this has the potential of creating redundancy in the process, it also causes subtle patterns to emerge, as will be seen in "signify-matches."

The workhorse function of the program is "match," shown in Figure 10.16. The arguments here are two sets of patterns the size of *pattern-size*. The function evaluates each sublist of the first list, determining whether the interval numbers of each sublist match or not. Its first attempt is explicit and shown in the expression "(member (first pattern-set-1) pattern-set-2)." Such an attempt avoids the necessity of further evaluation if the pattern from the first list is in the second list. Further computation is necessary through the use of "match-details" in the ensuing line if such a find does not occur.

Figure 10.16. The function "match."

```
:(match '((1 2 3)(4 5 6)) '((2 3 4)(8 9 10))) = ((1 2 3))


(defun match (pattern-set-1 pattern-set-2)
  (cond ((null pattern-set-1) nil)
        ((or (member (first pattern-set-1) pattern-set-2)
             (member 't (mapcar #'(lambda (x)
                                    (match-details (first pattern-set-1) x))
                           pattern-set-2)))
         (cons (first pattern-set-1)
               (match (rest pattern-set-1) pattern-set-2)))
        (t (match (rest pattern-set-1) pattern-set-2))))
```

One of the key functions of this program is "match-details," shown in Figure 10.17. It applies the variables to the matching process so that "almost" matches may occur. It takes two arguments, each of which equates to a list of intervals from two different works. The conditions of acceptance are shown in the "or" argument in line four of the code. Three possibilities exist: (1) the intervals will be the same (note this is not the same as the use of "member" above; in that case *all* of the

```
;(match-details '(2 3 4) '(3 4 5))  = T
;(match-details '(2 3 4) '(7 8 9)) = NIL


(defun match-details (pattern-1 pattern-2)
  (cond ((null pattern-1) t)
        ((null pattern-2) nil)
        ((or (eq (first pattern-1)(first pattern-2))
          (<= (abs (- (first pattern-1)(first pattern-2)))
                *range-tolerance*)
          (tolerate-errors pattern-1 pattern-2 *error-tolerance*))
         (match-details (rest pattern-1)(rest pattern-2)))
        (t nil)))
```

Figure 10.17. The function "match-details" used by the "pattern-match" program.

members of each list must be the same); (2) they will be off within the range of *range-tolerance*; and (3) they will be acceptable to "tolerate-errors," which uses the program variable *error-tolerance*. The variables for the runs shown have the default settings.

The function "tolerate-errors" shown in Figure 10.18 recurses through its first two arguments in parallel, reducing its third argument incrementally if no match is found. When *error-tolerance* is $\emptyset$, no match is found. The variable *error-tolerance* has the value of 1 for the runs shown. The function "signify-matches"

```
;(tolerate-errors '(1 2 3) '(1 2 -3) *error-tolerance*) = T
;(tolerate-errors '(1 2 3) '(1 -2 -3) *error-tolerance*) = NIL


(defun tolerate-errors (pattern-1 pattern-2 error-tolerance)
  (cond ((null pattern-1) t)
        ((zerop error-tolerance) nil)
        ((eq (first pattern-1)(first pattern-2))
         (tolerate-errors (rest pattern-1)
                          (rest pattern-2)
                          error-tolerance))
        (t (tolerate-errors (rest pattern-1)
                            (rest pattern-2)
                            (1- error-tolerance)))))
```

Figure 10.18. The function "tolerate-errors."

shown in Figure 10.19 counts the number of times a motive occurs in the *signature* list and returns it as a list of the number and the list. It then removes the list from the match list so that it will not repeat during recursion. This function is very helpful during composition in that signatures of low count can be struck from the process. The function runs in the previous figures clarify the process, but examples of the program in operation are required for one to understand how the variables work. Figure 10.20 shows sample output in intervals. Setting the variables too conservatively can produce meaningless results. Setting the variables too liberally, however, can produce signatures when there are none.

Figure 10.19. The function "signify-matches" as used in the "pattern-match" sequence.

```
;(signify-matches '((1 1 1)(1 1 1))) = ((2 (1 1 1)))

(defun signify-matches (match-list)
    (if (null match-list) nil
        (cons (list (count (first match-list) match-list :test 'list)
                    (first match-list))
            (signify-matches
                (remove (first match-list)
                        match-list
                        :test 'list)))))
```

Figure 10.20. Actual runs of the "pattern-match" program.

```
*range-tolerance* = 1
*error-tolerance* = 0
*pattern-size* = 5
(pattern-match (get 'mozart-K.533 'notes)(get 'mozart-K.280
'notes)) = ((2 (-2 1 -4 -3 -2)))
(pattern-match (get 'mozart-K.533 'notes)(get 'mozart-K.333
'notes)) = NIL
(setq *range-tolerance* 2) = 2
(pattern-match (get 'mozart-K.533 'notes)(get 'mozart-K.333
'notes)) = ((5 (5 -1 -1 -2 1)))
(pattern-match (get 'mozart-K. 280 'notes)(get 'mozart-K.333
'notes)) = ((2 -1 1 -4 -3 -2)))
```

One of the principal problems of this matcher is that it does not provide clear information as to how many matches have occurred within each of the works it analyzes. Therefore, one does not know if this is a true signature. For example, given the output of 8 as the number of times a pattern has occurred is not too useful if it equates to 7 and 1 matches in the works respectively. The numbers 4 and 4 as counts would produce more convincing results. Adding a feature to discern this and creating more variables would certainly enhance this program's ability to recognize pitch aspects of musical style. Altering this code to produce rhythm, dynamic, harmonic, texture, and other matchings could offer further refinement and develop more sophisticated tools. Utilizing the results of this code compositionally is a matter of poking signatures into computer-composed and styleless tonal music. This is described in the author's other publications listed in the bibliography as well as the works of many others. Composition of new works with signatures may be found in the author's book *Computers and Musical Style,* listed in the bibliography.

Grammars

Expert systems have created a renewed interest in a linguistic approach to music composition. This is principally due to the desire for programmers to base their programs on some kind of natural process. Since language uses sound, and order proceeds by analogous organizations to music, linguistics has received attention in recent years. While "music as a language" requires a substantial leap of faith not corroborated by a significant body of empirical evidence, studying linguistic models has proven useful to a number of composers.

Music grammar has, at present, been defined only crudely in terms of syntax and semantics. These definitions generally take the form of personal rather than universal representations of rules and values applicable during composition. Parsing helps understand written languages, however, and thus offers potential for parallels in music. Work in this area has proven fruitful, especially in GGDL (Generative Grammar Definition Language compiler) and EMI (Experiments in Music Intelligence, discussed later in this chapter).

Augmented Transition Network (ATN) parsing provides transformational rules to the context-free syntax of grammar. Of the many grammar types, only ATN allows the recursive possibilities inherent in LISP and is thus one approach of choice. Figure 10.21 shows a simple sentence parsed according to the rudimentary rules of ATN. In this figure, *s* refers to sentence part, *np* to noun phrase, and *vp* to verb phrase. The upper symbols show an alternative notation to the statements below.

It should be noted that ATN can also be very useful for reordering signatures as discovered by the program described in the previous section of this chapter. Context-sensitive ATN could, for example, place melodic signatures over the best

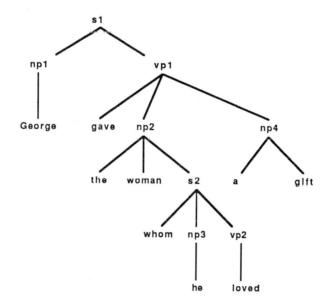

Figure 10.21. An example of sentence parsing.

matching harmony, connect signatures with other signatures at the appropriate registers, and/or affix cadential signatures at the proper points in a given phrase.

Many theorists have postulated musical parsing mechanisms appropriate for tonal grammars. Among these are Curtis Roads, Fred Lerdahl, and the author of this text. Typically they reference such concepts as noun phrase and verb phrase (the basic syntax of the English language). Figure 10.22 a to c presents crude but useful examples of the possibilities of parsing. Figure 10.22a shows a combination of a leap and its tonal resolution, followed by a stepwise progression to a traditional cadence. A simple progression in 10.22b demonstrates potential harmonic analysis.

Figure 10.22. Crude examples of musical parsing.

(a)

(b)

(c)   A1 C3   A3 C1 C2 C1 C1 O2 A1 O2 C1

In 10.22c, a twelve-tone row shows aspects of interval dependence. Note that all similar intervals have the same analysis. The letter/number combinations show repetition and variation of intervals in the relevant series.

    Parsing music requires that the language equivalents have meanings and that rules will restrict usage. Figure 10.23a lists one possible set. In this case, the initial symbol may be followed only by one of the symbols in the corresponding list. In 10.23b, a motive followed by three generated phrases demonstrates how these rules produce examples of style syntax. This gives an example of simple parsing and the varieties of syntactically correct replications of simple phrases. Note that each of the last three is an extended version of the first. Musical parsing may create straightforward variations or complex projections.

    One or more numbers representing defined parameters of the composition can then be assigned to the current definition. The fewer the possibilities, the more restrictive the composing process. For example, (a1 'entry '(4 3 2 1 −2 1 −3)) (a2 'entry '(−3 2 1 2 2 3)) (a3 'entry '(1 2 2 3 3)) rudimentarily demonstrates entries

Figure 10.23. Examples of symbolic musical parsing through a linguistic rules base.

(a)   (a1 = (c1 c2 o1 o2 o3 s1 s2))
        (a2 = (c1 c2 c3 o3 s2 s3))
        (a3 = (c2 c3 s3))
        (c1 = (a1 a2 a3 o2 o3))
        (c2 = (a1 a2 a3 o3))
        (c3 = (o2 o3 a2 a3))
        (o1 = (a1 a2 a3 c1 c2 c3 s1))
        (o2 = (a2 a3 c1 c2 c3 s1 s2 s3))
        (o3 = (a3 c2 c3 s2 s3))
        (s1 = (a1 a2 a3 o1 o2 o3))
        (s2 = (a2 a3 o1 o2 o3))
        (s3 = (a3 o2 o3))

(b)   (o1 c2 a3 s3) = (o1 a1 c2 a1 s2 a3 c3 a2 s3 o3)
                  (a1 o1 c1 o2 c2 a3 s3)
                  (a1 o1 c2 o3 a3 s3 a3 s3)

for one set of musical "words." This example is elastic and useful for testing. It restricts motion to small intervals. Since there may be many correct next intervals, the order of possibilities will have significant influence. Reordering can obviously be random or based on some mathematical formula. The Fibonacci series, or golden section (the series adds each of the two preceding numbers: 1, 1, 2, 3, 5, 8, 13 . . . n), has proven very successful.

Figure 10.24 gives an overview of one possible syntax relevant to sentence parsing and generation in English. The legend of Figure 10.25 shows only one of the several possibilities for representing hierarchical structure. Hierarchy descends through section and movement to the work's surface with structural relationship at each level. The system's linear and vertical structuring provide logical skeletal frames on which to create musical phrases. The musical example shows one possible translation of the phrase above.

Figure 10.26 shows a parser developed by K. S. Fu for syntax analysis of programmed languages. It is a top-down parsing algorithm consisting of generation and backtracking subalgorithms that can systematically trace out the programmed grammar of strings (lists of letters surrounded by double quotes ["]). This is used here to show parallel activity for linguistic application in fields other than music or language.

Graph grammars, especially context-driven grammars (another way to describe realization of syntactical representations), encourage pattern recognition and have been applied extensively in many diverse areas such as biology, chemistry, and economics. These grammars, to a degree, expand reductive mathematical processes by providing semantics to otherwise context-free environments. Grammars can thus provide the basic grist from which computers may draw material for the creation

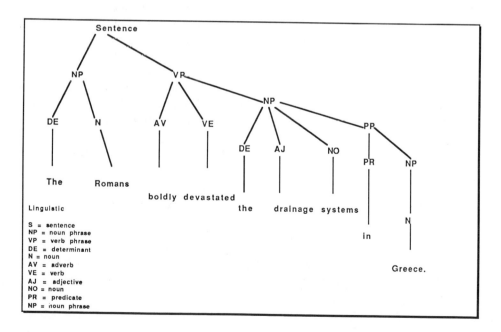

Linguistic

S = sentence
NP = noun phrase
VP = verb phrase
DE = determinant
N = noun
AV = adverb
VE = verb
AJ = adjective
NO = noun
PR = predicate
NP = noun phrase

Figure 10.24. Parse tree in English.

Figure 10.25. A parse tree using identifiers and musical example of computation.

of musically useful results, and can ensure that the results of composition will not be random. They appear reasonable in that composers involved in linguistics and automated music have created programs capable of basic style replication and rudimentary original composition in those styles.

Neural Networks

Neural networks, often called parallel distributed processing (PDP) or connectionist modeling, may be defined as hardware or programs that reinforce and diminish connections among internal nodes by how successfully they contribute to matches of recursed (back-propagated) data. The program sweeps a set of data through the net (often hundreds of times) so that patterns can be "learned." This simplistic explanation of a very complex phenomenon does make the important point that neural nets operate differently than expert systems. Peter Todd makes the distinction between expert systems and neural nets clear in the following comments:

> One of the major features of the PDP approach is that it replaces strict rule-following behavior with regularity-learning and generalization. This fundamental shift allows the development of new algorithmic composition methods that rely on learning the structure of existing musical examples and generalizing from these learned structures to compose new pieces. These methods contrast greatly with the majority of older schemes that simply follow a previously assembled set of compositional rules, resulting in brittle systems typically unable to appropriately handle unexpected musical situations.[1]

1. Todd, Peter. "A Connectionist Approach to Algorithmic Composition." *Computer Music Journal,* 13, no. 4 (1989), p. 27.

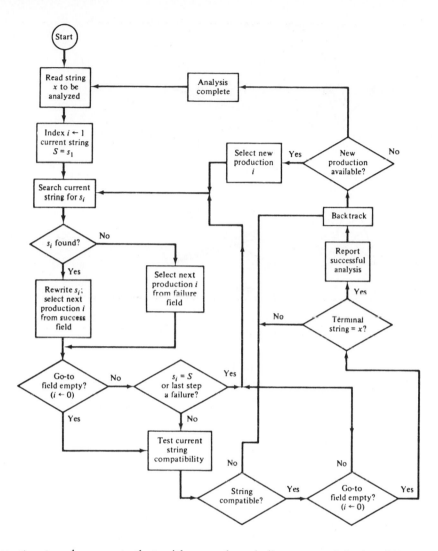

Figure 10.26. A programmed grammar with a syntax of programming languages. King Sun Fu, *Syntactic Pattern Recognition and Applications*, Copyright 1982, p. 192. Reprinted by permission of Prentice-Hall, Inc., Englewood Cliffs, New Jersey.

Current research suggests that with enough melodies a net might be able to replicate new works in the style of learned music. This could be accomplished in a number of ways. One method would be to stop the net at some point just before it has learned a work. The result may be enough in the style of the original as to represent a useful variant. Another method would be to teach a net two or more works in a given style and then request something in between. If, as in the first example, inexactness were introduced, interesting results might be produced.

Figure 10.27 shows a very simple net consisting of inputs and outputs separated by hidden units. Such networks begin with weights at each of the hidden units set randomly or to zero. When note representations are input to this kind of net, the hidden units make an initial attempt to replicate the input at the output level. When the output, initially random, is fed recursively back through the network after a comparison with the original input, those hidden units that seem to perform well

Figure 10.27. A simple neural net.

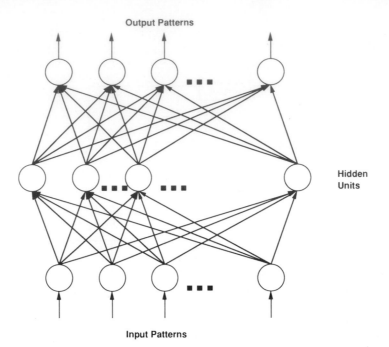

Output Patterns

Hidden Units

Input Patterns

are rewarded, and those that performed poorly are punished. This is accomplished by incrementally adding to or subtracting from the random weights of the hidden units.

Jamshed Bharucha has proposed a connectionist model of harmony where "each event in a musical sequence activates tone units and activation spreads via connecting links to parent chords and then to parent key units."[2] Peter Todd has developed networks that create new melodies out of what he terms "composition by plan manipulation" (see Bibliography). This involves networks producing new musical sequences based on perceived regularities in previously "learned" sequences. Wayne Bateman has observed the following:

Even if a compositional algorithm is stylistically "tight" enough to engender its output with readily identifiable stylistic features, the resulting music sounds mechanical and boring. Indeed one can offer no assurance that it is even possible to compose music according to an explicit, inflexible, formalized procedure that in the long run is artistically satisfying to most people.[3]

Performance considerations of neural nets are the focus of Barry Vercoe and Marvin Minsky's work at MIT's Media Laboratory. Here, hard-wired neural net "learned" accompaniments follow nuances of tempo indicated by human performers connected to the net via contact microphones. The ability of hard-wired neural nets (i.e., actual hardware, not software) to respond almost instantaneously makes them quite useful real-time musical tools.

2. Bharucha, Jamshed. "Music Cognition and Perceptual Facilitation: A Connectionist Framework." *Music Perception* 5, no. 1 (Fall 1987), pp. 1–30.

3. Bateman, Wayne. *Introduction to Computer Music* (New York: John Wiley and Sons, 1982), p. 238.

The future of musical neural nets appears promising at this time. Although little actual music has been produced, and that which has is fairly trivial, the connectionist concept is sophisticated and especially suited to music. Once problems of representation or how the data is entered into the net are solved, it should be possible for neural networks to create new music analogous to human composition. The quality of such efforts, however, remains suspect, as it does with all of the expert systems presented previously.

Current Programs

At the present time, many automated music or computer-assisted (CAC) programs are emerging, particularly in the microcomputer market. These often border on legitimate artificial intelligence (AI) potential. Most are based on straightforward random and improvisatory functions rather than being truly intelligent programs. Of these, M, written by David Zicarelli, Joel Chadabe, John Offenhartz, and Antony Widoff, has proven successful. Called "the intelligent composing and performing system," M stores composer-defined musical material as patterns and varies these according to such characteristics as orchestration and density. Figure 10.28 shows a sample screen from the M program.

Jam Factory, another program from Intelligent Music, follows more of an improvisatory structure based on an interactive sequencer-type system. Billed as a "real-time improvisation enhancement and performance system," users may work with the program while it is performing (real-time capabilities). Neither M nor Jam Factory have any real AI applications. However, they both have powerful algorithms that could serve as automated music engines.

Music Mouse, created by Laurie Spiegel, turns the Macintosh into what she calls "an intelligent instrument." The program utilizes the computer's "mouse" and

Figure 10.28. Screen from *M*, from Intelligent Music. Permission granted by Intelligent Music, Albany, New York.

allows the user to control a wide variety of sequencing note formations by physically moving the cursor while it is performing. The keyboard can then be used to control volume, tempo, tone control, pitch collection, transposition, and various MIDI parameters. The principal variables on the instrument are tempo and articulation and not pitch or loudness. Music mouse is an example of computer-assisted improvisation, automating parts of the process and leaving users free to shape and direct the flow of the music. Like Music Mouse, Instant Music for the Apple IIGS computer requires the user to hold down the button on the mouse while performing a work. Moving the cursor across the screen adds improvisational (called the "mousejam") changes to the music.

Linda Sorisio has developed a program called THE MUSES (acronym for THEory of MUSic Expert Systems). Primarily devised for music theorists, THE MUSES has potential for composition as well. Written on an IBM mainframe, the program utilizes nonlinguistic pattern recognition for the analysis of music in many styles. Sounds are typically entered into THE MUSES through a MIDI port by electronic instruments. Then, the program can apply many different timbral and pitch modifications before playback and analysis begins. It was designed to use processes in creating courseware for graduate students in music. It is written in IBM's own expert system tool for mainframes: the Expert System Environment utilizing Turbo Pascal. The intention was to devise a kind of computerized music theory professor.

Yaakov Kirschen's Music Creator software combines elements of different works in order to achieve new possibilities. It first stores the chords, melodies (pitch), and rhythms of the works to be used for combination. "Composing" involves three different works. By combining the rhythm of one with the melody of another and the chords of yet another, the program creates novel combinations of styles. To fit divergent examples together with some semblance of order, the program transposes the melody to fit with the harmonies. Because the composition has no random component in the process, the same choices always produce the same results. Different arrangements of the same works, however, create significantly different music. Music Creator often "composes" nonsensical pastiches. Occasionally, however, the chosen works match for a blending of styles into a novel and interesting musical result.

Experiments in Music Intelligence (EMI) is an object-oriented system written in LISP. It is designed to assist composers in their creative work. Based on natural language processing augmented transition network parsing (NLP-ATN), it assigns syntax definitions to dictionaries containing rules about when and where intervals may exist. A motive engine guarantees that composition will produce logical structures. Composers may explore many gradations of machine versus human control. Message passing and inheritance add depth by allowing the implications of a choice in one part of the composition to affect the nature of another (nonlinear composition).

One of EMI's programs is an elaboration of the algorithm presented previously in Figure 10.10. It creates music using a workstation approach such as that presented in Figure 10.29. Here, the left side of the graphic is for timbre creation and control, and the far lower right represents the computational or ordering of notes portion of the workstation.

THE WORKSTATION

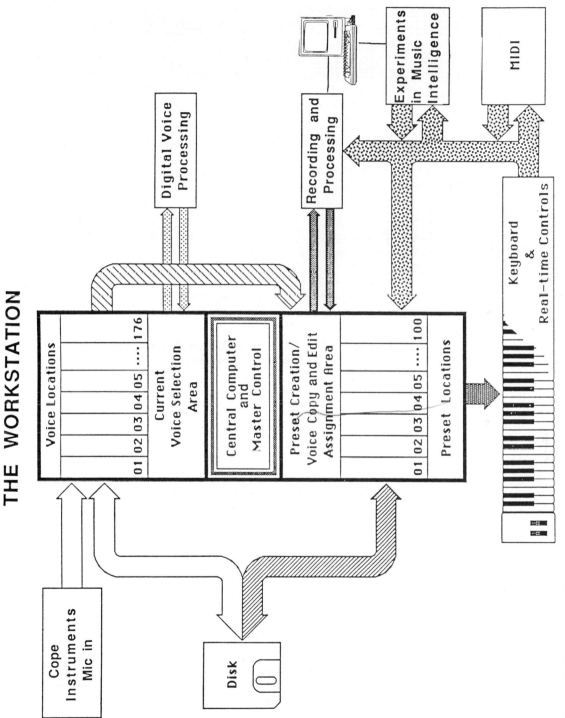

Figure 10.29. One possible workstation involving AI, sampling, MIDI, and natural language processing.

Figure 10.30. A machine-composed third movement theme (arguably) in the style of Wolfgang Amadeus Mozart.

Figures 10.30, 10.31, 10.33, and 10.34 are output from the EMI program. In Figure 10.30, a Mozart replicant (sonata type), the textures, harmonic protocol, and general melodic shape suggest Mozart's style. Note as well here the existence of a Mozart *signature* (the last bar dissonance), the result of pattern matching not unlike that described earlier in this chapter. Figure 10.31 gives an example of machine-composed Debussy. The results are presented in four staves due to limits of the notation program used to print the music, and not to any inherent program confusion. Note the relation of this machine-composed example to one of the works of Debussy input to the program's database: *Clair de lune* shown in Figure 10.32.

Figure 10.33 presents a kind of chorale in Stravinsky style not unlike that at the end of his *Symphony in C,* one of the works used for pattern matching. Figure 10.34 is from an EMI-created imitation of a Scott Joplin rag. Note the inherited syncopation and other characteristics of Joplin's style. The motion to a minor subdominant chord (here in bar 3) is unusual for Joplin, on the other hand, and may be an anomaly created by the expert system's own originality. For other and more extensive examples created by EMI, refer to the author's book *Computers and Musical Style* listed in the bibliography to this chapter.

Figure 10.31. The opening of a machine-composed prelude (arguably) in the style of Debussy.

Figure 10.32. The first two measures of Claude Debussy's *Clair de lune* on which Figure 10.31 is based.

Figure 10.33. A chorale-style machine-composed section of a larger work (arguably) in the style of Igor Stravinsky.

The League of Automated Composers (principally Jim Horton, Tim Perkis, John Bishoff, and Rich Gold) have involved mathematics and random sources. Their work includes ensemble pieces and usually employs electronic output. In *Network Piece* (1980), each of the group works out his materials independently, communicating the results from one minicomputer to another through digital-to-analog converters. Since one composer's work could influence another's, the outcome is a dialogue. Figure 10.35 shows the ensemble before a 1980 performance of *Network Piece*.

More recently, Bishoff and Perkis, along with Chris Brown, Scot Gresham-Lancaster, Phil Stone, and Mark Trayle, have created The Hub. This is a computer music "band" whose members are all designers and builders of their own hardware

Figure 10.34. Machine-composed Joplin rag theme.

Figure 10.35. The League of Automated Music Composers in performance in San Francisco on November 15, 1980. From the left: Jim Horton, Tim Perkis and John Bishoff. Photograph by John Grau (from Curtis Roads's 1985 book, p. 596, figure 335 [see bibliography for further information]).

Figure 10.36. Percussion Machine by Joe Jones, performed first at the Pocket Theatre in New York City on August 8, 1963.

and software instruments. The group electronically coordinates the activities of their individual systems through a central microcomputer, The Hub itself, as well as through ears, hands, and eyes. Their performances (June 6 and 7, 1987 in New York City) at the Clocktower and the Experimental Intermedia Foundation received wide acclaim. In program notes to the recital, Tim Perkis noted: "I see the aesthetic informing this work perhaps counter to other trends in computer music: instead of attempting to gain more individual control over every aspect of the music, we see more surprise through the lively and unpredictable response of these systems and hope to encourage an active response to surprise in hearing."

Joe Jones has created many automatic composing instruments. These range from mechanical orchestras of percussion batteries to his percussion machine shown in Figure 10.36 that looks more like an intrepid 'cellist with trappings. While the image may seem more theatrical than useful as a musical creator, such instruments have created novel if not effective works designed for "live" performance.

The Tsukuba Musical Robot, presented for the first time at the 1985 International Exposition in Tsukuba, Japan, is a fully implemented pianist capable of performing works either from sight or from a limited repertoire. Figure 10.37a shows this technical marvel during performance. Seated at a Yamaha digital organ, it scans scores with a videocamera and speaks with bystanders about its performance. Its control system consists of seventeen Z8001 and Z8002 sixteen-bit computers and fifty Z8094 eight-bit computers interconnected by fiberoptic data links. The robot's eye utilizes a charge-coupled device (CCD) camera and frame buffer with a resolution of 2,000 by 3,000 pixels. The limb design follows anthropomorphic models and consists of two-joint thumbs and four three-joint fingers moving at the speed of 1.5 m/sec. The robot is designed to accompany a human who sings into a microphone attached to the system. If the live performer is out of tune, the robot has been designed to adjust the synthesizer/organ accordingly to match the pitch level. Figure 10.37b shows the posture of the individual fingers at the keyboard.

Charles Ames spent six months developing Automated Music Composer. His system uses a Kurzweil 250 digital sampling keyboard and sound system with the user choosing the style of music desired: rock, standard jazz (*à la* Art Blakely), or

Figure 10.37. The Tsukuba *Musical Robot.*

a)

b)

Latin jazz. Ames-developed software creates original compositions within that style (usually taking many hours). Automated Music Composer was exhibited along with many other original music products for computers on a nationwide tour with Digital Equipment Corporation's "Robots and Beyond: The Age of Intelligent Machines."

Charles Ames has also developed a number of significant "constraint-based" programs for the development of automated music. Ames uses heuristic guidelines and form-generating procedures with the aesthetic goals of individual works in mind. He also employs mechanisms that maintain pitches in statistical balance by favoring the least-used pitch in any decision. Ames's *Crystals,* in particular, exemplifies his use of both AI processes and contextual sensitivity to produce successful compositions.

Otto Laske, one of the major proponents of musical intelligence as related to computers and automated music over the past few years, sums up many current views when he states,

> The question is: How can we transfer human musical expertise to a computer and represent it within the machine? How can we construct musical knowledge bases incrementally? How can we get the machine to explain its musical reasoning to a

Figure 10.38. Iannis Xenakis. Photo courtesy of Indiana University.

human being? There is nothing peculiar about musical expertise that would force us to use different methods from those used in artificial intelligence applications today to solve these very legitimate problems.[4]

Many are further convinced that by studying the problem of musical style through applications of pattern matching, we may find that grammars, neural nets and automated music have a significant impact on the development of a new universal style.

(For information on vectoral analysis and procedures see chapter 1.)

1. Historical Background: Iannis Xenakis was born in Braïla, Roumania, on May 29, 1922. Both of his parents were Greeks. He lived for ten years near the Danube before he moved with his family to Greece and obtained an education at a private college in Spetsai. He entered the Athens Polytechnic school, majoring in engineering, but soon became heavily involved with the Resistance. On January 1, 1945, he was badly wounded and blinded in his left eye. In 1947, Xenakis met Honegger, Milhaud, and Messiaen in Paris, with the latter encouraging him to go into music. He also met LeCorbusier, the architect, who accepted him as a collaborator, using Xenakis's

Vectoral Analysis: Iannis Xenakis: *Atrées*

4. C. Roads, "Symposium on Computer Music Composition," *Computer Music Journal* 10, no. 1 (Spring 1986), p. 56.

engineering talents. The two worked closely together on many projects, including the Baghdad stadium and the convent of La Tourette. In 1958, he helped with the design of the Philips pavilion at the Brussels Exposition (discussed in chapter 8 on analog electronic music), which further developed his ideas about architecture, acoustics, and music, ideas he finds inexorably linked. In 1966, he founded EMAMu (Equipe de Mathématique et d'Automatique Musicales) in Paris. He taught at Indiana University (Bloomington) during 1967–72, during which time he founded the Center for Musical Mathematics and Automation (similar to EMAMu). Most recently, he toured in America and Europe, giving classes in composition and attending performances of his music.

His works center around mathematical models and are often composed, per se, by machines (automated music). His writings (particularly *Formalized Music*) represent a standard reference for work relating to the early developments of computer composition. He has used probability laws, stochastics, Markovian chains, game theory, group theory, set theory, Boolean algebra, and Gaussian distributions as formalized projections and "galaxies." His music typically contains thick textures with many diverse elements sounding at once. Sometimes, as in *Metastasis* where the textures are glissandi, techniques are limited to one or two effects. More often, however, his computer programs will produce variations with astounding contrasts. As well, some works contain extended silences punctuated by seemingly random points or fragments of sound.

2. *Overview:* The *stochastic* and mathematical approach to music as represented in the music of Iannis Xenakis is often deeply rooted in a chance framework. Arbitrary materials feed into an extremely determinate composition system. The resultant structure is composer indeterminacy written out in traditional notation for predictable results. Xenakis describes his concepts and procedures in his book *Formalized Music:*

As a result of the impasse in serial music, as well as other causes, I originated in 1954 a music constructed from the principle of indeterminism; two years later I named it "Stochastic Music." The laws of the calculus of probabilities entered composition through musical necessity. But other paths also led to the same stochastic crossroads—first of all, natural events such as the collision of hail or rain with hard surfaces, or the song of cicadas in a summer field. These sonic events are made out of thousands of isolated sounds; this multitude of sounds, seen as a totality, is a new sonic event. This mass event is articulated and forms a plastic mold of time, which itself follows aleatory and stochastic laws. If one then wishes to form a large mass of point-notes, such as string pizzicati, one must know these mathematical laws, which, in any case, are no more than a tight and concise expression of chains of logical reasoning. Everyone has observed the sonic phenomena of a political crowd of dozens of hundreds of thousands of people. The human river shouts a slogan in a uniform rhythm. Then another slogan springs from the head of the demonstration; it spreads toward the tail, replacing the first. A wave of transition thus passes from the head to the tail. . . . The statistical laws of these events, separated from their political or moral context, are the same as those of the cicadas or the rain. They are the laws of the passage from complete order to total disorder in a continuous or explosive manner. They are stochastic laws.[5]

Some have argued that Xenakis's music is not indeterminate at all. Bernard Jacobson has written:

He uses chance, but his music leaves nothing to chance. This is not the paradox it might seem. To Xenakis—as indeed, to most philosophers—chance itself is a scientific concept. Central among the scientific laws he has applied to music is Bernoulli's Law of large numbers, which provides that as the number of repetitions of a given "chance" trial (such as flipping a coin) increases, so the probability that the results will tend to determinate end approaches certainty.[6]

Iannis Xenakis, using FORTRAN IV programming with the IBM-7090, has produced data for his free *stochastic music* detailed in his book *Formalized Music*. A number of his works for traditional instruments were composed with the aid of high-speed computations of probability theory made possible by computer application. These works include *ST/10–1, 080262* (1962, with first performance on May 24 of that year at the headquarters of IBM in France), *ST/48–1, 240162* (for large orchestra), *Atrées* (for ten soloists, 1962), and *Morsima-Amorsima* (for violin, 'cello, bass, and piano, 1962; the processes are described in the performance notes for this work). Pitches were calculated by the electronic brain 7090 IBM in Paris in obedience to a special stochastic (probabilist) "programme" devised by Xenakis. This was derived from the thesis of "minimum Rules of Composition," which he had already formulated in 1958 in *Achorripsis*. The "programme" is a complex of stochastic laws that the composer had been introducing into musical composition for a number of years. The computer defines all the sounds of a sequence, previously calculated, including the time of occurrence, kind of timbre (*arco, pizzicato, glissando,* etc.), instrument, pitch, the gradient of *glissando* (where it occurs), and the duration and dynamic of the emission of sound.[7]

Atrées (ST/10-3,060962) was completed in 1962 (the last six digits represent that date: 6, September, 1962) and composed with the same computer program known as ST (for stochastic) used for *ST/10* (1962; 10 = the number of performers), *Morsima-Amorsima, Achorripsis,* and *ST/48–1, 240162*. The work is fifteen minutes long, following a free form, at times dramatic, often halting and formidable. Pitches are fixed by determining the mean density of notes occurring during preconceived sequence lengths. Dynamic intensities derive from a chart of 44 values based on the dynamics *ppp, p, f,* and *ff,* with all other values existing only briefly within *crescendi*

5. Iannis Xenakis, *Formalized Music* (Bloomington: Indiana University Press, 1971), p. 9.

6. From the liner notes to Nonesuch Records H-71201 (*Akrata Pithoprakta*).

7. See Iannis Xenakis, *Morsima-Amorsima* (Boosey & Hawkes, 1967). From notes to the score.

$$(0 \le x \le x_0) = \int_0^{x_0} f(x)\, dx = 1 - e^{-cx_0} = F(x_0),$$

$$F(x_0) = \text{prob.}\ (0 \le y \le y_0) = y_0$$

$$1 - e^{-cx_0} = y_0$$

$$x_0 = -\frac{\ln\,(1 - y_0)}{c}$$

$$f(x)\, dx = ce^{-cx}\, dx.$$

and *diminuendi,* giving the work a constant feel of movement (since 40 of the 44 values have such changing dynamics) toward or away from these guideposts. Figure 10.39 gives an example of some of the mathematical theory behind this work.

The first formula represents an elementary law of probability (a density function) with the others showing the logic of producing a distribution function that can be translated into machine language. These programs were run on an IBM 7090 computer using punch cards, a process that could take (in the early 1960s) up to six months. The composer further ran many tests for errors in logic and orthography before actually translating his work into music notation. Figures 10.40 and 10.41 show examples of the FORTRAN IV language employment and the provisional results from one phase of the analysis program.

This work, like *Metastasis,* aptly demonstrates Xenakis's penchant for *glissandi* in his music. It also clearly emphasizes the fact that he uses the numbers (statistics) separate from musical meaning (i.e., the computer simply processes numbers). The composer relates to this with his comment: "There exists in all the arts what we may call rationalism in the etymological sense: the search for proportion" and "Now everything that is rule or repeated constraint is part of the mental machine."[8] He further refers to his use of science and art: "Computers resolve logical problems by heuristic methods. But computers are not really responsible for the introduction of mathematics into music; rather it is mathematics that makes use of the computer in composition."[9]

8. Xenakis, Iannis, "Free Stochastic Music from the Computer," in *Cybernetics, Arts and Ideas,* ed. by Jasia Reichardt, p. 124.

9. Ibid.

```
C     PROGRAM FREE STOCHASTIC MUSIC  (FORTRAN IV)                    XEN    6
C                                                                    XEN    7
C     GLOSSARY OF THE PRINCIPAL ABBREVIATIONS                        XEN    8
C                                                                    XEN    9
C     A - DURATION OF EACH SEQUENCE IN SECONDS                       XEN    9
C     A10,A20,A17,A35,A30 - NUMBERS FOR GLISSANDO CALCULATION        XEN   10
C     ALEA - PARAMETER USED TO ALTER THE RESULT OF A SECOND RUN WITH THEXEN  11
C     SAME INPUT DATA                                                XEN   12
C     ALFA(3) - THREE EXPRESSIONS ENTERING INTO THE THREE SPEED VALUES XEN  13
C     OF THE SLIDING TONES ( GLISSANDI )                             XEN   14
C     ALIM - MAXIMUM LIMIT OF SEQUENCE DURATION A                    XEN   15
C     (AMAX(I),I=1,KTR) TABLE OF AN EXPRESSION ENTERING INTO THE     XEN   16
C     CALCULATION OF THE NOTE LENGTH IN PART 8                       XEN   17
C     BF - DYNAMIC FORM NUMBER. THE LIST IS ESTABLISHED INDEPENDENTLY XEN  18
C     OF THIS PROGRAM AND IS SUBJECT TO MODIFICATION                 XEN   19
C     DELTA - THE RECIPROCAL OF THE MEAN DENSITY OF SOUND EVENTS DURING XEN 20
C     A SEQUENCE OF DURATION A                                       XEN   21
C     (E(I,J),I=1,KTR,J=1,KTE) - PROBABILITIES OF THE KTR TIMBRE CLASSESXEN 22
C     INTRODUCED AS INPUT DATA. DEPENDING ON THE CLASS NUMBER I=KR AND XEN 23
C     ON THE POWER J=U OBTAINED FROM V3*EXPF(U)=DA                   XEN   24
C     EPSI - EPSILON FOR ACCURACY IN CALCULATING PN AND E(I,J),WHICH XEN   25
C     IT IS ADVISABLE TO RETAIN.                                     XEN   26
C     (GN(I,J),I=1,KTR,J=1,KTS) - TABLE OF THE GIVEN LENGTH OF BREATH XEN  27
C     FOR EACH INSTRUMENT. DEPENDING ON CLASS I AND INSTRUMENT J     XEN   28
C     GTNA - GREATEST NUMBER OF NOTES IN THE SEQUENCE OF DURATION A  XEN   29
C     GTNS - GREATEST NUMBER OF NOTES IN KW LOOPS                    XEN   30
C     (HAMIN(I,J),HAMAX(I,J),HBMIN(I,J),HBMAX(I,J),I=1,KTR,J=1,KTS)  XEN   31
C     TABLE OF INSTRUMENT COMPASS LIMITS. DEPENDING ON TIMBRE CLASS I XEN  32
C     AND INSTRUMENT J.  TEST INSTRUCTION 480 IN PART 6 DETERMINES   XEN   33
C     WHETHER THE HA OR THE HB TABLE IS FOLLOWED. THE NUMBER 7 IS    XEN   34
C     ARBITRARY.                                                     XEN   35
C     JW - ORDINAL NUMBER OF THE SEQUENCE COMPUTED.                  XEN   36
C     KNL - NUMBER OF LINES PER PAGE OF THE PRINTED RESULT.KNL=50    XEN   37
C     KR1 - NUMBER IN THE CLASS KR=1 USED FOR PERCUSSION OR INSTRUMENTS XEN 38
C     WITHOUT A DEFINITE PITCH.                                      XEN   39
C     KTE - POWER OF THE EXPONENTIAL COEFFICIENT E SUCH THAT         XEN   40
C     DA(MAX)=V3*(E**(KTE-1))                                        XEN   41
C     KTR - NUMBER OF TIMBRE CLASSES                                 XEN   42
C     KW - MAXIMUM NUMBER OF JW                                      XEN   43
C     KTEST1,TAV1,ETC - EXPRESSIONS USEFUL IN CALCULATING HOW LONG THE XEN 44
C     VARIOUS PARTS OF THE PROGRAM WILL RUN.                         XEN   45
C     KT1 - ZERO IF THE PROGRAM IS BEING RUN. NONZERO DURING DEBUGGING XEN 46
C     KT2 - NUMBER OF LOOPS. EQUAL TO 15 BY ARBITRARY DEFINITION.    XEN   47
C     (MODI(IX8),IX8=7,1)  AUXILIARY FUNCTION TO INTERPOLATE VALUES IN XEN 48
C     THE TETA(256) TABLE (SEE PART 7)                               XEN   49
C     NA - NUMBER OF SOUNDS CALCULATED FOR THE SEQUENCE A(NA=DA*A)   XEN   50
C     (NT(I),I=1,KTR) NUMBER OF INSTRUMENTS ALLOCATED TO EACH OF THE XEN   51
C     KTR TIMBRE CLASSES.                                            XEN   52
C     (PN(I,J),I=1,KTR,J=1,KTS),(KTS=NT(I),I=1,KTR) TABLE OF PROBABILITYXEN 53
C     OF EACH INSTRUMENT OF THE CLASS I.                             XEN   54
C     (Q(I),I=1,KTR) PROBABILITIES OF THE KTR TIMBRE CLASSES. CONSIDEREDXEN 55
C     AS LINEAR FUNCTIONS OF THE DENSITY DA.                         XEN   56
C     (S(I),I=1,KTR) SUM OF THE SUCCESSIVE Q(I) PROBABILITIES. USED TO XEN 57
C     CHOOSE THE CLASS KR BY COMPARING IT TO A RANDOM NUMBER X1 (SEE XEN   58
C     PART 3, LOOP 380 AND PART 5, LOOP 430).                        XEN   59
C     SINA - SUM OF THE COMPUTED NOTES IN THE JW CLOUDS NA. ALWAYS LESS XEN 60
C     THAN GTNS ( SEE TEST IN PART 10 ).                             XEN   61
C     SQPI - SQUARE ROOT OF PI ( 3.14159...)                         XEN   62
C     TA - SOUND ATTACK TIME ABCISSA.                                XEN   63
C     TETA(256) - TABLE OF THE 256 VALUES OF THE INTEGRAL OF THE NORMAL XEN 64
C     DISTRIBUTION CURVE WHICH IS USEFUL IN CALCULATING GLISSANDO SPEED XEN 65
```

Figure 10.40. The principal glossary of Xenakis's stochastic music writing in FORTRAN IV (p. 145, *Formalized Music;* see Bibliography).

3. Orchestration Techniques: *Atrées* is scored for clarinet, bass clarinet, two French horns, percussion, two violins, viola, and 'cello (though there are various versions). The percussionist employs maracas, suspended cymbals, a gong, five temple-blocks, four tom-toms, and a vibraphone. Determination of which instruments play together at any given time is achieved by breaking them into timbre classes. For example, there exist classes for flute/clarinet, brass, struck-strings (*col legno*), bowed-strings, and *glissando*. Effects are treated similarly to instruments. As an example, the texture densities

Figure 10.41. Provisional results of one phase of the analysis (p. 153, *Formalized Music;* see Bibliography).

N	START	CLASS	INSTRM	PITCH	GLISS1	GLISS2	GLISS3	DURATION	DYNAM
1	0.00	7	1	34.0	0.0	0.0	0.0	0.00	3
2	0.10	10	1	43.2	0.0	0.0	0.0	0.41	50
3	0.11	6	8	81.3	0.0	0.0	0.0	0.63	21
4	0.13	6	3	47.0	0.0	0.0	0.0	0.18	10
5	0.18	1	4	0.0	0.0	0.0	0.0	1.90	29
6	0.25	9	1	48.7	0.0	0.0	0.0	0.51	35
7	0.33	6	7	11.4	0.0	0.0	0.0	0.37	42
8	0.34	9	1	38.1	0.0	0.0	0.0	0.00	59
9	0.40	1	1	0.0	0.0	0.0	0.0	2.20	45
10	0.41	6	9	55.0	0.0	0.0	0.0	1.07	0
11	0.76	6	7	11.5	0.0	0.0	0.0	0.40	7
12	0.90	8	2	23.2	0.0	0.0	0.0	0.00	19
13	1.00	7	2	26.9	0.0	0.0	0.0	0.00	6
14	1.09	10	1	46.2	0.0	0.0	0.0	0.32	57
15	1.09	6	2	68.5	0.0	0.0	0.0	0.71	25
16	1.23	6	3	46.9	0.0	0.0	0.0	0.64	32
17	1.42	6	1	44.0	0.0	0.0	0.0	0.44	1
18	1.57	10	1	36.2	0.0	0.0	0.0	0.22	21
19	1.65	4	2	32.5	0.0	0.0	0.0	1.09	13
20	1.78	6	8	72.6	0.0	0.0	0.0	0.06	60
21	1.92	6	3	38.9	0.0	0.0	0.0	0.55	60
22	1.94	5	1	74.6	71.0	-25.0	-71.0	0.80	62
23	2.18	4	1	32.6	0.0	0.0	0.0	1.50	50
24	2.18	6	6	50.9	0.0	0.0	0.0	0.60	26
25	2.19	1	12	0.0	0.0	0.0	0.0	4.58	24
26	2.20	9	1	49.3	0.0	0.0	0.0	0.02	58
27	2.23	9	1	51.0	0.0	0.0	0.0	0.22	13
28	2.32	7	1	36.9	0.0	0.0	0.0	0.00	43
29	2.33	4	1	31.8	0.0	0.0	0.0	1.38	56
30	2.54	1	6	0.0	0.0	0.0	0.0	0.28	14
31	2.57	11	2	12.2	0.0	0.0	0.0	1.69	40
32	2.71	9	1	48.5	0.0	0.0	0.0	0.37	55
33	2.80	1	5	0.0	0.0	0.0	0.0	1.50	58
34	3.28	5	2	15.4	49.0	5.0	-31.0	0.52	21
35	3.33	1	7	0.0	0.0	0.0	0.0	1.38	8
36	3.38	5	2	47.3	-71.0	-17.0	46.0	1.05	4
37	3.55	10	1	37.6	0.0	0.0	0.0	0.14	24
38	3.56	1	9	0.0	0.0	0.0	0.0	1.30	0
39	3.60	9	1	64.3	0.0	0.0	0.0	0.19	13
40	3.64	12	2	52.2	0.0	0.0	0.0	3.72	9
41	3.65	6	5	59.0	0.0	0.0	0.0	0.83	28
42	3.71	5	3	38.8	25.0	2.0	-15.0	0.00	11
43	3.80	6	8	75.6	0.0	0.0	0.0	0.43	17
44	3.87	6	2	51.5	0.0	0.0	0.0	0.77	57
45	3.89	6	7	12.1	0.0	0.0	0.0	0.39	2
46	4.15	5	2	43.0	-71.0	24.0	71.0	1.16	2
47	4.15	5	1	80.3	36.0	4.0	22.0	0.85	50
48	4.25	9	1	59.9	0.0	0.0	0.0	0.10	10
49	4.31	12	2	40.1	0.0	0.0	0.0	2.49	33
50	4.33	1	10	0.0	0.0	0.0	0.0	0.46	34

provided by the chart in Figure 10.42 show eight classes, four of which are instruments (played normally), with the other four being effects.

The vertical numbers refer to percentages (summing to 100) of each of the eight categories of timbres that contribute to the overall textural shape. The harp and clarinet have the least and most (respectively) deviation (2 and 26 percents). By and large, the patterns tend to imitate one another (partially out of necessity) with only the percussion moving somewhat independently at times.

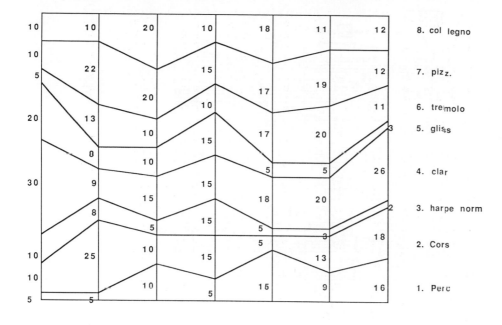

10	10	20	10	18	11	12	8. col legno
10	22		15		12		
5		20		17	19	12	7. pizz.
20	13	10	10			11	6. tremolo
		10	15	17	20		5. gliss
	0	10				3	
30	9		15	5	5	26	4. clar
	8	15		18	20		3. harpe norm
		5	15	5		2	
10	25	10	15	5	3	18	2. Cors
10				5	13		
10		10	5	16	9	16	1. Perc
5	5						

Figure 10.42. Percents of use utilized in *Atrées* (from *Cybernetics, Art and Ideas*, ed. by Jadis Reichardt, p. 128; see Bibliography).

$$P_z = 2/S \ (1 - Z/S)DZ$$

Figure 10.43. One probability formula used by Xenakis.

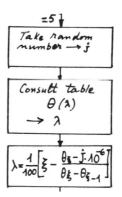

Figure 10.44. Example of aspects of Xenakis's algorithm for random processes.

4. Basic Techniques: Much of Xenakis's work with probability derives from a given voice's "memory" of a preceding pitch and choosing then from a given compass within a prescribed set of semitones (typically 86). This is given by the formula in Figure 10.43 where P_z is the probability of the interval z chosen from the compass s. Lengths of notes and even sliding speeds of glissandi are similarly determined. Part of an early flowchart of work in the ST series provides an example of the composer's processes (shown in Figure 10.44). The random number is used as a selection number from a table of correct possibilities. The formula creates values as a result of system-defined determinants.

Figure 10.45. First two bars from *ST/10-1, 080262*.

5. Vertical Models: Figure 10.45 shows the first two bars of *Atrées ST/10–1, 080262*. All twelve pitches exist here but clearly no rows or established protocol for their use. Centers (e.g., G♯ and E near the beginning) occur and pass so quickly that the word has little meaning. In fact, pitch itself seems elusive and often unimportant, owing to the rapidity of the changing harmonic rhythm. The texture varies on a microscale; that is, from instant to instant one is constantly provided with *change*. Polyrhythms abound (i.e., 6 against 5 against 4, etc., in the first half measure). Effects (harmonics, *pizzicato, tremolo, glissando*) occur simultaneously or in near proximity. Dynamics are volatile (subject to changes every note) and mixed in a nontraditional manner. Often this causes some instruments not to be heard during a performance. This level of complexity abounds in this and other of Xenakis's works, no doubt a reflection of the processes which contributed to its composition.

6. Horizontal Models: Figure 10.45 also provides an example of melodic order in *Atrées*. Only two melodic intervals are seconds (A–G♯ in the clarinet and C–C♯ in the viola), with most larger than an octave. Even when factoring in a pitch-class component, one finds few seconds or thirds. The pointillism thus achieved, however, is often clouded by the complex counterpoint taking place. It is difficult to follow any line independently from the others. Since each voice often changes timbres as well as pitches, this further confuses the issue.

7. Style: *Atrées ST/10–1, 080262* is a stochastically determined work based on probability calculations using an IBM 7090 computer. The complex process of developing programs for the work is as important as the piece itself. Writing the formulas, the resultant programs, and the charts of data from which the computer may choose possible notes requires intense scrutiny. Debugging the large functions properly is crucial if the process is to succeed. Translating the resultant data to music also claims great time and care to avoid mistakes. The result is a complex work demanding of its performers and audience alike. Some critics, confused by the pluralistic societies of new music, have dubbed Xenakis the founder of *maximalism.* Certainly this work, if not in size of orchestration in terms of event numbers per performer, ranks high in size.

This work, while similar to Webern's *Symphonie* (chapter 2) in terms of pointillism, varies with respect to texture and lack of premeditated pitch control. It is most different, however, when compared to Oliveros's *Sonic Meditations XIII* (chapter 6), which, by virtue of its outspoken simplicity and lack of tangible movement, represents the opposite extreme from Xenakis. Interestingly, however, *Atrées* holds more conceptual ties with Oliveros's work: for example, both were conceived with a high degree of indeterminacy, yet they have very predictable results in performance. Comparisons to the vectoral analysis found in chapter 5 proves very revealing, especially in the case where apparently opposite approaches to control reveal comparatively similar results.

Definition and Background

**Bibliography—
Chapter 10***

Further Readings

Ames, Charles. "Automated Composition in Retrospect 1956–1986." *Leonardo* 20, no. 2 (1987): pp. 169–185.
———. "Notes on Undulant." *Interface* 12, no. 3 (1983).
———. "AI in Music." *Encyclopedia of Artificial Intelligence.* New York: John Wiley and Sons, 1987.
———. "Statistics and Compositional Balance." *Perspectives of New Music* 28, no. 1 (1990): pp. 80–111.
Bateman, Wayne. *Introduction to Computer Music.* New York: John Wiley and Sons, 1982.
Clynes, Manfred, ed. *Music, Mind, and Brain.* New York: Penguin Press, 1982.
von Foerster, Heinz, and James Beauchamp, eds. *Music by Computers.* New York: John Wiley and Sons, 1969.
Garland, Peter. *The Music of James Tenney.* Santa Fe: SOUNDINGS Press, 1984.
Hiller, Lejaren. "Music Composed with Computers: A Historical Survey." In *The Computer and Music,* ed. H. Lincoln, chapter 4. Ithaca, N.Y.: Cornell University Press, 1970.
———. "Composing with Computers: A Progress Report." *Computer Music Journal* 5, no. 4 (1981): pp. 7–21.

*Addresses for record companies, periodicals, and music publishers mentioned in this Bibliography can be found in Appendix IV.

———. "Programming a Computer for Musical Composition." In *Computer Applications in Music,* ed. Gerald Lefkoff. Morgantown: West Virginia University Library, 1967.

Hiller, Lejaren, and Leonard Isaacson. *Experimental Music.* New York: McGraw-Hill, 1959.

Hofstadter, Douglas. *Godel, Escher, Bach.* New York: Random House, 1980.

Kivy, Peter. *Sound and Semblance: Reflections on Musical Representation.* Princeton, N.J.: Princeton University Press, 1984.

Koenig, Gottfried Michael. "Aesthetic Integration of Computer-Composed Scores." *Computer Music Journal* 7, no. 4 (1983): pp. 27–32.

———. "Project 1." *Electronic Music Reports* 1, no. 2 (1970).

Lansky, Paul. "A View from the Bus: When Machines Make Music." *Perspectives of New Music* 28, no. 2 (1990): pp. 102–11.

Lefkoff, Gerald, ed. *Computer Applications in Music.* Morgantown: West Virginia University Library, 1967.

Lincoln, Harry, ed. *The Computer and Music.* Ithaca, N.Y.: Cornell University Press, 1970.

Minsky, Marvin. *K-lines: A Theory of Memory.* Cambridge, Mass.: MIT AI Memo 516, 1979.

———. *The Society of Mind.* New York: Simon and Schuster, 1986.

Narmour, Eugene. *Beyond Schenkerism.* Chicago: University of Chicago Press, 1977.

Prieberg, Fred. *Musica ex Machina.* Berlin: Verlag Ullstein, 1960.

Reichardt, Jasia, ed. *Cybernetics, Art and Ideas.* Greenwich, Conn.: New York Graphic Society Ltd., 1971.

Roads, C. *Composers and the Computer.* Los Altos, Calif.: William Kaufmann, 1985.

Seay, Albert. "The Composer of Music and the Computer." *Computers and Automation* 13, no. 16 (1964).

Slawson, Wayne. *Sound Color.* Berkeley: University of California Press, 1985.

"Syncopation by Automation," *Data from ElectroData.* Pasadena: Electro-Data Division of Burroughs, Inc., 1956.

Truax, Barry. "General Techniques of Computer Composition Programming." *Numus-West* 4 (1973).

Expert Systems

Ames, Charles. "Crystals: Recursive Structures in Automated Composition." *Computer Music Journal* 6, no. 3 (1982): pp. 46–64.

Austin, Larry, and Eugene DeLisa. "Modeling Processes of Musical Invention." In *Proceedings of the International Computer Music Conference,* comp. James Beauchamp, pp. 206–11. San Francisco: Computer Music Association, 1987.

Barbaud, P. "Algorithmic Music." From a trade publication. Paris: *Systems Bulletin,* 1969.

Bateman, Wayne. *Introduction to Computer Music.* New York: John Wiley and Sons, 1982.

Bolognesi, Tommaso. "Automated Composition: Experiments with Self-Similar Music." *Computer Music Journal* 7, no. 1 (1983): pp. 25–36.

Caianiello, E. R. *Cybernetic Systems.* London: Research Studies Press, 1984.

Cope, David. *Computers and Musical Style.* Madison, Wis.: A-R Editions, 1991.

———. "Experiments in Music Intelligence." In *Proceedings of the International Computer Music Conference,* comp. James Beauchamp, pp. 174–81. San Francisco: Computer Music Association, 1987.

———. "An Expert System for Computer-Assisted Music Composition." *Computer Music Journal* 11, no. 4 (Winter 1987): pp. 30–46.

Dowling, W. Jay, and Dane L. Harwood. *Music Cognition.* New York: Academic Press, 1986.

Duisberg, Robert. "On the Role of Affect in Artificial Intelligence and Music." *Perspectives of New Music* 23, no. 1 (1984): pp. 6–37.

Evans, Brian. "Integration of Music and Graphics through Algorithmic Congruence." In *Proceedings of the International Computer Music Conference,* comp. James Beauchamp, pp. 17–24. San Francisco: Computer Music Association, 1987.

Forte, A. "Computer-implemented Analysis of Musical Structure." In *Computer Applications in Music,* ed. Gerald Lefkoff, pp. 20–34. Morgantown: West Virginia University Library, 1967.

Fry, C. "Flavors Band: A Language for Specifying Musical Style." *Computer Music Journal* 8, no. 4 (1984).

Garten, Brad. "Elthar—A Signal Processing Expert that Learns." In *Proceedings of the International Computer Music Conference,* comp. James Beauchamp, pp. 96–103. San Francisco: Computer Music Association, 1987.

Goldberg, Adele, and David Robson. *SMALLTALK-80: The Language and its Implementation.* Reading, Mass.: Addison-Wesley, 1983.

Greenberg, Gary. "Procedural Composition." In *Proceedings of the International Computer Music Conference,* comp. James Beauchamp, pp. 25–32. San Francisco: Computer Music Association, 1987.

Grossman, Gary. "Instruments, Cybernetics, and Computer Music." In *Proceedings of the International Computer Music Conference,* comp. James Beauchamp, pp. 212–19. San Francisco: Computer Music Association, 1987.

Hamel, Keith, Bruce Pennycook, Bill Ripley, and Eli Blevis. "Composition Design System: A Functional Approach to Composition." In *Proceedings of the International Computer Music Conference,* comp. James Beauchamp, pp. 33–39. San Francisco: Computer Music Association, 1987.

Holland, Simon. "New Cognitive Theories of Harmony Applied to Direct Manipulation Tools for Novices." In *Proceedings of the International Computer Music Conference,* comp. James Beauchamp, pp. 182–89. San Francisco: Computer Music Association, 1987.

Holtzman, S. R. "A Generative Grammar Definitional Language for Music." *Interface* 9, no. 1 (1982).

Koenig, Gottfried Michael. "PROJECT 2: A Programme for Musical Composition." *Electronic Music Reports* 1, no. 3 (1970).

Levitt, David. "Machine Tongues X: Constraint Languages." *Computer Music Journal* 8, no.1 (1984): pp. 9–21.

Lidov, D., and J. Gabura. "A Melody Writing Algorithm Using a Formal Language Model." *Computer Studies in the Humanities* 4, no. 4 (1973).

Lisle, Edward, R. and H. Christopher Longuet-Higgins. "Modelling Music Cognition." *Contemporary Music Review* 3, no. 1 (1989): pp. 15–28.

Longuet-Higgins, H. Christopher. *Mental Processes.* Cambridge, Mass.: The MIT Press, 1987.

Longuet-Higgins, H. C., and C. S. Lee. "The Rhythmic Interpretation of Monophonic Music." *Music Perception* 1, no. 4 (1984): pp. 424–41.

Newcomb, Steven R. "LASSO: An Intelligent Computer-based Tutorial in Sixteenth-Century Counterpoint." *Computer Music Journal* 9, no. 4 (1985): pp. 49–61.

Oppenheim, Daniel Vincent. "The P-G-G Environment for Music Composition." In *Proceedings of the International Computer Music Conference,* comp. James Beauchamp, pp. 40–48. San Francisco: Computer Music Association, 1987.

Polansky, Larry, David Rosenboom, and Phil Burk. "HMSL: Overview (Version 3.1) and Notes on Intelligent Instrument Design." In *Proceedings of the International Computer Music Conference,* comp. James Beauchamp, pp. 197–205. San Francisco: Computer Music Association, 1987.

Roads, Curtis. "The Tsukuba Musical Robot." *Computer Music Journal* 10, no. 2 (1986): pp. 39–43.

Rodet, Xavier, and Pierre Cointe. "FORMES: Composition and Scheduling of Processes." *Computer Music Journal* 8, no. 3 (1984): pp. 32–50.

Smoliar, Stephen W. "A Computer Aid for Schenkerian Analysis." *Computer Music Journal* 4, no. 2 (1980): pp. 41–59.

Truax, Barry. "The PODX System: Interactive Compositional Software for the DMX-1000." *Computer Music Journal* 9, no. 1 (1985): pp. 29–38.

Winsor, Phil. *Computer-Assisted Music Composition.* Princeton, N.J.: Petrocelli Books, 1987.

Yavelow, Christopher. "Composition or Improvisation? Only the Computer Knows." *AES 5th Annual Conference Proceedings.* Los Angeles: Audio Engineering Society, 1987.

An Example Program

Allen, John. *Anatomy of LISP.* New York: McGraw-Hill, 1978.

Barr, A., and E. Feigenbaum. *Handbook of Artificial Intelligence.* Stanford: Stanford Computer Science Department, 1979.

Carne, E. B. *Artificial Intelligence Techniques.* London: Macmillan, 1965.

Charniak, E., C. Riesbeck, and D. McDermott. *Artificial Intelligence Programming Techniques.* Hillsdale, N.J.: Lawrence Erlbaum Associates, 1979.

Charniak, Eugene, and Drew McDermott. *Introduction to Artificial Intelligence.* Reading, Mass.: Addison-Wesley, 1984.

Cope, David. *Computers and Musical Style.* Madison: Wis., A-R Editions, 1991.

———. "Pattern Matching as an Engine for the Computer Simulation of Musical Style." In *Proceedings of the International Computer Music Conference.* ed. Stephen Arnold and Graham Hair, pp. 288–94. San Francisco: Computer Music Association, 1990.

Ennals, R. *Artificial Intelligence.* West Sussex, England: John Wiley and Sons Ltd., 1985.

Fu, K. S. *Syntactic Pattern Recognition and Applications.* Englewood Cliffs, N.J.: Prentice-Hall, 1982.

Meehan, James R. "An Artificial Intelligence Approach to Tonal Music Theory." *Computer Music Journal* 4, no. 2 (1980): pp. 60–65.

Thomas, M. T. "VIVACE: A Rule-Based AI System for Composition." *Proceedings of the 1985 ICMC.* San Francisco: Computer Music Association.

Winston, P. H. *Artificial Intelligence.* 2d ed. Reading, Mass.: Addison-Wesley, 1984.

Winston, P. H., and B. K. P. Horn. *LISP.* 2d ed. Reading, Mass.: Addison-Wesley, 1984.

Grammars

Ames, Charles. "Crystals: Recursive Structures in Automated Composition." *Computer Music Journal* 6, no. 3 (1982): pp. 46–64.

Baroni, Mario, and Laura Callegari, eds. *Musical Grammars and Computer Analysis: Atti del Convegno (Modena, 4–6 Ottobre 1982).* Florence, Italy: L. S. Olschki, 1984.

Chomsky, Noam. *Aspects of the Theory of Syntax.* Cambridge, Mass.: MIT Press, 1965.
———. *Syntactic Structures.* The Hague: Mouton, 1957.
Cope, David. "An Expert System for Computer-Assisted Music Composition." *Computer Music Journal* 11, no. 4 (1987): pp. 30–46.
Dewdney, A. K. "Computer Recreations." *Scientific American* 256, no. 4 (April 1987).
Dodge, Charles. "Profile of A Musical Fractal." *Computer Music Journal* 12, no. 3 (1988): pp. 10–14.
Dodge, Charles, and Curtis Bahn. "Musical Fractals." *BYTE Magazine* (June 1986): pp. 185–96.
Fu, K. S. *Syntactic Pattern Recognition and Applications.* Englewood Cliffs, N.J.: Prentice-Hall, 1982.
Holtzman, S. R. "Using Generative Grammars for Music Composition." *Computer Music Journal* 5, no. 1 (1981): pp. 51–64.
Laske, Otto. "In Search of a Generative Grammar for Music." *Perspectives of New Music* 12, no. 1 (1973): pp. 351–78.
———. "Musical Semantics: A Procedural Point of View." *Proceedings of the International Conference on the Semiotics of Music.* Belgrade, 1973.
Lerdahl, Fred. "Cognitive Constraints on Compositional Systems." In *Generative Processes in Music,* ed. J. Sloboda, pp. 229–44. London: Oxford University Press, 1987.
Lerdahl, Fred, and Ray Jackendoff. "Toward a Formal Theory of Music." *Journal of Music Theory* 21, no. 1 (1977): pp. 111–72.
———. *A Generative Theory of Tonal Music.* Cambridge, Mass.: The MIT Press, 1983.
Roads, C. "Grammars as Representations for Music." In *Foundations of Computer Music,* ed. Curtis Roads and John Strawn, pp. 403–22. Cambridge, Mass.: MIT Press, 1985.
———. "Composing Grammars." *CMA Reports.* San Francisco: Computer Music Association, 1978.
———. "An Overview of Music Representations." In *Musical Grammars and Computer Analysis: Atti del Convegno (Modena, 4–6 Ottobre 1982),* ed. Mario Baroni and Laura Callegari, pp. 7–37. Florence, Italy: L. S. Olschki, 1984.
———. "Research in Music and Artificial Intelligence." *Computing Surveys* 17, no. 2 (1985).
Ruwet, N. "Théorie et Méthodes dans les études Musicales." *Musique en Jeu* 17 (1975).
Snell, James L. "Musical Grammars and Computer Analysis: A Review." *Perspectives of New Music* 23, no. 2 (1985): pp. 220–35.
Steedman, Mark J. "A Generative Grammar for Jazz Chord Sequences." *Music Perception* 2, no. 1 (1984).
Winograd, Terry. "Linguistics and the Computer Analysis of Tonal Harmony." *Journal of Music Theory* 12, no. 1 (1968): pp. 2–49.

Neural Networks

Bharucha, Jamshed. "Music Cognition and Perceptual Facilitation: A Connectionist Framework." *Music Perception* 5, no. 1 (Fall 1987): pp. 1–30.
Bharucha, Jamshed, and Peter Todd. "Modeling the Perception of Tonal Structure with Neural Nets." *Computer Music Journal* 13, no. 4 (Winter 1989): pp. 44–53.
Lischka, Christoph. "Connectionist Models of Musical Thinking." In *Proceedings of the International Computer Music Conference,* comp. James Beauchamp, pp. 190–96. San Francisco: Computer Music Association, 1987.
Scarborough, Ben Miller, and Jacqueline Jones. "Connectionist Models for Tonal Analysis." *Computer Music Journal* 13, no. 3 (Fall 1989): pp. 49–55.

Todd, Peter. "A Sequential Network Design for Musical Applications." *Proceedings of the 1988 Connectionist Models Summer School.* San Mateo, Calif.: Morgan Kaufmann, 1988.

———. "A Connectionist Approach to Algorithmic Composition." *Computer Music Journal* 13, no. 4 (Winter 1989): pp. 27–43.

Current Programs

Ames, Charles. "Automated Composition in Retrospect: 1956–1986." *Leonardo* 20, no. 2 (1987): pp. 169–85.

Cope, David. *Computers and Musical Style.* Madison, Wis.: A-R Editions, 1991.

Kirschen, Yaakov. *Music Creator.* Walnut, Calif.: JFY, 1989.

Laske, Otto. "KEITH: A Rule-System for Making Music-Analytical Discoveries." In *Musical Grammars and Computer Analysis: Atti del Convegno (Modena, 4–6 Ottobre 1982),* ed. Mario Baroni and Laura Callegari, pp. 165–99. Florence, Italy: L. S. Olschki, 1984.

Loy, Gareth. "Composing with Computers: A Survey of Some Compositional Formalisms and Music Programming Languages." In *Current Directions in Computer Music Research,* ed. Max Mathews and John R. Pierce, pp. 291–396 Cambridge, Mass.: MIT Press, 1989.

Meier, John. *Mozart,* Version 1.0. Santa Barbara, Calif.: Kinko's Academic Courseware Exchange, 1984.

Iannis Xenakis

Xenakis, Iannis. "Free Stochastic Music from the Computer." In *Cybernetics, Art and Ideas,* ed. Jasia Reichardt, pp. 111–23. Greenwich, Conn.: New York Graphic Society Ltd., 1971.

———. *Formalized Music.* Bloomington: Indiana University Press, 1971.

———. *Arts/Sciences: Alloys.* New York: Pendragon Press, 1985.

———. *Musique. Architecture.* Paris: Casterman, 1976.

Compact Discs, Recordings, and Publishers

Bischoff, John. *Lovely Little Records.* Lovely Records 101/106.

Brün, Herbert. *Gestures for Eleven* (1964). CRI s-321.

Cage, John, and Lejaren Hiller. *HPSCHD.* C. F. Peters. Nonesuch 71224.

Chadabe, Joel. *Daisy.* Opus One 16.

———. *Settings for Spirituals.* Lovely Music 1302.

Cope, David. *Out From This Breathing Earth* (1985). Opus One 129.

Hiller, Lejaren. *An Avalanche for Pitchman, Prima-Donna, Player Piano, Percussionist and Pre-Recorded Playback* (1968). Capra 1206.

Hiller, Lejaren. *Machine Music* (1964). Presser. Turnabout 34536.

Hiller, Lejaren, and Robert Baker. *Computer Cantata.* Theodore Presser. CRI SD-310.

Jaffe, David. *Silicon Valley Breakdown* (1982). Stanford S1.

Katzer, Georg. *La Mécanique et les Agents de l'Erosion.* Chant du Monde LDC-278044/45.

Lerdahl, Fred. *String Quartet No. 2* (1982). Laurel 128.

Scaletti, Carla. *sunSurgeAutomata* (1987). Centaur CRC-2045.

Xenakis, Iannis. *Akrata* (1965). Salabert. Nonesuch 71201.

———. *Atrées.* Salabert. EMI CVC 2086.

———. *Mikka* and *Mikka "S"* (1971 and 1976 respectively). Salabert. CP2 6.

———. *Morsima-Amorsima.* Salabert. Barclay 920217.

THE NEW
CONSERVATISM

Nowhere does the influence of oriental music upon occidental concepts appear so obviously and vigorously as it does in the new conservatism. Both Terry Riley and Philip Glass visited India, where they became fascinated by the ragas (melody-type), talas (repeated rhythmic patterns), gamaka (ornamentation), and tamburas (drone) they found there. Indian master sitarist Ravi Shankar had direct and indirect influences on these and other minimalist composers that has had a lasting effect on new music. The result has been a blend in the precision of performance (to wit, the Glass Ensemble) with heavily repeated materials using principally Western instruments and tunings.

As with most new developments in the *avant-garde,* if indeed the new conservatism could be so defined, the influence of John Cage must be acknowledged. While Debussy and others earlier on had crudely investigated the possible resources in the Orient, it was Cage who first (in 1947) began attending lectures of D. T. Suzuki. His studies of Zen and related Eastern philosophies greatly influenced him and hence the rest of the new music world. Those who worked directly with Cage, particularly Morton Feldman, whose soft and effete works show significant oriental influence, also created much stir. Lou Harrison (influenced by Henry Cowell) has developed extensive Southeast Asian gamelans for the performance of his work.

Today, while universality is the mainstay of the new conservatism, diversity abounds. In some cases, Steve Reich in particular, repeating materials shift in and out of phase, creating densely populated clouds of sound at times and monophonic lines in juxtaposition. In other cases, namely Philip Glass, the bar line sets the stage for changing meters for different lengths of repeating material. Still others, especially Terry Riley, use slow expansions or reductions that take place over long and mesmerizing spans of time. Some composers, La Monte Young and Harold Budd, distill the essence of the minimalism and create terse works more conceptual than sonic. Others adapt a perceived aimlessness in Indian and oriental musics and use them for triadic emphasis. In all cases, however, the influence is decidedly conspicuous.

A second source of influence apparent in the new conservatism is the search for a common style roughly analogous to the common-practice period which can speak to a general audience. Philip Glass comments: "[My music] is essentially concert music, which means inventing a new language as opposed to pop, which tends to be imitative. But the idea that concert music is only for a handful of people has only existed since the First World War. The language I've invented is not a purposely difficult one—it's a language of our time. I think people are beginning to hear that" (from an interview in the *Village Voice,* Sept. 18, 1964). Whether or not this new language has, in fact, been invented by him, or that we are speaking of it as a language at all, suggests the search for a common voice, a single mode through which composers can express their ideas without reinventing the wheel for each new work.

It should also be noted that the Beatles, and especially the work of George Harrison, invited oriental (especially Indian) music to enter the world of popular music (notably *Sgt. Pepper's Lonely Hearts Club Band).* An overlap or crossover between these two very different international cultures brought about an invitation for a similar crossing over within the world of concert music. This is most evident in the general popularity of, for example, the music of Glass and the success of New Age music.

Whether all of the music presented in this chapter could be considered cross-cultural remains to be seen. Whether future music will be defined by multicultural processes, techniques, instruments, or concepts is likewise impossible to infer. However, it is certain that much of the widespread adoption of basic minimalist and conservative tendencies has been influenced directly or indirectly by non-Western sources.

Minimalism

Frederic Rzewski's (founder of the *Musica Elettronica Viva*) *Coming Together* (1972) exemplifies minimalist techniques. The score contains 394 measures of continuous running sixteenth notes (no other rhythm occurs in the piece) over which a vocal line speaks the words of an inmate from the Attica Correction Facility. Figure 11.1 provides an example of the repetitious yet varied pulse and the G pitch centricity. Figure 11.2 shows the second and third measures of the work. Here, the first two sixteenths frame the motive and pulse in synchronization. The third, fourth, and fifth notes, however, extend the motive to three notes and cross the pulse at beat 2. The sixth and seventh notes are repetitions of the initial note with dual roles. For example, the G can be considered the end of the extended motive or the beginning

Figure 11.1. Measures 1 and 297 of Frederic Rzewski's *Coming Together* demonstrating the lack of significant variation in this minimalist work.

Figure 11.2. Measures 2 and 3 of Frederic Rzewski's *Coming Together.*

Figure 11.3. La Monte Young and Marian Zazeela performing *Dream Houses* in 1971. Copyright © La Monte Young & Marian Zazeela 1971. Courtesy: Heiner Friedrich. (Photo credit: Robert Adler.)

of the new version. While seemingly unimportant, these dual and even triple role inferences give the work its diversity. Notes 6 and 7 are linked to note 8 in such a way that the opening motive is repeated, but shifted with respect to beat. Notes 9, 10, and 11 repeat the variant of the motive, metrically altered. Careful evaluation of the two bars (less than 1/100th of the piece) shows a microcosm of actions and reactions, of cross accents and cross rhythms, all of which contrast the lack of development in new pitch and rhythm material. *Coming Together* is a striking work from the minimalist school that shows its power and potential.

Minimal music is also apparent in the music of Harold Budd. His *Lovely Thing (Piano),* in which one chord is played softly many times over a period of fifteen to twenty minutes; *One Sound* for string quartet; and *The Candy Apple Revision* (1970), which states simply, "D-flat Major," all classify as minimal compositions. About his approach, Budd remarks:

Ever since (a long time ago) I've pushed and pushed towards zero: Running it all down, a kind of on-going process of removal. There's an enormous difference, by the way, between Monotony and Boredom. Boredom, it seems to me, is trying to make something interesting. Monotony is making nothing interesting. And insofar as I feel all art to be utterly worthless (no redeeming social values), I'm interested in that what I do is pretty—("Terrifying," "Gripping," "Sensitive," "Relaxing," "Hypnotic," "Spiritual" all to the side for a moment)—an existential *prettiness;* a king of High-Art Uselessness. . . . [1]

---

1. From a letter to the author.

Much of minimal music actually is *maximal*[2] in duration. La Monte Young's New York City-based *Dream Houses* (1968) are media works of great duration (Alex Dea voice, Jon Hassell on horn, David Rosenboom, viola, and De Fracia Evans working slide projections). Like most minimal works these contain drones and slowly overlapping (focusing in and out) projections: a minimum of material. These works derive from earlier experiments such as *The Tortoise, His Dream and Journeys* (1964–), performed over extended periods of time by The Theatre of Eternal Music with John Cale, a member of the Velvet Underground rock group, on viola and Tony Conrad on violin.

→ Erik Satie's *Vexations* is a thirty-two bar piece to be played softly 840 times. His *musique d'ameublement* (1920) is also minimal music. This "furnishing music" co-composed by Satie and Darius Milhaud was played during intermissions, and programs announced: "We urge you to take no notice of it and to behave during the intervals *as if it did not exist.*"[3]

Composers such as Charlemagne Palestine and Yoshima Wada (whose large horns are created from "plumbing pipes") build on drones and/or slowly overlapping motives, creating a slowly evolving *somnambulistic* state. Max Neuhaus's underwater work, *Water Whistle,* utilizes eight to ten water-driven whistles and can be heard only if you are submerged in the same water as the whistles. Karlheinz Stockhausen's *aus den Sieben Tagen* (1968) is a verbal score containing only very brief performance directions such as "play single sounds with such dedication until you feel the warmth that radiates from you—play on and sustain it as long as you can."

Philip Corner is especially noted for his work with minimal concepts often lasting evenings, at other times lasting brief seconds. For example, his *One Note Once,* which is just that; the instrumentation being flexible. His *Metal Meditations* are often collaborations with others involved in the *Sounds out of Silent Spaces* series in New York City: Carole Weber, Julie Winter, Elaine Summers, Annea Lockwood, Alison Knowles,[4] Daniel Goode, and Charles Morrow, among others. These are evening-long events featuring composer-constructed and traditional instruments struck softly but with intense aural expression. These meditations also involve "total experience" with "ritual food events," slide projections, and lights. *Corner's One Note Once, Cage's 4'3",* and Young's *Compositions of 1960* all approach the ultimate minimal structure: 0 duration, 0 instruments, 0 performers, 0 audience.

Many composers feel that the *avant-garde* as such is dead, and that the works in the 1960s point to a return to simplicity, a return to the foundations of sound itself; pitch, duration, and silence. These composers and their works no longer achieve

---

2. The term *process* is also used to describe music that unfolds slowly, one that carries the thrust of invention by slowly processing one idea to another. Music in this genre, while appearing minimal, achieves "mileage" through constantly generating variations of a single idea.

3. Pierre-Daniel Templier, *Erik Satie,* trans. Elena French and David French, 1932 (originally published by Presses Universitaires de France). Cambridge, Mass.: The MIT Press, 1969, p. 45.

4. Knowles (along with Jaran Downey and Gunther Maier) has more recently been involved with *Other Media's* production of *Music in the Key of J* in New York City. This was broadcast on Teleprompter's Channel J (produced by Charles Morrow).

the "shock," immediacy, and notoriety that *avant-garde* works of the 1950s and 1960s characteristically received, nor the pretentious complexities of systems and scientific paraphernalia so in evidence with more mainstream academic-based composers' works. Steve Reich's *It's Gonna Rain* (1965), *Violin Phase* and *Piano Phase* (both 1967), and *Pulse Music* for phase-shifting gate, an instrument invented by the composer (1968–69), are notable.

The New Tonality

During the late 1960s, many composers also began to experiment with tonal resources. This reacquaintance is rooted in minimalism. Composers discovered that utilizing basic tonal materials in a constantly repeating fabric allowed their music to have continuity and to some extent new vitality without the phrase/cadence structure of the tonal common-practice period.

LaMonte Young's work in the very early sixties (see "Minimalism" section) influenced a diversity of composers. The simplicity of design and materials in Young's work, often based on justly tuned fifths, provided many composers with intriguing ideas suggesting further development: consonance and minimalism. James Fulkerson's *Triad,* for example, consists of a C major triad performed over a twelve- to twenty-hour period without variation. Robert Moran's *Illumination Nocturna* presents a C-rooted major thirteenth chord repeated slowly and softly for an extended period of time. This work, and his subsequent "trance music," represents other manifestations of this dronelike approach to triadic materials.

Terry Riley's *In C* (1964) gave a needed impetus and visibility to this new school of composition. The work is constructed from repeated and overlapped motives in the "key" of C moving, over a period of 45 to 90 minutes, to the key of E, back to C, and then to G. This is not the tonality one finds in late Romanticism; rather, it is a minimal work (the complete score can be placed on a single sheet) structured around continuously repeating octave Cs. Two major works followed *In C: Poppy Nogood and the Phantom Band* (1968) and *A Rainbow in Curved Air* (1969). Both of these works continued the explorations begun with *In C.* Each develops richer and more complex interrelationships of tonal materials less associated with drones and rhythmic repetition than *In C.*

Philip Glass began developing a similar kind of style in the late sixties with pieces like *Music in Fifths* (1969). This work evolves through expanding scalular cells in a kind of F-Dorian mode (three flats in the signature). He creates an "additive" structure common in his later works. For example, a three-note motive becomes four, then five, and so on, with the initial motive repeated on each reoccurrence. His opera *Einstein on the Beach* (1976) is a tonal work that continues to receive wide acclaim. His audience is as eclectic as his music, with rock and pop followers as well as traditional and experimental "serious" admirers. His work with the Philip Glass Ensemble has contributed enormously to this success. Minimal tonal music is very difficult to perform due to both its maximal length and intonation requirements. Glass's ensemble epitomizes the precision necessary for proper performance.

John Adams's *Shaker Loops* for strings (1978) and *Phrygian Gates* for piano (1978) utilize triadic source materials. Both works create the atmosphere of self-regenerative energy and, at the same time, lyric melodic curves traditionally associated with tonal music. Other composers committed to similar types of minimal/tonal composition include Beth Anderson, Gavin Bryers, Stuart Smith, William Duckworth and Phil Winsor (notably *Kyrie Eleison* for choir and tape drone, 1977).

In England, Cornelius Cardew's work with the Scratch Orchestra provided opportunity for both large-scale improvisation (performers were largely unskilled) and performances of simple tonal works. His enormous work *The Great Learning* (1971, particularly *Paragraph 2*) provide precedence for renewed tonal activity. Cardew was motivated by political beliefs and moved toward a more traditional tonal style with works such as *Soon,* based on Maoist-like texts and ideals. The music consists of single lines with "chording" similar to popular music while at the same time containing an unmistakable hint of Cardew's inimitable rhythmic subtleties and twists of phrase.

Lou Harrison has long persevered in this tonal realm. His *Mass to St. Anthony* (1962) is modal-tonal in key and sixteenth century in counterpoint. Even traditional cadences balance and direct the lines. Yet there is a subtle twentieth-century inflection throughout. His work with the American gamelan is the basis for a number of new works using rich quasi-tonal materials, though less traditionally Western in cadence and phrasing.

Robert Ashley's cryptic 1983 work *Perfect Lives (Private Parts)*—"an opera in seven episodes"—is tonal at least in basic pitch materials. Its composer-created text is "surrealistically" rooted in "sixties" nihilism as it comments on "Rodney's" life. Ashley's voice and the keyboard performance of Blue Gene Tyranny are so authentic in its recorded version (see Bibliography) as to challenge reproduction by any other performers. The cultural and anthropomorphic aspects of both the music and the poetry of this piece contextualize the tonal materials.

George Rochberg's career spans three periods: rigorous dodecaphony, Ivesian-like quotation, and his own brand of new conservatism. His twenty-three-minute *Trio* (piano, violin, 'cello) falls principally in the latter of these periods. The work begins and ends in E major. The nontonal syntax exploits the principle that successive chords contradict one another chromatically at least once, with common tones providing continuity (e.g., G major, G minor, F♯ major, E♭ major, etc.). Polytonality results from the direction of diatonic lines. The first movement spans the key-signatures of E, B♭, E, C, D♭, C, D♭, G, and E major respectively, though clearly all of the music presented is not within these centers. In fact, Rochberg relentlessly avoids the C triad when in the signature of C major. He provides "ghosts" with C as the common tone (i.e., F and A♭ major; F and C minor triads). Ostinato pedal tones on D and G in octaves provide the kind of tonal anticipation that serves as one of the most tasteful and successful aspects of this work. Ultimately, the composer provides the tonic pitch without, however, the full triad. Much of the work belies the signature-implied key; a midmovement section ends on a D♭ major triad in the signature of four sharps. The final movement propels the listener through the same key centers as the first movement, but with more bravura and direction. The skeletal attacks that succeed in driving the movement to a close create the *Trio's* most effective moments.

Each of the tonal idioms mentioned here bodes a virulent future for tonality in the last years of the twentieth century. The static and somnambulistic qualities of single resonant chords, though possibly less immediately conceivable as a style, could begin an entirely new language for tertian harmonies. Minimal tonal music, based on repetitions of ever-varying melodic fragments, is reaching wider audiences than most recent *avant-garde* styles. More and more composers seem infatuated with its potential. Even works that imitate traditional models of tonality, in either admiration or parody, have gained a significant following in recent years. If any aspect of twentieth-century music seems providential, it is most surely this recent trend toward consonance.

New Age Music

The widespread use of minimal techniques has led to the rise of what has been called *New Age* music. While many feel that New Age has more ties with *muzak* than with serious musical intent, one cannot ignore the fact that various forms of New Age music can be found in motion-picture soundtracks, new music concerts, radio stations (some devoted exclusively to it), and to opera and stage sound tracks. Since many of the performers and composers involved in New Age music have roots and traditions in jazz, it is not surprising to find that influence present in much of the work done to date. Its more radical protagonists claim effects from listener tranquility to serious changes in the mentally ill. Others insist that it mirrors the inner harmonies of humans. Some believe that the name derives from a proclamation of the sacred writings of India (Vedas) that tell of the incarnation of gifted musicians at the beginning of each new age in order to herald humanity's increasing ability to understand the mysteries of life. Others contend that it comes from ancient Egypt and even Atlantis where the cultures believed that certain musical notes could stimulate and awaken the *chakra* energy centers that lead to expanded awareness. Most agree that there is a kind of ancient/future aspect to whatever definition is assigned.

Unlike pure minimalism, New Age music does not necessarily involve constant repetitions. Rather, a constant dynamic state, consistent slow to medium tempi, and bluntly tonal environments persist. In progressive types of New Age, there are more attempts at unusual timbres, but the sense of suspended time pervades the music. Nonprogressive New Age music, on the other hand, often has distinct meters and traditional chord progressions. One critic summed up his views by saying that in New Age music "anything goes nowhere."

The simplest forms of New Age music employ natural sounds or their synthetic imitations. Don Campbell's *Lightening on the Moon,* for example, is based on a heartbeat and the overtone series. The composer claims that, in general, his music heals, educates, and creates well-being in its listeners. Many such composers refer to the pioneering work done by the French M.D. and hearing psychologist Alfred

A. Tomatis, who attempted to prove that physical health can be altered by the transmission of certain frequencies of sound to the brain. Known as the Tomatis method, his views suggest that serious health changes can occur by the use of auditory stimulation.

Such beliefs in the power of music have led some composers into cult traditions and studies of drugs that make the same claims on healing and raising of consciousness. Workshops, formed around the general topic of shaman exploration, occur regularly in certain New Age circles. Visits to *huichol,* a group of Native Americans, who use certain drugs to produce meditative and spiritually exalting hallucinations, sites in Mexico have provoked some to feel strongly that New Age music shares a ritual quality with other arts (notably dance) as expressed in these cultures.

Brian Eno has composed ambient music (self-proclaimed) for airports, businesses, and the home (notably *Ambience I*). Lists of ambient nature recordings now occur regularly in the Schwann record catalog and include the nonedited sounds of meadows, sailing, the sea, thunderstorms, heartbeats, the wind, Okefenokee Swamps, summer cornfields, and so forth. *Relax Video* (begun by Jacob Podber) produces videotapes of aquariums and fireplaces that stand as uncut, two-hour documentaries of one-camera, one-shot life exposures to the subject of their titles with a sound track of New Age compositions. His New Age production called *Ocean TV* is a minimalist production of waves crashing off the Long Island coast with no sound whatsoever. "God did a better job than I could have," the composer argues. Yanni Chryssolmallis (or just *Yanni*), in albums like "Keys to Imagination" and "Niki Nana" (both *Private Music* records) also composes inoffensive but interesting ambient music. Some have termed the style *new impressionism* to indicate the level "time suspension" in many of the works presented here.

Of the other New Age composers, Stephen Halpern (piano, usually with some combination of electronics and strings) and George Winston (mostly solo improvisatory piano) stand out. Halpern's *Comfort Zone,* for keyboards and strings, moves with typically meditative and inoffensive diatonicism through a variety of aimless scenes. Long themes roam above moderately moving passages formed of modal pedal points. Winston's *Winter into Spring* demonstrates the composer's freely improvisatory style. Here, the harmonic scheme often uses the circle of fifths with subtle shifts to chromatic but triadic sonorities. Mark Isham's film music (most notably *Never Cry Wolf*) exemplifies pure New Age techniques. Rarified long melodies are placed over simple triadic ostinati that usually center around a single key center with little variation or development.

The works of Vangelis, noted for film scores of *Blade Runner* and *Chariots of Fire*, exemplify the progressive side of New Age music. He uses long themes under which are effects produced from a variety of found (*musique concrète*) and created (usually synthesized) sounds. While this music varies distinctly from many New Age works, it retains the same conformity to nonmetric and time-suspended weightlessness. The timbres, though widely varying in source and type, all seem chosen by their associative but relaxed natures. His *Earth* and *To the Unknown Man* particularly emphasize these characteristics.

Figure 11.4. *New age* composer Vangelis Papathanassious.

Vangelis noted in an interview reported in *The Art of Electronic Music* by Tom Darter (see Bibliography): "You feel just like you have to start creating. It's like you feel when you have to go to the toilet. Then I just push the tape, and it happens when it happens. I don't know how it happens. I don't *want* to know. I don't *try* to know. It's like riding a bicycle. If you think, 'How am I going to do it?', you fall down. If you think about how to breathe, you choke. But when you do things dramatically they happen like that."

Composer Kitaro, like Vangelis, circumscribes large arcs of sound, usually a blend of electronic and live sounds. His *Toward the West* and *India* exemplify New Age progressiveness. Another progressive New Age composer, Upper Astral, overlays extremely long tonal melodies on punctuated triadic ostinati reminiscent in some ways of the *alberti bass* of previous centuries. This composer also employs sonic scenes of the surf, wind, and fountains. *Journey to the Edge of the Universe* epitomizes the use of these sources as do frequent synthesizer drones and filter band sweeps through the overtone series.

Whether New Age music, as both a concept and a reality, will truly develop into a form for future *development* or become a relative of background music for hospitals and bus stations will be seen during the rest of the decade. Many serious composers and highly qualified musicians are, at present, actively engaged in its creation. Its hallucinogenic qualities combined with a rising popularity among crossover artists have convinced many that it will remain an active force in new music. Some even suggest that a kind of new universal language may someday prevail and develop from this source. Composers claim that since any sound can be used, the form has arisen out of contemporary music over the past few decades. With the generally inoffensive tonal vocabulary and simple and long directed melodic lines, it also has a very solid root in the world of popular music.

Vectoral Analysis:
Philip Glass: *Einstein*
on the Beach

(For information on vectoral analysis and procedures see chapter 1.)

1. Historical Background: Philip Glass was born in Baltimore on January 31, 1937. He received his bachelor's degree from the University of Chicago in 1956 and then studied at Juilliard, where he earned another BA (1959) followed by an MA (1961). There he worked with William Bergsma and Vincent Persichetti. He had further studies with Darius Milhaud at the Aspen Music Festival during the summer of 1960 and with Nadia Boulanger on a Fulbright scholarship during 1963–65. From 1961 to 1963 he served as composer-in-residence for the Pittsburgh public schools under a Ford Foundation grant. Glass worked with Ravi Shankar in Paris in 1965, teaching him solfège and taking lessons in tabla from Shankar's associate, Allah Rakha. Inspired by the rhythmic and metric centricity of this music, he traveled to India for six months during 1965–66.

   On his return he collaborated in performances with Steve Reich and Arthur Murphy, finally developing his own group, the Philip Glass Ensemble, in 1968. He and his ensemble toured extensively during 1970 both in America and abroad. *Einstein on the Beach* was completed in 1975 as a collaboration between Glass and noted mixed-media conceptualist Robert Wilson. Its first performances in Europe proved quite successful. On November 21, 1976, the American premiere brought immediate attention and acclaim. In 1978 he was awarded a Rockefeller grant.

   He has completed two other operas: *Satyagraha* (1980) and *Akhnaten* (1984). These and *Einstein* roughly form a trilogy that Glass states is based on "historical figures who changed the course of world events through the wisdom and strength of their inner vision" (Gandhi and an Egyptian pharaoh in the latter cases respectively). His work, especially since 1965, is minimal in nature, with repetitions of pitch layered over a finely varied rhythmic base.

   Glass comments about his musical style in an interview with *Keyboard Magazine* (April, 1987): "I'm not interested in exotic and funny weird sounds. To me, that seems like an endless avenue; once you start on it, there's no telling where in the world it might lead. Maybe it's partly a generation thing too. I'm a pencil-and-paper composer. That's how I was taught to write music, and it's easier for me to conceptualize with a paper and pencil than it is with a machine."

2. Overview: *Einstein on the Beach* is an opera in four acts, nine scenes, and five "kneeplays" that occur at the beginning and end of each act. The work involves vocal and instrumental music, dance, and sets resembling traditional opera. However, there is no traditional plot here, no story to follow. Instead the work employs a sequence of events that develop the musical score more than a tangible direction. Indeed, even the text is surreal. For example, "I feel the earth move . . . I feel the tumbling down tumbling down. . . . There was a judge who like puts [sic] in a court. And the judge have like in what able jail what it could be a spanking." Stage action follows similar

Figure 11.5. Philip Glass.

Figure 11.6. From a performance of *Einstein on the Beach.*

discontinuity. Freud, Queen Victoria, Stalin, and Einstein (among others in the opera) are defined by a rhythmic parceling of the five-hour performance time.

The numbers 1, 2, and 3 figure heavily in the structural layout of the work. The first three acts have two scenes each, repeating twice the three elements of train, trial, and field. These elements appear in the final scenes of the last act as building for train, bed in the trial scene earlier, and the interior of a time/space/machine seen above the field of Acts 2 and 3. The stage is divided into three layers: foreground, middleground, and background, or downstage, centerstage, and upstage. These translate into sections called portrait, still-life, and landscape and intensities termed skin, flesh, and bones.

3. Orchestration Techniques: The ensemble for *Einstein* requires five to eight performers on electric organs, viola, 'cello, and soprano saxophones. Much of the work is in unison and at very fast and consistent *tempi,* demanding a high level of technical proficiency from the performers. Effects are nonexistent and timbre exploration minimal. In fact, the music is so sparse vertically at times that when straightforward harmonies do occur they produce extraordinary results even though they seldom extend beyond triads. Sparsity therefore conditions the listener, and Glass is able to get expansive results from only minor changes.

4. Basic Techniques: Glass employs repetition, addition/subtraction, and modes to create an often hypnotizing effect. The number of repeats follows either the score or, in the case of his ensemble performing, directions during the course of performance. Figure 11.7 shows measures 3 and 4 of Act 4, Scene 2, organ solo. Repeats are often extensive. The second measure shows the

Figure 11.7. From the score of *Einstein on the Beach;* measures 3 and 4 of Act 4, Scene 2.

additive procedure (seven to eight notes), the filling in of structural detail (the E between D and G at the end of the second measure) and the harmonic variation (A-C-E instead of C-E-A). The octave C drone is typical of Glass's work. Pedal tones, struck at the beginning of bars of constantly changing meters (though not explicitly shown), provide the underpinnings of the music's motion. The beat here (eighth notes) remains fixed as exactly as possible, providing the kind of locomotive charge that persists throughout.

5. Vertical Models: Figure 11.8 demonstrates a typical harmonic progression from *Einstein on the Beach.* Common tones proliferate. While triadic, the music does not follow other traditional voice-leading practices, though it does

Figure 11.8. From the second page of the score of *Einstein on the Beach*. This is a demonstration of harmonic progression.

move stepwise, a Glass trademark. There is virtually no contrary direction in the "voices," and the 6/4 chord at the end of this passage suspends every cadential tradition. The chromaticism follows that of Hovhaness and others by creating subtle key shifts between chords (i.e., difficult to explain the A major triad of measure 3 in the key of F minor of measures 1 and 2). The non triadic structure of measure 4 (A–D♯-B) outlines the dominant seventh of E major the final chord.

Glass has commented on this in an interview (Cole Cagne and Tracy Caras, *Soundpieces: Interviews with American Composers*—see Bibliography):

In *Einstein,* the kind of cadential formula that runs through it, the I-VI-IV♭-V-I progression that you hear in the Spaceship and the Knee Plays, the voicing and working out of that was done by somebody who knew very well how traditional harmony operated. I don't think that anyone who didn't have the training that I did could have written that. So even though my music seems so far away from her (Nadia Boulanger), it was only four or five years after studying with her that I began to find uses for the things that I had learned.

Figure 11.9. From the second page of the score of *Einstein on the Beach*.

6. Horizontal Models: Measures 16 through 20 of *Einstein* (shown in Figure 11.9) provide an apt model. Here the measures show metric divisions of 4/3/4/5/6 with no two measures of the same length. Nothing else changes here. The repeating pulse of the pedal point and the left hand (organ) C remain the same in each case. Given that each of these measures will be repeated many times during the actual performance, the constantly changing appearance of these measures is somewhat deceiving. Once a pattern has begun, one may be more than reasonably confident that it will immediately repeat many times; first exactly and then with slight variation, with these in turn repeating.

7. Style: Glass's *Einstein on the Beach* is a major example of minimalism in the freedom of nonliterary theater. The discontinuity between the various music, choreographic, set, and action elements creates a rich counterpoint at once

mesmerizing and confusing. Repetitious and slightly varied fragments of music of different lengths, often performed in unison or within consonant triadic harmonies, suggest a more traditional vocabulary with the exceptional lack of diversity providing a definite contemporary idiom. The success of this work and others in its genre with both concert hall and popular music enthusiasts has given rise to speculation that it may become the universal music language for the twenty-first century. Glass continues to compose music for the theater, movies, and his ensemble.

This work demonstrates favorable comparisons to the works analyzed in chapters 1 and 6 (especially "conceptualism"). It ignores the ongoing technological developments and innovation. The repetitive nature of Glass's style, and that of most of the music reviewed in this chapter, contrasts most sharply with the ideals expressed in chapters 5 and 12. "Indeterminacy," for example, suggests the exact opposite: a lack of repetition from event to event and even over the largest frame of sonic expression.

Bibliography— Chapter 11*

Further Readings

Sources

Schaeffer, John. *New Sounds, A Listener's Guide to New Music.* New York: Harper and Row, 1987.
Simms, Bryan R. *Music of the Twentieth Century, Style and Structure.* New York: Schirmer Books, 1986.

Minimalism

Mertens, Wim. *American Minimal Music.* New York: Kahn and Averill, 1983.
Reich, Steve. "Music is a Gradual Process." In *Anti-Illusion Catalog of the Whitney Museum.* New York: The Whitney Museum, 1969.
———. *Writings About Music.* New York: New York University Press, 1974.
Rzewski, Frederick. "Prose Music." In *Dictionary of Contemporary Music,* ed. John Vinton, pp. 593–95. New York: E. P. Dutton and Co., 1974.
Schwarz, K. Robert. "Steve Reich: Music as a Gradual Process." *Perspectives of New Music* 20, no. 1 (1981): pp. 225–86.
Scott, Stephen. "The Music of Steve Reich." *Numus West* 6 (1974).
Tame, David. *The Secret Power of Music.* Rochester, Vermont: Destiny Books, 1984.
Vandenbroeck, André. *Philosophical Geometry.* Rochester, Vt.: Inner Traditions International, Ltd., 1987.
Winckel, Fritz. *Music, Sound and Sensation, A Modern Exposition.* New York: Dover Publications, 1967.
Young, La Monte, and Marian Zazeela. *Selected Writings.* Munich: Heiner Friedrich, 1969.
———. "Sound is God: The Singing of Pran Nath." *Village Voice,* April 30, 1970.

*Addresses for record companies, periodicals, and music publishers mentioned in this Bibliography can be found in Appendix IV.

The New Tonality

Kupkovic, L. "The Role of Tonality in Contemporary and 'Up-to-date' Composition." *Tempo* 135 (1980): pp. 15–19.

Schwartz, K. Robert. "Steve Reich: Music as a Gradual Process." *Perspectives of New Music* 20, no. 1 (1981): pp. 225–86.

Young, La Monte, and Marian Zazeela. *Selected Writings*. Munich: Heiner Friederich, 1969.

New Age Music

Hamel, Peter Michael. *Through Music to the Self*. Dorset, England: Element Books, 1978.

Pavo, Roberto. *Future Now!* New York: Futurista Publications, 1987.

Philip Glass

Garland, D. "Creating Einstein on the Beach: Philip Glass and Robert Wilson speak to Maxime de la Falaise." *The Audience Magazine of BAM's Next Wave Festival* 2, no. 4 (1984): p. 1.

Glass, Philip. *Music by Philip Glass*. New York: Harper and Row, 1987.

Glass, Philip, and Robert Wilson. *Einstein on the Beach*. New York: EOS Enterprises, nd.

Jones, Robert T. "An Outburst of Minimalism!" *High Fidelity/Musical America* 33, no. 2 (1983): p. 26.

Palmer, R., and Philip Glass. *Einstein on the Beach*. Liner notes to the Tomato 4–2901, 1979 recording.

Rockwell, John. *All American Music: Composition in the Late Twentieth Century*. New York: Random House, 1983.

Adams, John. *Harmonielehre* (1985). Nonesuch 79115–2.

———. *Phrygian Gates*. New Albion NA 014.

———. *Shaker Loops*. New Albion NA 412 214–2PH.

Ashley, Robert. *Private Parts*. Lovely Music LML-1001.

Budd, Harold. *Coeur D'Orr* (1969). Advance 16.

———. *Oak of Golden Dreams* (1970). Advance 16.

Corner, Philip. *Ear Journeys: Water* (1977). Printed Editions.

———. *Rounds*. Soundings 3, no. 4, pp. 92–93.

Eno, Brian. *Ambient #2—The Plateau of Mirrors* (1980). Editions EG.

———. *Here Come the Warm Jets* (1973). Island 9268.

Glass, Philip. *Einstein on the Beach*. CBS M4K 38875.

———. *Music in Fifths*. Chatham Square CS-LP-1003.

———. *Music in Similar Motion* (1969). Chatham Square CS-LP-1003.

———. *Music with Changing Parts* (1970). Chatham Square CS-LP-1001/2.

———. *North Star*. Virgin 91013–2.

Halpern, Steven. *Connections*. Sound Rx SRX-7838.

Harrison, Lou. *Suite for 'Cello and Harp* (1949). New World 281.

Isham, Mark. *Vapor Drawings*. Windham Hill WD-1027.

Kitaro. *India*. Geffen 24085–2.

———. *Toward the West*. Geffen 24094–2.

Compact Discs, Recordings, and Publishers

Penguin Cafe Orchestra. *Music from the Penguin Cafe.* Editions EG EGED-27.

Reich, Steve. *Four Organs* (1970). Angel S-36059.

———. *It's Gonna Rain.* Columbia MS-7265.

———. *Music for 18 Musicians* (1976). ECM 11290–2.

Riley, Terry. *A Rainbow in Curved Air.* CBS MK-7315.

———. *In C.* CBS MK 7178.

———. *Poppy Nogood and the Phantom Band.* CBS MK-7315.

Rzewski, Frederick. *Coming Together.* Soundings 3, no. 4, Hungaraton HCD 12545.

———. *Variations on 'No Place To Go But Around' for Piano* (1973). Watt Works. Finnadar 9011.

Satie, Erik. *Complete Piano Music.* Denon CD-7485, –86, –87.

Upper Astral. *Journey to the Edge of the Universe.* Valley of the Sun Records.

Vangelis (Papathanassious). *Opera Sauvage.* Polydor 829663–1.

———. *The Mask.* Polydor 825245–2.

Winston, George. *Winter into Spring.* Windham Hill WH-1019.

Young, La Monte. *The Tortoise, his Dreams and Journeys* (1964). Shandar 83510.

———. *The Well-Tuned Piano* (1964–). Gramavision 18–8701–2.

THE POST-
AVANT-GARDE

12

The term *avant-garde* has become a designation for those composers or works displaying the newest technique or anti-technique such as chance music or sound (silence). The raison d'être of the *avant-garde* movement has centered around shock and "newness." Certainly such a movement begins to die when an event in any of its art forms becomes so new, so shocking, as to virtually negate anything from surpassing it. Rudolf Schwarzkogler, a Viennese artist born in 1940, attempted to accomplish such an event in the late 1960s. It seems, as we pick up the story by Robert Hughes of *Time,* that Schwarzkogler, a prime mover of the *avant-garde,* had decided that *his* art, at least, depended not on the application of paint, but on the removal of his own flesh:

> So he proceeded, inch by inch to amputate his own penis, while a photographer recorded the act as an art event. In 1972, the resulting prints were reverently exhibited in that biennial motor show of Western art, Documenta 5 at Kassel. Successive acts of self-amputation finally did Schwarzkogler in. . . . No doubt it could be argued by the proponents of body art . . . that Schwarzkogler's self-editing was not indulgent but brave, taking the audience's castration fears and reducing them to their most threatening quiddity. That the man was clearly as mad as a hatter, sick beyond rebuke, is not thought important; wasn't Von Gogh crazy too? But Schwarzkogler's gesture has a certain emblematic value. Having nothing to say, and nowhere to go but further out, he lopped himself and called it art.[1]

As the article states, Schwarzkogler is indeed dead, a victim of his own art. One is often reminded of Philip Corner's work entitled *"One anti-personnel type CBU bomb will be thrown into the audience"* (what kind of strange masochist would attend a program that had announced this work's performance?). While one finds the composer's suggestions asking the performers not to fulfill the probably small audience's desires, one wonders why some composer doesn't consider a world war as a next piece. The shock factor here is death, the "newness" that either of these

Evaluation

1. Robert Hughes, "The Decline and Fall of the Avant-Garde," *Time,* December 18, 1972, pp. 111–12.

be considered as art in the first place. Whether the act is real (as with Schwarz-kogler) or imagined (as with Corner), it seems topped only by multi-deaths, war, and finally complete annihilation. Since none of these seems real, at least in the form of artistic development, one is led to believe that at least for those of us who are aware of what has been happening in the arts, "newness" and "shock" are over, and with them, the prime movers, the superstructure of the *avant-garde* movement.

Philosophically the *avant-garde* remains one of the most conservative areas of musical thought: a concept in which, indeed, anything does *not* go. The very nature of the *avant-garde* concept binds the composer to reject the past and work within a multitude of limitations often surpassing those of the strictest of traditional contrapuntalists.

Sensing the oblivion inherent in such rejection of the past, a number of composers have begun to accept the philosophy projected, but not carried out, by the *avant-garde;* that is, truly "anything goes." Not a statement of rejection, this, but of affirmation: the post-*avant-garde*. While the phrase "anything goes" may immediately alienate those of us intent on saving the arts for (and in some cases from) people and significance, the words *with purpose* may be added. It is no longer the new sound, the new device, the new trick that is important, but the new *work*.

Antagonists of this philosophy generally neglect the true depth of such a direction: once the composer has become unprejudiced toward sound, Bach is no longer an enemy; the major triad, tonality, need no longer be avoided; dissonance need not be a requirement to be contemporary. Redefined, the post-*avant-garde* composer is *just* the composer, using anything that is necessary to fulfill the need to create music; accepting *all* sound and silence without being limited by current styles.

Likewise consistency, previously designated as the type of materials used (triads, noise, etc.), is implied and governed by the composer, not by period, audience, or fellow composers. The post-*avant-garde* composer has also challenged the listener's prejudices: can one truly accept all sound, all styles, all meaning in music? In effect, can one listen to Bach, to Webern, to Cage, to rock; not rejecting any?

The struggle, however taut it may have once seemed, grows less and less tangible with each passing year. The *post-avant-garde* works of this chapter, as different in sound and structure as they may seem, hold a fragile but distinctly recognizable common thread among them. Possibly Ben Johnston says it best in his article *On Context:* "Awareness makes free choice possible. Freedom requires responsiveness: responsibility."[2] Later in the same article his optimism is clearly focused:

> It is as though we have to cross a chasm. If we are to build a bridge over it we will have to anchor its ends far in the past and far in the future. Tradition thoroughly assimilated will help us anchor in the past; only a sharp eye for where we are going can help us anchor in the future. Technology will help us build the bridge, which will not impose upon nature but will be possible because we understand how things happen and cooperate rather than interfering.[3]

2. Ben Johnston, "On Context," *ASUC Proceedings 3* (1968), p. 35.
3. Ibid.

Certainly, there is no progress in music or art; that is, while an individual composer may get better with time, "newer" music with its complex new instruments for creating much more diverse sounds is no better than older music or any worse, for that matter. No invention, or creation, can "outdate" Machaut's *Mass* (c. 1360) as a newer car can, for instance, outdate the horse and buggy.

Techniques of Synthesis

There has existed, alongside the *avant-garde,* for the past thirty to forty years, a vast and somewhat sheltered mainstream of composers, often maddened, more often disgusted by what they saw and heard from the *avant-garde.* They have steadfastly held onto their historically justified techniques, and their ears. The *avant-garde* constantly shivered, however, above a pit of self-destruction. That difference, that canyon between the two divergent schools, is now the target of synthesis. The intelligent and talented composers on each side have realized that the radical claims of the initial proponents of both sides were not necessarily true.

One is reminded of the assertions set forth by two of the world's most renowned men of music: Igor Stravinsky, of *Le Sacre de Printemps* ("Very little tradition lies behind *Le Sacre* and no theory. I had only my ear to help me. . . . I am the vessel through which *Le Sacre* passed."[4]); and Pierre Boulez, the director of IRCAM in Paris ("Since the discovery by the Viennese, all composition other than twelve-tone is useless."[5]). Both men are, of course, incorrect; yet each viewpoint retains that grain of truth for which armies of artists and composers will clash for years. The last few years have witnessed the collapse of these camps surrounding the revisionist and the experimental.

We stand on the verge of one of the most creative and significant eras in the history of music. The prejudiced and insecure may still need shelter behind a mainstream door, yet those who now venture forth freely to take quiet advantage of the evident skills of both recent schools of thought (tradition and innovation, technique and intuition) are, will be, and have been braving an exciting new credible sensitivity into new music.

György Ligeti's *Requiem* is a four-movement work (twenty-six minutes in duration) for soprano and mezzo-soprano soloists, two choruses, and large orchestra. Composed during the years 1963 to 1965, the *Requiem* fuses two basic concepts. *Klangflächenkomposition* creates sound-mass that ebbs and flows through constant overlapping of timbre and spatial modulations evident in the extreme in his later *Lontano. Mikropolyphonie* creates highly complex densities of polyphonic motion in which no single voice dominates—only the overall fabric of resultant sound (notable in his *Aventures*). There is also a strong synthesis of traditional and *avant-garde* techniques. Conservative procedures are evidenced in the standard musical notation, text, extremely "determinate" articulations, and rhythmic complexities. Special effects include muting bassoons with handkerchiefs and the "Langlois effect"

4. Igor Stravinsky, "Apropos Le Sacre du Printemps," as printed on the cover of Columbia Records ML-5719.

5. David Cope and Galen Wilson, "An Interview with Pierre Boulez," *Composer* 1, no. 2 (September 1969), p. 83.

of squeezing the string with thumb and forefinger rather than pressing it normally against the fingerboard. The score is accompanied by a twenty-three-page booklet of incredibly exacting performance directions. Like his earlier *Aventures,* the *Requiem* occasionally moves from metered notation to "senza tempo" sections (especially in the third movement). Note that in Figure 4.10 (see chapter 4) his use of this effect is for *contrast.* In the *Requiem* the effect is quite the opposite, with even the bar lines being, in the composer's words, " . . . purely a means of synchronizing the individual parts."[6] Aside from its obvious synthesis of new and old, *Requiem* creates a composer-controlled "spatial movement." The composer has remarked about the work: "You have a drawing in two dimensions and you give it perspective. . . . I was constantly thinking of achieving this illusion of a musical space, which has only an acoustical existence in time."[7]

Witold Lutoslawski's *Symphony No. 3* (1983) is another good example of the post-*avant-garde.* Here the composer injects sweeping gestures of *glissandi* and scales into quasi-tonal and other more recognizably contrapuntal music. The effect is a fusing of *avant-garde* and more traditional styles. During the same year (1983) Krzysztof Penderecki's *Cello Concerto No. 2* was premiered. He too attempts to integrate his early gestural style (see the vectoral analysis of chapter 3) with quasi-romantic counterpoint of a highly chromatic but nonetheless unmistakably tonal nature. These works, along with others by Joseph Schwantner, Jacob Druckman, and others, have demonstrated a serious attempt to meld *avant-garde* and more traditional styles of music into a new common practice.

6. From the "Introductory Remarks" of the score: C. F. Peters: 30285.

7. "Conversations with Ligeti at Stanford," *Numus West* 2 (1972):19.

Figure 12.2. George Crumb. With permission.

George Crumb's *Ancient Voices of Children* (1970) is a twenty-seven-minute work for soprano, boy soprano, oboe, mandolin, harp, electric piano, and three percussionists. The work consists of five basic vocal movements separated twice by purely instrumental dances. The texts are by Federico Garcìa Lorca and sung in Spanish. The synthesis present in this work is evidenced by the composer's own words about the piece:

> In composing *Ancient Voices of Children* I was conscious of an urge to fuse various unrelated stylistic elements. I was intrigued by the idea of juxtaposing the seemingly incongruous: a suggestion of Flamenco with a Baroque quotation ("Bist du bei mir," from the Notebook of Anna Magdelena Bach), or a reminiscence of Mahler with a breath of the Orient. It later occurred to me that both Bach and Mahler drew upon many disparate sources in their own music without sacrificing "stylistic purity."[8]

Crumb's "stylistic purity" remains intact in this as well as his earlier works beginning with his *Five Pieces for Piano,* 1962. It is characterized by three particularly distinct features: (1) extremely defined and thinly exposed textures often consisting of solo lines (almost one-third of this work is for solo instruments), dramatic silences frequently expressed by square fermatas with duration in seconds (see Figure 12.3) and subtle motivic repetition and development; (2) the use of instruments and voice equally for their pitch and "special" timbral qualities. Crumb remarks,

> Certain special instrumental effects are used to heighten the "expressive intensity" e.g. "bending" the pitch of the piano by application of a chisel to the strings; . . . the mandolin has one set of strings tuned a quarter-tone low in order to give a special pungency to its tone.[9]

8. From the score: No. 66303. C. F. Peters.
9. Ibid.

Figure 12.3. George Crumb: *Ancient Voices of Children.* Copyright © by C. F. Peters Corp., 373 Park Avenue South, New York, N.Y., 10016. Reprint permission granted by the publisher.

and (3) the musical imagery—a reflection of the texts without programmatic connotations.

> I feel that the essential meaning of this poetry is concerned with the most primary things: life, death, love, the smell of the earth, the sounds of the wind and sea. These "*ur*-concepts" are embodied in language which is primitive and stark but which is capable of infinitely subtle nuance.[10]

Figure 12.3 shows the entire fourth movement of *Ancient Voices* and exemplifies the synthesis referred to earlier. The simple use of the whole-tone scale in the

10. Ibid.

opening vocal part beginning on C♯, the triadic harmonies, and the simple formal structure are all traditional. The marimba drones, the percussionists singing, and the Bach quote on the toy piano are all *avant-garde* in nature. The movement, and indeed the work, holds together with a high degree of continuity despite the contrasting material and styles.

Ellen Taaffe Zwilich's *Double Quartet,* a seminal twenty-one-minute work, convincingly demonstrates the composer's predilection for tight formal/modal structures and post-*avant-garde* synthesis. This four-movement works begins and ends in D. The opening, a dynamic and fast unison, defines the mode. The second movement begins in D minor with a transition to the third movement via a unison (leading-tone) C♯. This latter movement concludes on a D *dominant seventh* in 4/2 position. The fourth movement poses an F = F♯ contradiction with D again playing a very important role. The score centers on a kind of ambiguity between modes and key centers. The lexical implications in this (i.e., a chromatic tapestry without the rigors of a full-blown twelve-tone system) create a syntax that balances well with the quasi-tonal harmonic vocabulary. The orchestration employs an effective use of spatial modulations. In the performance notes, Zwilich suggests a seating arrangement that separates two string quartets by an apparent stage width. She then carefully creates a dialogue between the groups, at times complementary, more typically antiphonal.

Toshi Ichiyanagi's *Violin Concerto* is a three-movement, twenty-six minute *tour de force*. The soloist alternately converses with the orchestra and lapses into meditative soliloquies. The chromatic logic, not twelve-tone, does occasionally have actual rows (e.g., bar 46, solo violin: C-E♭-F♯-G-A-B♭-C♯-D-E-F-G♯-B transposed in bar 114 to: G-B♭-C♯-D-E-F-G♯-A-B-C-D♯-F♯ and thereafter occurring at a variety of pitch levels). Melodies typically ascend using only seconds and thirds. Ichiyanagi's lines tend toward continuous upward or downward motion or lapse into repeating figures that have no direction at all. Harmonic motion remains for the most part opaque. Either roots change so quickly that they blur distinction or they remain steady and without momentum, paralleling the contrast in his melodic writing. Voices tend to follow five, eight, or ten mutually exclusive pitch subsets. The composition, with the exception of a few freelance interchanges between orchestral soloists and the violin virtuoso, develops from the opening solo and effectively combines the melodic elements from each successive movement.

Henri Lazarof's *Second Concerto for Orchestra* (subtitled "Icarus") is a demanding twenty-two-minute three-movement work. Twelve-tone rows and near-rows abound. However, this is clearly not a dodecaphonic piece. The composer freely expresses intense chromaticism with an intuitive source. The harmonic vocabulary builds from the same foundation, and panchromatic chords can be found on almost every page of the score. The opening reveals an all-exclusive twelve-note pitch set that the composer varies freely throughout the work. His most frequently used technique involves presenting eleven notes of a row and then delaying the twelfth until (usually) it appears dramatically. For example, eleven notes are stated and repeated in the strings and percussion in bars 10 to 12 with a quadrupled twelfth pitch entry in the woodwinds. The beginning of the work also reveals a sentence-like phrase

Figure 12.4. Karel Husa.

structure that develops throughout the work. Often completely silent bars conclude the main thematic material. The principal motive of the work (C♯-F-G-A-B-C-E♭-G♭-A♭-B♭-D on the piano) announces each of the major sections. Vertical arrows and unevenly drawn stems without note-heads demonstrate notational synthesis techniques. The work gradually builds by slowly adding instruments to thundering climaxes that, after stopping abruptly, resolve.

Further Examples   György Kurtág's *Messages of the Late R. V. Troussova,* Op. 17, represents a significant post-*avant-garde* approach. Elements of instrument exploration, time suspension, and use of a variety of notations create an "atmospheric" style similar to that of Crumb yet distinctly that of Kurtág. The composer uses a gestural approach to timbre and cadence and generates a sense of breath through the use of extensive silence or soft sections.

Apotheosis of This Earth (1970) by Karel Husa, for concert band, is a work "physically" impelled by dynamics and textural momentum. Its synthesis is not easily heard because it is truly a work fused in every sense. Its three-movement structure (Apotheosis, Tragedy of Destruction, Postscript) employs sound-mass resultant of repetitive composite motives (see Figure 3.12 in chapter 3) and cumulatively sustained clusters which are often panchromatic, e.g., measure 149, where the horns and trumpets attack and slowly "unvelope" a twelve-note cluster. The final movement employs whispering with both repetitive consonance attacks and text ("this beautiful earth"). In *Apotheosis* one finds the fusion of *avant-garde* and traditional techniques so complete that neither is audible: a work of a unique and personal style.

Other works of varying degrees of synthesis include Donald Erb's *Symphony of Overtures* (1964) and Richard Toensing's *Doxologies I*. Both composers have evolved personal styles fused of elements equally *avant-garde* and traditional. The synthesis is complete: these works no longer "espouse" a single thought or gimmick nor express the fear of the use of any sonic material.

The author's *Threshold and Visions* (1979—a concerto for chamber orchestra) evolves a post-*avant-garde* idiom through synthesis of a diverse number of *avante-garde* techniques, including sound-mass, instrument exploration, and a free serial technique. The thirty-five-minute work is cast in five movements centered around a basic arch-type format.

Walter Mays's *Icarus* for large orchestra (1976) incorporates sound-mass, new instrumental techniques, electronic tape, improvisatory techniques, proportional notation, and indeterminate methods (stochastic). The large orchestration calling for well over one hundred players employs musical saw, bowed crotales, and electric organ to develop large volumes of complex sonic environments. David Felder's *Rondàge,* on the other hand, involves only five performers, fusing live electronics, sound-mass, structured improvisations, and new instrumental techniques into a comprehensively consistent vocabulary.

Barbara Kolb's *Soundings* is a complex work performable in two versions: chamber orchestra and tape prepared by the ensemble, or full orchestra divided into three groups directed by two conductors. The extensive program notes discuss the central conception of the work: "*Soundings* is a technique which makes it possible to ascertain the depth of water by measuring the interval of time between the sending of a signal and the return echo" with the resultant sounds developing ". . . a sea-change into something rich and strange."[11] A montage of triply overlaid contrapuntal textures results, each mini-orchestra or tape channel, depending on the version, being a separate but often simultaneous "sounding."

Soundings clearly divides into three major sections. The first section is characterized by a straightforward ostinato in the strings, repeating beat by beat throughout the entire passage, with slowly evolving patterns in first the original "sounding" and then the reflections. Tension is created by thickening texture and increased chromaticism toward a fast rush of sound slowly relaxing in a high *tremolo* in harp and solo violin. The second section is soloistic, conversational, and full of tightly woven musical gestures interplaying in often very thin textures. The final section reverts to the thick textures of the first, contrasts it in content with often long-held notes in rising chromatic lines but parallels it in direction, again driving to a loud climax sliced by an immediate *pianissimo* passage marked "in the distance."

Quotation

Quoting a fragment from another composer or style within the framework of one's own work became a prime focus for many composers in the *avant-garde*. It survives in the post-*avant-garde*. While hardly new since almost every composer has at one time or another quoted other music, from Bach's borrowed chants to Mahler's quotations of his own music, the use of strikingly different styles in the twentieth-century *avant-garde* has taken a decisively novel direction. The hymn quotes of Charles Ives as well as his free borrowings of any material to suit his message, evident in such works as *Central Park in the Dark* and *Symphony No. 4,* are often starkly

11. Barbara Kolb, *Soundings* (New York: Boosey & Hawkes, 1981).

presented against dissonant textures highlighting the cognizant drama present. Quite unlike the "theme and variations" quoting of previous centuries, this new actively polarized presentation of borrowed material results in "psychodrama."

Reasons for such quoting vary from composer to composer and often from work to work by the same composer. George Rochberg speaks of his usage:

> The centerpiece of my *Music for the Magic Theatre* is a transcription, that is, a completely new version, of a Mozart adagio. I decided to repeat it in my own way because I loved it. People who understand, love it because they know it began with Mozart and ended with me. People who don't understand think it's by Mozart.[12]

Peter Maxwell Davies's use of Handel quotes in *Eight Songs for a Mad King* (1969) results in a strange periodization (of George III) as well as superimposed *collage* effect (especially in "Comfort Ye, Comfort Ye My People," of Song ♯7). Michael Colgrass achieves an Ivesian *montage* in *As Quiet As* (1966) for orchestra by using a multitude of effectively varied quotes framed by a background of subtle clouds of modulating chords.

Mauricio Kagel superimposes quote upon quote from Beethoven in his *Ludwig van* (1970), creating, like Lukas Foss in his *Baroque Variations* (1967) and Stockhausen in his *Opus 1970,* a surrealistic intertwining of raw material stylistically consistent but rhythmically and texturally deranged. Each is contextually dramatic as additive overlays contribute to the increasing cognizant tension of "composer" intention.

The third movement of Luciano Berio's *Sinfonia* (1968) for eight soloists and orchestra, quoting extensively from Mahler and Debussy among others, possesses dramatic power through its use of striking text, likewise quoting from a number of sources, including Samuel Beckett, and driving musical force (see analysis at the end of this chapter). Certainly more innocent, at least in its length and continuity, is George Crumb's use of a short Bach fragment in his *Ancient Voices of Children* (1970, shown earlier in this chapter). The performance (on a toy piano) complete with Baroque ornaments is possibly one of the most powerful quotes in recent music, though the dynamics of the movement barely rise above *mezzoforte.*

Phil Winsor's *Orgel I,* for pipe organ and prerecorded tape, includes some performer choice (e.g., *which* Bach fugue, prelude, etc.) yet the incredible diversity creates a constant rationale of forged opposites. Figure 12.6 shows page X, a page of directed choices from which at points in the score (not shown) the performer may choose items within a prescribed time limit. The tape, made by the performer, contributes further overlays of the given material, resulting in massive densities of crowded triadic clashes. Each listener will, of course, recognize from experience only a percentage of the quotes. However, their often simultaneously polarized styles, and indeed the listener's inherent quest for message, create intense drama.

---

12. George Rochberg, "No Center," *Composer* 2, no. 1 (September, 1969), p. 89.

Figure 12.5. Phil Winsor.
Photo by Julia Winsor.

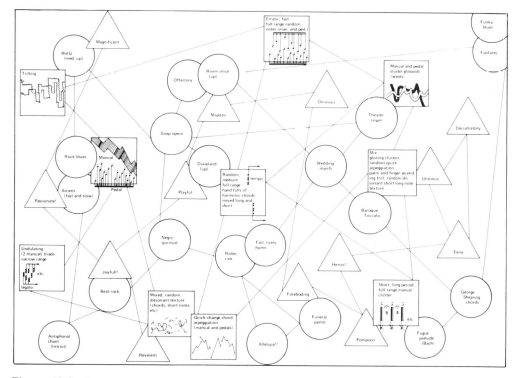

Figure 12.6. Phil Winsor's *ORGEL I* (page X). Copyright © 1975 by Pembroke Music Co., Inc. New York. International Copyright Secured. 62 Cooper Square, New York, N.Y. 10003. Copying or reproducing this publication in whole or in part violates the Federal Copyright Law. All rights reserved including public performance for profit. Used by permission.

It is no longer possible to avoid the implications of the post-*avant-garde*. Whether they be, in the final analysis, friend or enemy (or both), one must know and acknowledge them. Nothing is gained by ignorance. Varèse's comments are most apropos:

> My fight for the liberation of sound and for my right to make music with any sound and all sounds has sometimes been construed as a desire to disparage and even to discard the great music of the past. But that is where my roots are. No matter how original, how different a composer may seem, he has only grafted a little bit of himself on the old plant. But this he should be allowed to do without being accused of wanting to kill the plant. He only wants to produce a new flower. . . .[13]

Vectoral Analysis: Luciano Berio: *Sinfonia*

(For information on vectoral analysis and procedures, see chapter 1.)

1. Historical Background: Luciano Berio (b. 1925, Oneglia, Italy) was a cofounder with Bruno Maderna of the electronic music studio in Milan (1955). He later taught at the Juilliard School of Music (until 1973) and Mills College in Oakland, California, and he has been director of the electronic music studio at IRCAM in Paris.

   Berio's music separates into two major periods, though there is a defined continuity throughout his compositional career: (1) through the mid-fifties, a post-Western serialism prevails with *Chamber Music* (1952) as a good example; and (2) through the late seventies, an eclectic theater approach is expressed through electronic means (e.g., *Visage,* 1961) and more recently through large instrumental works (e.g., *Sinfonia,* 1968 and *Coro,* 1976 for voices and instruments). Other important works include *Circles* (for soprano, harp, and two percussion ensembles, 1962; see example in chapter 5), *Omaggio a Joyce* (1958), *Differences* (for five instruments and tape, 1959), and *Opera* (large "opera," 1972, with a revised version completed in 1977).

   Berio is most known for his extraordinary music-theater works, many of which were greatly influenced by the abilities of Cathy Berberian, who for a number of years was married to Berio. Her gymnastic vocal talents fused with Berio's dramatic and lyric style to create *Visage* and particularly *Recital* (1971), a singular study of a singer's mental breakdown. Other works dedicated to Cathy Berberian include *Circles* and *Epifanie* (1960).

2. Overview: *Sinfonia* was originally composed in four movements and later (in 1968) altered to include a fifth. Some maintain that the latter was added at a conductor's request for a "flashy" final movement. The work was commissioned by the New York Philharmonic Orchestra and dedicated to Leonard Bernstein (the conductor). It is scored for large orchestra (see Orchestration Techniques) and eight voices performed most notably since the premiere by the Swingle Singers.

13. As quoted in *Contemporary Composers on Contemporary Music.* Elliott Schwartz and Barney Childs, eds. (New York: Holt, Rinehart and Winston, 1967), p. 201.

Figure 12.7. Luciano Berio. BMI Archives. Used by permission.

The first movement is cast in two large sections melded together through a transition. The opening of the work, ominously provoked by three tam-tams, sets repeated notes in motion. These vacillate through a variety of homorhythmic and heterophonic rhythmic variants utilizing timbral development (e.g., slow vowel changes in the voices; use of mutes in brass). This opening material is followed by similar groupings (i.e., initialization/pitch repetition/development) of successively shorter and shorter duration. A second section emerges innocuously from this stretto by a short burst in the background from the piano. These outbursts increase in importance until finally they take over completely, forming the nucleus of the second main section characterized by loud quick blasts of sound followed by silences. These develop into an orchestral tutti. Occasionally one or more of the notes rings after being set in motion by the fast bursts. This allows Berio, in the final few measures, to recollect the opening or first section briefly in an illusion of a three-part form. Berio has cleverly allowed the second section to "grow" from the second part of the first section. The end of the movement resembles the first part of the first section.

The second movement subtitled "O King" is continuous organic form centered on the simple text: "Martin Luther King." Except for the vowel exchange carried over from the first movement, this is the only text for the movement. The idea from the first movement (excitation) continues in the piano, whose sudden single attacks on certain notes initiate the held soft pitches by the singers. The material centers on F, and a variety of chromatic scales emerge around this pivotal point (hybrid chromatic gestures, whole-tone scales, etc.). The end of the movement suggests a brief return to the blasts at the end of the first movement, implying, as the first does to itself, a cyclical use of materials. At the outset of the movement, all materials move upward from F, and at the end of the movement, all materials work down from the same F.

The third movement is an Ivesian barrage of quotations. Figure 12.8 shows a portion of the movement. The text here reads: "But now it's done, it's over, we've had our chance. There was even, for a second, hope of resurrection, or almost." It seems to encapsulate the almost narrative "stream-of-consciousness" flow of the work. Eclecticism abounds in both text and music. Text examples are drawn from such sources as Claude Levi-Strauss's book *Du Cru et du Cuit* (on Brazilian-origin myths of water), Samuel Beckett, and Berio's own words all set with performance directions in English, such as "impatient," "indignant," and "bewildered"—these taken, for example, from just four bars on page 12. Music quotes are prevalent throughout the third movement and include fragments from Debussy's *La Mer,* references to Berio's own music (primarily *Epifanie* and *Sequenza IV*), as well as quotations from "Bach, Schoenberg, Ravel, Strauss, Berlioz, Brahms, Berg, Hindemith, Beethoven, Wagner, Stravinsky, Boulez, Stockhausen, Globokar, Pousseur, Ives. . . ."[14] The major quote, however, is from Mahler's Second Symphony (Scherzo), which runs throughout the movement in one form or another. "As a structural point of reference, Mahler is to the totality of the music of this section what Beckett is to the text."[15] The Beckett referred to is *The Unnameable.* Aside from the diverse juxtapositions of contrasting elements, the movement tends to shift around three centerpins: a short upbeat motion followed by a crashing cluster chords. Between these flow the overkill of musical information for which the work has become so noted.

Berio refers to the "expedition-like quality" of this movement:

This third part of *Sinfonia* has a skeleton which is the scherzo from Mahler's *Second Symphony*—a skeleton that often reemerges fully fleshed out, then disappears, then comes back again. . . . But it's never alone: it's accompanied throughout by the "history of music" that it itself recalls for me, with all its many levels and references—or at least those bits of history that I was able to keep a grip on, granted that often there's anything up to four different references going on at the same time. So the scherzo of Mahler's *Second Symphony* becomes a generator of harmonic functions and of musical references that are pertinent to them which appear, disappear, pursue their own courses, return to Mahler, cross paths, transform themselves into Mahler or hide behind it. The references to Bach, Brahms, Boulez, Berlioz, Schoenberg, Stravinsky, Strauss, Stockhausen, etc. are therefore *also* signals which indicate which harmonic country we are going through, like bookmarkers, or little flags in different colours stuck into a map to indicate salient points during an expedition full of surprises.[16]

14. From liner notes by the composer, Columbia MS 7268.

15. Ibid.

16. From *Luciano Berio: Two Interviews* (with Rossana Dalmonte and Bálint András Varga) (London: Marion Boyars, 1985), p. 19.

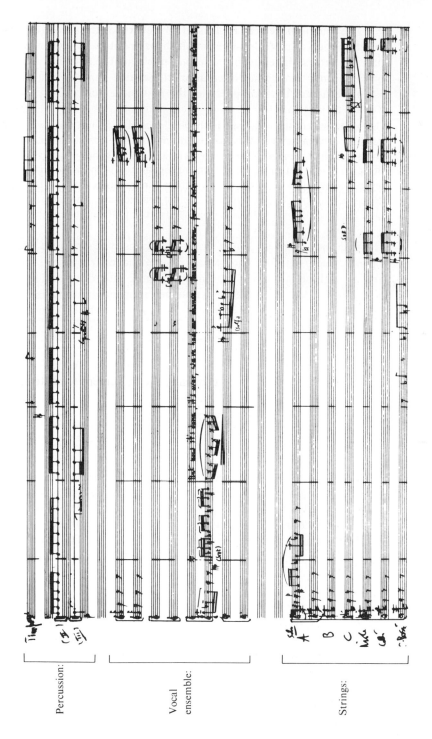

Percussion:

Vocal ensemble:

Strings:

The fourth movement returns to the reverie of the second and is a reaggregation of materials used in all three previous movements. The material grows higher as in the second movement, particularly enveloping the major second/minor third intervallic set. Sudden bursts of sound suggest recapitulation of the second part of the first movement.

The treatments of the vocal part in the first, second and fourth sections of *Sinfonia* resemble each other in that the text is not immediately perceivable as such. The words and their components undergo a musical analysis that is integral to the total musical structure of voice and instrument together. It is precisely because the varying degree of perceptibility of the text at different moments is a part of the musical structure that the words and phrases are not printed here. The experience of "not quite hearing" them is to be conceived as essential to the nature of the work itself.[17]

The fifth movement is set in a single variations type structure introduced by a piano/voice/flute *soli* trio section. The music, characterized by materials similar to those in the first movement, is more integrated and involves less contrast. The text continues to expose heterophonic multiple language collage, with clusters waxing and waning in an interlocking repeated pitch, or vacillating *tremolo* style.

In its five-movement form, *Sinfonia* is an arch form:

$$I \quad II \quad III \quad IV \quad V$$

with the centerpiece (movement III) a striking compilation of diverse materials surrounded by two quiet, almost passive sections and bounded externally by two agitated and dramatic movements.

3. Orchestration Techniques: *Sinfonia* employs an orchestra of eighty-one players and eight vocalists. The stage layout is given in the performance notes and includes a diagram of spatial locations for each of the orchestral groups. The violins divide into three (not the usual two) sections and are spaced diagonally from left to right, across the stage. The three percussionists are situated as far apart as possible, with percussion I in the center. The vocalists usually stand directly in front of the conductor and need amplification to be heard.

   Berio gives the percussion and particularly the piano a very large role in the orchestra. Orchestration involves some doubling and incorporates a sectional approach (i.e., rare solos). Few effects are used (muting and harmonics are the exceptions) and balance is obtained by careful handling of dynamics.

4. Basic Techniques: While quotation and texts play an important role in *Sinfonia,* the underlying core of consistent materials and vocabulary ties the

17. Ibid.

Figure 12.9. Luciano Berio: *Sinfonia*, examples of rhythmic development.

work together. These center rhythmically around expanding and contracting rhythmic units, metrically evolved through an interplay of duple and triple elements. Figure 12.9 is an example from the first few bars.

These escalate to involved rhythmic schemes around repeated couplets or two-note groupings recurring in an environment of constantly shifting rhythmic design. Pitch seems lessened in importance by the large structures of sound (discussed more fully under Vertical and Horizontal Models) that are primarily based in seconds and thirds with leaps developed out of their octave transpositions: sevenths, ninths, and so on.

Figure 12.10. Luciano Berio: *Sinfonia*, examples of vertical sonorities.

5. Vertical Models: As mentioned earlier, harmonic structures in *Sinfonia* seem to be built primarily out of seconds and thirds. Figure 12.10 shows six of these in ascending order of complexity and dissonance.

The first is a frequently repeated harmony found at the end of the first and fifth movements in the voices (again suggesting arch form) and in a number of other locations throughout the piece. It consists of a minor triad with a major seventh. The second example, like the first, is generally consonant with suggestions of a whole-tone scale extracted from the opening of the second movement. Example 3, from the fourth movement, begins to show deepening complexity and illustrates the growth of dependency on the intervals of seconds and thirds. Note the beginning of contradictory chromatism: D♭ and D♮. Example 4, from the second movement, creates similar tension with slight variations, while example 5, from the beginning of the first movement, deepens the dissonance. The final example, from one of the large constructs of the third movement, is a near panchromatic (ten different notes) structure, again of stacked seconds and thirds. There is clearly no systematic application of specific rules, but rather an imaginative and intuitive approach to intervallic development.

6. Horizontal Models: Most of the vertical structures mentioned above arise out of slowly adding notes horizontally. All chord structures seen in Figure 12.10, except 1 and 6, were created by adding notes from the bottom in orders that incorporate no leap larger than a third. These are typical of the melodic/harmonic style that Berio incorporates throughout *Sinfonia*.

7. Style: *Sinfonia* is a prime example of the post-*avant-garde* musical style. It is a contrapuntal work developing elements of quotation, clusters, improvisation (brief but important vocal ornamentations), and serial techniques. The culmination of these diverse elements in a *gestalt* represents the essence of the post-*avant-garde*.

It would seem that such diverse elements as the work talking about itself as in "Keep going, going on, call that going, call that on. But wait. He is barely moving, now almost still. Should I make my introductions?"—at which point the singers are introduced by name while the music continues could not possibly make sense. Berio uses nearly every conceivable sonority from major thirds, triads, and lush ninth chords to cluster the use of massive dramatic bursts of sound within delicate frames of textures (the first movement primarily). However, reflecting a society gone mad with self-preoccupation, *Sinfonia* forcefully drives its musical/dramatic point home, leaving few listeners with less than a profound disturbance borne of having indeed heard the through-composed expression of *self* without restraint. The work does indeed have continuity and a kind of frightening "madness," a macrocosm of dramatic fusion. While traditional in notation, material for quotes, form, and rhythmic flow, it is as well a highly *avant-garde* work in text, "act" of quoting, and eclectic, harmonic, and melodic idioms, and is a striking example of the post-*avant-garde*.

This work, with its dramatic and often "stream-of-consciousness" feel, resembles the Peter Maxwell Davies work analyzed in chapter 4. Both rely on quotation of various composers as well as a free use of available resources. It also compares favorably with Penderecki's *Capriccio* of chapter 3's vectoral analysis, though not so explicitly (drama and unordered pitch components primarily). This work relies significantly on many of the experiments in the realms of electronic music (chapter 8), utilizing them, however, in its imaginative use of timbre with traditional instruments.

Postlude

In chapter 1, the author attempted to explore the various relationships between the arts and cultural trends of the late nineteenth century in terms of the origins of the *avant garde*. It is no accident that art parallels the tempo of world events. The comparisons hold true today. In obvious cases such as technology, the relevance appears so striking as to be impossible to refute. Forty-six percent of all musical instruments sold in 1986 were electronic in construction. The digital revolution is exploding onto new fronts daily. The accessibility of personal computers has provided a technology to all musicians that ten years ago was available only in university research centers. This is true in the other arts as well. Computer lighting boards and digitally processed graphic arts programs have given rise to a whole new generation of technically minded creators and producers.

In less obvious areas, one finds the concepts of specialization and economy as important points of comparison. Styles have not only fragmented into various schools of thought and aesthetic, these schools further have separated into single views of individuals. Many composers, seeking to find a true language, write consecutive works in widely different modes without concern. Gone are the simplicities of a pen-and-paper mode of composing; now typesetting software and laster printers have brought desktop publishing possibilities to the home. The economics of keeping up technologically have become a major factor even for the "notes on paper" composers. The use of sampled sounds, digital editing, and storage as well as production will be the greatest single evolution of the late twentieth century. These will have a profound effect on performance groups of all kinds. Ensembles and orchestras, which hitherto have depended (at least in part) for their income on the commercial world, whether radio, TV, or live performance, will find the competition stiff. Sampling systems will, as their synthesizer cousins have already proven, drop significantly in price over the next few years. An increase in quality will allow any composer anywhere to perform large-scale works without large-scale performance resources.

On subtler levels, one finds the conservatism exemplified in chapter 11 in every arena: politics, religion (fundamentalist), visual arts, architecture, motion pictures, and so on. There is a sense of rondoic return to an earlier period where simplicity abounded and music and all of the arts were a part of cultural heritage and distinctly not in the rarified air of academia or a concert hall setting.

Musical style, as well as instrumentation, shows a distinct return to former aesthetics. One finds, for example, long tapering lines reminiscent of Mahler in New Age music. Quasi-tonal progressions abound freely in a variety of new music forms that only ten years ago would have seemed very out of place. Effects, from the "noises" of Russolo to the early efforts in electronic music, have come full circle with sampling devices that imitate traditional instruments. Rhythm, once fragmented by pointillism, has returned in many styles to a steady and predictable metric pulse, sometimes even employing motor-rhythms as in the works of Philip Glass. The free use of pitch class has diminished significantly, with lines returning to more traditional and predominantly stepwise motion so prevalent even in turn-of-the-century music. Interest in diverse tuning systems, combinations of various media, indeterminacy, and cluster chords have waned significantly since their inceptions in the 1940s and earlier. Even the challenge to tonal harmony seems exhausted, with few who resist the simple graces of triadic consonances on a systematic basis.

While exact counterparts may stretch the point, some are irresistible. Glass and Satie, for example, or Crumb and Ives, New Age and impressionism, while not obviously presenting clear parallels, do not beg the point. Even techniques of artificial intelligence and music suggest the introspection so inherent in Schoenberg's self-studies toward serialism and the work of Busoni and others in scientific applications to style. Most important, however, is the *ethos* of a period where, with technological advances expanding horizons in a multitude of directions, composers retrench into a reexamination of ages past where subtle hierarchies and nuances of musical structure predominated and individuality emanated from personal statement within a style, not from the shock and newness of the style.

Visionary Roberto Pavo has predicted the many changes he feels will take place during the next few decades: "Mice attached to TV sets with Mac-like menus where visual and sonic images can be frozen, digitized, edited and printed in just a few seconds. The body will have all manner of contraptions attached to it including alpha-state Walkmen-like radio-tape-players and automatic massage units as well as the already extant electronic organs; talking machines everywhere, even toaster ovens; intelligent machines will run our houses, our businesses, even our lives—they will even tell our fortunes and our horoscopes (and we'll believe them). They will compose our music, write novels, create videos, fight our wars, run our space program and, generally speaking, our future. It's all fantastic" (from *Future Now!;* see Bibliography).

George Crumb sums it up succinctly in his article titled "Music: Does It Have a Future?": "I am optimistic about the future of music. I frequently hear our present period described as uncertain, confused, chaotic. The two decades from 1950 to 1970 have been described as 'the rise and fall of the musical *avant-garde*,' the implication being that nothing at all worthwhile was accomplished during those years. My own feeling is that music can never cease evolving; it will continually re-invent the world in its own terms."[18]

As the author looks back over twenty years and six editions of *New Directions in Music,* what is clear is that good music takes the same drive and skills it always did and the same patience on the part of its audience to understand it. New technologies, electronic performance potentials, conservative or *avant-garde* styles do not guarantee quality—only composers can do that.

Bibliography— Chapter 12*

Further Readings

Evaluation

Cage, John. "The Future of Music." *Numus West* 5 (1974).
Cope, David. "A Post Avant-Garde." *Composer* 3, no. 2 (1972): pp. 61–65.
Johnson, Tom. "Exotic Music: borrowing is not so bad." *Village Voice* 25, 1980.
Johnston, Ben. "On Context." *ASUC Proceedings* 3 (1968): pp. 32–36.
Rochberg, George. "The New Image of Music." *Perspectives of New Music* 2, no. 1 (1963): pp. 1–10.
Salzman, Eric. *Twentieth-Century Music: An Introduction.* 3d ed. Englewood Cliffs, N.J.: Prentice-Hall, 1988.

Techniques of Synthesis

Burrows, David. "Music and the Biology of Time." *Perspectives of New Music* 11, no. 1 (1972): pp. 1–10.
Cope, David. "Footnotes." *Composer* 4, no. 2 (1973): pp. 52–54.
Gillespie, Don, ed. *George Crumb: Profile of a Composer.* New York: C. F. Peters, 1986.
Kaufman, Harold. "Ligeti's Zweites Streichquartet." *Melos* 37 (1970).
Ligeti, György. "Metamorphosis of Musical Form." *Die Reihe* 7 (1960): pp. 5–19.
Ligeti, György, *Witold Lutoslawski, and Ingvar Lidholm. Three Aspects of New Music* (from a composition seminar in Stockholm). Stockholm: Nordiska Musikförlaget, 1968.

18. George Crumb, "Music: Does It Have a Future?" In *George Crumb, Profile of a Composer* (New York: C. F. Peters, 1986), p. 19.

*Addresses for record companies, periodicals, and music publishers mentioned in this Bibliography can be found in Appendix IV.

Further Examples

Cope, David. "Biography of George Crumb." In *George Crumb: Profile of a Composer,"* pp. 8–15. New York: C. F. Peters, 1986.

Crumb, George. "Music: Does It Have a Future?" In *George Crumb: Profile of a Composer,* pp. 16–19. New York: C. F. Peters, 1986.

Ives, Charles. "Music and Its Future." In *American Composers on American Music,* ed. Henry Cowell, New York: Unger Publishing Co., 1962.

"Musician of the Month: Karel Husa." *Musical America* (August 1969): p. 5.

Stucky, Steven. *Lutoslawski and his Music.* Cambridge: Cambridge University Press, 1981.

Quotation

Harbison, John. "Peter Maxwell Davies' Taverner." *Perspectives of New Music* 11, no. 1 (1972): pp. 233–40.

Henze, Hans Werner. *Music and Politics.* London: Faber and Faber, 1982.

Luciano Berio

Dalmonte, Rossana, and Bálint András Varga. *Luciano Berio: Two Interviews.* Translated and edited by David Osmond-Smith. New York: Marion Boyars, 1985.

Poissenot, Jacques M. "Luciano Berio." In *Dictionary of Contemporary Music,* ed. John Vinton, pp. 78–79. New York: E. P. Dutton and Co., 1974.

Santi, Piero. "Luciano Berio." *Die Reihe* 4 (1958): pp. 98–102.

Postlude

Pavo, Roberto. *Future Now.* New York: Futurista Publications, 1987.

Compact Discs, Recordings, and Publishers

Berio, Luciano. *Coro.* Universal Edition. DG 2531 270.
———. *Epifanie* (1961). Universal Edition. RCA LSC-3189.
———. *Sequenza IV* (1966). Universal Edition. Candide 31015.
———. *Sinfonia.* Universal Edition. Erato ECD 88151.
Cope, David. *Concert for Piano and Orchestra* (1981). Opus One 82.
———. *Re-birth* (1975). Seesaw Music Corp. Cornell CUWE-16A.
———. *Threshold and Visions.* New York: Alexander Broude. Folkways FTS 33452.
Crumb, George. *Ancient Voices of Children.* Peters. Nonesuch 9 79149–2.
———. *Makrokosmos III* (1974). Peters. AMU 038.
Davies, Peter Maxwell. *Eight Songs for a Mad King.* Boosey and Hawkes. Nonesuch H-71285.
del Tredici, David. *Final Alice* (1976). London LDR-71018.
Druckman, Jacob. *Windows* (1972). MCA Music. CRI S-457.
Erb, Donald. *Symphony of Overtures.* Galaxy Music. Turnabout 34433.
Felder, David. *Rondáge* (1977). Alexander Broude.
Gubaidulina, Denisov. *March.* MCA MLD 32113.
Husa, Karel. *Apotheosis of This Earth* (1970). Associated Music Publishers. Golden Crest 4134.
———. *Sonata for Violin and Piano* (1975). Grenadilla 1032.
Ives, Charles. *Central Park in the Dark* (1906). AMP. CBS MK 42381(64).

Kolb, Barbara. *Soundings* (1981). Boosey & Hawkes.

Ligeti, György. *Adventures* (1966). Peters. DG 423 244–2.

———. *Le Grand Macabre* (1978). Wergo 60085.

———. *Lontano* (1967). Schott. Wergo WER 60163–50.

———. *Melodien for Orchestra* (1971). Decca Head 12.

———. *Requiem*. Peters. Wergo 60 045–50.

Nono, Luigi. *Canti di Vita e d'amore* (1962). Ars Viva. Wergo 60067.

Rochberg, George. *Violin Concerto* (1974). Columbia M-35149.

Schnittke, Alfred. *A Paganini*. DG 415 484–2GH.

———. *Quartet for Strings I* (1966). BIS CD467.

Schwantner, Joseph. *Aftertones of Infinity* (1978). New World NW 381–2.

Stravinsky, Igor. *Variations Aldous Huxley in Memoriam* (1964). Boosey and Hawkes. Columbia MS-7386.

Takemitsu, Toru. *November Steps* (1967). Peters. CBS Sony 58 DC 282–2.

Toensing, Richard. *Doxologies I*. Cornell University 9.

GLOSSARY OF TERMS

This is an alphabetical listing of those terms used in the text that may need further clarification. An asterisk (*) after a term within a definition signifies that the word so starred is itself defined within this glossary.

additive synthesis the creation of timbres by plotting the amplitude envelopes of the fundamental and harmonics of a timbre.

algorithmic music music based on algorithms defined as step-by-step procedures (often shown as block diagrams with interconnecting lines) and usually produced by a computer.

amplifier an instrument used to increase the power of a sound or signal.

amplitude equivalent to the "loudness" of a pitch; the dynamics of sound.

amplitude modulation (AM) a periodic variation of amplitude* creating *tremolo*.

antimusic a term denoting those works the concept or implication of which is "opposed to" the traditional meaning of music. In current terms, it refers to those compositions that either

(1) include no reference to sound in their scores; (2) destroy one or more of the traditional composer/performer/audience relationships; or (3) are impossible to perform and exist only in concept.

atonality literally, away from tonality, or no tonality. Atonality is truly impossible to obtain, as any group of sounds will by acoustical principles have one or more strongest tones (tone center = tonality), just as they will have form (intended or not). *Pantonality** (inclusive of all tonalities) has for the most part replaced the term *atonality* in reference to twelve-tone music (dodecaphony*).

augmentation expanding the duration of a rhythmic set without disturbing the relationship of elements (e.g., doubling or tripling the value of each note).

autonomous music Xenakis's term for music that does not employ "strategy" or "games" in its performance. This would include all of traditional music and all *indeterminate* music* that does not result from group conflict (*heteronomous music** is the opposite term).

avant-garde   a French term literally meaning *advance guard* or *vanguard;* in the arts, applies to those who work in the newest areas of creativity. It may come to mean in music a certain period (such as "modern") roughly covering the years 1935–1975. Thus the term post-*avant-garde* means after the earlier period: no longer can anything be really "new."

band-pass filter   an electronic filtering device that allows a certain band to pass while rejecting all the remaining frequencies; often applied to white sound* in order to create a wide variety of timbres.

band-reject filter   an electronic filtering device that eliminates a particular band (group) of frequencies while allowing the remainder to pass.

Bauhaus   an art school in Germany founded in 1919 by Walter Gropius, and closed in 1933 in which the various art forms and crafts were taught interdisciplin-arily. Faculty included Paul Klee, Vasily Kandinsky, and Mies van der Rohe (among others of like prominence), and was instrumental in encouraging the development of many of the media forms extant today.

binary   a term used to denote a numbering system in "base 2." Only two numbers need be used (0,1), and can be represented by any system capable of two states. To create linear* numbers (1,2,3 . . . etc.), a code is created defined by columns proceeding to the left by increments following an exponential series (. . . 16, 8, 4, 2, 1). In this way, any number can be represented and operated upon. (0 0 0 1 = 1; 0 0 1 0 = 2; 0 0 1 1 = 3; 0 1 0 0 = 4; etc.). This concept is important for digital computers.

black sound   used to denote silences as opposed to white sound* (inclusive of all frequencies).

brake drum   the housing of the braking mechanism of an automobile; also used as a percussion instrument.

chance music   often used synonymously with *indeterminate* *music,* it means any music in which there is a "chance" result whether it be by composer, performer, or both.

circular bowing   on string instruments, a procedure whereby the bow is kept in motion, regardless of bow direction change, by a circular action of the bow across the string.

circular breathing   on wind instruments, the ability of the performer to breathe in through the nose while expelling air through the mouth, thereby needing no rests or "breaks" to regain breath. Performers well versed in this procedure can play continuously for great lengths of time.

classic electronic music   electronic music created primarily by "splicing" one sound to the next rather than by using keyboards and sequencers.

cluster   a chord that contains two or more intervals of a major second or less.

combinatoriality   a twelve-tone technique wherein hexachords* of different versions of the same row can be exchanged to create new rows (still twelve different pitches). Forms of newly created rows can be used simultaneously with the original to avoid unisons, octaves, etc., often characteristic of contrapuntal dodecaphonic* techniques.

computer-generated sound   timbres produced by computational means by either additive* or FM synthesis.*

contact microphone   a certain type of microphone that requires physical contact for reproduction of sound.

cross-coupling   a tape-recorder technique of attaching the playback of one channel to the record of another channel and vice versa to create a reiteration of attack with built-in decay,* usually employed in live-electronic music.*

DAC   digital-to-analog converter. An instrument designed to translate digital* information into analog sound (primarily conversion of numbers into voltages and smoothing the result into continuous voltages for sound production).

dada   international movement (beginning around 1916) that some feel originated with the poet Tristan Tzara. It included artists such as Man Ray and Marcel Duchamp among others, and attacked all conventional standards and aesthetics of "art." Exemplified by redefining machine-produced objects as works of art, by collages of newspapers, etc., it was (and some feel it still is) one generating force behind the *avant-garde.*

decay   that aspect of a tone's envelope* in which the amplitude decreases.

digital computer   a computer whose information is stored and processed in binary* numbers.

dodecaphonic   a term commonly used to refer to twelve-tone music.

drift   in electronic music, any unintentional shift of frequency due to equipment inaccuracy. All analog oscillators* and generators* necessarily include a small amount of drift.

envelope   the amplitude* characteristics of a signal. Most typically: attack, initial decay,* sustain, and final decay.* Envelope generators control both the amount and duration of each of these characteristics.

equal temperament   dividing the octave into twelve equal parts. Based on the twelfth root of two, this system represents to some composers an artificial solution to the problems encountered in just* intonation.

feedback   a result of cross-coupling.* Literally, any electronic device in which sound is fed back through the system one or more times to produce echoes or, depending on gain* adjustment, an increase of the sound to limits of system tolerance.

filter   an electronic instrument designed to allow selection of frequencies from a signal: band-pass,* band-reject,* for example.

Fluxus   a group of *avant-garde** composers beginning in the 1960s with intentional direction toward danger and boredom as viable concepts of art.

FM synthesis   the artificial creation of harmonics via sidebands of complex spectral frequency modulation.*

fractal   a self-replicating object that regenerates at succeeding smaller and larger levels.

frequency modulation (FM)   a periodic variation of frequency, creating vibrato.

Futurists   Italian group of composers (1912–20) employing a wide variety of noise*-making instruments.

gain   amount of amplification. Variable gain would be the "loudness" knob on any sound-producing device (e.g., amplifier*).

generator   sound source of all types of electronic signals except sine waves.*

gesamtkunstwerk   German term meaning literally "complete art work." Used to denote the nineteenth-century view of opera (particularly Wagner's), the composer creating and controlling all aspects of the work—staging, music, lyrics, dance, etc.—and all aspects contributing equally to the total effect.

graphic   in music, those scores that are more oriented toward visual incitement than communication of directions through traditional symbols.

hardware   a computer term used to denote actual instrument technology as opposed to programmatic (software*) technology. Colloquially, hardware refers to "hard" physical instruments while software refers to programs.

heteronomous music   music that utilizes "games" and "strategy" during performance, producing *conflict* and indeterminate* results. Term primarily used by Xenakis.

heterophony   "hetero" = several; phony = sounds. This term identifies music that contains many variations of a melody simultaneously.

hexachord   in its simplest form, a six-note chord. Commonly used in twelve-tone music to construct various further computations of the row.

improvisation   music that involves some performer freedom during performance within a certain set of parameters* created by the composer. As opposed to indeterminate* music, improvisation suggests (often demands) that the performer draw upon techniques and intuition based on previous experience within a set stylistic framework.

indeterminacy   act of composer, performer, and/or both in which the outcome is unpredictable. In general, unlike improvisation, where the performer is asked to draw upon previous experience and techniques, indeterminacy requires a *real* "letting of sounds be themselves," as John Cage has put it, with performers and performing situations allowing any sound to exist within the framework set by the composer. The term *aleatoric* is sometimes used to denote indeterminacy.

interface   any instrument that allows two different instruments to communicate. In computer music (especially computer-generated sound*) the digital-to-analog (D/A) *interface* allows the digital computer to produce analog sounds on tape. A MIDI *interface* allows many different digital instruments to communicate to one another.

inversion   stating something upside-down. In twelve-tone music this refers to rearranging an entire row exactly by calculating up intervals downward and vice versa.

isorhythm   a compositional technique of Gothic music (c. twelfth to fifteenth century, primarily in Machaut) in which a set rhythm is repeatedly applied throughout the composition to set melodies (isomelos) of different numbers of notes.

just tuning   tuning systems based on the overtone series.* The intervals of the fifth and the major third are calculated (ratios 3:2 and 5:4, respectively) from the series and projected into scales.

klangfarbenmelodien   German term denoting color pointillism*: individual notes have distinctly different timbre, further separated by range.

klangflächenkomposition   sound-mass* that ebbs and flows through constant overlapping of timbre* and spatial* modulation.

linear   literal meaning: pertaining to line. In traditional music *linear* refers to melodic or contrapuntal flow. In electronic terminology *linear* refers to a "straight" line flow as opposed to exponential accelerated flow.

live-electronic   sound created by a performer working "live" using electronic instruments in a concert situation. "Live" also refers to an approach opposite to that of composing electronic music on tape by splicing procedures (classical*).

matrix   a box of 144 squares that provides all versions of a twelve-tone row. The original is placed across the top with the inversion top to bottom; all notes are then filled in according to transpositions. This is an important device for analysis and composition of twelve-tone music.

microtone   an interval that is less than an equal-tempered half-step. Quarter tones* are one example.

MIDI   an acronym for Musical Instrument Digital Interface, the default standard in the music industry for digital instrument communication.

mikropolyphonie   highly complex densities of polyphonic motion in which no single voice dominates.

mixer   an electronic instrument designed to combine signals by algebraically summing their amplitudes.

modulation   a process in which any aspect of a sound or signal is varied (e.g., amplitude modulation* and frequency modulation*).

montage   a visual overlapping of images.

multimedia   a work that employs two or more traditionally separate art forms. "Happenings" are multimedia events that are more or less aleatorically conceived.

multiphonics   the technique (particularly on wind instruments) of obtaining two or more sounds simultaneously. Obtained by control of the overtone* series so that one or more of the partials becomes prominent enough to be heard as a separate tone. Another voice can be added by humming.

musique concrète   music that employs nonelectronic sounds on tape. The tape recorder is most commonly the compositional tool, and sounds are manipulated after recording to achieve the desired effect.

noise   traditionally defined as undesirable sound. Today, however, as composers continually employ sounds that were in the past "disliked" or considered "nonmusical," it has come roughly to mean those sounds whose complexity is such that individual frequencies are no longer determinable and/or audible.

oscillator   an electronic instrument designed to create sine waves.*

oscilloscope   a device used to show via cathode-ray tubes the characteristics of incoming signals (amplitude,* frequency, etc.).

ostinato   a grouping of notes that is repeated many times.

overtone   all sounds except sinusoidal forms contain small secondary pitches called overtones, the alteration or filtering* of which alters timbre.

panchromatic   inclusive of all chromatic tones. Usually used to refer to cluster* chords in which all or most of the twelve pitches occur.

pandiatonicism   inclusive of all diatonic (or key-scale) notes. Pandiatonic clusters* include all seven scale notes (e.g., a white key forearm cluster on piano = key of C pandiatonic cluster).

pantonality   inclusive of all tonalities. Like atonality* it is impossible to achieve, and thus very loosely applied to twelve-tone music.

parameter   any characteristic element or concept (of sound) that can be controlled.

pitch class   the set of pitches related to a given pitch by octave transposition (e.g., all B's belong to the same pitch class).

pointillism   a term derived from the graphic arts; as applied to music, each sound becomes more an entity in itself, separated distinctly from those before and after by space (frequency), distance (silence), and/or timbre.

potentiometer (pot)   a variable resistor used to control the energy in a system. Most usually found as a volume control.

prepared piano   a piano the timbre of which has been altered by the placing of various objects between, on, or around the strings inside the instrument.

process music music created by overlaying short motives of different lengths. The "process" is as important as the resultant variations.

program computer software* designed by the programmer to initialize and control the computer in specific operations. In composition, programs are set up in advance to create the parameters* of the computer's "musical" language as well as act as interface* between the "programmer" and the computer.

psychoacoustics the study of sound and its complexity, and its communication both physically and psychologically to humans.

pulse wave any waveform that instantaneously moves from a negative to a positive function. This includes all square and rectangular wave forms.

quarter tone one-half the distance between two tones that are a semitone (half-step) apart.

real-time a term used to denote composition time equivalent to performance time as opposed to abstract or nonreal time.

retrograde literally meaning "backward." In twelve-tone music, a row is permutated in twelve retrogrades (R) or readings of the original versions backward.

ring modulator a signal multiplier circuit, combining signals to produce the sum and difference of their frequencies, with only the resultant sidebands exiting.

sampling the ability of a computer to calculate as points the characteristics of a waveform. The higher the sampling rate, the better

the resultant fidelity of sound in analog output through speakers (45K per second usually the minimum).

sequencer a device capable of storing programmed control voltages in order to "play" them at any given speed.

serialization the ordered and intellectual logic applied to any or all aspects of compositional technique.

sine wave a tone that contains no overtones.*

software computer programs.* As opposed to hardware,* software refers to programs and data; i.e., "soft" as opposed to "hard" instruments (e.g. the computer).

sound-mass a block of sound in which individual pitches are no longer important and/or perceptible. Used instead of *noise** to avoid negative connotations.

spatial modulation the compositional technique of moving sound evenly and continuously from one physical location to another.

splicer an instrument to cut and place together segments of tape for synchronization. It is used extensively in classic* electronic music.

square wave a pulse wave* with equal positive and negative energy.

stochastic music mathematician Jacques Bernoulli's term from the Greek meaning, literally, "target." Stochastic laws imply that the more numerous indeterminate* activities become, the more determinate their outcome. These are often improvisatory or indeterminate in isolation, but in mass create the same construct of sound-mass*, *mikropolyphonie**, and/or *klangflächenkomposition.**

strategic music heteronomous* music composed of "live-performance" games.

synthesizer an electronic device used to artificially create timbres.

tetrachord a group of four notes. Often used to designate one of the three groups of four notes of a twelve-tone row.

timbre modulation the compositional technique of moving sound continuously and evenly from one timbre to another.

triangle wave waveform that, when viewed on an oscilloscope,* takes the shape of a triangle. It contains every other overtone.*

trichord any group of three notes. Often used to designate one of four groups of three notes of a twelve-tone row.

vibrato frequency modulation.* This is different from the *tremolo* created by amplitude modulation.*

vocoder an instrument designed to code sounds (speech) into digital information for communication over cables or by radio (subsequently decoded upon reception). It is now used by some composers to create new sounds by modifying traditional ones.

voltage control the ability of one module in a synthesizer to control another. A vital concept for electronic music allowing many techniques (AM,* FM,* etc.) to take place without manual control.

white sound sometimes referred to as white noise; sound that contains all possible frequencies (called white, from white—inclusive of all colors—light). Often used in conjunction with various filters* to create a wide variety of timbres.

wind sound sculptures sculptures designed to allow wind to create sound; similar to Oriental wind chimes.

BIOGRAPHICAL DATA

A listing of many of the composers discussed in this book, with brief biographies and/or current information about each, appear here in alphabetical sequence. Omissions are due either to lack of definite information concerning the composer, and/or necessarily limited space. Only non-USA birthplaces are listed.

ANDRIESSEN, Louis (b. 1939, Utrecht, Holland) is a leading composer of Holland where he currently has served as musical advisor to the Globe theater group of Amsterdam.

ANTHEIL, George (1900–59) was noted as America's *Bad Boy of Music* (book by Antheil published in 1945), and during the twenties and thirties as one of the most confusing figures in the world of music. His *Ballet mécanique* (inclusive of airplane motors, doorbells, and the like) is considered by many to be a milestone of the *avant-garde*. His music is as stylistically diverse as his character.

ASHLEY, Robert (b. 1930) was cofounder of ONCE (at one time an annual festival of new music in Ann Arbor, Michigan) and coordinator of the ONCE Group. He is active as both composer and performer of new music and holds degrees from the University of Michigan and the Manhattan School of Music.

AUSTIN, Larry (b. 1930) was the founding editor of *Source: Music of the Avant-Garde,* a biannual publication devoted to the music of the *avant-garde*. He is currently teaching in the music department at North Texas State University. His works have appeared as part of a number of important festivals, including the New York Philharmonic 1964 *Avant-Garde* Series and the 1965 Rome *Nuova Consonanza.*

BABBITT, Milton (b. 1916) was professor of music at Princeton University and a director of the Columbia-Princeton Electronic Music Center. Educated in mathematics as well as in music, he was particularly well suited for the complicated intricacies of programming and detailed acoustical knowledge necessary for composition using the Mark II Synthesizer. As one of the major representatives of American music, his work has received numerous performances throughout the world. He retains all possible control over compositional elements whether his materials be electronic or instrumental.

BEHRMAN, David (b. 1937) was cofounder of the Sonic Arts Group (performers of live-electronic music) and a producer of recordings of new music for CBS and Odyssey Records. As composer/performer, he has participated in many festivals of new music, including the Angry Arts Festival in New York, and the Lincoln Center Library New Music Concerts. He continues to organize and support concerts and recordings of *avant-garde* music both here and abroad. He currently works with live computer music (via microprocessors).

BERIO, Luciano (b. 1925, Italy) founded the electronic studio at the Italian Radio in Milan with Bruno Maderna in 1955. A prolific composer and conductor, he lived in the U.S. and taught at Juilliard School of Music until 1973. He now conducts and composes in Europe and his music continues to rely on an intuitive "dramatic" approach.

BOULEZ, Pierre (b. 1925, France) was founder (in 1953) of the new music series *Domaine Musicale,* and continues to be active in his support of new music. In 1970, he took up duties as head conductor of the New York Philharmonic, replacing Leonard Bernstein. A prolific composer and author, his music and approach continues to be a major influence in the European *avant-garde.* He founded and currently heads IRCAM in Paris.

BRANT, Henry (b. 1913), whose first works appeared in the then *avant-garde* publication *New Music Quarterly* (early 1930s), continues to contribute as both theorist and composer to the spatial composing techniques now finding great popularity in the multimedia, electronic, and theatrical arenas.

BROWN, Earl (b. 1926) has been composer-in-residence at several universities, including the University of California at Berkeley, the University of Southern California, and the Peabody Conservatory of Music. During the 1950s his association with John Cage led to his use of indeterminate techniques. This, together with influences derived from Alex Calder's mobiles, led him further toward graphic and mobile-type structures, a composite of indeterminate and improvisatory techniques.

BUDD, Harold (b. 1936), whose works have appeared at FFLEM (First Festival of Live Electronic Music), has enjoyed numerous performances by Bertram Turetzky among others. He has also composed for documentary and art films. His music and philosophies are influenced in part by recent art, especially "minimal art."

BUSSOTTI, Sylvano (b. 1931, Italy) is active as a composer and promoter of *avant-garde* music, notably at the Cologne series *Music of our Time,* the Munich series *New Music,* and the Florence concerts *Vita Musicale Contemporanea.* His scores are primarily graphic with emphasis on live performing/composing situations.

CAGE, John (b. 1912) is unquestionably the world's leading exponent of the *avant-garde.* His writings (*Silence, A Year from Monday,* and *Notations,* among others) and music continue to explore and experiment with the basic concepts, techniques, and philosophy of all the *avant-garde* forms presented here. His percussion concerts in early 1936 (Seattle), his experiments about the same time with prepared piano techniques, and his first compositions on tape (1951), along with the inclusion of chance operations involved in compositional process, culminated in a 25-year retrospective concert of his music in Town Hall (New York) in 1958. He continues to make extensive U.S. and European lecture tours. Very few concerts of new music have failed to include the name, music, or at least the influence of John Cage.

CARTER, Elliott (b. 1908), under the encouragement of Charles Ives, studied at Harvard with Walter Piston and in Paris with Nadia Boulanger. He has taught at Juilliard, Columbia, Cornell, Yale, and other schools and is particularly noted for his rigid and iconoclastic views of rhythm (metric modulation) and harmonic space. His works, like those of Carl Ruggles, are composed very slowly (usually at the rate of one every one or two years), and are regarded by their performers (he does not compose electronic music) as *extremely* difficult. His *Double Concerto* and the *Concerto for Orchestra* are considered by many to be the most difficult in orchestral literature.

CHIARI, Giuseppe (b. 1926, Italy) was coorganizer (with Sylvano Bussotti) of the *Musica e Segno* and a member of *Gruppo 70* in Florence. An active member of the European *avant-garde* movement, his works were performed at the 1963 *Internazionale Nuova Musica* at Palermo, the Festival of the *Avant-Garde* in New York, and several *Fluxus* festivals. His concepts point toward a new theatrical form of music dependent on inclusion of all aural materials.

CHILDS, Barney (b. 1926) is a graduate of Stanford University (Ph.D.) and studied at Oxford University as a Rhodes Scholar. His many awards include the Koussevitsky Memorial Award in 1954. His endeavors for Advance Records has furthered the cause and works of new music. His works involve improvisatory and some indeterminate methods, often including audience participation but avoiding the overly theatrical.

COWELL, Henry (1897–1965) was editor of *New Music* from 1927 until the mid-forties (the periodical continued until the 1950s with Cowell on the executive board), a publication devoted to the innovative scores of that period. His 1930 book *New Musical Resources* is devoted to the new possibilities of harmony and rhythm that would later form a cornerstone for *avant-garde* experimentation. He promoted new music with great vitality and composed prolifically in countless styles and with considerable diversity, freely open to new and creative ideas.

CRUMB, George (b. 1929) studied at the University of Michigan with Ross Lee Finney and currently teaches at the University of Pennsylvania in Philadelphia. His *Echoes of Time and the River* for orchestra won the 1968 Pulitzer Prize. His scores are unique both musically and in notation (all of his published works are autograph scores, as his manuscript is incredibly meticulous [see examples in the body of this book]).

CURRAN, Alvin (b. 1938) has been a recipient of both the Bearns Prize and BMI Student Composers award. He is an active member of *Musica Elettronica Viva* in Italy

(live-electronic performance group); his recent music is theatrical and concerned with new sounds, both electronic and nonelectronic in origin.

DAVIDOVSKY, Mario (b. 1934, Argentina) currently composes and teaches in New York City. His *Synchronisms No. 6* for piano and tape won the 1971 Pulitzer Prize. Like Carter and Ruggles, he composes very slowly and his electronic works are *classical* in construction. He was active for many years in the Columbia-Princeton Electronic Music Center.

DAVIES, Peter Maxwell (b. 1934, England) resides in England and has been active with *The Fires of London* and the *Pierrot Players*. His music, like that of Berio, is highly eclectic and dramatic.

DRUCKMAN, Jacob (b. 1928) teaches at the Yale School of Music and has been active in the Columbia-Princeton Electronic Music Center. His *Windows* for orchestra received a Pulitzer Prize in 1972. A great deal of his music, especially the *Animus* series, is for traditional instruments and tape. He has also been involved in the creation of new sounds for traditional instruments, and their resultant notations.

DUCKWORTH, William (b. 1943) founded and was president of the Association of Independent Composers and Performers, dedicated to the performance of new music. He currently teaches at Bucknell University. His music often employs process techniques.

ERB, Donald (b. 1927) has received grants from the Ford and Guggenheim foundations and from

the National Council on the Arts. He is currently on the faculty of Indiana University. His music often employs both live and taped electronic sounds in combination with performers on traditional instruments. His works are performed widely both here and abroad and are recorded on Nonesuch and Ars Nova discs.

FELCIANO, Richard (b. 1930) currently teaches at the University of California at Berkeley and has received grants from the Ford (two), Fulbright, and Guggenheim foundations. His works are primarily for traditional instruments and tape and are published by E. C. Schirmer in Boston.

FELDMAN, Morton (1926–1986) was one of the major influences on young composers, through both his music and his writings about music. His works generally require very soft dynamics and are published by C. F. Peters and recorded on Columbia, Odyssey, and Time records. His work, though influenced by painting (especially the works of Pollock and Kline) and dance (Merce Cunningham), constantly underplays the theatrical.

FOSS, Lukas (b. 1922) is conductor of the Brooklyn Philharmonic Orchestra. His music revolves around controlled improvisation based on historical concepts of live performance-creation combined with intentionally used "non-musical" sounds for drama and expression.

GLASS, Philip (b. 1937) studied at the University of Chicago and at Juilliard with Bergsma, Persichetti, and Milhand. He is known for his three major operas (especially *Einstein on the Beach*) and the film score for *Koyaanisqatsi.* He champions a minimal (repeating with slight variation) and triadic style.

HAUBENSTOCK-RAMATI, Roman (b. 1919, Poland) studied at the University of Cracow and is living as a freelance composer in Vienna. His music is predominantly indeterminate.

HILLER, Lejaren (b. 1924) studied with Milton Babbitt and Roger Sessions at Princeton while achieving his Ph.D. in chemistry. After 1955 he turned toward composition and with Leonard Isaacson began experiments in computer music (first at the University of Illinois and later at *SUNY,* Buffalo).

HUSA, Karel (b. 1921, Prague) studied at the Prague Conservatory as well as at the Ecole Normale de Musique in Paris (composition with Arthur Honegger). Since 1954 he has taught at Cornell University. His music is a fusion of the traditional and *avant-garde,* and his *Music for Prague* and *Apotheosis of this Earth* have made the concert band a more viable ensemble for contemporary composers.

ICHIYANAGI, Toshi (b. 1933, Japan) formed a new music performing group called *New Direction* in 1963. His works have been performed both here and abroad, notably by David Tudor. His music often is graphic and live-electronic. In the last few years, his concepts have turned to mixed media in the form of environmental works.

IVES, Charles (1874–1954) was (and still is) a major influence on almost every facet of *avant-garde* tradition. Almost everything done in the *avant-garde* (whether directly traceable to him or not in terms of lineage) seems predated by Ives by many years.

JOHNSTON, Ben (b. 1926) taught for many years at the University of Illinois and has received a Guggenheim Fellowship and grants from the University of Illinois and the National Council on the Arts and Humanities. His writings have appeared in *Perspectives of New Music* and *Composer.* His music is highly structured and often utilizes unique sound sources and microtones.

KAGEL, Mauricio (b. 1931, Argentina) resides in Cologne, where he serves as composer/conductor for the *Ensemble for New Music.* Many of his works involve written directions rather than notes, employ some improvisatory and aleatoric elements, and are based primarily on theatrical concepts.

KNOWLES, Alison (b. 1933) is a visual/performance/graphic artist. Her work has been influential in environmental media (e.g., *The Hour of Dust,* 1968–71). She works in New York City.

KRAFT, William (b. 1923) has been a percussionist with the Los Angeles Philharmonic Orchestra. He has studied with Otto Luening, Vladimir Ussachevsky, and Henry Cowell, among others, and has written extensively not only for percussion but for full orchestra as well. His *Contextures: Riots-Decade '60* is a classic intermedia orchestral composition.

KRENEK, Ernst (b. 1900, Germany) began his composing career as a twelve-tone composer. He has never ceased to explore all available materials and concepts of his craft. His music is intellectual and complex with an approach directed toward individualizing each work in both concept and sound.

LENTZ, Daniel (b. 1942) has had numerous performances of his works both here and abroad. His music, generally graphic and dramatic (multimedia), often expresses political messages, and his unusual use of colors to represent instruments and/or effects gives both the visual and aural image of his works a marked individuality.

LIGETI, György (b. 1923, Transylvania) worked from 1957 to 1958 in the Studio for Electronic Music of WDR in Cologne. Since 1961 he has been professor of composition at the Hochschule für Musik in Stockholm. Though largely nonelectronic, his music has explored the vast sonic possibilities of traditional orchestral and choral instruments. Despite the fact that his ideas are extremely complex, he continues to employ traditional notation and exact composer control. He has attained wide acclaim as a leader of the *avant-garde* both through his recordings on DG and exposure in the soundtrack of the motion picture *2001: A Space Odyssey.*

LUENING, Otto (b. 1900) is a leading representative of electronic music in America. His ideas of the early 1950s continue to represent effective techniques and procedures for contemporary composers. His historical surveys of electronic music remain a primary source of information on the origins and development of this medium. He was codirector of the Columbia-Princeton Electronic Center. His music freely includes all sound sources available, especially *musique concrète*.

LUNETTA, Stanley (b. 1937) was a member of the *New Music Ensemble* and, aside from his work as percussionist (Sacramento Symphony Orchestra), has composed many *avant-garde* works. His music is theatrical and employs multimedia techniques. Through his association and performances with David Tudor and Larry Austin, he has been instrumental in advancing the cause of new music in America.

LUTOSLAWSKI, Witold (b. 1913, Poland) is both an active conductor and a composer in Poland. Most of his early works were destroyed in World War II. His works today are a strong fusion of *avant-garde* and traditional techniques. He works very slowly (a large work every two years or so) and has used indeterminate and improvisatory procedures. He attributes much of his style to a hearing of Cage's *Concert for Piano and Orchestra* (divulged in a conversation with the author).

MacKENZIE, I. A. (1894–1969) was an early exponent of experimental ideas involved with novel instrument exploration and philosophical concepts of ego and art. His music, though for the most part without notation or significant audience approval, concentrates on fantasy vs. reality.

MADERNA, Bruno (b. 1920, Italy–d. 1974) was an active conductor of new music (testament are the large number of recordings and premieres of new works he conducted in both Europe and America), as well as a composer. In 1961 he founded the Darmstadt International Chamber Ensemble, which he conducted until his death.

MORAN, Robert (b. 1937) is a freelance composer in New York City. His works often involve humor as well as drama. Primarily a composer of mixed-media compositions, Moran has also been active in performing a good deal of new music (such as the puppet operas of Satie and many others when he was director of the West Coast Music Ensemble, 1968–73).

MUMMA, Gordon (b. 1935) was a member of the Sonic Arts Union (live-electronic music) and is a composer/performer actively concerned with the preservation of live performance and a controlled theatrical/gesture situation. His music is found on the *Music of Our Time* series (Odyssey Records) and Lovely Music. He is a professor of music at the University of California at Santa Cruz.

OLIVEROS, Pauline (b. 1932) is a composer of electronic, live-electronic, and multimedia compositions and an articulate experimentalist. Her works appear on the *Music of Our Time* series (Odyssey Records) and Columbia Records, and her articles in *Source, Composer* and *Printed Editions*.

PARTCH, Harry (1901–1974) received many grants, including those from the Carnegie Corporation, the Fromm Foundation, and the University of Illinois. A virtually unknown experimentalist in new tunings and instruments for many years, his works and ideas have recently gained wide notice, consideration, and success. His book *Genesis of a Music* and his works serve as a storehouse of new concepts and performing techniques. He lived in San Diego and taught part-time at the University of California until his death.

PENDERECKI, Krzysztof (b. 1933, Poland) has won awards from the Polish Union of Composers and UNESCO (1960) and is a graduate of the University of Cracow. His music explores the vast possibilities of sonic material available within traditional concert bodies (e.g., orchestra, choir). More recently his music follows neo-Romantic techniques.

POUSSEUR, Henri (b. 1929, Belgium) worked at the Brussels electronic music studio. He is a graduate of the Liège and Brussels conservatories. Most of his music is electronic, and much of it explores the numerous sonic and acoustical possibilities of tape with live performers (especially orchestra).

REICH, Steve (b. 1936) founded (along with Terry Riley) the phase-music school of composition (principally with the works *It's Gonna Rain* [1965] and *Piano Phase* [1967]).

REYNOLDS, Roger (b. 1934) was cofounder of ONCE and has received Fulbright, Guggenheim, and Rockefeller Foundation fellowships. He teaches at the University of California in San Diego. His works are available from C. F. Peters and are recorded on Nonesuch Records.

ROCHBERG, George (b. 1918) has since 1960 been on the staff at the University of Pennsylvania in Philadelphia. He used "quotes" freely and a liberal approach to serial techniques. Most recently his work has followed neoclassic stylistic principles.

SATIE, Erik (b. 1866, France–d. 1925) was one of the most influential composers of the *avant-garde*. Composers such as John Cage, Robert Moran, and many others have given Satie the highest plaudits in terms of his influence on new music. These influences take the form of ultra-simplicity, new time concepts (i.e., *Vexations*), and intermedia. A number of biographies are available and have been listed in the appropriate chapter bibliographies.

SCRIABIN, Alexander (b. 1872, Russia–d. 1915) was influential in the use of media forms. Biographical information is available in almost any book on twentieth-century music.

STOCKHAUSEN, Karlheinz (b. 1928, Germany) experimented with electronic music in the mid-fifties, co-editorship of *Die Reihe,* and prolific compositions utilizing electronic sound sources on tape performed over numerous speakers placed acoustically and compositionally in and around the audience. These works have placed him at the forefront of the European *avant-garde*. His life and works are discussed at length in *Kontrapunkte 6* (P. J. Tonger-Rodenkirchen/Rhein). His writings about music are prolific and complex.

SUBOTNICK, Morton (b. 1933) teaches at the California Institute of the Arts in Valencia. He was one of the cofounders of the San Francisco Tape Center and has worked in the Columbia (New York) electronic studio. His more recent compositions involve "ghost" electronics.

USSACHEVSKY, Vladimir (b. 1911, Russia–d. 1990), together with Otto Luening, presented one of the first American tape music concerts in 1952, and was one of the foremost exponents of *musique concrète* in this country. He taught at Columbia University in New York.

VARÈSE, Edgard (b. 1885, France–d. 1965) spent the last forty years of his life working in New York City. His early predictions and pioneering work with tape and electronic sounds, along with his original approach to concepts of music, mark him as one of the major experimentalists and creators of our time. His music is available from G. Schirmer.

WOLFF, Christian (b. 1934, France) teaches at Dartmouth University. His association in the early fifties with Cage and Feldman led to the development of very personal indeterminate procedures, often notated graphically but sometimes traditionally. His works are published by C. F. Peters and recorded on Time and Odyssey records.

WUORINEN, Charles (b. 1938) is an active composer and pianist. Most of his works (recorded on CRI, Nonesuch, and Advance records) require immense performer virtuosity and are explicit in notation.

XENAKIS, Iannis (b. 1922, Rumania) received his early training in science at the Ausbildung am Polytechnikaus in Athens, Greece. From 1947 until 1959 he worked with the famed architect Le Corbusier. His approach to composition is founded primarily on mathematical principles and explores fields of new sounds using traditional instruments and notation. His music is recorded on Columbia, Angel, Vanguard, and Nonesuch records.

YOUNG, La Monte (b. 1935) is one of the most highly original composers of the *avant-garde*. He studied briefly with Karlheinz Stockhausen in Germany and is a freelance composer in New York City. His *Dream Houses* and other mixed-media works, as well as the innovative compositions of 1960, have made him, along with John Cage, one of the most energetic exponents of new music both in America and abroad.

Further biographical information on these as well as many other contemporary composers listed in this book is available in *Dictionary of Contemporary Music,* edited by John Vinton (New York: E. P. Dutton & Co., 1974, 834 pp.).

III · NOTATIONS

The objective of this appendix is to provide a skeleton outline of new music notations developed over the past fifteen to thirty years that have become somewhat standard. It is a minimal sketch, intended to illuminate some of the examples in the book. It gives samples of viable solutions to problems posed by *avant-garde* music, and, it is hoped, will stimulate the reader to research this area in greater depth.

Introduction

Most scores over the past thirty years include "performance instructions" that describe the new symbols evolved by the composer for the work. It is usually separate, sometimes multipaged, and often full of symbols in direct conflict with similar symbols of other composers. Until the late sixties there seemed an almost endless stream of "artistic" endeavors—as numerous as composers and works attempting new directions. Since the publication of the *Darmstädter Beiträge zur Neuen Musik* in 1965 there has been a slow but steady pull toward codification of symbology. The short bibliography that follows this introduction indicates a host of articles and books dedicated to this ever-changing subject.

One of the most important new[1] *concepts* employed in new music is that of *proportional notation.* In most music since 1600 bar lines serve a variety of purposes:

1. To keep performers together
2. To provide (in some music) primary and secondary implied accents for *dance suites* and the like
3. To make the *reading* of music more feasible (even a Clementi *Sonatina* becomes a "nightmare" upon the removal of bar lines)

Contemporary composers often feel that these bar lines conflict with their ideas of freeing musical line, form, drive, and rhythm from imposed "square-ness" and repetition. While some of these composers have solved their problems within a metered structure (i.e., Elliott Carter, *metric modulation;* György Ligeti, involved and intricate rhythmic entrances, etc.), others have felt that the only solution was to dispense with the bar line entirely. *Proportional notation* is a barless structure in which the rhythm of the work is derived from the performer "proportioning" left-to-right visual reading speed with the time allotted for the given section. Toru Takemitsu's *Voice* (Figure 4.4) uses small vertical slashes through the upper portion of the staff to indicate approximately 4½ seconds of playing time.

---

1. The word "new" is used here with caution: indeed proportionality existed *before* metered notations in many medieval works. In fact, it is probably the oldest concept of music notation. However, it is the new *way* in which the term is used that is of interest here.

Others, like Penderecki (see Figure 3.9—*Threnody*), use large blocks of space that equal a certain duration of time. The performer then reads at a speed *proportional* to the time given for performance (i.e., if an entrance begins about one-third through a 30-second section the performer waits 10 seconds before entering, etc.). This system eradicates the limits and implied accents of bar lines. At the same time, however, it introduces a certain degree of flexibility in that each performer reads the score differently, therefore giving more "chance" possibilities to the performance.

Some composers, like George Crumb, for example (see Figure 12.3), use tempo marks without bar lines. At the same time most of these composers write in a very *thin* soloistic style so that the need for bar lines is minimal (less than, say, trying to perform *Le Sacre du Printemps* without bar lines). In any event, different composers use notations for different reasons. Many mix proportional and metered notations within the same work (see Figure 4.10—Ligeti's *Aventures*), thereby taking advantage of the benefits of both systems. While to the untrained eye these types of scores may appear unnecessarily difficult and/ or obscure, they have become standard practice.

Following a short bibliography (completely annotated bibliographies on the subject are available in many other sources) is a list of somewhat standard new music notations. Again, this is a bare outline only, and does not in any way pretend to be comprehensive or to make any major codifying suggestions (this is the subject of another of this author's books: *New Music Notation,* referred to below).

Brief Bibliography

Bartolozzi, Bruno. *New Sounds for Woodwind.* London: Oxford University Press, 1967, revised 1980.

————. "Proposals for Changes in Musical Notation." *Journal of Music Theory* 5, no. 2 (1961): pp. 297–301.

Behrman, David. "What Indeterminate Notation Determines." *Perspectives of New Music* 3, no. 2 (Spring-Summer 1965): pp. 58–73.

Brindle, Reginald Smith. *Contemporary Percussion.* London: Oxford University Press, 1970.

Cage, John. *Notations.* New York: Something Else Press, 1969.

Cope, David. *New Music Notation.* Dubuque, Iowa: Kendall/Hunt Publishing Company, 1976.

Cowell, Henry. *New Musical Resources.* New York: Alfred A. Knopf, 1930.

Darmstädter Beiträge zur Neuen Musik. Mainz: B. Schott's Söhne, 1965.

Eimert, Herbert; Fritz Enkel; and Karlheinz Stockhausen. *Problems of Electronic Music Notation.* Ottawa: National Research Council of Canada, 1956.

Howell, Thomas. *The Avant-Garde Flute: A Handbook for Composers and Flutists.* Berkeley: University of California Press, 1974.

Karkoschka, Erhard. *Notation in New Music.* New York: Praeger Publishers, 1972.

Kontarsky, Aloys. "Notation for Piano." *Perspectives of New Music* 10, no. 2 (1972): pp. 72–91.

Pooler, Frank, and Brent Pierce. *New Choral Notation.* New York: Walton Music Corp., 1973.

Read, Gardner. *Source Book of Proposed Music Notation Reforms.* New York: Greenwood Press, 1987.

Rehfeldt, Phillip. "Clarinet Resources and Performance." *Proceedings* 7, no. 8, American Society of University Composers (1974).

Salzedo, Carlos. *Modern Study of the Harp.* New York: G. Schirmer, 1921.

Stone, Kurt. "New Music Notation: Why?" *Musical America* 24, no. 7 (July 1974).

————. *Music Notation in the Twentieth Century: A Practical Guidebook.* New York: W. W. Norton, 1980.

Turetzky, Bertram. *The Contemporary Contrabass.* Berkeley: University of California Press, 1974.

Yates, Peter. "The Proof of the Notation." *Twentieth-Century Music.* New York: Pantheon Books, 1967.

A) Pitch meaning	Symbol	One composer among the many who use this type of notation
quarter-tones	↑ ↓ = (¼ up or down)	*Béla Bartók*
	♯ ♭ ♮ = (¼ up)	*Mauricio Kagel*
	(sharpen) (flatten)	
	↑ ♯♯ ♭ ↓	*Krzysztof Penderecki*
	(¼) (¾) (¼) (¾)	
highest and lowest pitch	↑ ↓	*Krzysztof Penderecki*
clusters	♮ or ♯ (cluster symbols)	*Henry Cowell*
silent pitches	◇	*Arnold Schoenberg*
(to be held down on the piano for ring-off of overtones when other tones are struck)		

B) Rhythm

half dot	•♩• = (♩ ♪)	*George Crumb*
repetition of whole groups of notes	• — • — • — • — •	*Krzysztof Penderecki*
slow/even speed-up of pitches		*Karel Husa*
slow/even decrease of speed of pitches		*Karel Husa*

long fermata with duration
shown in seconds

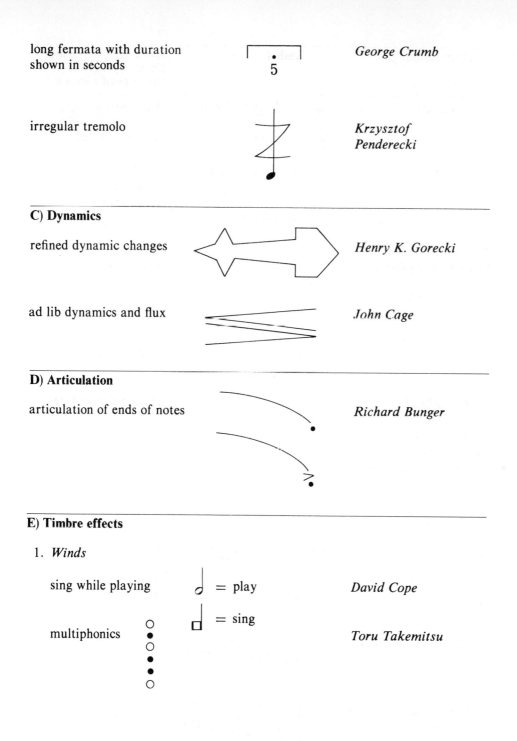

George Crumb

irregular tremolo

Krzysztof
Penderecki

C) Dynamics

refined dynamic changes

Henry K. Gorecki

ad lib dynamics and flux

John Cage

D) Articulation

articulation of ends of notes

Richard Bunger

E) Timbre effects

1. *Winds*

sing while playing   = play   *David Cope*

    = sing

multiphonics   *Toru Takemitsu*

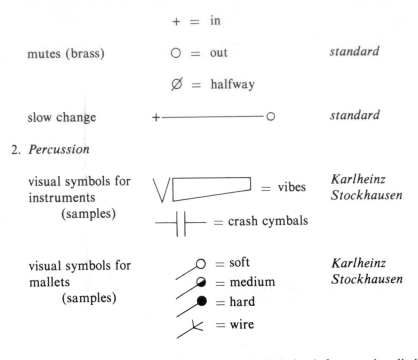

mutes (brass)	+ = in O = out Ø = halfway	*standard*
slow change	+————————O	*standard*

2. *Percussion*

visual symbols for instruments (samples)	= vibes = crash cymbals	*Karlheinz Stockhausen*
visual symbols for mallets (samples)	= soft = medium = hard = wire	*Karlheinz Stockhausen*

(for these last two see Reginald Smith Brindle's book for complete listing)

3. *Harp*

rolling surf effect		*Carlos Salzedo*

(for a complete listing of such effects and notations, see
Carlos Salzedo's book in the preceding bibliography)

4. *Piano*

glissando inside over strings		*Henry Cowell*
glissando inside over one string		*Henry Cowell*
mute		*George Crumb*

5. *Strings*

mute on   *Pierre Boulez*

mute off   *Pierre Boulez*

play between tailpiece
and bridge   *Krzysztof Penderecki*

6. *Vocal*

falsetto   *Krzysztof Penderecki*

spoken   *György Ligeti*

breath/inhale   *György Ligeti*

breath/exhale   *György Ligeti*

laughter   *Krzysztof Penderecki*

Note that a number of contemporary scores leave out staves of instruments with empty bars. This contributes to the "new" look of many of the scores of Crumb, Penderecki, and many others shown in this book. Likewise, when non-pitch-related activity is being employed, one-line staves are often used—quite unfamiliar in appearance to those who are used to the standard five-line staff.

IV · SOURCE ADDRESSES

The purpose of this appendix is to furnish addresses of record companies, music periodicals, and music publishers that dedicate a large part of their services to the promotion of contemporary and *avant-garde* music. The lists are provided to aid the reader in these ways:

1. to obtain works and equipment (hardware and software) for further study and research (since the author has by no means been comprehensive in coverage of *all* works in given areas);
2. to become acquainted with the large number of sources not ordinarily found in music, record, and bookstores or even in many university libraries; and
3. to help support the dissemination of new music by making the names and addresses of its supporters that much more available.

The lists are by no means complete for a variety of reasons:

1. lack of space (with apologies to all those companies who do support new music yet whose names, for one reason or another, were not included in the list);
2. availability to the general public (i.e., Columbia Records does indeed support new music, but their name has not been included in this list as their records are available at any retail record store);
3. new music proportion to output: the emphasis here must of necessity be on companies that devote a *major* portion of their production to new music; and
4. emphasis on listing those companies from which the examples in the book were taken, thus giving the reader the opportunity to obtain the score, record, piece of equipment, or book discussed with comparative ease.

Record Companies

Advance: c/o Music Dept., University of Redlands, Redlands, CA 92374

Advent: 23366 Commerce Park Rd., Cleveland, OH 44122

Albany Records: P.O. Box 5011, Albany, NY 12205

Avant: c/o Crystal Records, 2235 Willida Lane, Sedro Woolly, WA 98284

Bay Cities: 9336 Washington Blvd., Culver City, CA 90230

Bowdoin College Music: 6 W. 95th St., New York, NY 10025

CAPRA: 500 Broadway, New York, NY 10012

CDCM: P.O. Box 560102, Dallas, TX 75356-0102

Celestial Harmonies: 4549 East Fort Lowell, Tucson, AZ 85712

Cornell University: Lincoln Hall, Ithaca, NY 14850

CRI: 170 W. 74th St., New York, NY 10023

Crystal: 2235 Willida Lane, Sedro Woolly, WA 98284

Desto: c/o CMS Records, 4685 Manhattan College 120, Bronx, NY 10471

Deutsche Grammophone: 825 8th Ave., New York, NY 10019

DMP Records: Bristol Court, Melbourne, FL 32904

ECM: 825 8th Ave., New York, NY 10019

Finnadar: 75 Rockefeller Plaza, New York, NY 10019

Flying Fish Records: 1304 West Schubert, Chicago, IL 60614

Folkways: c/o Rounder Records, One Camp St., Cambridge, MA 02140

Golden Crest: 220 Broadway, Huntington Station, NY 11746

Harmonia Mundi: 3364 S. Robertson Blvd., Los Angeles, CA 90034

Hungaraton: 24–02 40th Ave., Long Island City, NY 11101

Louisville: First Edition Records, 609 Main St., Louisville, KY 40202

Mainstream: 1700 Broadway, New York, NY 10019

Music of the World: Box 285, Brooklyn, NY 11209

Nonesuch: 75 Rockefeller Plaza, New York, NY 10019

Now: 224 S. Lebanon St., Lebanon, IN 46052

Odyssey: 51 W. 52nd St., New York, NY 10019

Opus One: Box 604, Greenville, MA 04441

Orion: 486 Dawson Dr., Camarillo, CA 90265

Owl: Box 4536, Boulder, CO 80302

Point Park: Wood and Blvd. of the Allies, Pittsburgh, PA 15222

Private Music: 1133 Avenue of the Americas, New York, NY 10036

Redwood: 6400 Hollis St., Emeryville, CA 94608

Serenus: 9 Airport Drive, Hopedale, MA 01747

Smithsonian Collection: 1250 W. Northwest Highway, Suite 505, Palatine, IL 60067

Trilogy: 723 7th Ave., New York, NY 10017

Wergo: (See Harmonia Mundi)

WIM: (See Crystal)

Windham Hill: Box 9388, Stanford, CA 94305

Periodicals

Canadian Composer: 159 Bay St., Toronto 1, Canada

Computer Music Journal: MIT Press, 28 Carlton St., Cambridge, MA 02142

Contemporary Music Newsletter: Dept. of Music, New York University, Washington Square, New York, NY 10003

Darmstädter Beiträge zur Neuen Musik: B. Schotts Sohne, Weihergarten 12, Postfach 1403, 6500 Mainz, Germany

Electronic Musician: 6400 Hollis St. #12, Emeryville, CA 94608

Electronotes: 60 Sheraton Drive, Ithaca, NY 14850

Interface: heerweg 347b Lisse, Netherlands

Interval: Box 8027, San Diego, CA 92102

Journal of Music Theory: Yale University, New Haven, CT 06520

Journal Seamus 2550 Beverly Blvd. Los Angeles, CA 90057

Keyboard: 500 Howard St., San Francisco, CA 94105

Konzerte Mit Neuer Musik: Rundfunkplatz 1, 8 Munich 2, Germany

Melos: B. Schotts Söhne, Weihergarten 12, Postfach 1403, 6500 Mainz, Germany

Music Technology: 7361 Topanga Canyon Blvd., Canoga Park, CA 91303

Musician: P.O. Box 701, 31 Commercial St., Gloucester, MA 01930

Music in Poland: ZAIKS 2, Hupoteczna Str., Warsaw, Poland

Musical America: 1 Astor Plaza, New York, NY 10036

Nutida Musik: Sveriges Radio, S-105, 10 Stockholm, Sweden

Perspectives of New Music: Dept. of Music, Univ. of Washington, Seattle, WA 98195

die Reihe (back issues): c/o Theodore Presser Co., Bryn Mawr, Pa.

Sonda: Juventudes Musicales, Madrid, Spain

Sonorum Speculum: Donemus 51, Jacob Obrechtstraat, Amsterdam, Netherlands

Sonological Reports: Utrecht State University, Utrecht, Netherlands

Soundings: 948 Canyon Rd., Santa Fe, NM 87501

Studio Sound: Link House, Dingwall Ave., Croydon CR9 2TA, Great Britain

Tempo: c/o Boosey and Hawkes Ltd., 295 Regent St., London, England W1A 1BR

There are a number of other magazines which carry regular columns dealing with new music and/or magazines dealing with more mainstream musical trends. Names and addresses of such magazines can be found in either *Directory of the Music Industry,* 1418 Lake St., Evanston, IL 60204, or *Directory of the World of Music,* Music Information Service, 310 Madison Ave., New York, NY 10017.

Music Publishers

It is very difficult to be complete in this area without filling several hundred pages with addresses. To avoid this, the author has listed only major U.S. music publishers, many of which handle the music of numerous European companies dealing with new music (C. F. Peters, for example, aside from its own nine companies, represents forty publishers of new music from around the world). These "umbrella" publishers are noted with an asterisk. Catalogs and lists of music available from almost all new music publishers are available from these "major" companies.

Music distributors are also included in this list and designated by an asterisk. These companies distribute catalogs of publishers from around the world.

The Internationales Musikinstitut Darmstadt Informationszentrum fur zeitgenossische Musik Katalog der Abteilung Noten (Druck and Herstellung: Druckerei und Verlag Jacob Helene KG., Pfungstadt, Ostendstrasse 10, Germany) is a fairly comprehensive listing of new music and publishers (issued annually).

Along with the listing of major publishers and distributors are a number of smaller companies that deal almost exclusively in new and *avant-garde* music. These companies for the most part are not represented through distributors. Other such publisher addresses may be obtained from the *Directory of the World of Music,* Music Information Service, 310 Madison Ave., New York, NY 10017, or *Directory of the Music Industry,* 1418 Lake St., Evanston, IL 60204.

ASCAP (1 Lincoln Plaza, New York, NY 10023), BMI (40 W. 57th St., New York, NY 10019), and Sesac (10 Columbus Circle, New York, NY 10019) all have publishers' names and addresses (of their own affiliated "performance rights" publishers).

Associated Music Publishers: 866 3rd Ave., New York, NY 10022

Augsburg: 426 S. 5th St., Minneapolis, MN 55415

Baerenreiter-Verlag: Heindrich Schutz Allee 35, 35 Kossel, Germany

Belwin Mills: 16 W. 61st St., New York, NY 10023

B. H. Blackwell Ltd.: 48–51 Broadstreet, Oxford, England OX1 3BQ

Bowdoin College Music Press: Brunswick, ME 04011

Brass Press: 136 Eighth Avenue North, Nashville, TN 37203

Alexander Broude, Inc.: 225 West 57th St., New York, NY 10019

J. W. Chester, Ltd.: Eagle Court, London, E.C.1, England

Composers' Facsimile Edition: 170 W. 74th St., New York, NY 10023

Composers' Press Inc.: 1211 Ditmas Ave., Brooklyn, NY 10018

Dorn Productions: P.O. Box 704, Islington, MA 02009

Carl Fischer, Inc.: 62 Cooper Square, New York, NY 10003

Galaxy Music: 2121 Broadway, New York, NY 10023

Otto Harrassowitz: Postfach 349, 6200 Wiesbaben 1, Germany

Lingua Press: 6417 La Jolla Scenic Drive South, La Jolla, CA 92037

Edward Marks: 1790 Broadway, New York, NY 10019

MCA Music: 225 Park Ave. South, New York, NY 10003

Mills Music, Inc.: 1619 Broadway, New York, NY 10019

Moeck Verlag: D31 Celle, Postfach 143, Germany

C. F. Peters: 373 Park Ave. South, New York, NY 10016

Theodore Presser: Bryn Mawr, PA 19010

E. C. Schirmer Music Co.: 112 S. St., Boston, MA 02111

G. Schirmer: 866 3rd Ave., New York, NY 10022

Seesaw Music Corp. (also Okra Music): 1966 Broadway, New York, NY 10019

Smith Publications: 2617 Gwyndale Ave., Baltimore, MD 21207

Universal Edition: 195 Allwood Rd., Clifton, NJ 07012

Walton Music: 17 W. 60th St., New York, NY 10023

Wilhelm Hansen Group: Gothersgade 9–11, DK 1123 Copenhagen K, Denmark

Hardware

Akai: P.O. Box 2344, Fort Worth, TX 76113

Alesis Studio Electronics: 3630 Holdrege Ave., Los Angeles, CA 90016

Analytic Systems Group Inc.: P.O. Box 621, Amherst, NY 14226

Axxess: Box 8435, Ft. Collins, CO 80525

Art Inc.: 215 Tremont St., Rochester, NY 14608

Casio: 15 Gardner Road, Fairfield, NJ 07006

Clarity: Nelson Lane, Garrison, NY 10524

J. L. Cooper Electronics: 1931 Pontius Avenue, West Los Angeles, CA 90025

Decillionix: P.O. Box 70985, Sunnyvale, CA 94086

DigiTech: 5639 South Riley Lane, Salt Lake City, UT 84107

Drew Engineering: 35 Indiana St., Rochester, NY 14609

D. Drum: 1201 US Highway 1 Suite #280, N. Palm Beach, FL 33408

Drum Workshop: 2697 Lavery Ct. 16, Dept. MI, Newbury Park, CA 91320

Ensoniq: 155 Great Valley Parkway, Malvern, PA 19355

E-mu Systems: 1600 Green Hills Rd., Scotts Valley, CA 95066

Europa Technology: 1638 W. Washington Blvd., Venice, CA 90291

Eventide Inc.: One Alsan Way, Little Ferry, NJ 07643

Fairlight Instruments: 2945 Westwood Blvd., Los Angeles, CA 90064

Fender Musical Instruments: 1130 Columbia Street, Brea, CA 92621

Forte Music: Box 6322, San Jose, CA 95150

Garfield Electronics: P.O. Box 1941, Burbank, CA 91507

Gentle Electric: Dept. P, P.O. Box 132, Delta, CO 81416

Harris Sound, Inc.: 6640 Sunset Blvd., Suite #110, Hollywood, CA 90028

Hohner Inc.: P.O. Box 15035, Richmond, VA 23227

IMS: 1552 Laurel St., San Carlos, CA 94070

Industrial Systems: 9811 Owensmouth Suite #10, Chatsworth, CA 91311

Kawai: Dept. KM, P.O. Box 438, 24200 S. Vermont, Harbor City, CA 90710

Korg: 89 Frost St., Westbury, NY 11590

K-Muse: 18653 Ventura Blvd., Suite #359, Tarzana, CA 91356

Kurzweil Music Systems: 13336 Alondra Blvd., Cerritos, CA 90701

Lexicon Inc.: 60 Turner Street, Waltham, MA 02154

Mellotron: 36 Main St., Port Washington, NY 11050

Moog Electronics: 2500 Walden Avenue, Buffalo, NY 14225

New England Digital Corporation: Waltham, MA 02154

Oberheim Electronics: 2250 S. Barrington Ave., Los Angeles, CA 90064

Roland Corp.: 7200 Dominion Circle, Los Angeles, CA 90040

Sequential: 3051 North First Street, San Jose, CA 95134

Simmons Group Centre, Inc.: 23917 Craftsman Road, Calabasas, CA 91302

Standard Productions: 1314 34th Ave., San Francisco, CA 94122

Syncordion: 117 Cedar Lane, Englewood, NJ 07631

Technics: 1 Panasonic Way, Secaucus, NJ 07094

TOA Electronics, Inc.: 480 Carlton Court, South San Francisco, CA 94080

Voyce Music: P.O. Box 27862, San Diego, CA 92128

Voyetra Technologies: 420 Mt. Pleasant Ave., Mamaroneck, NY 10543

WERSI: 1720 Hempstead Road, P.O. Box 5318, Lancaster, PA 17601

Yamaha: Nippon Gakki Co. Ltd., Hamamatsu, Japan

Software

Bacchus Software Systems: 2210 Wilshire Blvd. #330, Santa Monica, CA 90403

Decillionix: P.O. Box 70985, Sunnyvale, CA 95086

DigiDesign Inc.: 920 Commercial Street, Palo Alto, CA 94303

Digital Music Services: 23010 Lake Forest, Suite D334, Laguna Hills, CA 92653

Dr. T's Music Software: 66 Louise Road, Chestnut Hill, MA 02167

Electronic Arts: 2755 Campus Drive, San Mateo, CA 94403

Enharmonik: P.O. Box 22243, Sacramento, CA 95822

Great Wave Software: P.O. Box 5847, Stanford, CA 94305

Hayden Software: 18 Haviland, Boston, MA 02115

Hippopotamus Software, Inc.: 985 University Ave #12, Los Gatos, CA 95030

Hybrid Arts, Inc.: 11920 West Olympic Blvd., Los Angeles, CA 90064

Imaja: P.O. Box 638, Middletown, CT 06457

Intelligent Music: P.O. Box 8748, Albany, NY 12208

Joreth Music: Box 20, Evansham, Worchester, WRII5EG, U.K.

Magnetic Music: P.O. Box 328, Rhinebeck, NY 12572

Mark of the Unicorn: 222 Third Street, Cambridge, MA 02142

McNifty Central (Impulse): 6860 Shingle Creek Pkwy #110, Minneapolis, MN 12540

Jim Miller: P.O. Box 648, Honaunau, HI 96726

Mimetics: P.O. Box 60238, Station A, Palo Alto, CA 94306

Music Data: Box 28001, Crystal, MN 55428

Music Works: 18 Haviland, Boston, MA 02115

Note Worthy Software: 13119 Pleasant Place, Burnsville, MN 55337

Opcode Systems: 3641 Haven, Suite A, Menlo Park, CA 94025

Passport: 625 Miramontes Street, Half Moon Bay, CA 94019

Roland Corporation: 7200 Dominion Circle, Los Angeles, CA 90840

SFX Computer Software: 1 Hunter Road, North Weldon Industrial Estate, Corby, Northhamptonshire, England

Southworth Music Systems, Inc.: Box 275 RD 1, Harvard, MA 01451

Syntech Corporation: 5699 Kanan Road, Agoura, CA 91301

Triangle Audio: P.O. Box 1108, Sterling, VA 22170

Voyetra Technologies: 333 Fifth Ave., Pelham, NY 10803

World Class Software: 1500 Valley River Drive, Suite 250, Eugene, OR 97401

MIDI Organizations and Publications

International MIDI Association: 11857 Hartsook St., North Hollywood, CA 91607

MIDI Manufacturers Association: 7200 Dominion Circle, Los Angeles, CA 90040

Index

Adams, John, 336, 345
Adler, Guido, 47
Aeolian Chamber Players, 98
Ahlstrom, David, 188
Albright, William, 93, 95, 121, 250
aleatory, 127, 128, 318. *See also* stochastic
    music; contingency, music of;
    indeterminacy
algorithms, 292, 296, 305, 306, 308–10,
    369. *See also* automated music
Allen, Terry, 183
Ames, Charles, 310, 315–16, 325
Amirkhanian, Charles, 81, 174, 189. *See
    also* text sound music
AMM, 129
Andersen, Eric, 173, **175**
Anderson, Beth, 174, 336
Anderson, Laurie, 104, 121, 189, 209
Anderson, Ruth, 50, 52, 250
Andriessen, Louis, 151, **152,** 162, 374
Antheil, George, 80–81, 118, 121, 374
    Ballet mécanique, 80, 121
antiart, 165–67, 183
antimusic, 155, 369
Appleton, John, 247, 248, 249, 250, 285,
    289
archicembalo, 67
archiorgano, 67
architecture, new music and. *See* Fuller,
    Buckminster; Gropius, Walter; Le
    Corbusier; Pavilion; van der Rohe,
    Mies; Xenakis, Iannis
Aristotle, 130
ars combinatoria, 287. *See also*
    Musikalisches Würfelspiel
Art Ensemble of Chicago, 127, 208
art, new music and. *See* antiart; Bauhaus;
    Breton, André; Calder, Alexander;
    concept art; cubism; dadaism; Dali,
    Salvadore; expressionism; *futurists;*
    impressionism (art); Kandinsky,

Vassily; Klee, Paul; minimal art;
    Motherwell, Robert; Picasso, Pablo;
    Pollock, Jackson; Rauschenberg,
    Robert; Ray, Man; Rouault,
    Georges; Schwarzkogler, Arnold;
    Seurat, Georges; surrealism; Tzara,
    Tristan; van Gogh, Vincent; Warhol,
    Andy
artificial intelligence. *See* algorithms;
    automated music; Experiments in
    Musical Intelligence (EMI); neural
    networks
Ashley, Robert, 128, 155, **170,** 174, 194,
    208, 237, 345, 374
    Perfect Lives (Private Parts), 336
    *Public Opinion Descends Upon the
        Demonstrators,* 198, 213, 215
    Wolfman, 162, 170, 189
Astral, Upper, 339, 346
Atelier 17, 183
atonality, 40, 369
Augmented Transition Network (ATN),
    303, 310
Austin, Larry, 88, 128, 173, 188, 213, 292,
    326, 374, 378
    Accidents, 162, 189
    Bass, 215
    The Maze, 121
    Sonata Concertante, 285
automated music, **220,** 287–330. *See also*
    algorithms; computer-assisted
    composition
Automated Music Composer, 310, 315–16
automatic instruments. *See Automated
    Music Composer;* computer-assisted
    composition (CAC); DATATRON;
    Disklavier, mellotron; wind-sound
    sculptures
autonomous music, 369. *See also* Xenakis,
    Iannis
Ayler, Albert, 127, 162

---

*Pages that are bold face denote a reference in a figure legend: pages with a *n* indicate a footnote.

Hiller, Lejaren, 228, 251, 254, 282, 285, 290–92, 325–26, 330, 377
  HPSCHD, 214, 215, 291, 330
  MUSICOMP and, 255
Hindemith, Paul, **16, 18,** 28, 136, 217, 360
Hobart, Jim, 105
Hodkinson, Sydney, 83
Hoffman, E. T. A., 217, 287
Hoffmann, Richard, 285
Hofstetter, Fred, 262
Holliger, Heinz, 86, 98–99, 122
Holst, Gustav, 232
Honegger, Arthur, 221, 317, 377
Houlik, James, 86
Hovhaness, Alan, 110, 122, 343
Howe, Hubert, 254, 255, 283
Hub, The, 313, 315
Hubbard, Freddie, 127
Hunkins, Arthur, 262
Husa, Karel, **354,** 367, 382
  Apotheosis of this Earth, 61, **64–65,** 78, 105, 122, 354, 367
Huse, Peter, 185
Hykes, David, 92, 163
hymns, 228, 290

Ice T, 231
I Ching, 124, **126,** 139
Ichiyanagi, Toshi, 251, 353, 377
Ignace, Paul, 124, **125,** 166, 200, 203
impressionism (art), 1
impressionism (music), 6, 8, 11, 13, 117, 338, 365
improvisation, 102, 124–34, 137, 151, 160–61, 195, 336, 349, 355, 364, 371, 376
  clusters and, 60
  computer programs and, 309–10
  theater and, 105
Improvisation Chamber Ensemble, 128
indeterminacy, 50, 124, 127, 134–64, 167, 168, 195, 318, 344, 349, 365, 371. *See also* I Ching
industrial music, 231–32
interface. *See* Musical Instrument Digital Interface (MIDI)
inter-media, 193, 194, 198–207, 213, 377, 379
International MIDI Association, 268. *See also* MIDI Manufacturers Association
Institute for Research and Coordination of Acoustics/Music (IRCAM), 108–9, **110, 111,** 256, 278, 349, 358, 375
Isaacson, Leonard, 228, 282, 290, 291, 326, 377
Isham, Mark, 209, 338, 345
Ives, Charles, xi, **8,** 28, 30, 45, 78, 79, 336, 356, 360, 365, 367, 375, 377
  The Cage, 18

Central Park in the Dark, 216, 355, 367
  Majority, 54, 78, 79
  Symphony No. 4, 105
  Three Quarter-Tone Pieces, 67, 78
  Three Places in New England, **17,** 28, 78
  The Unanswered Question, 105

Jackendoff, Ray, 28, 293–94, **295,** 329
Jacobson, Bernard, 167, 319
Jam Factory, 309
jazz, 86, 95, 117, 127–28, 208–9, 210, 310, 315–16, 337, 338
Johns, Jasper, 157
Johnson, Bengt-Emil, 174
Johnson, Roger, 188, 189
Johnson, Tom, 122, 173, **174,** 188, 366
Johnson, Wayne, 128
Johnston, Ben, 65–66, 76, 78, 79, 93, 120, 122, 348, 366, 377
Jolivet, Andre, 278
Jones, David Evan, 286
Jones, Joe, 174, 315
Jones, Kevin, 292
Joplin, Scott, 312, **314**
Joyce, James, 1
just intonation, 64, 67, 372

Kagel, Mauricio, 76, 83, 90, 95, 214, 215, 216, 251, 377, 382
  clusters and, 55
  1898, 141, 163
  Improvisation Ajoutée, 60, 163
  Ludwig van, 216, 356
  Match, 203, 216
  Rrrrrrr. . . . , 163
  Sonant, 59, 78, 133
Kandinsky, Wassily, 1, **3,** 165, 370
Kaprow, Allan, 197–98, 214
Kasemets, Udo, 50, 215, 216
Kayn, Roland, 155, 160, 164
Ketoff, Paul, 232
Killam, Rosemary, 262
King, Martin Luther, 359
King Crimson, 231
Kiss, 197
Kitaro, 339, 345
Kiva Ensemble, 99, **102**
klangfarbenmelodien, 47, 49, 372
klangflächenkomposition, 349, 372, 373
Klaviatur-Spaerophon, 218
Klee, Paul, 370
Klein, Martin, 290
Knowles, Alison, **175,** 188, 216, 334, 377
Koenig, Gottfried Michael, 290, 326, 327
Kolb, Barbara, 355, 368
Kontarsky, Aloys, 93, 226, 381
Korte, Karl, 122, 251
Kosugi, Takehisa, 174n

Kotik, Petr, 165, 292
Kraft, William, 88, **89,** 90
Krauze, Sigmund, 198
Krenek, Ernst, 52, 223
Kuhn, Wolfgang, 262
Kupferman, Meyer, 83, 122, 251
Kurtág, György, 354
Kurtz, Eugene, 83

Lacy, Steve, 127
LaFaro, Scott, 127
Lalli, Laura Tedeschini, 292
Lalo, Edouard, 109
laser, 197. *See also* multimedia
Laske, Otto, 200, 210, 270–72, 372
Layton, Billy Jim, 162
Lazarof, Henri, 353
Lebel, Jean-Jacques, 198
Le Brun, Marc, 283
Le Corbusier, 194, 242–43, 379
Lederman, Norman, 177
Led Zeppelin, 197
Leedy, Douglas, 102, 122, 155, 190
Lentz, Daniel, 171–72, 188, 198
Lerdahl, Fred, 28, 293–94, **295,** 303, 329, 330
Levi-Strauss, Claude, 360
Levy, Robert, 86
Lewin, David, 51, 77
Lewis, George, 127
Liebermann, Rolf, 78
Ligeti, György, 69, 83, 86, 90, 95, **350,** 366, 380, 385
  Articulation, 251
  Atmosphères, 61, 78, 122
  Aventures, 71, 78, 79, 91, 122, 349–50, 368, 381
  Lontano, 61, 69, 78, 105, 108, 122, 349, 368
  Lux Aeterna, 78
  Melodien for Orchestra, 368
  Requiem, 78, 349–50, 368
  Volumnia, 78
LISP, 268, 296, 298–302, 303, 310, 328
Liszt, Franz, 109
live electronic music, 232, 236–41, 242
Lockwood, Annea, 251, 334
Logothetis, Anestis, 153, 164
Lomon, Ruth, 112, 122
Lorrain, Denis, 292
Lorton, Paul, 262
Lucas, Theodore, 61, **62,**
Lucier, Alvin, 128, 237, **238,** 251
  North American Time Capsule, 238, 251
  Queen of the South, 112, 238
Luening, Otto, 217, 221, 228, 229, 232, **233,** 247, 251, 252, 377, 379
Lunetta, Stanley, 61, **63,** 128, 171